Victoria Crosses on the Western Front August 1914–April 1915

Victoria Crosses on the Western Front August 1914–April 1915

Mons to Hill 60

Paul Oldfield

Pen & Sword
MILITARY

First published in Great Britain in 2014 by
Pen & Sword Military
an imprint of
Pen & Sword Books Ltd
47 Church Street
Barnsley
South Yorkshire
S70 2AS

ISBN 978 1 78303 043 9

A CIP catalogue record for this book is available from the British Library

Typeset in Ehrhardt by
Mac Style, Bridlington, East Yorkshire
Printed and bound in the UK by
CPI Group (UK) Ltd, Croydon, CRO 4YY

Pen & Sword Books Ltd incorporates the imprints of Pen & Sword Archaeology, Atlas, Aviation, Battleground, Discovery, Family History, History, Maritime, Military, Naval, Politics, Railways, Select, Social History, Transport, True Crime, and Claymore Press, Frontline Books, Leo Cooper, Praetorian Press, Remember When, Seaforth Publishing and Wharncliffe.

For a complete list of Pen & Sword titles please contact
PEN & SWORD BOOKS LIMITED
47 Church Street, Barnsley, South Yorkshire, S70 2AS, England
E-mail: enquiries@pen-and-sword.co.uk
Website: www.pen-and-sword.co.uk

Contents

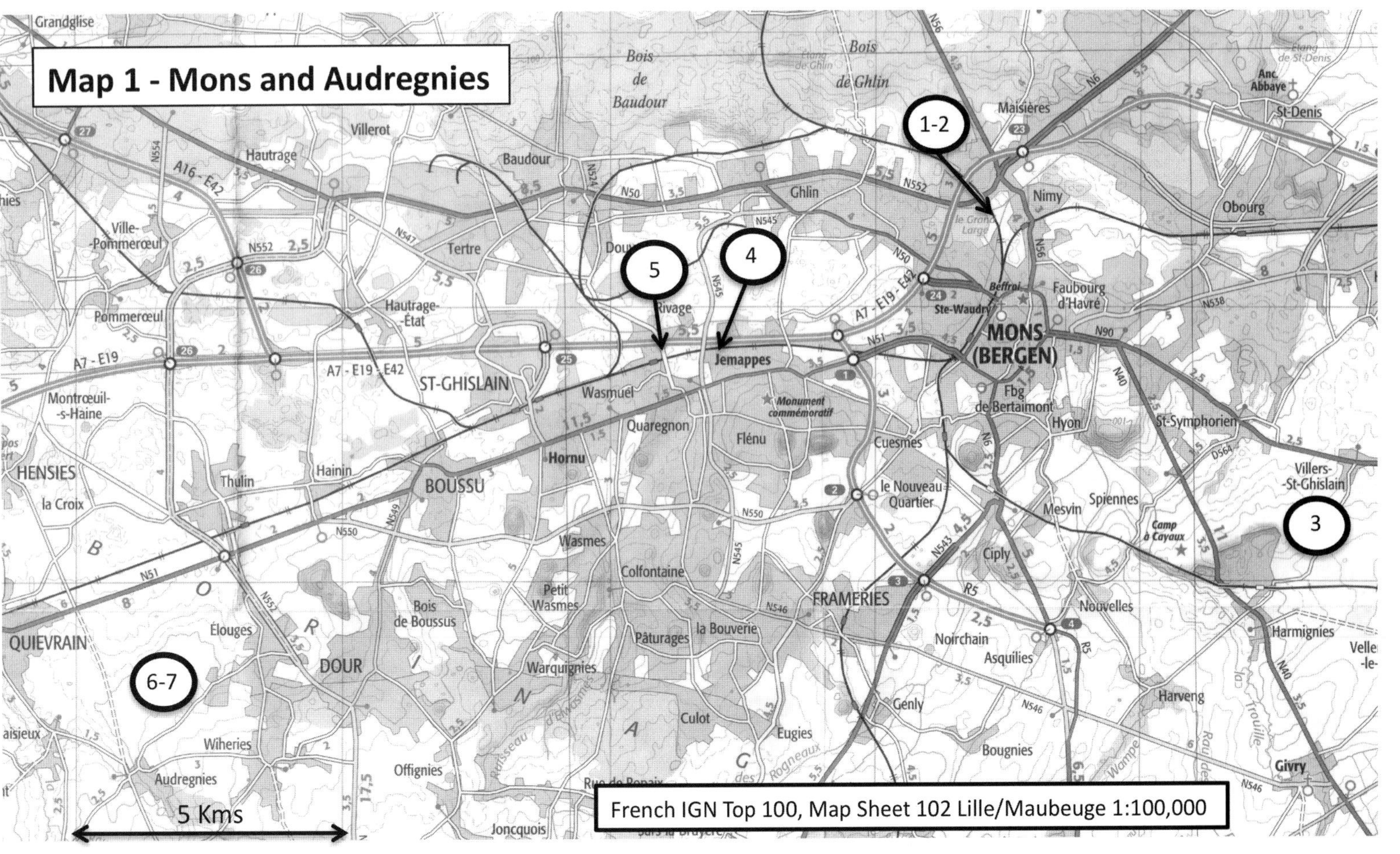
Map 1 - Mons and Audregnies
1-2
3
4
5
6-7
MONS
(BERGEN)
Jemappes
Nimy
Maisières
Obourg
St-Denis
Ghlin
Bois de Ghlin
Bois de Baudour
Baudour
Villerot
Hautrage
Tertre
Hautrage-État
Ville-Pommerœul
Pommerœul
Montrœuil-s-Haine
HENSIES
la Croix
Thulin
Hainin
ST-GHISLAIN
BOUSSU
Hornu
Wasmuel
Quaregnon
Flénu
Rivage
Cuesmes
le Nouveau Quartier
Faubourg d'Havré
Fbg de Bertaimont
Hyon
St-Symphorien
Villers-St-Ghislain
Spiennes
Mesvin
Ciply
Camp à Cayaux
FRAMERIES
Nouvelles
Harmignies
Givry
Harveng
Noirchain
Asquilies
Bougnies
Genly
Eugies
la Bouverie
Pâturages
Colfontaine
Wasmes
Petit Wasmes
Warquignies
Culot
Bois de Boussus
Offignies
DOUR
Élouges
Wiheries
Audregnies
QUIEVRAIN
Joncquois
Grandglise
Monument commémoratif
Beffroi
Ste-Waudru
A7 - E19 - E42
A16 - E42
5 Kms
French IGN Top 100, Map Sheet 102 Lille/Maubeuge 1:100,000

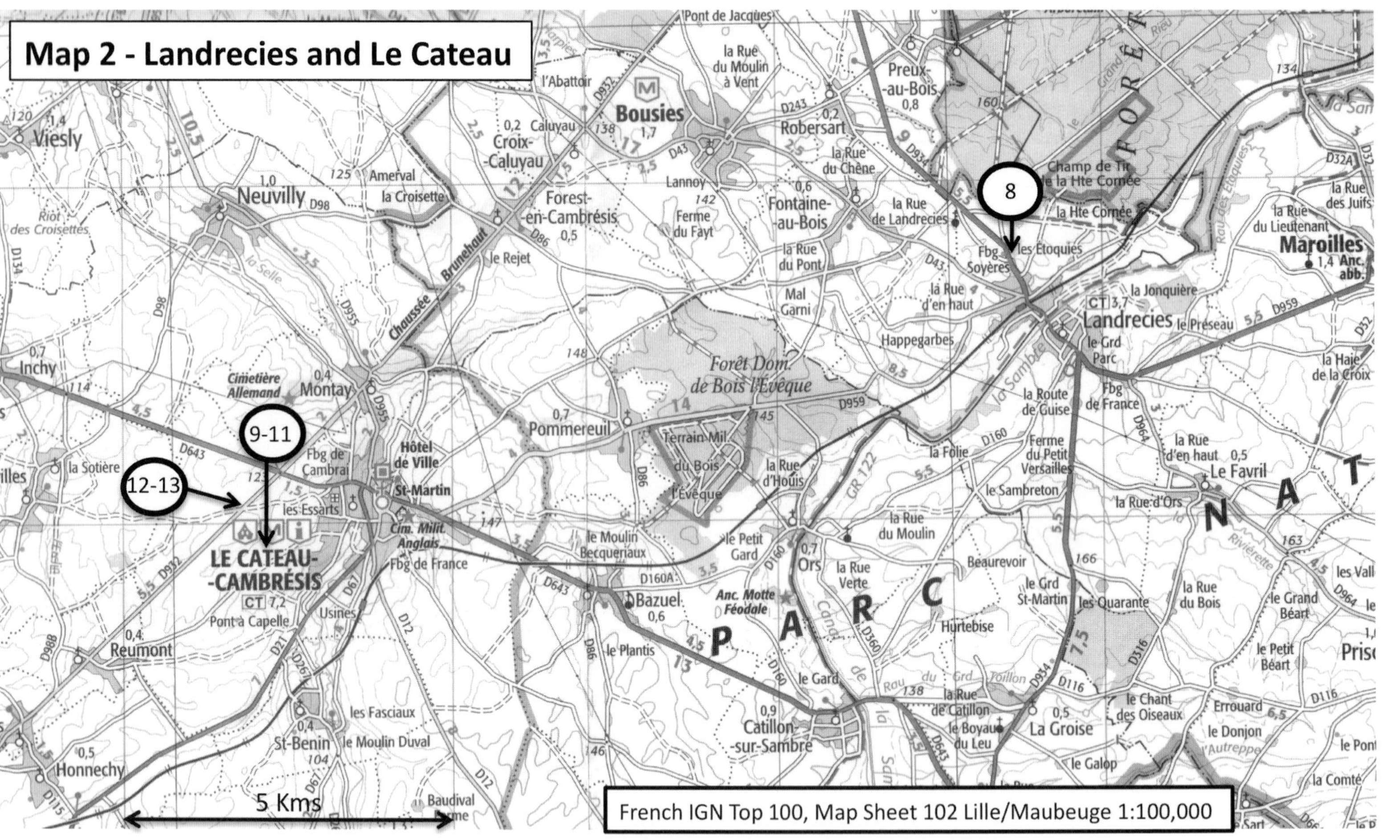
Map 2 - Landrecies and Le Cateau
8
9-11
12-13
5 Kms
French IGN Top 100, Map Sheet 102 Lille/Maubeuge 1:100,000
Viesly
Neuvilly
Inchy
Montay
LE CATEAU-
-CAMBRÉSIS
Reumont
Honnechy
St-Benin
Pommereuil
Forêt Dom.
de Bois l'Évêque
Bousies
Robersart
Preux-
-au-Bois
Fontaine-
-au-Bois
Forest-
-en-Cambrésis
Croix-
-Caluyau
Landrecies
Maroilles
Le Favril
Ors
Bazuel
Catillon-
-sur-Sambre
La Groise
Chaussée Brunehaut

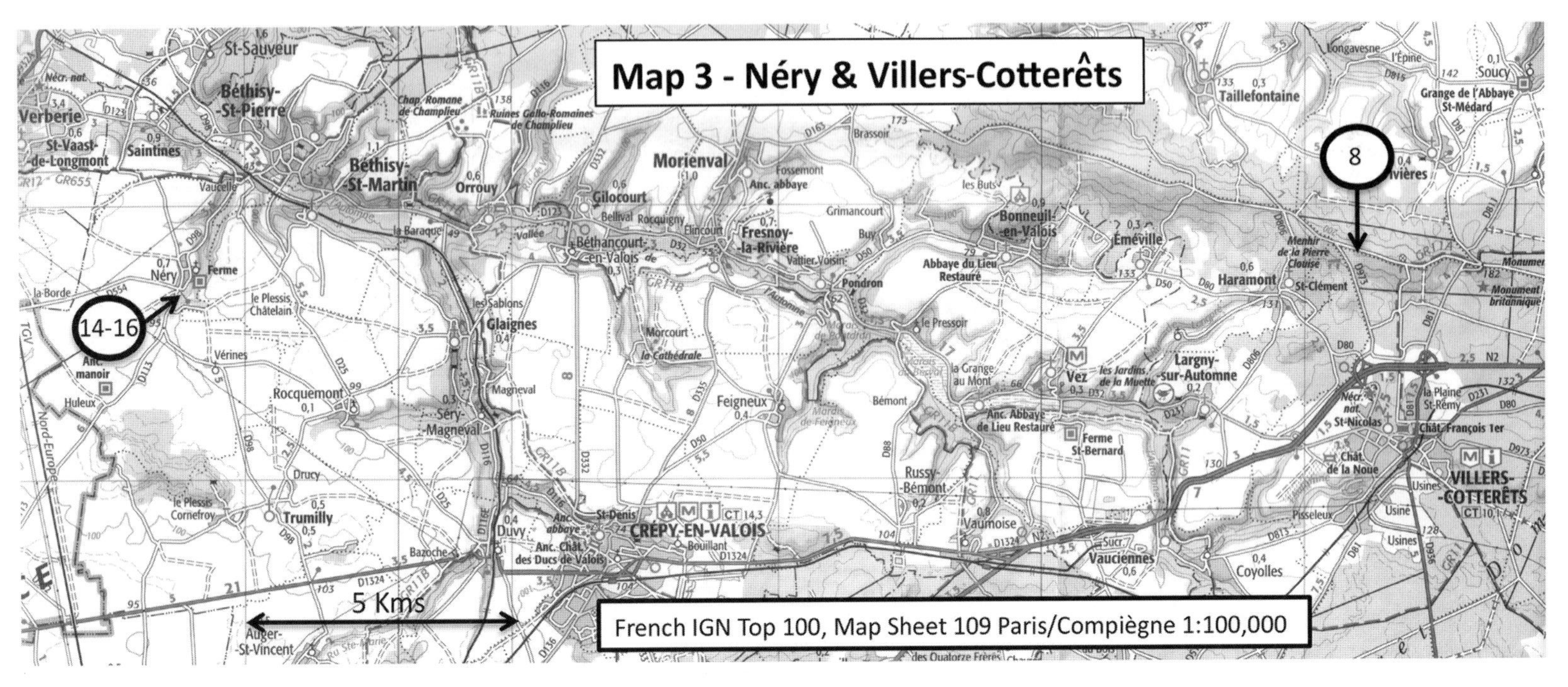
Map 3 - Néry & Villers-Cotterêts
8
14-16
5 Kms
French IGN Top 100, Map Sheet 109 Paris/Compiègne 1:100,000
Néry
Verberie
Saintines
Béthisy-St-Pierre
Béthisy-St-Martin
Orrouy
Gilocourt
Morienval
Fresnoy-la-Rivière
Bonneuil-en-Valois
Éméville
Haramont
Vez
Largny-sur-Automne
Crépy-en-Valois
Villers-Cotterêts

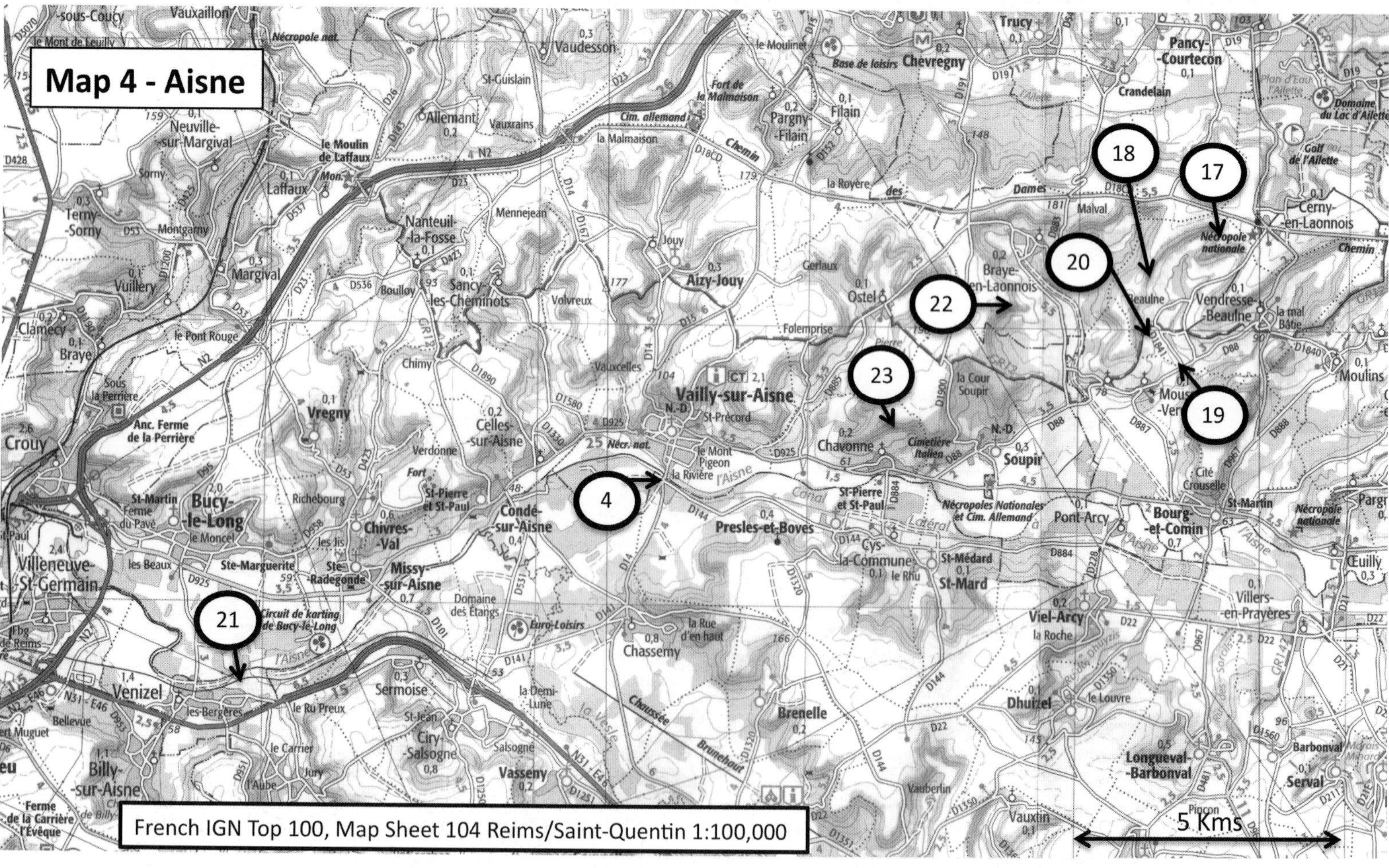
Map 4 - Aisne
17
18
19
20
22
23
4
21
French IGN Top 100, Map Sheet 104 Reims/Saint-Quentin 1:100,000
5 Kms

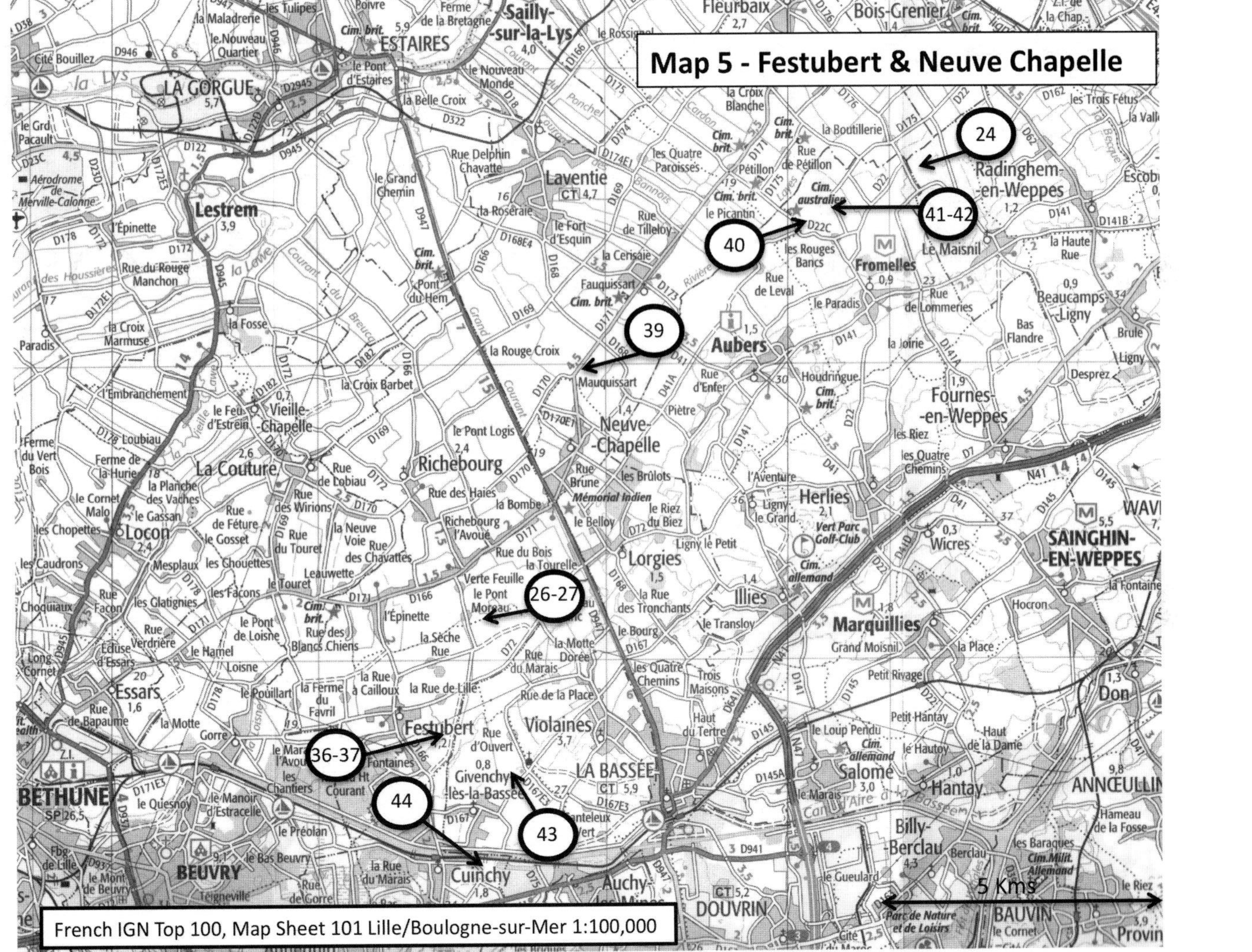
Map 5 - Festubert & Neuve Chapelle
24
41-42
40
39
26-27
36-37
44
43
5 Kms
French IGN Top 100, Map Sheet 101 Lille/Boulogne-sur-Mer 1:100,000

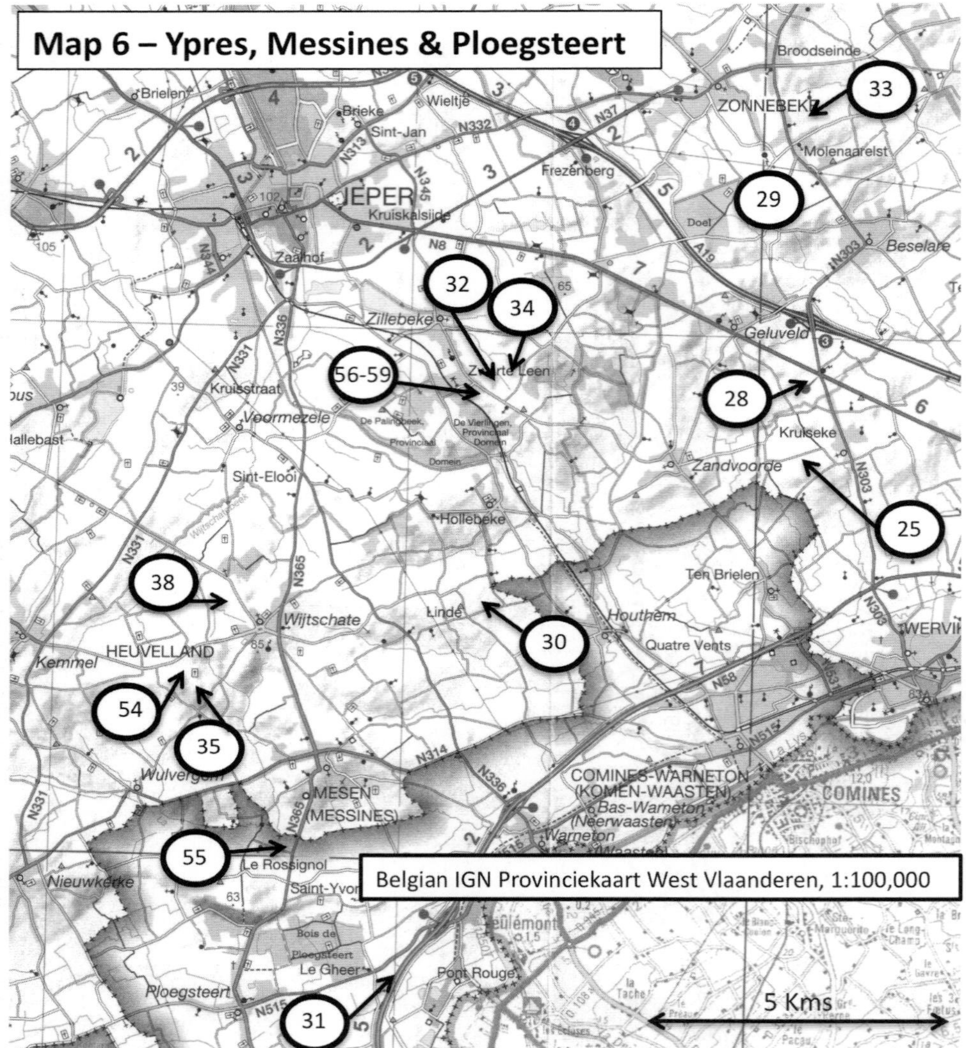
Map 6 – Ypres, Messines & Ploegsteert
Belgian IGN Provinciekaart West Vlaanderen, 1:100,000
5 Kms
33
29
32
34
56-59
28
25
38
30
54
35
55
31
IEPER
ZONNEBEKE
Broodseinde
Molenaarelst
Frezenberg
Wieltje
Brieke
Sint-Jan
Brielen
Kruiskalsijde
Zaalhof
Zillebeke
Beselare
Geluveld
Kruiseke
Zandvoorde
Kruisstraat
Voormezele
Sint-Elooi
Hollebeke
Ten Brielen
Houthem
Quatre Vents
Wijtschate
Linde
HEUVELLAND
Kemmel
Wulvergem
MESEN
(MESSINES)
COMINES-WARNETON
(KOMEN-WAASTEN)
Bas-Warneton
(Neerwaasten)
Warneton
COMINES
Le Rossignol
Saint-Yvon
Nieuwkerke
Bois de Ploegsteert
Le Gheer
Ploegsteert
Pont Rouge
Doel
De Palingbeek Provinciaal Domein
De Vierlingen Provinciaal Domein

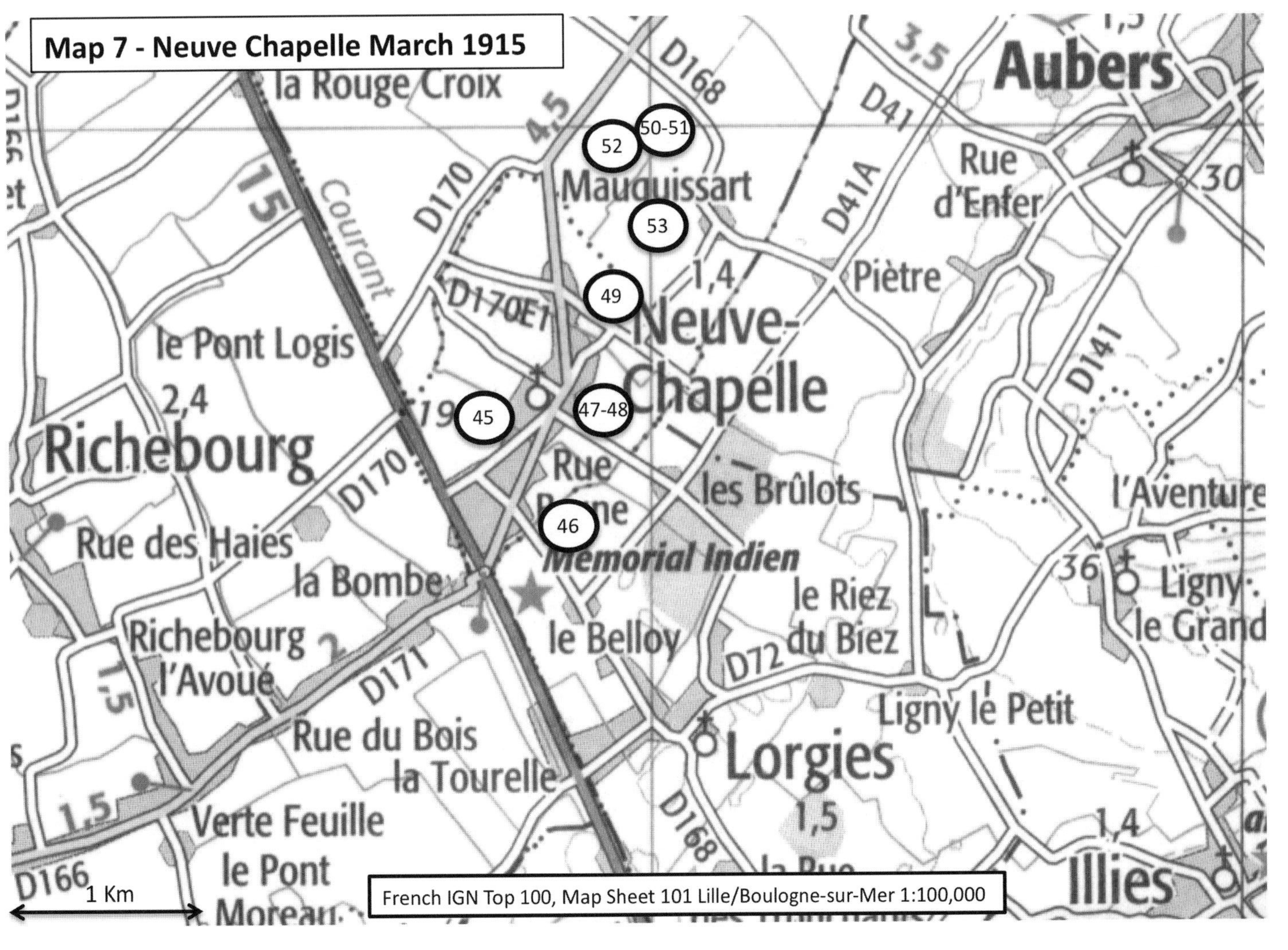
Map 7 - Neuve Chapelle March 1915
la Rouge Croix
Aubers
Rue d'Enfer
Mauquissart
Piètre
Neuve-Chapelle
le Pont Logis
Richebourg
Courant
Rue des Haies
la Bombe
Richebourg l'Avoué
Rue du Bois
la Tourelle
Verte Feuille
le Pont Moreau
les Brûlots
Memorial Indien
le Belloy
le Riez du Biez
l'Aventure
Ligny le Grand
Ligny le Petit
Lorgies
Illies
D168
D41
D41A
D170
D170E1
D141
D72
D171
D166
50-51
52
53
49
47-48
45
46
1 Km
French IGN Top 100, Map Sheet 101 Lille/Boulogne-sur-Mer 1:100,000

Abbreviations

ACF	Army Cadet Force
ADC	Aide-de-Camp
ADS	Advanced Dressing Station
AMS	Army Medical Services
ARP	Air Raid Precautions
ASC	Army Service Corps
Att'd	Attached
Bdsmn	Bandsman
BEF	British Expeditionary Force
BGRA	Brigadier General Royal Artillery
BQMS	Battery Quartermaster Sergeant
Brig-Gen	Brigadier General
BSM	Battery Sergeant Major
Bt	Baronet
Bty	Battery (artillery unit of 4–8 guns)
Capt	Captain
CB	Companion of the Order of the Bath
CBE	Commander of the Order of the British Empire
ChB	Bachelor of Surgery
CIGS	Chief of the Imperial General Staff
C-in-C	Commander-in-Chief
CMG	Companion of the Order of St Michael & St George
CMS	Church Mission Society
CO	Commanding Officer
Col	Colonel
Cpl	Corporal
CQMS	Company Quartermaster Sergeant
CRA	Commander Royal Artillery
CRE	Commander Royal Engineers
CSgt	Colour Sergeant
CSM	Company Sergeant Major
CWGC	Commonwealth War Graves Commission
DCLI	Duke of Cornwall's Light Infantry
DCM	Distinguished Conduct Medal

DD	Doctor of Divinity
DFC	Distinguished Flying Cross
DG	Dragoon Guards
DL	Deputy Lieutenant
Dmr	Drummer
DSC	Distinguished Service Cross
DSM	Distinguished Service Medal
DSO	Distinguished Service Order
Dvr	Driver
FM	Field Marshal
FRCS	Fellow of the Royal College of Surgeons
GC	George Cross
GCB	Knight Grand Cross of the Order of the Bath
GCMG	Knight Grand Cross of the Order of St Michael & St George
Gen	General
GOC	General Officer Commanding
GSO1, 2 or 3	General Staff Officer Grade 1 (Lt Col), 2 (Maj) or 3 (Capt)
HLI	Highland Light Infantry
HMT	Her/His Majesty's Transport
IDSM	Indian Distinguished Service Medal
IMS	Indian Medical Services
IOM	Indian Order of Merit
JP	Justice of the Peace
KBE	Knight Commander of the Most Excellent Order of the British
KCB	Knight Commander of the Order of the Bath
KCVO	Knight Commander of the Royal Victorian Order
Kms	Kilometres
KOSB	King's Own Scottish Borderers
KOYLI	King's Own Yorkshire Light Infantry
KRRC	King's Royal Rifle Corps
LCpl	Lance Corporal
LDV	Local Defence Volunteers (predecessor of Home Guard)
LG	London Gazette
LRCP	Licentiate of the Royal College of Physicians
Lt	Lieutenant
Lt Col	Lieutenant Colonel
Lt Gen	Lieutenant General
Maj	Major
Maj Gen	Major General
MB	Bachelor of Medicine
MBE	Member of the Order of the British Empire
MC	Military Cross

MGC	Machine Gun Corps
MGRA	Major General Royal Artillery
MID	Mentioned in Despatches
MM	Military Medal
MO	Medical Officer
MP	Member of Parliament
MRCP	Member of the Royal College of Physicians
MRCS	Member of the Royal College of Surgeons
MSM	Meritorious Service Medal
MT	Motor Transport
MVO	Member of the Royal Victorian Order
OBE	Officer of the Order of the British Empire
OBI	Order of British India
OP	Observation Post
OTC	Officers' Training Corps
PC	Privy Counsellor
Pte	Private
RA	Royal Artillery
RAF	Royal Air Force
RAFVR	Royal Air Force Volunteer Reserve
RAMC	Royal Army Medical Corps
RCAMC	Royal Canadian Army Medical Corps
RE	Royal Engineers
RFA	Royal Field Artillery
RFC	Royal Flying Corps
RGA	Royal Garrison Artillery
RHA	Royal Horse Artillery
RHG	Royal Horse Guards
RMA	Royal Military Academy
RMS	Royal Mail Ship
RN	Royal Navy
RNR	Royal Naval Reserve
RSM	Regimental Sergeant Major
SAC	South Africa Constabulary
Sect	Section (sub-unit of ten infantrymen or two artillery guns)
Sgt	Sergeant
SMS	Seiner Majestät Schiff (German for 'His Majesty's Ship')
SPG	Society for Propogating the Gospel
Spr	Sapper
TA	Territorial Army
TD	Territorial Decoration
TF	Territorial Force

USAAF	United States Army Air Force
VAD	Voluntary Aid Detachment
VC	Victoria Cross
VTC	Volunteer Training Corps
WO1 or 2	Warrant Officer Class 1 or 2

Introduction

While tramping over various battlefields I often wondered exactly where such and such Victoria Cross had been won. This book, the research for which commenced in 1988, aims to fill that gap. It is designed for the battlefield visitor as well as the armchair reader. Each account provides background information to explain the broad strategic and tactical situation, before examining the VC action in detail. Each is supported by a map to allow a visitor to stand on or close to the spot and at least one photograph of the site. Detailed biographies help to understand the man behind the Cross.

Some accounts are the result of resolving conflicting war diaries and other documents, including regimental histories and therefore some long accepted facts are challenged. At this early stage of the war mapping was often ad hoc. War diaries contain little of the detailed topographical information that came later with accurate trench maps and a sophisticated grid reference system. To identify some sites it has been necessary to search not only unit war diaries and histories, but also those of parent formations and flanking units.

As far as possible chapters and sections within them follow the titles of battles, actions and affairs as decided by the post-war Battle Nomenclature Committee. VCs are numbered chronologically 1, 2, 3 … 59 from 23rd August 1914 – 21st April 1915. As far as possible they are described in the same order, but when a number of actions were fought simultaneously, the VCs will be covered out of sequence on a geographical basis.

Refer to the master maps to find the general area for each VC. If visiting the battlefields it is advisable to purchase maps from the respective French and Belgian 'Institut Géographique National'. The French IGN Top 100 and Belgian IGN Provinciekaart at 1:100,000 scale are ideal for motoring, but 1:50,000, 1:25,000 or 1:20,000 scale maps are necessary for more detailed work, e.g. French IGN Serie Bleue and Belgian IGN Topografische Kaart. They are obtainable from the respective IGN or through reputable map suppliers on-line.

Ranks are as used on the day. Grave references have been shortened, e.g. 'Plot II, Row A, Grave 10' will appear as 'II A 10'. There are some abbreviations, many in common usage, but if unsure refer to the list.

Thanks are due to too many people and organizations to mention. All are acknowledged in 'Sources', but I would like to single out my fellow researchers in the 'Victoria Cross Database Users Group', who have provided information and other assistance selflessly over many years. They are Doug and Richard Arman, Vic Tambling and Alan Jordan, assisted by Alasdair Macintyre, who is the son of a WW1 VC. I would also like to acknowledge the support and assistance of a small but dedicated support team … my family.

Paul Oldfield
Wiltshire
September 2013

Chapter One

The Retreat from Mons

Battle of Mons, 23rd August 1914

1 Lt Maurice Dease, 4th Royal Fusiliers (9th Brigade, 3rd Division), Nimy, Mons, Belgium
2 Pte Sidney Godley, 4th Royal Fusiliers (9th Brigade, 3rd Division), Nimy, Mons, Belgium
3 Cpl Charles Garforth, 15th Hussars (3rd Division), Harmignies, Belgium
4 Capt Theodore Wright, 57th Field Company RE (3rd Division), Mariette, Belgium
5 LCpl Charles Jarvis, 57th Field Company RE (3rd Division), Jemappes, Belgium

When Britain declared war on Germany on 4th August 1914, detailed plans to move the British Expeditionary Force (BEF) to the continent were set in motion. The BEF began crossing to France on 9th August and, having completed its concentration south of Mauberge, took its position on the left

The invading Germans, having seized Brussels, swung southwest with the intention of capturing Paris and pinning the French Army against their own frontier defences from the rear. The BEF concentrated around Mauberge, before advancing into Belgium on the left flank of the French Fifth Army. On the evening of 22nd August 1914 the Germans were pressing forward with the Allies probing towards them. The scene was set for a massive encounter battle the following day.

of the Allied line. It advanced into Belgium as German and Allied forces moved towards each other in a vast meeting engagement. Although unknown at the time, the BEF was closing with the German First Army under von Kluck; the outside of the Schlieffen Plan's enormous right hook designed to outflank Paris.

On 21st August a British bicycle patrol encountered Germans near Obourg and Private John Parr, 4th Middlesex, became the first British soldier to be killed in action in the war. He is buried in St Symphorien Military Cemetery (I A 10) with many others killed during the Battle of Mons. Next morning, a 4th Dragoon Guards' picket near Casteau pursued a German cavalry patrol and Corporal Edward Thomas fired the first British shot of the war.

During the night of 22nd/23rd August 1914, the BEF completed its move forward to the line of the Mons-Condé Canal (Canal du Centre), with I Corps on the right and II Corps on the left. On the right of II Corps was 3rd Division, holding the line from Harmignies, seven kilometres southeast of Mons, via Obourg on the canal, then westwards to Mariette. The intention was to continue the advance next morning, but it became clear the enemy was in vastly superior numbers and Sir John French ordered the line of the canal to be held. The canal loop at Nimy jutting out to the north was the most difficult part of the line to defend.

At dawn on Sunday 23rd August 1914, German artillery fired the opening salvoes of the Battle of Mons. Soon after British troops were in action on the continent of Europe for the first time since Waterloo in 1815. At 9.00 a.m., German infantry advanced against the British positions in the Obourg/Nimy area, intending to seize four bridges over the Canal.

The opening positions of the Battle of Mons on 23rd August 1914. The weakness of the salient caused by the Canal loop at Nimy is evident (Official History 1914, Volume 1, Maps).

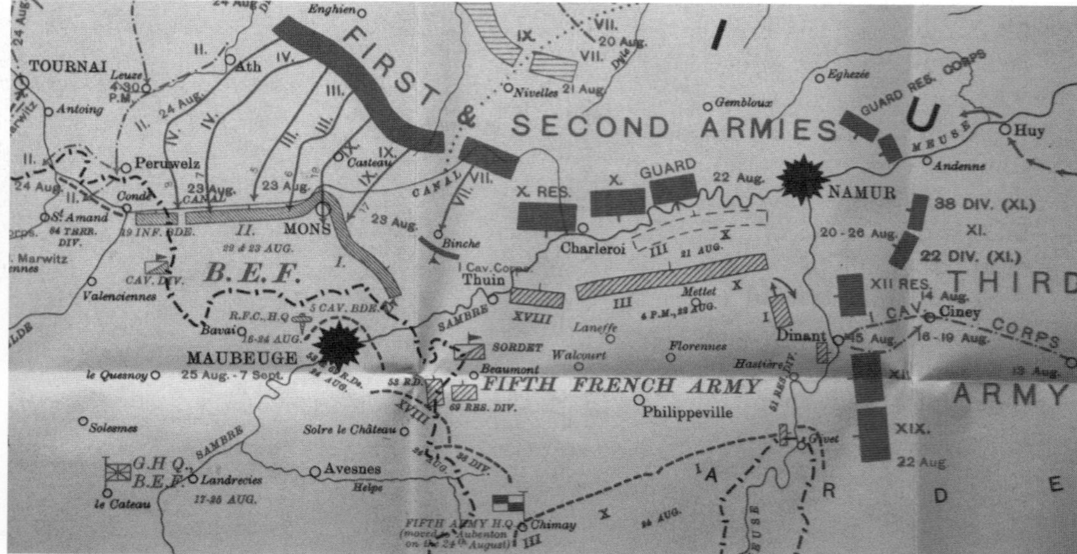

The Mons-Condé Canal at Obourg, a few miles east of Nimy, showing the original width in 1914. The Canal was widened in the late 1930s and many of the original features were lost.

4th Royal Fusiliers held the northwest tip of the canal loop with 4th Middlesex to the east at Obourg. Z Company was on the left at the road bridge leading to Ghlin and Y Company, commanded by Captain L F Ashburner DSO MVO (MID for this action), was split between the railway and road bridges at Nimy. X Company was in support at Nimy station while W Company formed the Battalion reserve in the north of Mons town.

Y Company had two platoons at each bridge, with Company HQ at the railway bridge. **Lieutenant Maurice Dease**, the Battalion machine-gun officer, set up his two guns either side of the railway bridge. The gun on the left was on top of the embankment where it had an excellent field of fire across the canal to the northwest and could counter any attempt to rush the bridge itself. The gun on the right was dug into the embankment. The makeshift emplacements were protected with railway sleepers and sacks filled with shingle taken from the nearby flourmill.

4th Royal Fusiliers in the Grand Palace at Mons. This scene has changed little since. There are many cafes and restaurants in and around the Place, but it is best to park a little way out and walk in. The main architectural features are the 15th Century Town Hall and the 17th Century Belfry nearby.

Shortly after dawn a German cavalry patrol approached the road bridge, which was swung across the line of the canal, preventing the horsemen from getting over. They suffered a number of casualties from rifle fire and a wounded officer was captured; he turned out to be Leutnant von Armin, son of the Commander of IV Army Corps. Around 7.00 a.m., a German aircraft flew in front of 4th Royal Fusiliers' positions.

The Germans realised the canal loop at Nimy was the weakest point in the British line. Concealing themselves in the plantations north of the canal they poured heavy fire into the British positions before attacking the bridges with four infantry battalions, supported by cavalry and artillery. The Fusiliers met the closely packed Germans converging on the bridges with a hail of small arms fire. The ability of pre-war Regular infantrymen to fire 15 aimed shots a minute at 300 yards proved devastating. Coincidentally, the standard was introduced by CO 4th Royal Fusiliers, Lieutenant Colonel N R McMahon DSO, when he was Chief Instructor of the School of Musketry. The Germans were forced back into

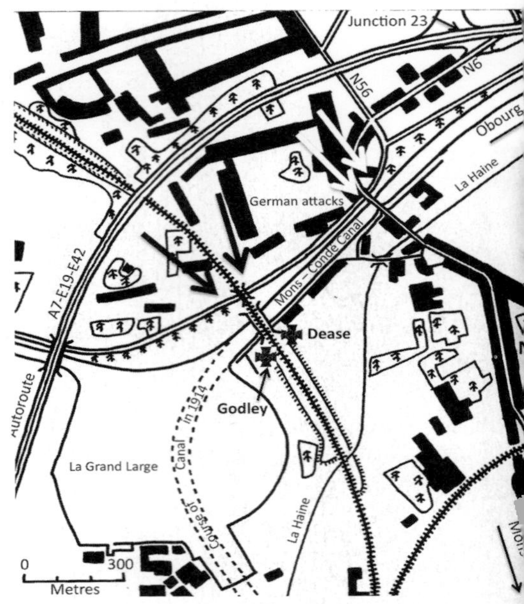

Leave the A7-E19-E42 Autoroute at Junction 23 for Nimy/Maisieres. Follow the N6 south towards Mons. 180m after crossing over the Canal, turn right and immediately right again over a small bridge. After 250m the narrow road reaches the Canal bank. Follow it to the left for 300m to the railway bridge. There is plenty of parking space, but beware other cars speeding along this stretch. The line of the Canal was altered west of the railway bridge when it was widened in the late 1930s.

Nimy railway bridge. The Germans destroyed the original in 1918. The rebuilt bridge was replaced by a longer and larger structure when the Canal was widened in the late 1930s. Sidney Godley and 50 other survivors of the battle including Captain Ashburner, returned for the inauguration of the new bridge in April 1939; it was the last of seven visits Godley made to Nimy. The bridge was destroyed again in 1944.

View from the left machine-gun emplacement. In 1914 the bridge was a simpler flat structure, affording a much clearer field of fire. Climbing onto the embankment should be undertaken with extreme caution. Fast trains cross the bridge frequently in both directions with little warning of their approach.

The German view of the right machine-gun emplacement dug into the embankment. Use the pedestrian walkway to gain access to the north side of the Canal.

the cover of the plantations with heavy casualties. However, the Fusiliers' position was far from secure; they remained under constant artillery and rifle fire and were heavily outnumbered.

Dease intended controlling the two machine-guns from a trench 50m behind, but the crews suffered numerous casualties and he made frequent journeys forward to sort out the problems. Around 9.00 a.m. he was hit below the knee while attending the left gun. Refusing to go for aid, he crawled to the right gun where he was shot in the side. Lieutenant Frederick Steele (died 25th–27th October 1914 and commemorated on the Le Touret Memorial), the platoon commander at the bridge, managed to persuade Dease to stay in cover for a while, but when the guns fell silent again he went to check on his men. Having replaced the wounded gunners, he continued to control their fire in full view of the enemy.

Half an hour later the attack resumed, with the Germans coming on in extended order. Although this attack was also checked, the situation at the bridge was critical. To the right, 4th Middlesex and 1st Gordon Highlanders were also under heavy pressure. On the left the Germans had closed up to the long straight section of the canal west of Mons. Lieutenant Joseph Mead's platoon in Mons was sent to reinforce Ashburner, but Mead was wounded and killed shortly afterwards (St Symphorien Military Cemetery V B 3). Captain W A C Bowden-Smith then went up with Lieutenant Everard Smith's platoon, but within ten minutes these officers had also been hit and subsequently died (Bowden-Smith died as a prisoner on 28th August and is buried in Cement House Cemetery, Langemarck-Poelcapelle (XVIII D 1-16); Smith is buried in St Symphorien Military Cemetery (II A 5)).

By midday the Germans had worked their way close to the canal, from where they poured rifle and machine-gun fire into the beleaguered Fusilier's positions. By then Dease had been hit in the neck and possibly other places as well, but he continued doggedly to control his guns from the middle of the bridge, assisted by Sergeant Haylock (or Haycock), who was also hit and had to be carried to the rear. From this point accounts of the action differ over precise details. At some time Dease may have taken over the right gun after rolling the injured gunner down the bank to make space. In view of his wounds it is more likely that when both guns fell silent the Section Corporal, Parminter, took over on the right until he was wounded in the head and rolled down the bank. By then Dease was out of action and all his men were dead or badly wounded.

Under the bridge on the south side of the Canal is a memorial to 4th Royal Fusiliers and the two Victoria Crosses. It survived the Second World War having been hidden by local people, but it had to be replaced in 2012 when the original was stolen.

Steele (MID for this action) realised that both guns were silent and asked for volunteers who knew how to operate them. **Private Sidney Godley** came forward. Despite being wounded he had supplied ammunition to the guns throughout the morning. There are a number of versions of what happened next. In one account Godley cleared the left emplacement of three bodies and brought the machine-gun back into action, but other accounts specify the right gun. Under Steele's control, Godley continued firing for two more hours.

By the afternoon the British position was becoming increasingly untenable. To the east, German units were crossing the canal in force and the French Fifth Army withdrew unexpectedly, threatening the entire BEF right flank. At Nimy, in an incredible act of courage, Musketier Oskar Niemeyer swam to the middle of the canal under heavy fire to open the swing road bridge. Although he was killed (St Symphorien Military Cemetery), his actions allowed the Germans to increase pressure against 4th Royal Fusiliers.

The Battalion received the order to withdraw at 1.10 p.m. and this was confirmed 30 minutes later. Again accounts differ on what happened subsequently. Steele stated that Godley fired under his control until hit in the head and the gun was irreparably damaged; he was then allowed to go to the rear. In other versions Godley continued to man the machine-gun at Steele's request, while the rest of the Company withdrew.

Godley was reputedly the last man left at the bridge, except for the dead and wounded who could not be carried. The machine-gun water jacket was riddled with bullets and eventually became unusable. When he could do no more, Godley is reputed to have smashed the machine-gun and thrown it into the canal, but in view of suffering over 20 wounds this seems unlikely, particularly as he could only crawl back to the main road afterwards. From there two civilians carried him to the hospital in Mons and he spent the rest of the war in captivity.

During the retirement from the canal, Steele is reputed to have carried Dease to the rear, but his own account states that Dease had to be left behind. By 3.30 p.m., when Dease died, most of the Battalion was clear of Mons and retiring in good

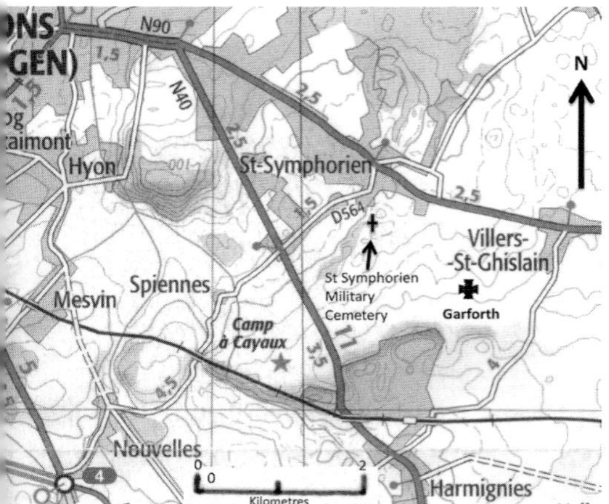

Accounts of Charles Garforth's VC action on 23rd August 1914 are too imprecise to identify the location with any accuracy. All that is known is that it took place near Harmignies and Villers-Saint-Ghislain. Close by is the beautiful St Symphorien Military Cemetery, containing the first and last British war dead and the last Canadian to die. Maurice Dease is buried there, as is August Neimeier. The land was donated by Jean Houzeau de Lehaie during the war and the cemetery was laid out by the Germans. As a combined British-German cemetery containing 229 British and 284 German graves, it is unique on the Western Front. (Extract from French IGN Top 100, Sheet 102 Lille/Maubeuge)

order to a new line to the south. The day's fighting cost 4th Royal Fusiliers 45 killed or died of wounds and 67 wounded, most having to be abandoned.

While the Royal Fusiliers battled it out at Nimy, 3rd Division Cavalry (A Squadron, 15th Hussars), had been busy on the right flank. During the previous night 1 and 2 Troops had bivouacked at Bonnet and 3 and 4 Troops at Hyon. In the morning 3 and 4 Troops were ordered to reconnoitre Havre and Bray under Capt Wells. 3 Troop came into contact with the advancing Germans at Havre, reporting a battalion each of artillery and infantry and a cavalry brigade. 4 Troop moved via Bray to Binche linking up with 1 Troop on the way. They were engaged at Binche by Uhlans, wounding Lieutenant Rogerson, and were then fired on by artillery and only managed to extract themselves with artillery assistance.

4 Troop went to Mons to assist the infantry and participated in a rearguard action falling back on Villers St Ghislain. During this tricky operation elements of the Squadron found themselves trapped by a wire fence at Harmignies. German machine-guns were firing down the fence line and the situation was potentially disastrous. With complete disregard for their own safety **Corporal Charles Garforth** and Lance Corporal Ball dashed to the fence and cut several gaps to allow the horsemen to escape. Ball was later taken prisoner.

The rearguard action continued until 8.00 p.m. when 4 Troop broke contact to escort a battery to safety at Nouvelles, where it spent the night. Next morning, after

The area north of Harmignies looking towards Villers-Saint-Ghislain, where Charles Garforth won his VC on 23rd August 1914.

concentrating at Framieres, the Squadron commenced the retreat with the rest of the BEF. During the next fortnight, Garforth was involved in two other incidents that, together with his actions on 23rd August, resulted in the award of the VC. Accounts disagree about the exact dates of the other incidents, varying from 2nd to 7th September. However, the majority of the evidence indicates they took place on the 6th and 7th.

On the afternoon of 6th September near Dammartin, southeast of Senlis, A Squadron took over patrolling duties forward of the Divisional outpost line from the Divisional Cyclist Company. Patrols were ordered to act boldly and push forward. Sergeant Scarterfield's (MID for this action) patrol came into contact with two enemy squadrons. Some Germans opened fire while others made ready to charge the British patrol. There was no alternative other than to gallop off towards safety. While jumping a ditch, Scarterfield's horse was hit and fell, pinning him to the ground. Garforth turned back despite the heavy enemy fire, managed to pull Scarterfield clear of the dead animal and then carried him to safety on his own horse. Next day Garforth was again on patrol near Meaux, south east of Dammartin. On this occasion Sergeant Lewis had his horse shot under him. Garforth drew the enemy's machine-gun fire away from Lewis and covered his withdrawal with three minutes of rapid rifle fire.

Meanwhile on 23rd August, at 2.30 a.m. orders had been issued to prepare all bridges over the canal for demolition. 56th Field Company RE on 3rd Division's right had no time to destroy the bridges in its sector before the enemy was upon them. 57th Field Company RE on the left had more time to prepare its eight allocated bridges. However, two Sections were engaged on other tasks and there was a shortage of leads and explosives. To make matters worse, instantaneous

The area in which 57th Field Company tried to destroy the canal bridges has changed completely since 1914. The A7-E19-E42 Autoroute marks the line of the former canal and the subsidiary canal is a drainage channel, the Haine. No trace of the original bridges and locks remain.

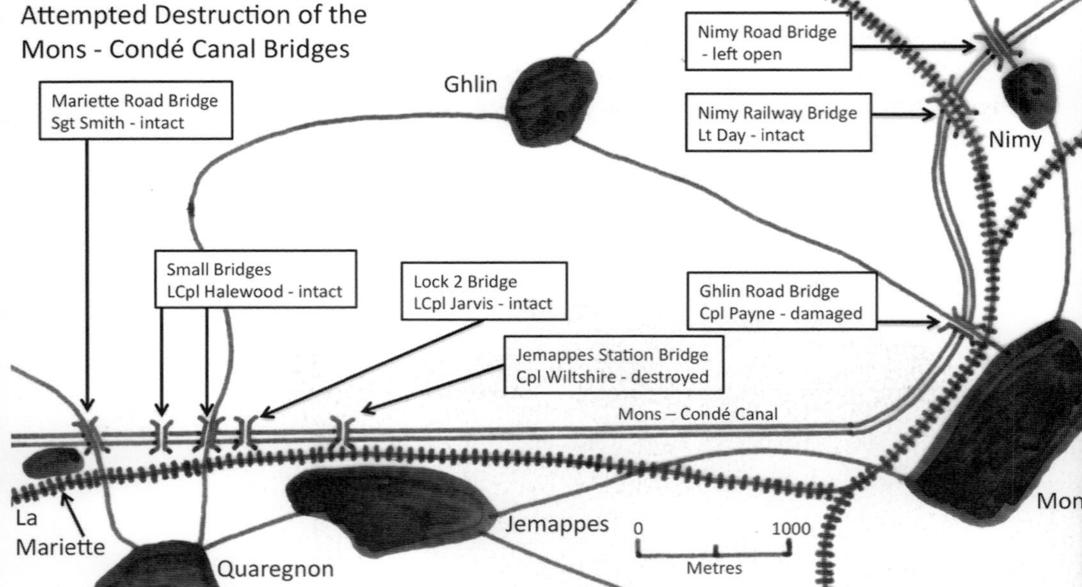

An original drop bridge still in place near Ville sur Haine, similar to the one Lance Corporal Jarvis tried to destroy at Jemappes.

In the foreground is the site of Lock 2 looking eastwards along the line of the former subsidiary canal. The main canal is now covered by the Autoroute marked by the streetlights behind the bushes on the left. In the centre distance is the Belfry in Mons. The mast on the right is at Jemappes station. To reach the site of Lock 2, park at the station, walk through the underpass to the far platform and beyond it is the Haine. Turn left (west) and walk along the cycle path for 1 km to just before the road bridge.

fuses had been withdrawn just before mobilisation and there was only one electrical exploder per Section. Despite the problems, the Sappers set about their difficult task.

Lieutenant Day's party was allocated the three bridges at Nimy and Mons, but had insufficient explosives for all three. They therefore ignored the road bridge at Nimy as it was swung across the canal. Day was wounded and taken prisoner before he had time to connect all the charges to the Nimy railway bridge. Corporal Payne managed to connect his charges to the Ghlin road bridge northwest of Mons, but without an exploder it was impossible to set off all six fuses simultaneously. As a result this bridge was probably damaged, but not destroyed.

Further west, at 7.15 a.m., Lieutenant Boulnois was given eight men, a cart load of explosives and one exploder to deal with the five bridges from Jemappes station to Mariette. These bridges were of the drop type (rather than swing) and 12-15m in length. Boulnois allotted men to bridges as they passed each one and arranged to return to set off the charges with the only available exploder. Corporal Wiltshire and a sapper were allocated the Jemappes station bridge. The Lock 2 bridge near Jemappes was allotted to **Lance Corporal Charles Jarvis** and Sapper Neary. The two small bridges just west of Lock 2 fell to Lance Corporal Halewood and a sapper, while the main road bridge at Mariette was allocated to Sergeant Smith and Sapper Daball.

The station at Jemappes from the north. The car park is on the south side and the structure on the right is the underpass. The Haine is behind the camera.

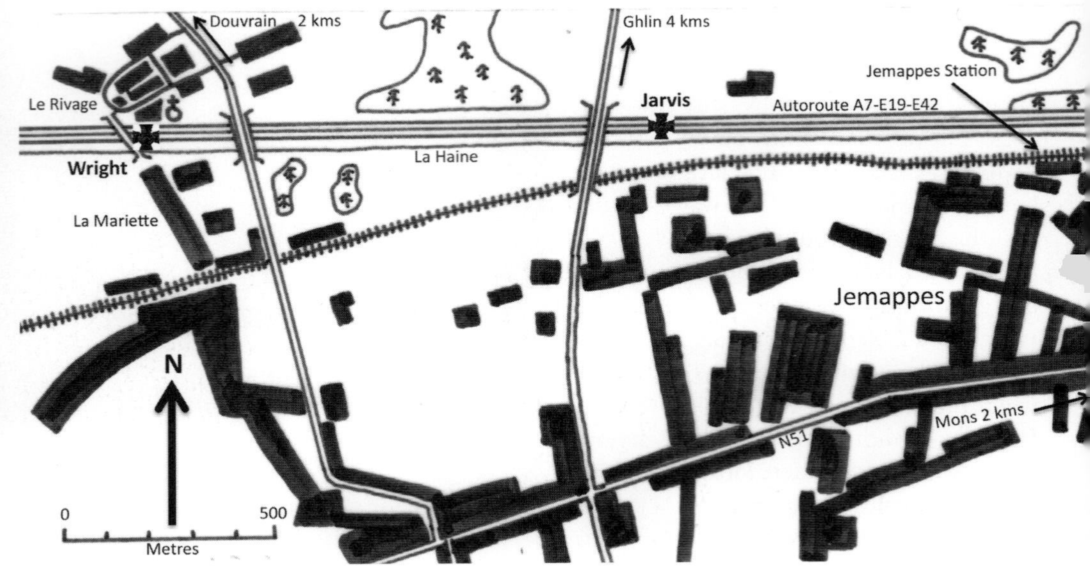

To reach the site of Lock 2, park at Jemappes Station, walk through the underpass to the far platform and beyond it is the Haine. Turn left (west) and walk along the cycle path for about a kilometre to just before the road bridge. To view the bridge at Mariette, cross the road bridge heading north and turn first left into Le Rivage following the one-way system through the village. Park at the footbridge, which leads to La Mariette, walk over it to stand above the Haine bridge in 1914. This is the site of the road.

Jarvis enlisted the help of two soldiers from B Company, 1st Royal Scots Fusiliers, defending the bridge. Using a small boat, which the infantrymen held in position, the two sappers fixed 22 gun cotton slabs to the three main girder supports. As they worked, the enemy fire intensified and Jarvis sent the infantrymen back into cover. He then sent Neary to find Corporal Wiltshire, whom he understood had the exploder at the Jemappes station bridge. Although under heavy fire, Jarvis completed the work on his own, making occasional dashes back to the infantry barricade to fetch extra explosives and run out the leads.

Enemy pressure at the bridge continued to increase and the company commander, Captain Thomas Trail (DSO for this action), went off on a donkey to find reinforcements and ammunition, while his men were forced to fall back 20m from the canal. Keeping well down in the boat Jarvis pulled himself along the bank and then crawled over it to safety. **Captain Theodore Wright**, the Divisional Adjutant RE, who had been detailed to supervise 57th Field Company's preparations, arrived. While attempting to cross the 20m of open ground south of the canal, Wright was

Jemappes station is out of view on the left. The cycle path follows the line of the Haine on the right, with the Autoroute beyond the bushes. Follow this path for about 1 km to the site of Lock 2 just before the second bridge.

wounded in the head by shrapnel and then departed to find out what was happening elsewhere. The situation was becoming critical and there was a danger that the infantry would have to withdraw further, but Jarvis could not destroy the bridge until the exploder arrived.

A lifting bridge over the canal west of Jemappes in 1914. The large building on the right can still be seen alongside the Autoroute.

At about 2.00 p.m., Boulnois and Smith were checking on progress at the bridges when they ran into Wright coming from Lock 2. While conversing they flagged down a dispatch rider looking for 1st Royal Scots Fusiliers and learned that orders for a general retirement had been issued. Although no orders had been received to destroy the bridges, it was clear this must be done as a matter of urgency. However, they had only one exploder with which to destroy five bridges. Leaving Boulnois to get on as best he could, Wright set off in a car to order the destruction of the bridges being prepared by Day at Nimy.

A contemporary photograph from the Belfry in Mons along the line of the Canal west of the town towards Jemappes. Mons station is below the canal.

Boulnois reached his easternmost bridge at Jemappes station, but CO 1st Royal Scots Fusiliers was not keen to blow it in the absence of orders from Divisional HQ. Around 3.00 p.m. the situation became so desperate that the CO relented. The exploder was connected to the leads laid by Corporal Wiltshire and the bridge was destroyed. Boulnois decided to omit the next three bridges, including Jarvis' at Lock 2, and go directly to the main road bridge at Mariette. On the way he and Smith again met Wright and it was decided hastily that Wright and Smith would go to the Mariette bridge, while Boulnois did what he could at the remaining three bridges between Mariette and Jemappes. At one of Lance Corporal Halewood's bridges, Boulnois managed to connect the leads to the electricity supply in a nearby house. However, just as he completed the preparations the power supply failed and he could do nothing. Lock 2 and the other bridge were overlooked completely in the confusion.

The modern bridge at Mariette looking east from the site of the 1914 bridge.

At the Mariette bridge, Wright and Smith discovered that the free ends of the explosive leads reached only as far as the towpath, which was separated from the infantry positions (B Company, 1st Northumberland Fusiliers), by a subsidiary canal (4.5-6m wide), running parallel with the main waterway. With longer leads tied around him, Wright managed to reach the girder bridge over the smaller canal and gained shelter underneath it. Then under the bridge, he swung hand over hand to reach the far bank, but every time he lifted his head to the level of the towpath he was fired on from only 30m away. It was impossible to reach the leads and he began to swing back under the bridge. Utterly exhausted, he fell into the water, from where he was rescued by Smith.

Due to a series of unfortunate circumstances only one bridge (Jemappes station) out of the eight allocated to 57th Field Company was destroyed. However, this does not detract from the exceptional gallantry displayed by Captain Wright, Lance Corporal Jarvis and others in attempting to destroy them. Jarvis' VC citation states that he blew up the Lock 2 bridge, but other evidence suggests that this did not occur.

Site of the pontoon bridge over the River Aisne at Vailly where Theodore Wright was mortally wounded on 14th September 1914.

On 14th September, at Vailly on the River Aisne, Captain Wright was assisting the passage of 5th Cavalry Brigade over a pontoon bridge built by 56th and 57th Field Companies the previous night. While supervising repairs to the bridge he was constantly exposed to heavy enemy fire and was eventually mortally wounded as he assisted some injured men into shelter.

Action of Elouges, 24th August 1914

6 Capt Francis Grenfell, 9th Lancers (2nd Cavalry Brigade, Cavalry Division), Audregnies, Belgium
7 Maj Ernest Alexander, 119 Battery RFA (5th Division), Elouges, Belgium

The unexpected withdrawal of the French Fifth Army on the BEF's right flank on 23rd August and increasing pressure from overwhelming numbers of German troops, necessitated pulling back from the Mons-Condé Canal. From dawn on 24th August the German IV Corps tried to envelop the retreating BEF's left flank, held by 5th Division (II Corps). The Divisional Commander ordered a rearguard (1st Norfolk, 1st Cheshire and 119 Battery RFA), to occupy the high ground west of

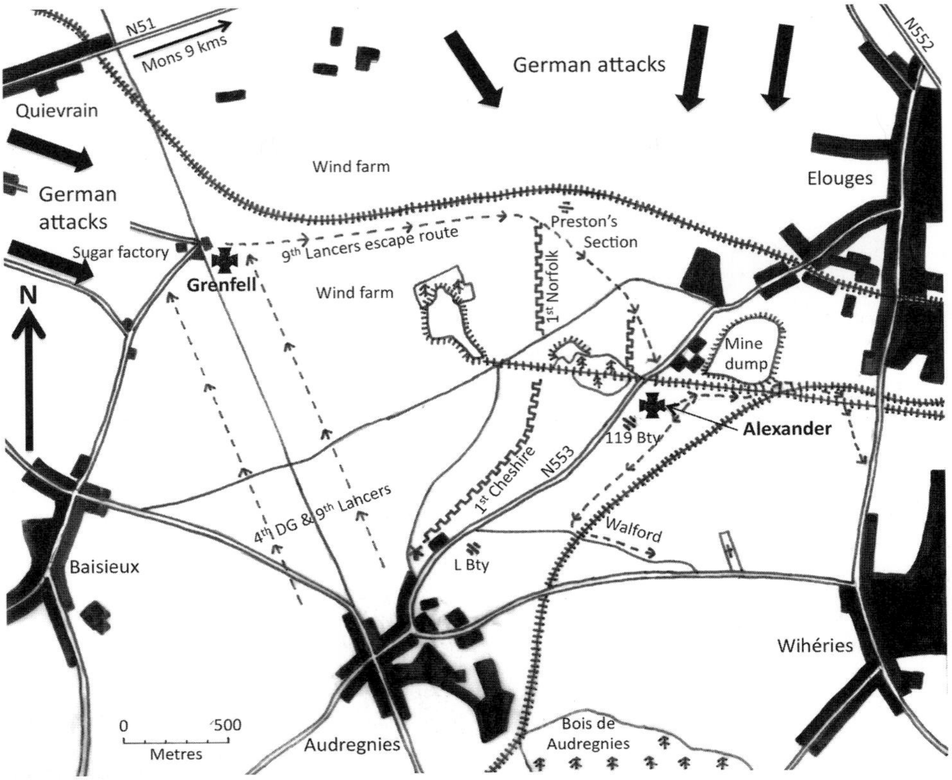

On 24th August 1914 the area of the rearguard action was covered in mines, spoil heaps and a number of light railways. The mines have gone, but the spoil heaps (mainly wooded) and the railway embankments remain. The road between Elouges and Audregnies offers excellent views to the north and northwest, but it can be extremely fast. If you stop (there are normally places to pull in a car), ensure you get right off the roadway. The sugar factory can be approached along the Roman Road from Audregnies, but it is quite rough in places and only recommended for cross-country vehicles; easier access is from the west through Baisieux, where there is a café.

Elouges, facing northwest towards Quievrain. Two British cavalry brigades were also in the area. At 12.30 p.m., before the rearguard was ready, a concerted attack developed from the direction of Quievrain and Baisieux.

2nd Cavalry Brigade had been in action since 4.00 a.m., conducting a fighting withdrawal through Elouges. It was ordered to block the enemy by reoccupying positions vacated earlier to the north of Audregnies. While moving into these positions a strong enemy attack developed from Quievrain. The situation was critical; if the Germans broke through before the rearguard was prepared, it could have resulted in the destruction of the entire 5th Division. 9th Lancers, with 4th Dragoon Guards and 18th Hussars in support, was ordered to halt the attack at all costs.

Looking north along the Roman Road, astride which 9th Lancers and two troops of 4th Dragoon Guards advanced against the flank of IV German Corps. The sugar factory is behind the camera.

The cavalry would not have charged the whole distance, some 1,500m. To do so would have risked arriving at the enemy positions on exhausted horses. In any case obstacles such as this sunken lane across the line of advance would have slowed progress to a walk in places.

The sugar factory from the north. B Squadron, 9th Lancers took cover around it and nearby spoil heaps to engage the advancing Germans after the charge petered out.

A cavalry charge, although a desperate measure against unbroken infantry, was the only way of stopping the enemy in the time available. Setting off from north of Audregnies, 9th Lancers and two troops of 4th Dragoon Guards, advanced astride the Roman road towards the enemy flank. When still 450m away, they were halted by a wire fence and engaged by nine enemy batteries and heavy small arms fire. The Germans suffered little damage as a result of the charge, but the psychological effect delayed their advance for some hours. The British artillery did great execution amongst the massed German ranks and gave the rearguard a much needed respite to prepare rudimentary positions on the high ground. Meanwhile the rest of the Division slipped away.

The fence that halted the Lancers has been the subject of some controversy. In 1921, local people knew nothing about it; indeed some insisted it never existed. Whatever it was may never be known, but it was certainly not positioned by the advancing Germans.

When the 9th Lancers charge petered out, **Captain Francis Grenfell** kept B Squadron together. They took cover behind small slagheaps and around a sugar factory about 1,250m southeast of Quievrain, where they dismounted and engaged the enemy with their rifles. About 2.30 p.m. the Germans resumed their attack and

The cavalry's escape route from the sugar factory looking east with the light railway embankment on the left (now a cycle track). 1st Norfolk held the high ground from the embankment to the right where the tree covered spoil heap marks the site of a mine in 1914.

The reverse view of the previous picture with the sugar factory on the left and the railway embankment on the right. The construction of the wind farm altered the view significantly, but did provide a number of convenient tracks to areas of the battlefield that were previously inaccessible.

the Lancers were forced to retire eastwards towards Elouges under the cover of a light railway embankment. Grenfell chose to ride along the embankment and was wounded in the hand and thigh. Earlier in the day his horse had been killed while bullets had passed harmlessly through his boots and tunic.

The Germans then threw twelve battalions against the rearguard, but were driven back by the infantry with support from L Battery RHA (awarded three VCs a week later at Néry) and a section of 119 Battery under Lieutenant COD Preston. This section was forced to retire under fire, but came back into action 450m to the right of the rest of the Battery, where it engaged targets until they were closer than 200m. Just before the Germans surrounded it, Preston pulled back but, moving along a road in front of the rest of the Battery, became mixed up with the retiring cavalry.

One of the lead horses was shot and Sergeant McCartney dismounted to cut it free. Preston extracted the section from the cavalry and came back into action again. When the Germans were 700m away he sent one gun out of action and was wounded for the second time. McCartney went back to assist with the other gun and, once Preston had been evacuated for treatment, got both guns away.

Meanwhile the rest of 119 Battery had come out on top in a duel with two enemy batteries. The German advance was checked again but, as the forward troops withdrew, two sections of the Battery were exposed to heavy flanking fire from nearby mine dumps. Earlier in the afternoon, Captain J C Walford had wisely moved the wagon lines into a hollow alongside a railway embankment, where they were sheltered from the enemy fire. **Major Ernest Alexander**, commanding 119 Battery, got his men into the hollow while he went to obtain permission to withdraw from Lieutenant Colonel Ballard of 1st Norfolk, commanding the rearguard. Meanwhile Battery Sergeant Major F Smyth organised some gunners on the embankment to engage the enemy with their rifles. Two cavalry machine-guns joined them.

Alexander returned with authority to pull back but, due to the close proximity of the enemy, it was not possible to use the horse teams in the hollow. The only option was to run the guns back into

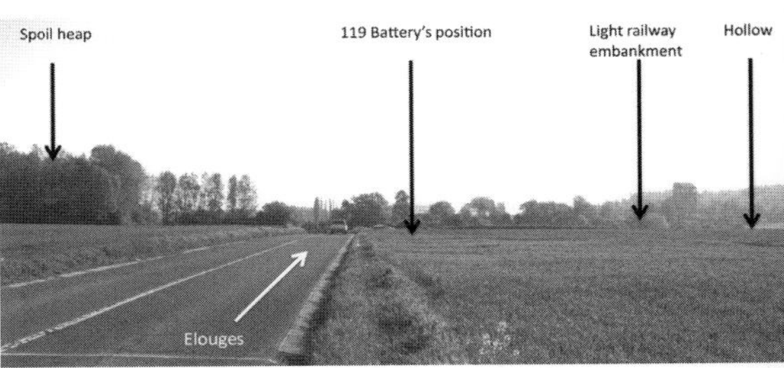

Looking east along the road from Audregnies towards Elouges. 119th Battery was to the right of the road, firing across it to the northwest. The gunners came under fire from German infantry on the tree covered spoil heap on the left. Alexander got his men and the guns into the cover of the hollow on the right below the derelict industrial building, which stands alongside another disused light railway embankment.

The route taken to run the guns into the hollow.

cover by hand. Despite the heavy fire, Alexander led the men back across 300m of open ground to manhandle the guns into the cover of the embankment. This was a most difficult, dangerous and arduous task. With so few men due to casualties and over heavy ground they could only move one gun at a time.

Alexander had succeeded in recovering one gun when B Squadron, 9th Lancers arrived. Grenfell readily accepted Alexander's appeal for assistance and calmly went off to find an escape route for the guns. He then rode back to where his men were sheltering and reminded them of when the Regiment had rescued the guns at the Battle of Maiwand in Afghanistan in 1880. Every man came forward; approximately eleven officers and forty troopers. Covered by a few men firing from the embankment, the cavalrymen and a dozen or so gunners raced over two fields and slowly manhandled the guns and limbers into safety. A number of journeys had to be made before everything was recovered. During this time they were exposed to three German batteries, as well as heavy small arms fire from the mine dumps.

One of the guns being moved by Grenfell's team was lifted off the ground when a shell landed beneath it, but fortunately it failed to explode. Grenfell was wounded again, this time in the face, but carried on. With the guns in the cover of the embankment and temporarily out of view of the Germans, the drivers were able to limber up. Alexander went back to rescue a wounded man then split the Battery in two to get away. He sent the guns and some wagons east in the cover of the railway embankment, which they had to cross before reaching the road, thereby exposing themselves to the enemy fire for about 300m. Walford took the rest of the wagons and the limbers by a different route over a level crossing. Alexander satisfied himself everyone and everything that could be moved had got away before leaving himself behind the guns.

Only one wagon and a limber were lost, but 119 Battery suffered forty-six casualties, including ten killed, and lost forty-three horses during the day. 9th Lancers had fourteen killed. Grenfell refused treatment and rode back sixteen kms with his men, despite having been in continuous action since dawn. An officer of 4th Dragoon Guards saw him on the journey, "*…with a bleeding hand tied up in a bandana handkerchief and bullet holes through his clothes, but very exhilarated*". At 7.00 p.m., completely exhausted, he collapsed and was picked up by a car driven by the Duke of Westminster. He was taken to Bavay, where his wounds were dressed by nuns and that night he slept in the Duke's bed at Le Cateau.

On the battlefield, 1st Norfolk received the order to retire to avoid being enveloped. This was achieved, but 100 wounded men had to be left behind. Three messengers sent with withdrawal orders to 1st Cheshire failed to reach the Battalion. The reserve company at Audregnies was sent back by a staff officer, but the rest and a small party of 1st Norfolk were forced back to the Audregnies road. By aggressive action a short respite was gained and some troops got away through Bois d'Audregnies. When the Germans returned to the attack, 1st Cheshire was split into three groups and fought on until almost 7.00 p.m. Short of ammunition, the survivors were overwhelmed and surrendered to 72nd Regiment of IV Corps.

From the centre of 1st Cheshire's position north of the Audregnies - Elouges road looking northwest. Baisieux church is on the left with the sugar factory in the centre and the light railway embankment used by the cavalry to make good their escape on the right.

The rearguard had done its job well against an entire German corps. The majority of 5th Division managed to slip away; but the cost had been heavy with 1st Norfolk losing over 250 men, including fifty-four killed, and 1st Cheshire over 700, although only fifty-eight were killed, the majority being taken prisoner.

Affair of Landrecies, 25-26th August 1914

8 LCpl George Wyatt, 3rd Coldstream Guards (4th (Guards) Brigade, 2nd Division), Landrecies & Villers – Cotterêts, France

During the retreat from Mons, 2nd and 3rd Coldstream Guards formed the rearguard for 4th (Guards) Brigade. At 7.00 p.m. on 24th August 1914, 3rd Coldstream Guards billeted at Malgarni, southeast of Bavay, having been under arms for 32 hours. Soon after 4 a.m. on the 25th the Battalion marched off towards Landrecies. It was hot and water was short, but with the enemy close behind it was imperative to cross the Sambre bridges before they were blown. By 9.45 a.m. the men were so exhausted they were covering only three and a half kilometres an hour and more than ninety had dropped out. The CO realised if he continued as instructed he would have no men left and ordered normal rest halts to be taken.

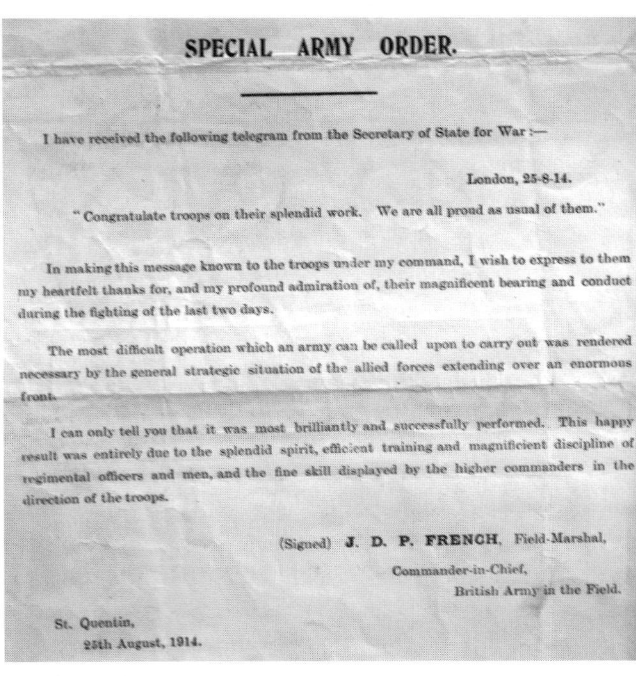

SPECIAL ARMY ORDER.

I have received the following telegram from the Secretary of State for War :—

London, 25-8-14.

"Congratulate troops on their splendid work. We are all proud as usual of them."

In making this message known to the troops under my command, I wish to express to them my heartfelt thanks for, and my profound admiration of, their magnificent bearing and conduct during the fighting of the last two days.

The most difficult operation which an army can be called upon to carry out was rendered necessary by the general strategic situation of the allied forces extending over an enormous front.

I can only tell you that it was most brilliantly and successfully performed. This happy result was entirely due to the splendid spirit, efficient training and magnificient discipline of regimental officers and men, and the fine skill displayed by the higher commanders in the direction of the troops.

(Signed) J. D. P. FRENCH, Field-Marshal,
Commander-in-Chief,
British Army in the Field.

St. Quentin,
25th August, 1914.

Field Marshal French's congratulatory message to the BEF on 25th August 1914.

Reaching Landrecies at 1.00 p.m., the Battalion went into billets in the barracks northwest of the Sambre and

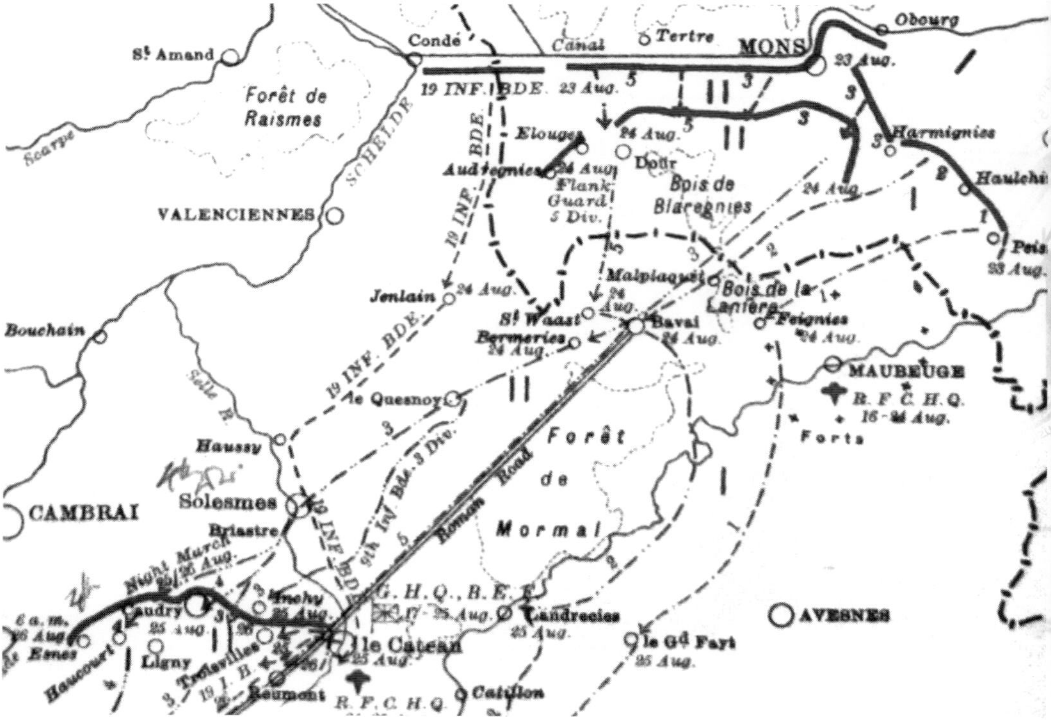

The early stages of the retreat from Mons. Landrecies is on the southern edge of the Foret de Mormal, which effectively split I Corps from II Corps (Official History 1914, Volume 1, Maps).

by early evening the whole Brigade was resting. There were no reports of Germans in the immediate area, but the Forest of Mormal dominated the north of the town and a surprise attack could have been launched from it. The Sambre bridges were therefore guarded, those in Landrecies being the responsibility of 4th (Guards) Brigade. 3rd Coldstream Guards provided an outpost at a railway crossing in the northwest of the town. French cavalry was reported to be operating to the north, but otherwise the situation was quiet.

The road junction picketed by 3rd Coldstream Guards. On the left is the memorial arch. The road on the right running past the water tower leads towards the Forest of Mormal, part of which can be seen in the distance.

The former French Army barracks in Landrecies.

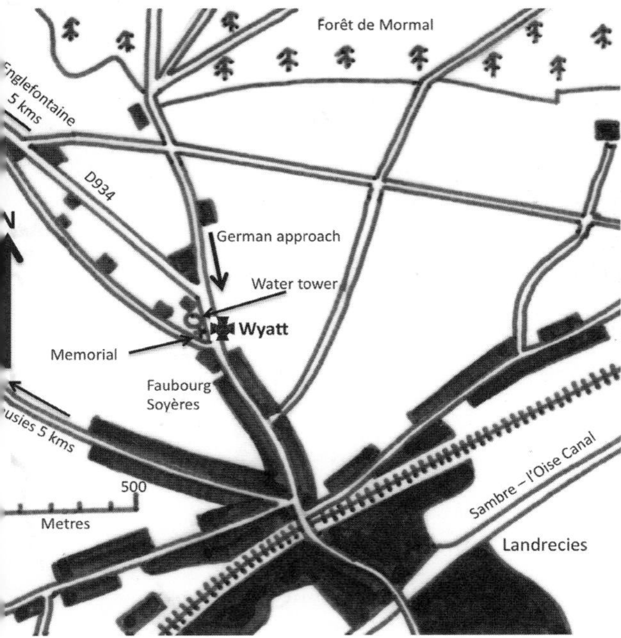

Landrecies has a number of shops, cafes and restaurants, making it a convenient place to take a break during a tour of the nearby battlefields. Leave the town northwards on the D934 and 600m after the railway crossing is a memorial arch on the left. There are places to park on either side of the road. The arch stands at the junction picketed by 3rd Coldstream Guards and commemorates the stand made here on the night of 25/26th August 1914.

At 5.30 p.m. some civilians rushed into the town, reporting the enemy was advancing out of the Forest. Two companies of 3rd Coldstream Guards under Captain Heywood rushed to a road junction at Faubourg Soyère, 600m beyond the railway, but mounted patrols failed to find the enemy. It is possible the civilians sighted a German patrol which, having entered the town and finding it full of British troops, had beaten a hasty retreat.

Taking it to be a false alarm, sentries were posted and the troops settled down to rest again. No 2 Company formed a picket at Faubourg Soyère, with two machine-guns covering the flanks and wire stretched across the road. Darkness was falling at 7.00 p.m. when a warning was given of approaching Uhlans, followed by 1,000 infantry supported by artillery. A cavalry patrol approached the picket and was driven off, leaving two dead.

Shortly afterwards No 3 Company under Captain Monck, relieved No 2 Company. A report was received from civilians that French cavalry was approaching from the direction of the Forest. When troops were heard moving along the road about 7.30 p.m. it did not cause undue alarm. However, these troops were Germans singing French songs. The sentry's challenge

The picket position looking towards the Forest of Mormal. The burning barn extinguished by Wyatt was on the left side of the right hand road.

This house still bears scars from the fighting.

The German view of 3rd Coldstream Guards' position as they advanced towards Landrecies. The light coloured cottage on the right may be the one behind which 3rd Coldstream Guards sheltered from fire being directed down this road.

was answered with, *"Ne tirez pas; nous sommes Francais"*. Monck went forward to investigate and the leading 'French' officer shone his torch directly into Monck's face. A British torch shone out from the picket line and although the front rank appeared to be in French or Belgian uniforms, those behind were definitely Germans. The game was up, but the Germans rushed the picket before Monck's order to open fire could be obeyed. Monck was knocked over in the rush, as was the machine-gun after the gunner, Private Robson, was bayoneted (Landrecies Communal Cemetery, B 6). Despite the surprise, the picket recovered quickly and forced the enemy back with volleys of shots and in hand-to-hand fighting. The machine-gun was recovered.

No.1 Company was immediately sent to reinforce the position while the rest of the Battalion guarded the other entry points into the town. 2nd Grenadier Guards and two sections of artillery set up a fallback position at the railway crossing. The Germans charged again and again, but on each occasion they were forced back by steady rifle and machine-gun fire. At 8.30 p.m. a German field gun joined in the fight. Its fire was accurate, but the enemy infantry aimed too high in the poor light. There is a report that the Germans were using grenades, but at that early stage in the war it seems unlikely.

The memorial stone under the arch at Faubourg Soyere. Major Matheson was second-in-command of 3rd Coldstream Guards. He took forward three platoons of No.1 Company to reinforce No.2 Company. When Wyatt was asked by a newspaper why he did it, he replied, "*Because Major Matheson told me to.*" Matheson was later CO and went on to command 46th Brigade and 20th, 4th & Guards Divisions during the war. He retired in 1935 as General Sir Torquhil George Matheson, 5th Baronet KCB CMG.

Leave Villers-Cotterêts north on the D81 into Forêt Domanial de Retz. Two kilometres north of the N2 the road swings right and on the right is the 'Guards Grave, Villers-Cotterêts Forest', which contains the remains of 78 identified members of 4th (Guards) Brigade and 20 unknowns. One man buried there is 2nd Lieutenant George Edward Cecil. Continue along the D81. As the road bends to the left is a memorial to Cecil erected by his mother after the war. Immediately after the memorial turn left onto Rond de la Reine and park at the house on the right. Rond de la Reine is one of numerous tracks and rides criss-crossing these woods.

A barn stood on the left side of the lane leading towards the Forest. The Germans tried to set up a machine-gun at the end of the lane to fire into the British positions, but the Coldstreams negated this by pulling back a few metres into the cover of a cottage. Soon after a German shell set fire to the straw in the barn and the light enabled the enemy to direct more accurate fire into the British. With the enemy only 25m away **Lance Corporal George Wyatt** dashed out with a pitchfork, tossed out the burning straw from the barn and beat out the flames. Shellfire rekindled the fire and again Wyatt went out and put out the flames. In darkness the enemy fire became inaccurate and the opportunity to overwhelm the picket passed.

Fighting went on into the night and at about 1.00 a.m., the CO, Lieutenant Colonel Fielding, brought up a howitzer from 60th Battery. With its third round it scored a direct hit on the enemy gun, silencing it and effectively bringing the Affair at Landrecies to a close. The action cost 3rd Coldstream Guards 124 casualties, but the losses would have been greater had Wyatt not extinguished the flames.

On 1st September, at Villers-Cotterêts, 4th (Guards) Brigade was covering the withdrawal of 2nd Division. 3rd Coldstream Guards was widely dispersed from north of Soucy westwards to cover the many approaches through the dense woodland. No 1 Company was on the right, No 2 in the centre and No 4 on the left with No 3 in reserve. The plan was for companies to retire in succession from the left when ordered.

As Nos.1 and 2 Companies fell, back a number of Uhlans appeared to the front and were fired upon. No 4 Company observed a farm cart crossing its front and believed it carried refugees until a machine-gun aboard opened fire. It caused no damage and the Company fell back in good order. The Battalion fell back through

Vivières to the ride known as Rond de la Reine running east to west through Forêt Domanial de Retz. 2nd Grenadier Guards held the east and 3rd Coldstream Guards the west, blocking the road to Haramont. The Battalion was stretched to cover the long frontage, which resulted in large gaps, particularly between Nos 2 and 4 Companies. The CO went to see the Brigadier-General who authorised No 4 Company to close up to No 2 Company. The right of 2nd Grenadier Guards filled the resultant gap.

Rond de la Reine in the Forêt Domanial de Retz north of Villers-Cotterêts, scene of confused fighting on 1st September 1914.

The Germans chose this moment to attack and opened fire at close range. There was no time to fill the gap between Nos 2 and 4 Companies. A German machine-gun enfiladed the Coldstream position along the broad main ride along the ridgeline. Falling back, but fighting all the away, the Battalion became mixed up with elements of other units. Arriving at the railway line (since removed) north of Villers-Cotterêts, 2nd Coldstream Guards took over the rearguard and soon afterwards the whole Brigade fell back through 5th Brigade. During this confused action Wyatt was wounded in the head, but went on firing until he could no longer see through the blood in his eyes. The MO bandaged Wyatt and ordered him to go to the rear, but he went straight back to his position and continued the fight instead.

Battle of Le Cateau, 26th August 1914

9 Capt Douglas Reynolds, 37 (Howitzer) Battery RFA (5th Division), Le Cateau and Pisserloup, France

10 Dvr Job Drain, 37 (Howitzer) Battery RFA (5th Division), Le Cateau, France

11 Dvr Frederick Luke, 37 (Howitzer) Battery RFA (5th Division), Le Cateau, France

12 Maj Charles Yate, 2nd KOYLI (13th Brigade, 5th Division), Le Cateau, France

13 LCpl Frederick Holmes, 2nd KOYLI (13th Brigade, 5th Division), Le Cateau, France

On the night of 25th/26th August 1914, General Sir Horace Smith-Dorien's II Corps rested around Le Cateau, intending to continue the retreat the following morning. During the day a gap had opened between I Corps and II Corps as they separated to pass either side of the Forest of Mormal. This was exacerbated when I Corps was forced to pull back earlier than expected at 2 a.m. on 26th August. At that time, some of II Corps' troops were still completing the previous day's march. Smith-Dorien realised if he continued to pull back he risked the entire BEF being

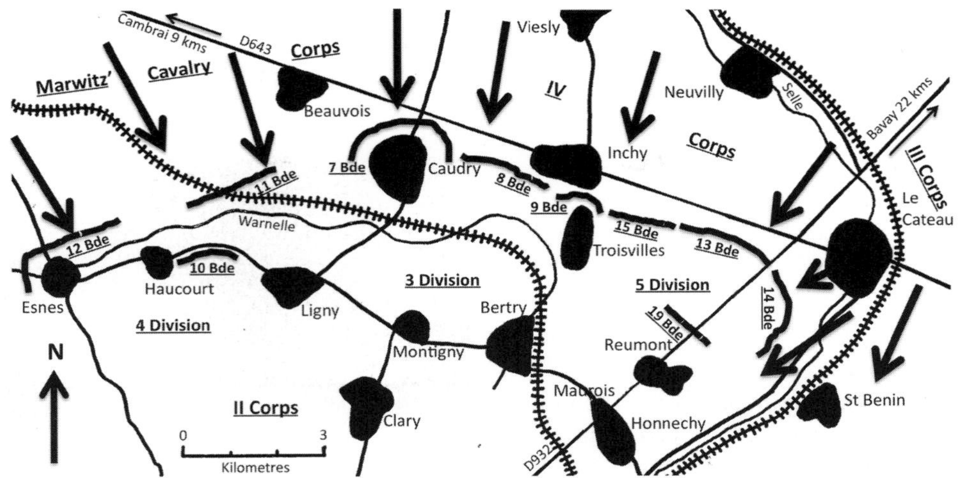

Although heavily outnumbered, II Corps fought a delaying action at Le Cateau on 26th August 1914. Both flanks were threatened with envelopment, particularly on the right, where five VCs were awarded. Le Cateau has a number of hotels, shops, cafés and restaurants. The town library at 9 Rue du Marché aux Chevaux houses a 3.7" Howitzer of 1932 vintage presented by 93 (Le Cateau) Battery, successor to 37 (Howitzer) Battery. Le Cateau is also the birthplace of the artist Matisse and there is a museum dedicated to him.

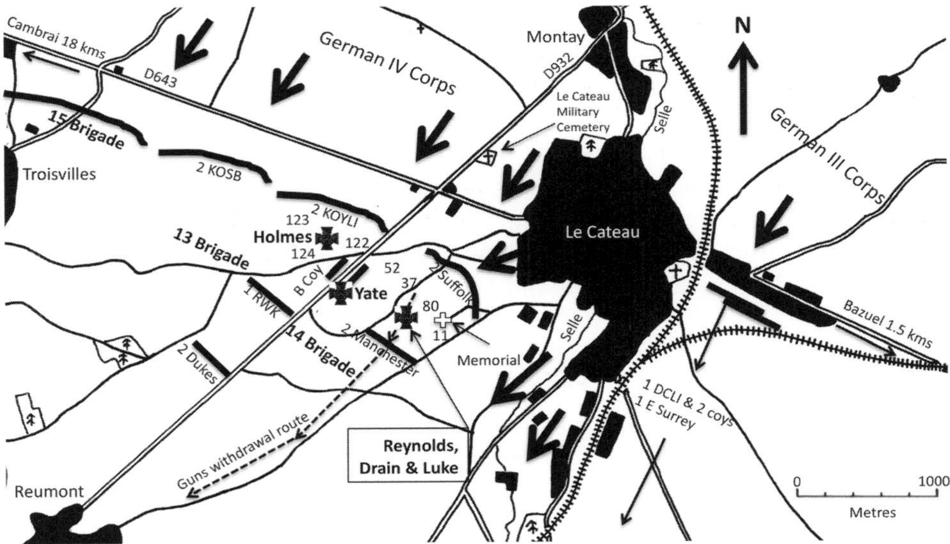

Most of 5th Division's sector of the Le Cateau battlefield can be viewed from the northern end of B Company, 2nd KOYLI's position, where the track from Le Cateau to Troisvilles crosses the D932. This is a very fast road and it is advisable to get off it completely on the west side of this junction before alighting, while ensuring the track remains accessible for farm vehicles. The same track to the east leads to 37 (Howitzer) Battery's position, but is only driveable in a cross-country vehicle usually. It is worth the walk to see the ground. Units of 13th and 14th Brigades are shown, but others have been omitted for clarity. Unit titles are abbreviated and only gun battery numbers are shown.

enveloped and destroyed. He therefore decided to fight a holding action to gain time.

The troops awoke at 4.00 a.m. expecting to march off and were surprised when ordered to stand fast. The position was less than ideal; some units had poor fields of fire and could be approached quite closely from dead ground. There was little

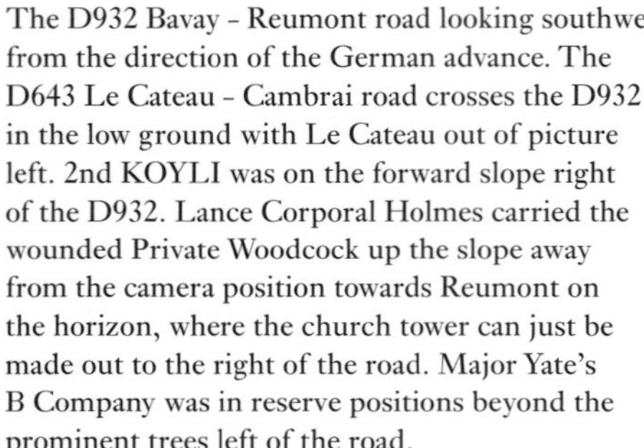
The D932 Bavay - Reumont road looking southwest from the direction of the German advance. The D643 Le Cateau - Cambrai road crosses the D932 in the low ground with Le Cateau out of picture left. 2nd KOYLI was on the forward slope right of the D932. Lance Corporal Holmes carried the wounded Private Woodcock up the slope away from the camera position towards Reumont on the horizon, where the church tower can just be made out to the right of the road. Major Yate's B Company was in reserve positions beyond the prominent trees left of the road.

The D932 looking northeast towards the advancing Germans. B Company, 2nd KOYLI was sited in ditches either side of the road from this position to just before the trees on the right, which can be seen in the previous picture. The track running right from these trees leads to 37 (Howitzer) Battery's position. On the other side of the road the car is parked at the entrance to the track to Troisvilles.

time to dig proper defences, as around 6.00 a.m. the first German patrols entered Le Cateau. At 6.30 a.m. two battalions of 14th Brigade (1st DCLI and half 1st East Surrey) were surprised as they tried to clear Le Cateau and fought their way out along the Selle valley. Unaware of the order to stand, they played no part in the main action and the rest of the Brigade fought the battle at just over half strength. As the early morning mist cleared, a dozen batteries opened fire on the British positions.

5th Division was holding II Corps' open right flank with 15th Brigade left, 13th Brigade centre and 14th Brigade right. The latter was supported by XV Brigade RFA (11, 52 and 80 Batteries) with 37 (Howitzer) Battery attached. The order to stand did not reach the Division until 5 a.m. The position ran along an east-west ridge falling away to the east and north towards Le Cateau and the Cambrai road. 13th Brigade had 2nd KOSB left and 2nd KOYLI right facing north close to the Cambrai road. To its right was 14th Brigade, holding the vital high ground southwest of Le Cateau with 2nd Suffolk, 2nd Manchester and half of 1st East Surrey.

37 Battery had billeted at Reumont the previous night and knew nothing of the decision to stand until ordered to move forward at 4.00 a.m. By 5.00 a.m. the Battery was in its allotted but exposed position astride a track leading to the main Reumont road, close to B Company, 2nd KOYLI. 11, 52 and 80 Batteries came up in line a little later. All were very exposed within the infantry positions, but because of the shape of the ground they had difficulty clearing the crest to the front when firing at close range

Looking east towards Le Cateau over B Company, 2nd KOYLI's position alongside the D932. The prominent spire left of centre is in the town, demonstrating the depth of dead ground on this flank, which allowed large bodies of German troops to manoeuvre close to the British positions before being exposed to their fire. On the left is the track from Le Cateau to Troisvilles. The guns of XV Brigade were on the high ground on the right, mainly on the reverse (right) slope, making it difficult to engage close range targets to the east and north.

targets. The gunners began to dig in, but made little progress before coming under rifle fire and were soon being sought by the enemy artillery. At 6.50 a.m., 37 Battery's commander, Major Jones, and BSM Morrow were wounded in the OP, but remained at duty. At 9.00 a.m. shells fell on the Battery's horse teams and these were withdrawn towards Reumont, but not before about 50 horses had been lost.

2nd KOYLI had three companies forward south of the Le Cateau – Cambrai road (D643). C Company was east of the Reumont road (D932) and A and D Companies were west of it with B Company and Battalion HQ some way to the rear. The Battalion expected to pull back by 11.00 a.m. in accordance with the original plan and prepared for only a short rearguard action. However, at 6.00 a.m. new orders were received, *"There will now be no retirement for the fighting troops; fill up your trenches with water, food and ammunition as far as you can."* C Company handed over to 14th Brigade and crossed the Reumont road to take up positions west of A Company.

B Company, commanded by **Major Charles Yate**, with the Battalion machine-gun section on its right flank, moved forward a little, but remained some distance behind the rest of the Battalion. It was sited in ditches either side of the Reumont road facing southeast to provide enfilade protection to 14th Brigade and cover the open right flank. The roadside to the north was higher than the south, allowing B Company to fire from both ditches simultaneously. A culvert under the road was used to communicate between the two lines. However, the sunken track to

The junction of the D932 with the Troisvilles track on the right; a relatively safe place to park off the main road. B Company, 2nd KOYLI's positions ran from here alongside the road almost to the crest.

The high ground southwest of Le Cateau, out of view left, held by 2nd Suffolk and 2nd Manchester. There is a memorial to these Battalions, together with 2nd Argyll & Sutherland Highlanders and XV Brigade RFA in the small copse on the right. The memorial can be reached from Le Cateau by driving south along Avenue des Essarts following signs for Collège J Rostand. Turn right into Chemin du Reumont, passing the Collège on the left before taking a minor track on the right for 200m to the memorial. Park before the memorial as turning close to it is difficult.

Troisvilles was full of artillery limbers and horse teams, effectively cutting the Battalion in two.

2nd Suffolk (14th Brigade) was pushed off the ridge southwest of Le Cateau, but retook it before losing it again. From about 10.00 a.m. German batteries began firing from the east into the flank of the troops close to the Reumont road, who were then under fire from two sides. Shortly afterwards the German infantry began to advance. The guns of 37 and 52 Batteries and the 2nd KOYLI machine-guns cut swathes through the German ranks as the range decreased from 1,800m to 700m. During pauses in these attacks German machine-guns caused many casualties amongst the defending British troops. 37 Battery destroyed at least two enemy batteries, which had been firing shrapnel into 14th Brigade's positions but, as the day wore on, the Germans brought up more batteries and the intensity of fire increased, as did British casualties.

At 11.15 a.m. two companies of 2nd Manchester passed between 37 and 52 Batteries to assist 2nd Suffolk. Fifteen minutes later, German batteries sought out 11, then 80 and finally 37 Batteries with airburst shrapnel shells. Two gunners in 37 Battery's centre section were knocked out and Sergeant T J Brown ignored three wounds to assist Lieutenant Earle in forming two detachments with the remaining four men. Earle was saved from serious injury when shrapnel hit the metal ring of his braces. Thinking XV Brigade had been silenced, the enemy guns switched attention to XXVIII Brigade supporting 13th Brigade on the other side of the Reumont road.

Withdrawal was imperative if 5th Division was to survive. In preparation, some of the guns were ordered back, but not without heavy losses. 11 Battery lost two guns, 80 Battery one and the whole of 52 Battery's guns had to be abandoned. There was some reluctance and delay in carrying out the withdrawal because of the way orders came down by word of mouth and also because of the previous order that there would be no retirement. 37 Battery had almost run out of ammunition and was under fire from two enemy batteries at Inchy, when informal orders came to withdraw about 2.00 p.m. **Captain Douglas Reynolds** went off on foot with a rifle to search for the horse teams. While away he was overtaken by men from another battery together with some of the left section of 37 Battery. He accompanied them back to their positions before resuming his search for the horse teams.

View from the OP over Le Cateau.

Meanwhile, BQMS O'Keefe led forward three teams, one of which was blown up, but the other two managed to recover A and B sub-sections. Reynolds returned with two teams from 52 and 80 Batteries. There was some doubt whether the large trail eye of 37 Battery's 4.5" Howitzers would fit over 52 and 80 Batteries' 18 Pounder limber hook, but it worked and they withdrew C and D sub-sections. Reynolds ordered E and F sub-sections to be disabled and abandoned before withdrawing with the rest of his men to Reumont, two miles to the southwest. Reynolds sent a sergeant and then Lieutenant Earle to persuade Major Jones to fall back from the OP; he refused until all howitzers had been recovered. Earle returned to Reynolds, who had obtained permission from the CRA to try to save the two left section howitzers. Reynolds had no difficulty in getting sixteen volunteers (three officers and thirteen other ranks) to make up two more teams and hurried back to the front.

The Germans gained ground steadily, but a brief respite was gained by a 2nd Manchester machine-gun. Taking advantage of this, Reynolds galloped his teams over the last 900m to the abandoned howitzers. At this time they were not under fire. The Germans were only 100m away, many on the ridge where they had just overrun the OP. They waved their arms and shouted at the approaching teams, presumably attempting to get them to surrender. The audacity of the action caught the Germans by surprise, gaining the gunners precious seconds to reach the howitzers without being fired upon. The Germans then opened a hail of rifle and artillery fire, but the gunners stuck resolutely to their task.

The team commanded by Lieutenant Earle with E sub-section, had driven less than 50m when the centre pair of horses was shot down. Earle and Sergeant Brown, both of whom were wounded, jumped down to separate the dead horses from the rest of the team. Earle's arm was shattered by a bullet and he stepped back to allow someone else to help. The wheelers were also shot and Earle, seeing it was impossible to move the howitzer, ordered it abandoned for the second time. Earle was hit again, this time in the head. Despite the intensity of the German fire, Gunner Fraser went back to recover his greatcoat.

The Left section (E and F sub-sections) of 37 Battery was right of this track leading to Reumont, which is just out of view on the right horizon. The Germans had reached the high ground on the left by the time the rescue attempt was made. F sub-section was limbered up, crossed to the left of this track and made off cross-country for another track to reach Reumont.

The other team was commanded by 2nd Lieutenant Morgan. **Driver Frederick Luke** skilfully manoeuvred the limber hook directly over the trail eye of the F sub-section howitzer. Sergeant Butterworth and Gunners Baker and Garlick quickly limbered it up, but as they made off to gain the track leading to Reumont, Gunner BG Cobey on the centre pair of horses was shot dead (La Ferté-sous-Jouarre Memorial). Cobey's whip was thrown into the air and caught by Reynolds, who rode alongside the rider-less pair to guide them. Luke rode on the leading pair and **Driver Job Drain** on the wheelers. Some astonished Germans were charged down as the team made its escape between 3.00 p.m. and 3.15 p.m.

Sergeant Bower went back to rescue the wounded Earle and put him on a horse. When it was hit, Bower transferred Earle to a bareback Clydesdale for a very uncomfortable ride to the aid station. Later, Bower was taking a lift on the trail of a gun when Reynolds saw him. The trail was covered in blood and Reynolds asked if he was wounded. When Bower replied it was Earle's blood, Reynolds said he should get off and walk. Despite his great bravery and support for any man whom he believed had suffered an injustice, Reynolds was rather cold and stern. Bower received no recognition for his actions.

Having reached relative safety, the survivors marched all night to arrive at St Quentin at 6.00 a.m. next morning. In addition to the three VCs, the Battery was awarded two DSOs (Major Jones and Lieutenant Earle), two DCMs (Sergeant Brown and Trumpeter Waldron) and a Croix de Guerre (Gunner Fraser). Reynolds also received the Legion d'Honneur. Some accounts claim Trumpeter SGF Waldron was only 15 when he was awarded the DCM, but his birth was registered in the last quarter of 1897, making him almost 17, which is still quite an amazing achievement. Without detracting from 37 Battery's achievement, the rescue of the howitzers has overshadowed the outstanding bravery exhibited by the other batteries in XV Brigade.

While heavy fighting took place to his front and right, Yate was careful not to reveal B Company's position. Eventually a worthwhile target of two massed infantry battalions presented itself. He allowed them to advance 100m down a forward slope before opening rapid fire. From then on B Company was in action until the end of the battle. The German battalions broke and retired behind the crest, but half an hour later advanced again, more cautiously this time, and threatened to envelop the right flank.

Pressure increased from midday, particularly after 2nd Suffolk had been overwhelmed on the right flank around 2.45 p.m. B Company came under enfilade fire from the right and soon after the Germans brought up a battery of machine-guns along the Cambrai road, which caused serious problems for 2nd KOYLI, for the rest of the day. One machine-gun with B Company was knocked out, having disrupted the enemy enfilading 2nd Suffolk's position. The other gun was brought back over the Reumont road after 14th Brigade retired around 2.20 p.m. However, it became separated from its tripod as the Germans swept the ground with concentrated rifle fire and the crew had to destroy the gun.

On the left of 2nd KOYLI the forward companies were reinforced by their support platoons, but it was inevitable the position would be lost due to the intense

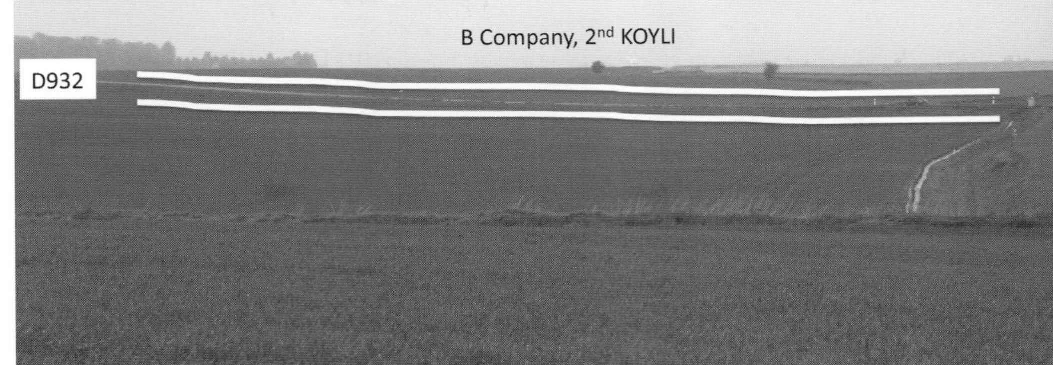

Having pushed 14th Brigade off the high ground, this was the German view of B Company, 2nd KOYLI's position along the D932. Notice how the shape of the ground allowed the troops on the far side of the road to fire over the heads of those on the near side.

pressure. The line was slowly rolled up from west to east, with the survivors of each platoon falling back as best they could to their support platoon trenches. Ammunition ran low despite half the Battalion's reserve being distributed before the action commenced. Just before 3.00 p.m. the whole of the ridge west of Le Cateau was held by the Germans and shortly after it was learned that 1st Royal West Kent, 13th Brigade's reserve, had pulled back to a new position further to the rear. 2nd KOSB on the left had also been pushed back, leaving 2nd KOYLI holding a salient with the enemy on three sides.

The Germans kept up constant pressure along the whole of 5th Division's front and threatened to envelop the right flank. At about the same time as the last 37 Battery howitzer was being galloped away, 2nd KOYLI received the order to pull back. Reserve positions were abandoned while other positions to the rear were occupied to cover the withdrawal of the forward troops. However, the Germans were so close and their fire so intense that retirement for some was impossible.

A Company was in the angle formed by the Cambrai and Reumont roads. When the order to withdraw arrived it was clear that the move would be extremely hazardous. By 4.00 p.m. the survivors were running back under close enemy fire. **Lance Corporal Frederick Holmes** heard a cry for help from Bugler HN Woodcock, whose legs were broken at the knee. Holmes picked Woodcock up and carried him 100m, but then had to strip off his equipment in order to carry Woodcock over his shoulder.

Holmes is reputed to have carried Woodcock for 3.5 kms until handing him over to the stretcher-bearers. Woodcock survived almost to the end of the war, but was killed on 19th August 1918 (Heath Cemetery, Harbonnieres III F 2). Holmes ran back towards the old position and came upon a gun limbered up and ready to move, with its crew lying dead and wounded around it. Holmes put a wounded trumpeter on one of the horses, mounted the leading pair and moved off just as the enemy closed in. He managed to get away, but at one point had to use his bayonet to escape. After running back for five kms he stopped to rest the horses at a stream. Holmes eventually met up with a battery and did not rejoin his Battalion until 30th August.

B Company's fire initially forced the Germans back. German field guns were firing from only 800m away, but despite their superiority the enemy was hesitant about closing in for the kill. They tried to dislodge Yate's men by sounding 'Cease Fire' on a bugle, but rapid fire was the only response. The Germans then tried to negotiate surrender under the white flag. This attracted even more fire, but despite the tenacity of the defenders their position rapidly became untenable.

A company of 2nd KOSB on Yate's left was overrun and then B Company's survivors were rushed from all sides. Yate was the only officer left. With all ammunition expended he led the surviving 19 men from an original strength of 220 in a final desperate bayonet charge. At the end only three men were standing. Yate was overcome from behind and by 4.30 p.m. all resistance had ended. The day after the battle, Major Gray, Royal Irish Fusiliers, marching down the road into captivity, counted 62 dead in B Company's position. However, the CWGC record only 48 fatalities in 2nd KOYLI on 25/26th August 1914 (most have no known grave and are commemorated on La Ferté-sous-Jouarre Memorial). The Battalion suffered 592 casualties, including 310 prisoners, of whom 170 were wounded. However, their desperate action gained sufficient time for the reserve battalions to slip away.

Across II Corps' and 4th Divisions front the troops held their ground despite being heavily outnumbered, but by mid-afternoon both flanks were in danger of collapsing. French cavalry arrived to protect the left and the entire Corps began a coordinated but extremely tricky withdrawal to St Quentin. The battle resulted in about 8,000 casualties, but it allowed the BEF to fall back in good order.

On 9th September, Captain Reynolds again distinguished himself during the Battle of the Marne near Pisseloup, a hamlet 1 km north of the Marne and 15 kms southwest of Chateau Thierry, where a hostile battery prevented troops advancing. Creeping forward he discovered its precise location and, although very close, directed the fire of his own howitzers to destroy the enemy battery, thus allowing the advance to continue.

Affair of Néry, 1st September 1914

14 Capt Edward Bradbury, L Battery RHA (Cavalry Division)
15 BSM George Dorrell, L Battery RHA (Cavalry Division)
16 Sgt David Nelson, L Battery RHA (Cavalry Division)

After Le Cateau the German First Army (von Kluck) continued to advance towards the lower Seine, west of Paris, while Von Bulow's Second Army marched directly on the capital. On 29th August, the French Fifth Army checked the German Second Army's advance at Guise. Next day the German First Army turned southeast to attempt the destruction of the French Fifth Army and in so doing missed a chance to destroy the French Sixth Army north of Paris. Instead of finding the French Fifth Army on 1st September, von Kluck caught up with the BEF, which resulted in the British fighting a number of actions, including one at Néry.

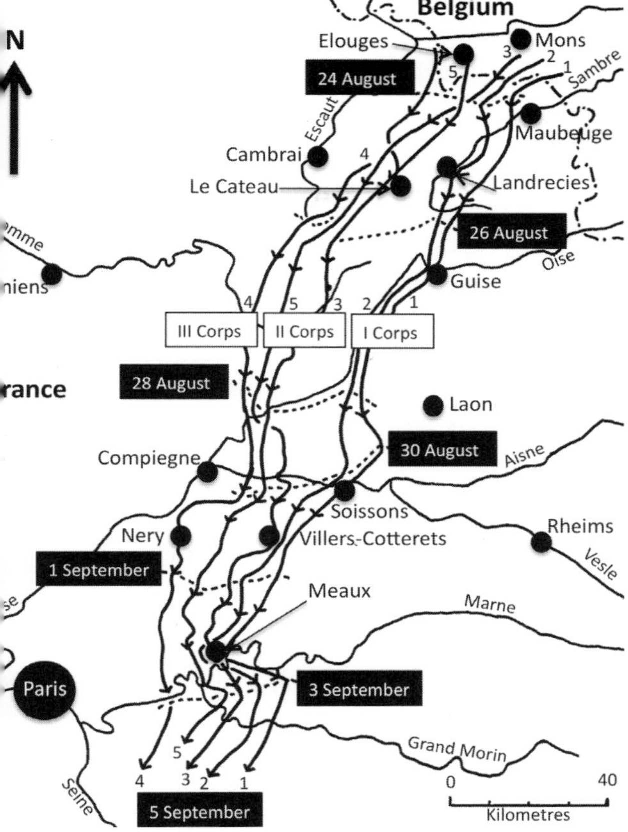

The routes taken by the five infantry divisions (in three Corps) of the BEF during the Retreat from Mons, 23rd August - 5th September 1914. Only the major rivers and significant towns/ cities have been included. The line reached every other night is shown by a dotted line and the date.

The BEF had managed to rest on 29th August and resumed the retreat the following day. On the 31st the cavalry protected the BEF's left flank by moving along the west bank of the Oise. That night each formation was allocated an area in which to billet, but GHQ's orders did not specify a front to be held or boundaries between formations and the ambiguity led to misunderstandings. French units occupied most of the area allocated to the Cavalry Division and only 2nd Cavalry Brigade was able to billet west of the Oise.

1st Cavalry Brigade and L Battery RHA were ordered to bivouac at Néry, at the western end of the II Corps area, close to the newly formed III Corps (4th Division & 19th Brigade). The Brigade commander, Brigadier-General Charles J Briggs CB, made a reasonable assumption that III Corps was providing protective outposts to the north and only ordered local sentries posted. However, III Corps units covered little more than their own billets and there were no II Corps units east of Néry until Crepy en Valois, a gap of eight kilometres. Briggs was not to know this. Indeed, with contact established west of the Oise with the French Sixth Army and the French Fifth Army's successful action at Guise, it seemed likely that the night and next day would be relatively uneventful. They would be anything but!

The situation late on 31st August 1914 showing the BEF's bivouac areas. Note the gaps between formations. The dotted line is the route taken by the German 4th Cavalry Division through the night ('Journal of the Royal Artillery' Volume LIV).

The village of Néry is largely as it was in 1914. There are no facilities, but there are hotels and restaurants in Verberie nearby, where some of the dead are buried. The main points of the battlefield can be walked in under two hours and it is worth the effort to understand the ground. Park at the church opposite the Mairie, which has some information on the action, but the opening times are irregular (Mon, Wed, Fri & Sat 1000-1200; Tue & Thu 1600-1830). Flanking the church are the farms where 11th Hussars billeted. Behind the church this track leads down into the ravine separating Néry from the high ground to the east where the Germans were positioned. The trees have grown considerably and the vegetation is much thicker than in 1914, but even then the ravine was a significant obstacle on horseback. Walk along the ravine to the south and climb out to Feu Farm. To the east is le Plessis Châtelain, HQ of the German 4th Cavalry Division during the action. Turn west to pass the site of the German guns and continue on the Feu Farm access track to reach the main road. At the junction the sugar factory is left and up the sunken road to the right (not as deep as in 1914) is Néry with the L Battery field just before the crossroads on the right. On the other side of the crossroads are various memorials and information boards. Continue north along the main street, passing the site of HQ 1st Cavalry Brigade, to reach the village cemetery where some of the dead are buried, including Captain Edward Bradbury VC.

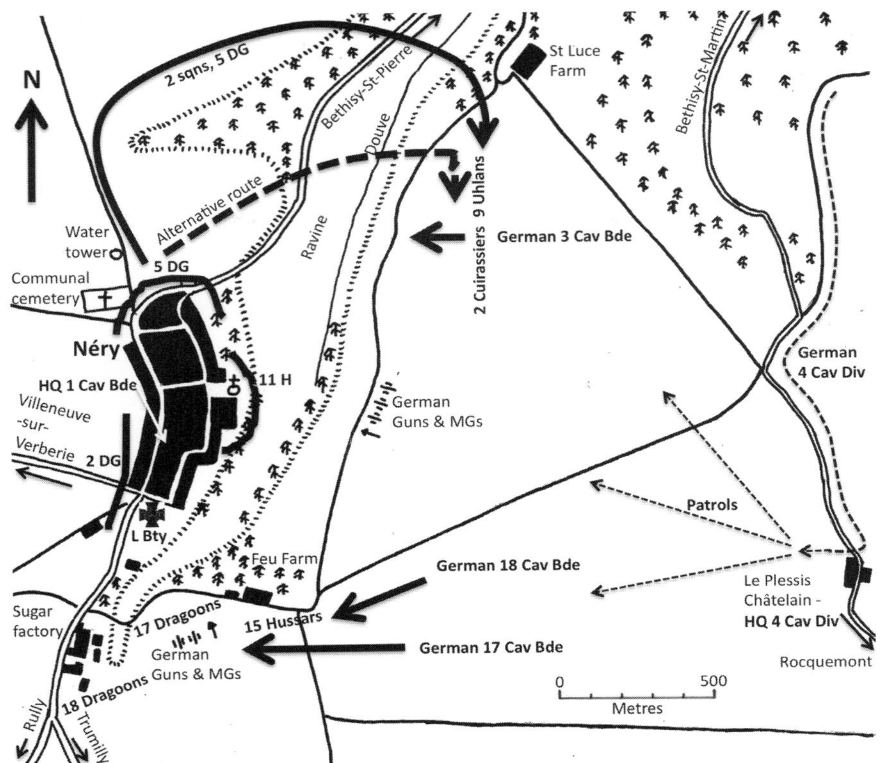

The early part of the action at Néry on 1st September 1914. 2nd Lieutenant Tailby's patrol encountered the Germans south of St Luce Farm. He escaped to the northeast and re-entered Néry along the Bethisy-St-Pierre road. When the action commenced the majority of the German guns were opposite the church, where they came under the concentrated machine-gun and rifle fire of the 11th Hussars and were forced to move south to join the other guns at Feu Farm. A mounted action by two squadrons of 5th Dragoon Guards effectively halted 3rd German Cavalry Brigade's attack towards the north of the village and from then on the main action centred on the L Battery field. The route taken by 5th Dragoon Guards is not known precisely. Suffice to say it hit the 3rd German Cavalry Brigade in the flank from the north or northeast.

Néry was divided into billeting areas, with 5th Dragoon Guards to the north, 11th Hussars in the centre, based around two farms near the church overlooking the ravine to the east and 2nd Dragoon Guards (Queen's Bays) to the southwest. L Battery, which had already distinguished itself at Elouges, Le Cateau and in the rearguard actions that followed, was in a field south of the village, with the sugar factory as its headquarters. The men were exhausted having been retreating and fighting for nine continuous days. As soon as the horses had been attended to and local defences arranged, the men dropped down to sleep.

A few miles northwest of Néry, 4th Division had a number of sharp encounters with the advancing Germans during the night, but this was not known to HQ 1st Cavalry Brigade. Indeed when a farm labourer rode into the village that evening and announced the Forêt de Compiègne to the north was thick with Germans he was jeered by the inhabitants. Early in the morning a civilian reported a strong German force at Bethisy, but this was passed to HQ II Corps at Crépy instead of

HQ III Corps at Verberie. It eventually reached III Corps via GHQ, but not before battle was joined.

The march was to resume at 4.30 a.m., so at 2.30 a.m. the men rose to prepare. Due to the heavy mist the battery commander, Major Sclater-Booth (DSO for this action), was told that the march would not begin until 5.00 a.m. He therefore ordered the poles to be dropped and the horses watered at the sugar factory. Around 5.00 a.m. the march was delayed again.

The German 4th Cavalry Division, part of II Cavalry Corps preceding the advance of First Army, pressed on through the night in an attempt to find the left flank of the French Fifth Army and bring it to battle next morning. The German units rested for a while in the villages of Bethisy-St-Pierre and Bethisy-St-Martin. As mist began to rise at 4.00 a.m., patrols were sent ahead, one returning at 5.00 a.m. with news that the British were in Néry and totally unprepared to defend it. Lieutenant General Otto von Garnier ordered an immediate attack.

An 11th Hussars patrol led by 2nd Lieutenant Tailby (his first patrol), set off with Corporal Parker and five men from the north-eastern exit of Néry. They were to gain the high ground of the eastern plateau and make a sweep southwards before re-entering the village. Patrols from 5th Dragoon Guards and the Queens's Bays made similar sweeps to the north and south respectively, but returned having seen nothing.

Tailby had almost completed his patrol and was about a mile from Néry when

The sugar factory from the west.

The farm south of the church occupied by 11th Hussars as it looked in 1914. This is private property, but a similar view can be seen today through the gate.

The crossroads at the southern end of Néry with the sunken road on the right leading down the hill to the sugar factory in the distance; it was used as cover by the Queen's Bays during the action. The field on the far side of the road is where L Battery was drawn up. The lone bush beside the wall on the left is where the haystacks stood in September 1914. The German guns were beyond the trees behind the modern barn left of centre.

Néry church from the east with the tops of the trees in the ravine in front. This is the direction in which the first German patrols approached.

the mist cleared a little and 150m away he saw a column of dismounted German cavalry. The Germans did not see them until a zealous trooper dismounted and opened fire. Tailby and his men galloped off as they were outnumbered and the German cavalry leapt into their saddles to give chase. The Germans barred the direct return to Néry so Tailby took his patrol northeast at first and gained the edge of the plateau. Plunging down the slope, Tailby's horse went head over heels. Fortunately the Germans gave up the pursuit and Corporal Parker returned with Tailby's horse. They galloped on down the hill and outside an estaminet Tailby saw a German cloak and rifle. The woman there told him three Germans had just bolted. Tailby grabbed the cloak to prove the Germans were close and asked for directions to Néry on the Bethisy road, which they reached near the railway crossing. They galloped into the village at 5.30 a.m. Tailby sent Corporal Parker to alert 5th Dragoon Guards, who did not believe the news, while he rushed on to report to his CO, Lieutenant Colonel T Pitman. Pitman immediately went to Brigade HQ to ensure Briggs was aware of the situation.

At 5.40 a.m. the mist began to lift and from the high ground to the south and east the Germans could scarcely believe their eyes as they looked over Néry. There was 1st Cavalry Brigade making ready to move off, totally unprepared to fight a battle. The Germans had a golden opportunity to deal a crushing blow and opened fire with rifles, machine-guns and twelve artillery pieces. In Néry there was utter chaos as men and horses ran about seeking cover, but some men recovered quickly and within seconds fire was being returned. One of the first shells exploded above Brigade HQ and the time fuse came through the roof. Briggs picked it up, noted it was German and the range was set for 800m. He immediately sent motorcycle despatch riders to warn HQ Cavalry Division and HQ 4th Division that 1st Cavalry Brigade was under attack. Briggs gave 5th Dragoon Guards a free hand to operate against the enemy flank and 11th Hussars extended its front northwards to compensate. Briggs then went round the positions and was seen assisting a machine-gun team at one time near L Battery. His Brigade Major, Major JS Cawley, was mortally wounded near him (Néry Communal Cemetery).

The main street through Néry from the north. HQ 1st Cavalry Brigade was in the building at the end of the street on the left.

The German guns caused most damage. Some were located directly east of Néry, but were very close to 11th Hussars and were raked by the fire of its machine-gun section. It seems likely that these guns moved soon after the start of the action and joined the others south of the village between the sugar factory and Feu Farm, from where they could engage the main British opposition. L Battery and the Queen's Bays took the brunt of this fire.

Feu Farm from the south. The German guns were on the far left of this field firing into Néry in the left distance across the ravine hidden by the trees.

Sclater-Booth was at Brigade HQ on the east side of the main street when the firing started, but the route to the Battery was blocked by stampeding Queen's Bays horses. The carnage was awful and soon the street was full of dead and dying animals. He eventually crossed the street and reached a point from where he could see L Battery. Running to rejoin it, he shouted to Trumpeter Gould to sound the 'Alarm', but before he could comply, a shell exploded directly in front of them. Sclater-Booth did not recover consciousness for five hours and was temporarily blinded. Although badly shaken and dazed, Gould managed to sound the 'Alarm', although by then it was somewhat superfluous.

Contemporary photograph from in front of the German gun position looking north over Néry. L Battery was beyond the trees on the left. The track from the sugar factory to Feu Farm is out of sight in a slight dip across the middle ground.

Captain Edward Bradbury had been chatting with the other L Battery officers near some haystacks when the first shell burst above the Battery, followed by a hail of Maxim and rifle fire. Bradbury called out, *"Come On! Who's for the guns?"*, and ran towards them in the field. The officers and men near Bradbury joined him in trying to free the six guns from their horse teams. One gun was overturned on the road bank by the panicking horses and a second had its spokes blown out by a

A similar picture to the previous, taken lower down in the ravine with the sugar factory - Feu Farm track in the foreground. L Battery was on the high ground behind the trees on the left.

The crossroads south of Nery looking north along the main street towards HQ 1st Cavalry Brigade. This street was the scene of utter chaos and carnage, preventing Major Sclater-Booth returning to L Battery in the field on the right. There are a number of memorials and information boards on the far side of the crossroads.

shell rendering it useless. A third gun was destroyed and its crew killed by a direct hit, while another had its wheels damaged and its horse team killed. However, it and the remaining two guns were freed and turned to face the enemy artillery about 900m away. Bradbury took command of one gun, Lieutenant Giffard another (Légion d'Honneur for this action) and Lieutenants Mundy (MID for this action) and Campbell the third. Behind them, the machine-guns of the Queen's Bays came into action and later those of 11th Hussars also moved to the southeast corner of the village.

Accounts vary at this point. One says the first gun to fire was D sub-section commanded by Lieutenant Campbell, who was laying with Bombardier Perrett loading. As more men arrived, Campbell handed this gun over to Lieutenant Giffard and with Perrett ran to help free C sub-section. D sub-section was then manned by Sergeant Fortune and others and had barely recommenced firing when it was hit by a shell, killing or wounding most of the detachment, including Fortune (Néry Communal Cemetery).

C sub-section was cut away from the dead horses and was soon in action with Campbell laying, Perrett No 1, Gunner Miller No 2 and another gunner as No 4, with Driver Mansfield and others bringing ammunition. After firing a few rounds it was hit. Miller was killed (Néry Communal Cemetery) and Mansfield and Perrett wounded. Campbell bandaged Perrett's head wound, then managed to get away with Lieutenant Mundy to join the crew of the third gun. Another version states that Campbell's gun was destroyed before it fired a single round. However, both agree that Campbell and Mundy then joined Bradbury's gun.

Lieutenant Giffard had been trotting a lame horse in the sunken lane leading to the sugar factory when the battle commenced. He is reported to have run to B sub-section with Sergeant DP Phillips and Gunner WJ Richardson. They managed to fire off eight rounds before the gun was hit. Giffard was severely wounded and the rest of the crew killed (Phillips and Richardson are buried in Nery Communal or Verberie National Cemeteries) or wounded, leaving only Bradbury's gun in action. However, this version contradicts other accounts, which say that Giffard took over D sub-section from Campbell.

Sergeant David Nelson was initially stunned by the ferocity of the onslaught, but recovered quickly and called on Gunner Darbyshire to help him bring F sub-section into action. This was achieved quicker than the other guns because its horse team was being watered at the sugar factory. Nelson and Darbyshire were joined almost immediately by Captain Bradbury, Lieutenants Campbell and Mundy, Corporal Payne and Driver Osborne. They quickly used up the ammunition in the limber and had to carry rounds over the shell torn ground from the wagons 20m to the rear. The Germans continued to pour steady and accurate fire into the field. After 20 minutes, Darbyshire was badly concussed and his ears and nose were bleeding from the blast. Campbell replaced him as layer, but a few minutes later he was blown five metres from the gun and killed as a shell exploded just above the shield (Néry Communal Cemetery). Perrett came round to see Campbell lying dead nearby and was hit again by a machine-gun bullet in the arm. The gun was then crewed by Bradbury laying, Nelson range setter and Mundy observer.

Fortunino Matania's painting conveys something of the death and destruction wreaked upon L Battery, but not the full horror. For example the body of Captain Bradbury slumped against the dead horse has both legs intact.

A shell fatally wounded Mundy (Baron Communal Cemetery) and Payne (La Ferté-sous-Jouarre Memorial) and wounded Nelson in the right leg and side, but he stuck to his duties. Darbyshire and Osborne (both awarded the French Médaille Militaire for this action) did a splendid job, repeatedly crossing the field to collect ammunition.

At first L Battery was engaged by four enemy guns, but as the last gun refused to be silenced and began to score hits on the German artillery, more guns were switched against it. Nelson left a vivid account of the action in his diary, *"During the awful carnage the moaning of dying men and horses audible amidst the terrific thundering of cannon; the scenes in most cases beyond description. One man in full view of me had his head cut clean off his body. Another was literally blown to pieces, another was practically severed at the breast, loins, knees and ankles. One horse had its head and neck completely severed from the shoulders."*

Contemporary view from L Battery's field towards the German gun positions, showing how little vegetation there was at the time of the battle. The sugar factory chimney is on the right and Feu Farm is just out of view left.

Although the dual was unequal, the gunners did not flinch. **Sergeant Major George Dorrell,** who had been engaging the enemy with a rifle, joined the gun team about 7.15 a.m. He replaced Bradbury, who went to find more ammunition. As Bradbury returned he was cut down by a shell and both legs were severed above the knee. Although he knew he was dying he continued to encourage the others. Darbyshire and Osborne were knocked out by the same shell as Bradbury, but survived (Bombardier H G Darbyshire died on 12th July 1915 and is buried in Lancashire Landing Cemetery (D 108), Gallipoli).

Dorrell and Nelson were then alone, but kept up a steady fire until 7.30 a.m., when they had used all the available ammunition. They then continued the battle with their rifles. At one time Nelson was taken away for attention, but returned to assist the Queen's Bays in refilling their machine-gun belts. Another account states that when relieving troops arrived the two were slumped against the shield of the gun, utterly exhausted.

Meanwhile, to the north, 5th Dragoon Guards left one squadron to secure the northeast end of the village and Lieutenant Colonel GK Ansell led two squadrons in a wide sweep to St Luce Farm to outflank the enemy. They fell upon the German 3rd Cavalry Brigade (2nd Cuirassiers and 9th Uhlans) preparing to attack across the ravine into the north of the village. Ansell counter-attacked immediately and the mist helped disguise his weakness in the ensuing fire fight. Having thrown the Germans into confusion he pulled back before they realised how weak his force was. Ansell was killed (Verberie French National Cemetery D 96), but the German

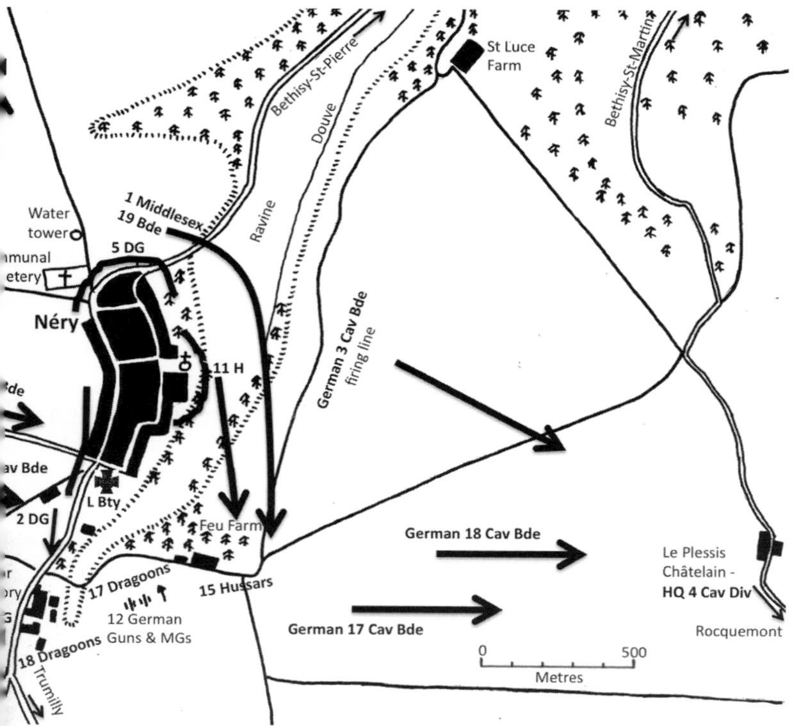

The end of the action as reinforcements arrived. 1st Middlesex (19th Brigade) outflanked the German guns and forced them to begin retiring. C Squadron, 11th Hussars pursued the withdrawing Germans back to le Plessis Châtelain, while other forces arrived from the west and southwest to complete the relief of 1st Cavalry Brigade.

3rd Cavalry Brigade was thrown onto the defensive and played little further part in the action.

The sugar factory viewed from the direction of the German 17th Cavalry Brigade advance. Néry is out of view right.

To the south the German 17th Cavalry Brigade (17th and 18th Dragoons) advanced on the sugar factory held by a troop of the Queen's Bays until it was shelled out of the buildings. The majority of the Queen's Bays established a firing line along the sunken road behind L Battery from where they were able to pour effective fire into the German gun positions. Lance Corporal Webb of the Queen's Bays actually fired a machine-gun planted on his own knees (MID). The dismounted Germans were halted at the head of the ravine by brisk small arms fire. They had left their ammunition column well behind in order to move more swiftly and as a result were forced to conserve ammunition.

18th German Cavalry Brigade (15th and 16th Hussars) was ordered to make a mounted attack on the southern end of the village. 16th Hussars was halted by the thick foliage and steepness of the ravine and dismounted, just as I Battery RHA came into action. 15th Hussars, attacking further north, came under fire from the village and almost crashed into the rear of the 18th Dragoons firing line. They dismounted and prepared to advance on foot with their carbines to assist the Dragoons.

As soon as Major General Allenby, commanding the Cavalry Division, received news about the attack at Néry, he set off with 4th Cavalry Brigade and I Battery RHA, intending to sweep around Néry and enter it from the south. Four guns of I Battery (a section of D Battery was attached making eight guns in total) came into action about 1,800m from the German guns at 8 a.m. Three German guns swung round to engage I Battery and this relieved some of the pressure on Néry. A troop of Royal Horse Guards charged a dismounted party of Germans on the southern flank. Although the troop was driven back, it was clear to the Germans that substantial British reinforcements were close. The tables were very quickly being turned.

The Germans attempted to get two machine-guns into the sugar factory to enfilade the Queen's Bays positions near L Battery, but I Battery knocked them out before they came into action. Lieutenant CN Champion de Crespigny led fifteen men of the Queen's Bays against the sugar factory. De Crespigny was mortally wounded (Hatfield Peverel (St Andrew) Churchyard, Essex), but Sergeant Major Fraser kept the men together and managed to prevent the Germans getting any further forward. The Germans used the sugar factory owner, the mayor and some workers as a human shield. The British troops did their best to fire between the civilians and some Germans were hit, but inevitably so too were some civilians and one woman died.

19th Brigade also moved on Néry, with 1st Middlesex leading. In coordination with Briggs, D Company, in the lead, advanced along the eastern side of the ravine to fire

The L Battery field from the sugar factory. If the Germans had succeeded in setting up two machine-guns here they would have been able to fire into the rear and flank of the Queen's Bays lining the upper end of the sunken road.

on the German guns from the flank. After two minutes rapid fire by the infantry, added to the fire of I Battery, the Germans left the guns and D Company rushed forward. Four German guns and the Guards Machine-Gun Company were saved, but eight guns had to be abandoned because the fire of I Battery and various units' machine-guns prevented the horse teams reaching them.

With more British reinforcements arriving as the Germans ran short of ammunition, the prospect of being cut off and overwhelmed loomed. Von Garnier decided to break off the engagement and retire to the east. By 8.45 a.m. the battle was over. A company of 1st Middlesex and a squadron of dismounted Queen's Bays cleared the sugar factory of about twenty remaining German troops. C Squadron 11th Hussars set off in pursuit and captured the hamlet of le Plessis Châtelein, where the German 4th Cavalry Division HQ had been located. Its orders were not to exploit far, as there was no support available. C Squadron returned to Néry with 110 prisoners. Other units arrived, particularly from 10th Brigade, but took no part in the battle.

Soldiers of 1st Middlesex were amongst the first to reach the carnage in L Battery's field. A corporal found Bradbury and Perrett lying by the gun wheel where they had fallen. He offered his water bottle to Bradbury who passed it to Perrett, who could not drink due to a face wound. Bradbury took a few sips then slumped back. Sergeant Nelson, despite his wounds, found a few unwounded men and a door from the village to carry Bradbury away. Bradbury had them cover his lower body with a blanket to hide the stumps of his legs and made them promise to return for Perrett. As he was being taken to the aid station near the village cemetery, he passed the CO of the Queen's Bays and called out with a grin, *"Hello Colonel, they've hotted us up a bit, haven't they!"* He knew he was dying and asked to be taken inside the cemetery so others would not witness his agony. A Colour Sergeant of 1st Royal Warwickshire found him a little later while searching for wounded to evacuate

Le Plessis Chatelein, where HQ 4th German Cavalry Division was established during the battle from the eastern end of Feu Farm.

to Baron. Bradbury was still alive and was made as comfortable as possible in a farm cart packed with straw for the journey, but died soon afterwards.

Néry Communal Cemetery where Captain Bradbury was taken to die. The memorial stone in the centre is flanked by six grave stones either side, although only seven of the twelve are buried here. This is repeated at Verberie Military Cemetery where the other five are buried.

Only three of the eight German guns were worth recovering and were displayed on Horse Guards Parade as being captured at Le Cateau! The other five were rendered useless before being abandoned. L Battery under Dorrell cannibalised limbers and wagons to fit serviceable wheels to their six guns so they could be towed away. I Battery rendered assistance. By noon the troops had reorganised and the retirement south resumed. Néry was abandoned. Many of the wounded were taken to Baron, 16 kms to the south, where the Germans later took them prisoner. Nelson escaped, but the French overran the hospital a few days later and the other wounded were evacuated to Britain.

Although 1st Cavalry Brigade had been surprised, it recovered quickly and prevented the German 4th Cavalry Division getting into the British rear areas and wreaking havoc. What started as a certain victory for the Germans ended in a major set back. However, the cost was high. The British lost 55 killed or died of wounds, 91 wounded and 380 horses. Of these, L Battery lost 18 men killed and seven more died of wounds. Another 29 were wounded and 150 horses lost. Unusually there are common memorials to twelve L Battery men at Néry Communal Cemetery and Verberie Military Cemetery. Seven were buried at Néry and five at Verberie, but precisely who is in which grave is unclear. German casualties were 180, including 78 prisoners, 230 horses and eight guns.

Memorial to three officers of 1st Cavalry Brigade killed during the battle at Néry Communal Cemetery. Captain Bradbury's grave is on the right against the cemetery wall.

Dorrell and the other survivors joined XIV Brigade RFA Ammunition Column (4th Division) and on 19th October returned to Woolwich to a rapturous reception. F sub-section is understood to be the Néry gun in the Imperial War Museum.

Chapter Two

Battle of the Aisne 1914

Capture of the Aisne Heights, 14th-15th September 1914

17 Pte Ross Tollerton, 1st Cameron Highlanders (1st (Guards) Brigade, 1st Division), Chivy, France
18 LCpl William C Fuller, 2nd Welsh (3rd Brigade, 1st Division), Chivy, France
19 Bdr Ernest Horlock, 113th Battery RFA (1st Division), Vendresse, France
20 Pte George Wilson, 2nd HLI (5th Brigade, 2nd Division), Verneuil, France
21 Capt William Johnston, 59th Field Company RE (5th Division), Missy-sur-Aisne, France

Having been checked by the French Fifth Army at Guise on 29th August and fighting a number of engagements against the BEF on 1st September, the Germans attempted to force the French away from Paris to the southeast. By 4th September this had failed, the Allies gained the initiative and Joffre issued orders to go over to the offensive. The Battle of the Marne (5th-12th September) brought the long

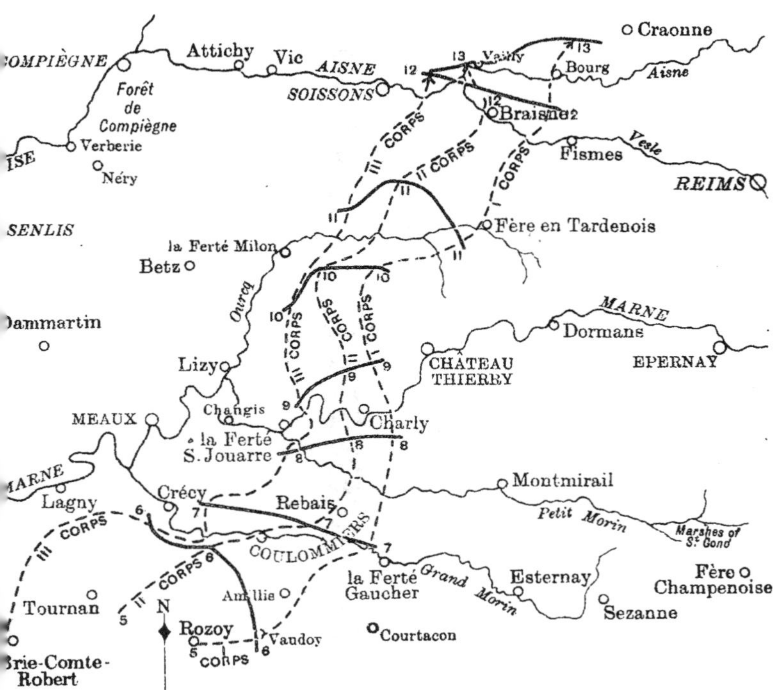

The long retreat from Mons ended on 5th September 1914. The Allies went onto the offensive and the Germans were pushed back over the Aisne and Vesle rivers. On 13th September, the BEF seized crossings over the Aisne and next day attempted to take the heights above the river. (Official History 1914, Volume 1)

The Aisne between Venizel and Missy at Moulin des Roches where 17th Field Company RE operated a pontoon ferry.

The Aisne valley from the Chemin des Dames ridge.

German advance through Belgium and France to an end. The amended Schlieffen Plan had failed to seize Paris and knock France out of the war. The unpalatable prospect for Germany of a long war on two fronts became reality. By 10th September the Germans were falling back on the Aisne and Vesle rivers.

On 8th September, the BEF advanced into a 40 kms wide gap between the German First and Second Armies and crossed the Marne next day. By 12th September the BEF was on the heights south of the Aisne and an audacious night operation by 11th Brigade secured a crossing over the river at Venizel. The gap between First and Second German Armies was still 29 kms wide, filled by only three cavalry divisions. Von Moltke decided to stand on the Aisne and arranged for corps at Maubeuge and Brussels to rush to fill the gap.

In front of the British, the Germans dug in along the northern heights commanding the Aisne, a slow flowing but deep river up to 60m wide. It presented a serious obstacle, as fording was not possible and the bridges were covered by German artillery. Orders were issued late on 12th September for the three corps of the BEF to force crossings over the river and then gain the Chemin des Dames ridge, which lay between the valleys of the Aisne and the Ailette, some eight kilometres to the north. The ridge is approximately 1,000m wide across its flat top, with a series of spurs and deep re-entrants running away to north and south. These features were of great significance in the ensuing fighting.

On Sunday 13th September, the BEF crossed the Aisne and established itself on the north bank. Haig's I Corps on the right had the largest bridgehead, but II Corps (centre) and III Corps (left) also made lodgements. Sir John French was unsure if the Germans would choose to hold the Chemin des Dames or merely delay his advance with rearguard actions. He therefore ordered a general advance to find out, *"The Army will continue the pursuit tomorrow at 6.00 a.m. and act vigorously against the retreating enemy"*.

Divisions set off next morning in column of route with the advanced guards expecting to meet only German rearguards. Instead they found the Germans entrenched in strength, with heavy artillery support. As a result, divisions came into

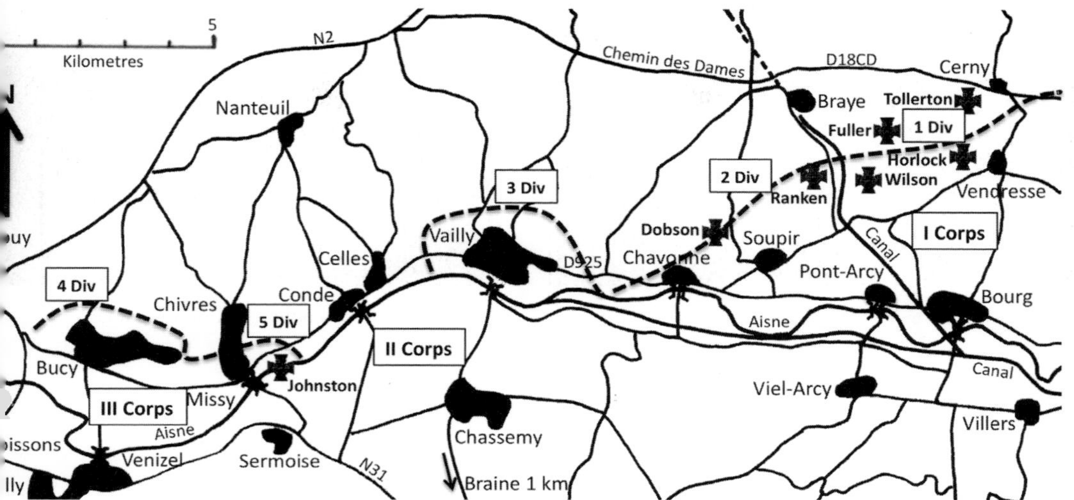

On 13th September 1914, the BEF forced crossings over the Aisne and established bridgeheads on the north bank. The three Corps had varying degrees of success, with I Corps on the right having the best of it. The five VCs awarded for the fighting on 14th–15th September are shown, together with those on the 19th and 28th before the BEF began to disengage and move north to Flanders.

action piecemeal with little coordination between formations. Thick mist increased difficulties and reduced artillery support to the minimum.

Patrols in the 1st Division (I Corps) area north of Troyon discovered the Germans dug in on the axis of the Division's advance at the sugar factory at Cerny and the crossroads to the northwest. 2nd Brigade was ordered to seize this objective in a pre-dawn preliminary operation. 1st (Guards) Brigade would then continue the advance with 3rd Brigade in reserve. The attack began at 3.00 a.m. It was pitch dark, raining heavily and very misty. Troyon was occupied by 2nd KRRC at 4.00 a.m. and some trenches to the north were also taken. Resistance stiffened and, by 6.30 a.m., 2nd Royal Sussex had deployed to the left of 2nd KRRC and 1st Northamptonshire to the right. By 7.00 a.m. the whole of 2nd Brigade was involved in the fighting. At first, the attack on the sugar factory made little progress, but 2nd Royal Sussex moved two companies round to the west to take the position in the flank and enfilade the Germans holding up 2nd KRRC. The garrison at the sugar factory surrendered and a German battery entrenched to the east was destroyed while attempting to withdraw.

1st Loyal North Lancashire came up to support 2nd Royal Sussex and 2nd KRRC, while 1st Northamptonshire worked forward on the right of the Brigade. Around 9.00 a.m., 2nd Brigade was digging in on the top of the flat ridge, but the Germans were quick to counter-attack. 1st (Guards) Brigade was sent to the left to outflank the enemy, while 2nd Cavalry Brigade secured the right flank. The British guns were not yet in position, but could have done little with visibility limited to a few metres. However, the enemy artillery already had the range and caused heavy

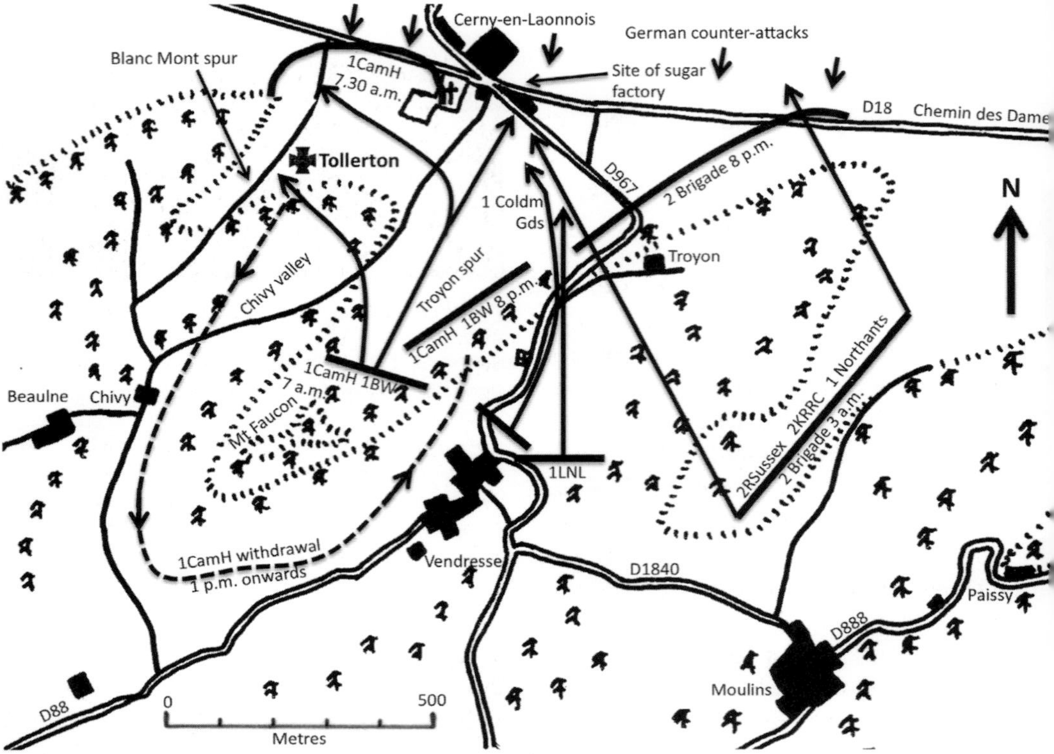

The site of Ross Tollerton's VC action can be reached in two ways. Park at the Necropole Nationale on the D18, west of Cerny-en-Laonnois and walk 450m west along the D18 to a track running south along the Blanc Mont spur. It is possible to park a single vehicle here, but try to avoid blocking the track entrance for long. Alternatively, park 600m southwest of Cerny on the Chivy road and walk west along the edge of the fields and slope to Blanc Mont spur.

casualties amongst the leading British battalions.

In 1st (Guards) Brigade, 1st Coldstream Guards moved up through the woods to the left of 2nd Brigade, while 1st Cameron Highlanders and 1st Black Watch found their way onto the southwest end of the Troyon spur. On the left, 1st Cameron Highlanders formed up in the cover of a wood on the spur between Chivy and Vendresse, with 1st Black Watch on its right. The Camerons moved off at 7.00 a.m., with A Company leading on the right and D Company on the left. The Battalion's objective was the high ground in the area of the sugar factory, but as it advanced out of the cover of the wood it came under

The Cerny crossroads, objective of 2nd Brigade on 14th September 1914. The attack came in from the left. The site of the sugar factory is behind the camera. The road to the left of the chapel runs past French and German cemeteries (Necropole Nationale) and continues along the top of the Chemin des Dames ridge. This is the area of the failed Nivelle Offensive in April 1917 that led to the French army mutinies.

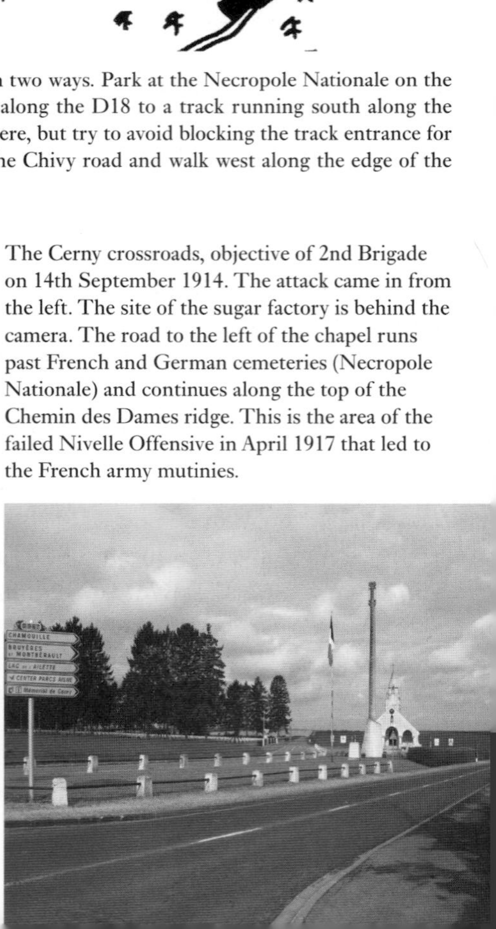

heavy enfilade fire from the right. The Battalion veered left, partly in response to the fire, but also to meet a German counter-attack developing from that flank. About 8.00 a.m., 1st Coldstream Guards reached the top of the spur and found 1st Cameron Highlanders and 1st Black Watch already there. The Camerons took up positions at the head of the Chivy valley, with 1st Coldstream Guards and 2nd Brigade on the right and a company of the Black Watch on the left. However, two Cameron platoons continued towards the original objective on the Chemin des Dames, reached it and took up positions there. Meanwhile the rest of 1st Cameron Highlanders and 1st Coldstream Guards attacked northwards. They suffered heavy losses, but reached the Chemin des Dames and a Coldstream company went on to Cerny and a wood beyond.

1st Cameron Highlanders' machine-gun section and B and C Companies were sent to Le Blanc Mont spur to cover the Brigade's open left flank. In outline the Camerons' position was arc shaped, with the left facing northwest and the right northeast. At about 7.30 a.m. a major counter-attack began to develop from the north of Le Blanc Mont. To add to the confusion, the Cameron companies were totally intermingled and under fire from friendly troops behind them due to the poor visibility.

At about 8.00 a.m. a heavy attack was launched against the Battalion and the right had to fall back to the cover of the Chemin des Dames road bank. At 11.30 a.m. the right was again forced back from near the sugar factory. Casualties mounted steadily and a shortage of ammunition made retirement inevitable.

Looking southwest along the road from Cerny (behind camera) to Chivy. The Troyon spur is on the left. 1st Cameron Highlanders formed up in the cover of the wood in the left distance prior to advancing towards the sugar factory. Earlier that morning a 9th Lancers patrol, led by Lieutenant Riversdale Grenfell, ran into a German picket on this road and Grenfell was killed. His brother Francis was awarded the VC for his part in the action at Elouges on 24th August.

Having reached this point, 1st Cameron Highlanders was hit by heavy fire from the right and veered towards the Blanc Mont spur in the distance.

Looking south along the Blanc Mont spur from the Chemin des Dames. 1st Cameron Highlanders advanced from the left to reach this position.

At 1.00 p.m. the Germans launched another counter-attack against the whole frontage of 1st (Guards) and 2nd Brigades. 2nd Royal Sussex was pushed out of the sugar factory and this exposed the right flank of 1st Cameron Highlanders. Two companies of 1st Gloucestershire (3rd Brigade) were sent to stabilise the front.

Gradually giving up ground, 1st Cameron Highlanders fell back into the Chivy valley, covered by the 1st Gloucestershire companies. A party of 50 men became separated and when its ammunition ran out it too fell back behind the crest of the ridge, where it was overwhelmed and destroyed. The remnants of the Battalion swung east to take up positions for the night, facing northwest along the Troyon spur, north of Vendresse. Stragglers came in and by nightfall about 200 had been gathered.

Lieutenant James Matheson (B Company) had been seriously wounded on the Blanc Mont spur in the initial attack northwest of the Chivy – Cerny road. He fell face first into soft earth and almost suffocated. **Private Ross Tollerton** and Lance Sergeant George Geddes turned Matheson over and managed to get him onto Tollerton's back. Geddes was shot dead (La Ferté-sous-Jouarre Memorial), but at great personal risk Tollerton carried Matheson into the cover of a corn stook. He then returned to the firing line and was wounded in the right temple and hand.

When the order to retire was given, Tollerton stayed with Matheson despite being surrounded by Germans. He continued his vigil for two days and nights, patiently waiting for a chance to carry the officer back to the British

From the southern end of the Blanc Mont spur looking towards the top of the Troyon spur over the ground 1st Cameron Highlanders advanced across in the original attack. Just below the top of the Troyon spur on the left is the Cerny - Chivy road.

The Chemin des Dames road bank used by 1st Cameron Highlanders for cover, with the Cerny crossroads in the background.

Tollerton carried Matheson into the cover of a corn stook in this field at the southern end of the Blanc Mont spur. 1st Cameron Highlanders fell back into the valley in the background in which the hamlets of Chivy and Beaulne nestle. The southern end of the Beaulne spur is on the right and Mont Faucon is on the left.

lines. It was cold and frequent rain showers soaked them through. Wounded again, weakened by loss of blood and having eaten nothing since the morning of the attack, Tollerton would have been lucky to make it back on his own. It was impossible for him to carry Matheson as well. In the late afternoon of the 16th the Germans pulled back a little. Seeing British troops digging in some distance away, Tollerton staggered towards them, although he was hardly able to stand, and a stretcher party went to recover Matheson. Both survived their ordeal, but Matheson never recovered completely and died in 1933.

At 10.00 a.m., 3rd Brigade (less 1st Royal West Surrey, diverted to Paissy as right flank guard) was ordered from its reserve position near Moulins to extend the line to the left of 1st (Guards) Brigade southeast of Troyon. It was to gain the Chemin des Dames above Chivy and link up with 2nd Division on the left. Just before 10.30 a.m. the Brigade advanced under shellfire in a north-westerly direction, crossing the Chivy valley towards the Mont de Beaulne spur. On the right was 1st South Wales Borderers, on the left 2nd Welsh, two companies of 1st Gloucestershire were in Brigade reserve, while the other two were in reserve to 1st Division.

Arriving at Mont Faucon, a strong German counter-attack was seen advancing along the spur northeast of Chivy in a south-westerly direction into 2nd Division's flank. The Brigade Commander's account indicates this was the Le Blanc Mont spur,

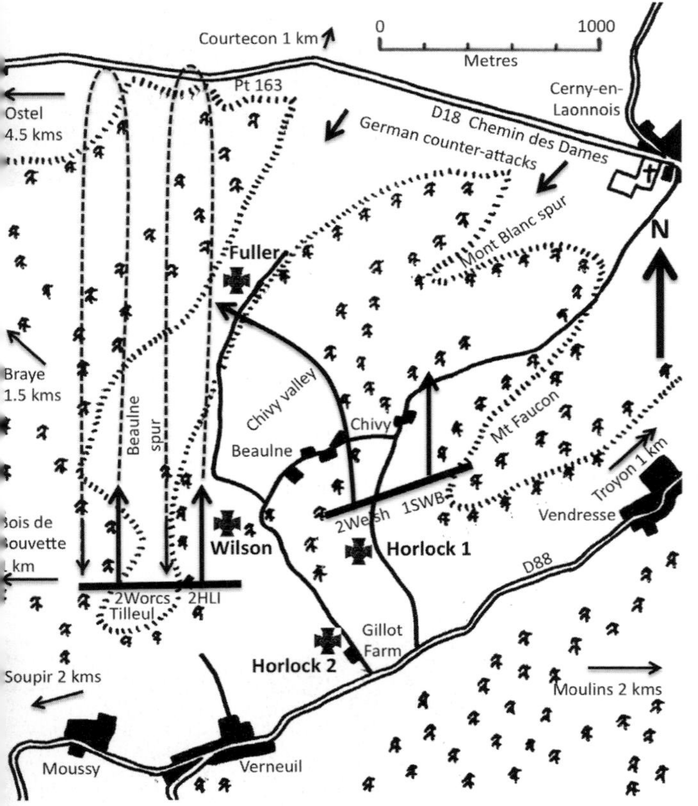

The sites of Ernest Horlock's and George Wilson's VC actions can be reached easily on the minor roads in the area. West of Beaulne is a track running northwest then north towards the top of the Beaulne spur. It can be driven with care for the first 300m or so and there is ample space to park without impeding farm vehicles. A cross-country vehicle will get to the top without difficulty, but it is best to walk the last 500m to gain better views of where William Fuller's VC action took place.

From the south-eastern slope of the Beaulne spur looking east over the Chivy valley to Mont Faucon, with Beaulne in the low ground. When the German counter-attack was seen, 2nd Welsh changed direction to head across this valley to engage the enemy on the Beaulne spur up the slope on the left. It advanced more quickly and became separated from 1st South Wales Borderers, which ran into the thick woods in the centre and on the left. In the left far distance is the Chemin des Dames ridge.

but the Brigade HQ war diary specifies the Beaulne spur, which is generally accepted to be the next spur to the west. Commander 3rd Brigade could see 2nd Division's guns exposed at the end of the spur and ordered 1st South Wales Borderers and 2nd Welsh to attack. The machine-guns of the attacking battalions were brigaded together and the attack was supported by 113 and 40 (Howitzer) Batteries.

2nd Welsh on the left advanced more quickly and became separated from 1st South Wales Borderers, which ran into thick woods. The supporting machine-guns managed to take a German trench in enfilade and cleared it, also knocking out a German machine-gun. 1st South Wales Borderers lost touch with 1st (Guards) Brigade on its right.

Once the mist lifted, the British guns were able to bear on the enemy and, together with flanking fire from 5th Brigade (2nd Division) on the left, caused heavy German casualties. About 1.00 p.m. it was clear 1st (Guards) Brigade on the right was under pressure and some platoons fell back having suffered heavy losses. 1st South Wales Borderers was ordered to push on to try to relieve the pressure by advancing north of Chivy. German artillery fire became heavier and more accurate.

About the same time 2nd Welsh advanced to the southeast slopes of the Beaulne spur, supported by the artillery, where it came under fire from German infantry in the cover of corn stooks 130m away. The enemy was rushed and cleared out at bayonet point. The Welsh were then advancing at right angles to their original direction and, as they crossed the track running along the top of the spur, were hit by a hurricane of enfilade artillery fire and forced to halt.

On nearing the crest the commander of B Company, Captain Mark Haggard, ordered his men to lie down in cover

The southeast slope of the Mont de Beaulne spur up which 2nd Welsh advanced and came under fire from Germans who were in the cover of corn stooks.

Looking north along the top of the Beaulne spur. As 2nd Welsh crossed this track from right to left it came under heavy enfilade fire and was forced to halt. William Fuller's VC action was in the field on the left.

while he went forward to reconnoitre the enemy position. On returning he ordered a bayonet charge, which was held up by heavy fire, in particular from a machine-gun. Accompanied by three men, one of whom was **Lance Corporal William Fuller,** Haggard charged the gun and shot a number of its crew with his rifle before being hit several times himself, one round passing through his stomach and exiting through his right side. Two of the others were also hit, one being killed. Despite his wounds and the shellfire, Haggard continued to encourage his men, *"Stick it the Welsh"*. He then called to Fuller, *"I'm done, get back"*. At first Fuller obeyed, but then disregarded the heavy fire and carried Haggard back 100m to the shelter of the ridge.

Having dressed Haggard's wounds, Fuller went into the open to recover the officer's rifle. Assisted by Private Snooks and Lieutenant Melvin, the machine-gun officer, he carried Haggard 1,200m to a dressing station in a barn (possibly in Beaulne). Heavy shellfire continued to pour down, but Fuller stuck to his duties and did what he could for Haggard. He also helped 60 French civilians sheltering in the cellar of the adjoining farmhouse, until wagons were sent to take them away. Despite Fuller's efforts, Haggard (nephew of the author Sir Rider Haggard), died late the following afternoon (Vendresse British Cemetery I G 11).

The positions gained by 3rd Brigade were held against counter-attacks until about 4.30 p.m., when orders were received for a general advance. 1st South Wales Borderers was directed on the Chemin des Dames southwest of Cerny, while 2nd Welsh made for the track junction with the

Captain Mark Haggard's grave in Vendresse British Cemetery, a few kilometres from where he was mortally wounded.

When 113 Battery moved forward to support the infantry in the Chivy valley, its first position was on the crest in the centre below Mont Faucon on the right. Once the counter-attack had been repulsed the guns were moved to the camera position northwest of Gillot Farm.

Reverse view of the previous picture from the first gun position with Gillot Farm on the left.

main road to the west. By dusk little progress had been made and the Chemin des Dames remained in German hands. The battalions were ordered to establish outposts – 1st South Wales Borderers on the right from the Chivy road, 550m south of the main road, with 1st Gloucestershire in the centre and 2nd Welsh on the left on the Beaulne spur and at the head of the Chivy valley.

Having been in action east of Vendresse in the morning, 113 Battery moved forward to support the infantry in the Chivy valley. As the Battery emerged over the crest at 11.00 a.m., the commander, Major Ellershaw, observed the German counter-attack against 3rd Brigade on the Beaulne spur. The guns came into action in an open field and inflicted terrible casualties on the enemy at a range of 1,800m. Once the first onslaught had been repulsed, the guns were moved under fire to a more suitable position about 450m away. The Battery played an important part in beating back a major counter-attack against 1st (Guards) and 2nd Brigades at 1.00 p.m. and continued in action throughout the day expending 950 rounds. It appears not to have had any casualties, despite being under heavy fire at times. At 6 p.m. nine men went forward to reconnoitre a new position. It proved to be untenable, but they encountered a group of Germans and took 50 prisoners and two machine-guns. That night the Battery bivouacked at a farm at Courtonne, about one kilometre south of Verneuil.

It is not clear where 113 Battery came into action on 15th September, but one of the three fatalities suffered that day (Bombardier G S Coultish) was buried in Vendresse Churchyard, indicating it was close to the positions used, the previous day. The other two men who died are commemorated on the La Ferte-sous-Jouarre Memorial (Sergeants A Crouch and VOG Lineham).

The Germans quickly found the range and a shell landed under **Bombardier Ernest Horlock's** gun. It killed the Number 1 and sprayed Horlock with splinters in the right thigh. He walked to the dressing station and, having been treated, the doctor ordered him to get into an ambulance going to the field hospital. However, Horlock reasoned if he was fit enough to walk to the ambulance he was still of use to the Battery and went back to continue laying his gun. He was hit in the back a few minutes later. When he arrived at the dressing station the doctor angrily demanded to know why he had not gone to the field hospital as ordered. Horlock said he could not find the ambulance. The doctor then reasoned if Horlock could walk from the Battery to the dressing station he could walk to the field hospital. Once the wound had been dressed, Horlock was put in the custody of an orderly and packed off on foot. He persuaded the orderly he would be better employed at the dressing station and, when he turned back, Horlock reasoned if he was fit enough to walk to hospital, he could walk back to the Battery, which he did. He was wounded a third time, on this occasion in the arm, and feared that a further appearance at the dressing station would be too much for the doctor, so continued to serve his gun until the Battery went out of action that evening.

2nd Division was directed to seize the line Ostel – Courtecon, two kilometres west of Cerny-en-Laonnois on the Chemin des Dames. 4th (Guards) Brigade on the left was to occupy the top of the Soupir spur at Croix sans Tete or Point 197 (188 on modern maps). 6th Brigade on the right was to pass through 5th Brigade and occupy the top of the ridge. 5th Brigade was in reserve initially, having gained a bridgehead over the Aisne the previous day.

4th (Guards) Brigade did not start until 10.00 a.m. due to traffic congestion at Pont d'Arcy. 2nd Connaught Rangers had been detached from 5th Brigade to Soupir late on 13th September and at 5.30 a.m. on the 14th pushed two companies onto the high ground at La Cour Soupir Farm (see maps for the VCs awarded to Ranken and Dobson a few days later). Around 10.30 a.m. the Germans attacked in force and 2nd Connaught Rangers was hard pressed to hold them east and west of the Farm, even with the support of 2nd Grenadier Guards when it arrived. 3rd Coldstream Guards eventually alleviated the pressure and later the rest of the Brigade arrived. A number of attempts were made to continue the advance on Point 197, but there was little progress and 4th (Guards) Brigade dug in along the Chavonne – Point 197 road.

At 5.00 a.m., 6th Brigade crossed the Aisne by pontoon bridges at Pont Arcy. 1st KRRC was split – A & D Companies guarded the left flank towards La Bouvette Wood, where they made contact with 4th (Guards) Brigade, while B & C Companies acted as right flank guard along the Beaulne spur. At 10.30 a.m., 6th Brigade commenced its attack, with 1st Royal Berkshire and 1st King's leading. Both flanks came under very heavy fire from artillery at Braye and machine-guns in La Bouvette Wood and another wood 600m north of Tilleul. B and C Companies, 1st KRRC charged the latter, suffered heavy casualties, lost a machine-gun and had to fall back. 1st Royal Berkshire got ahead of 1st King's, but by midday the leading battalions were at the base of the ridge near Braye, where they were halted by fire from tiers of trenches in front of Les Grelines Farm and from both flanks. An attempt by 2nd Worcestershire (5th Brigade) to clear the enemy on the right from the flank failed. Heavy fighting followed, during which the Germans pushed the Brigade back to only 800m from Moussy.

Having crossed the Aisne on the 13th, 5th Brigade established an outpost line from northeast of Verneuil to northwest of Moussy. Heavy firing was heard from 5.00 a.m. from the direction of Troyon and the Moussy area was shelled from the high ground north of Braye. From 8.30 a.m. Verneuil was being shelled and at 9.45 a.m. shrapnel began bursting over the ridge at Tilleul. At 10.35 a.m. the Germans began a small advance and for the rest of the day made half-hearted attacks.

The wood north of Moussy-Verneuil (out of picture left) at the southern tip of le Tilleul spur attacked by 2nd HLI on the afternoon of 14th September 1914. During this action Lieutenant Sir Archibald Gibson-Craig was killed. In the background is the Aisne valley.

2nd HLI started the day by reinforcing Tilleul. Around noon C and D Companies advanced with 2nd Worcestershire on the left to reinforce the half of 1st KRRC acting as 6th Brigade's right flank guard. 2nd HLI attacked a small wood north of Moussy-Verneuil on le Tilleul spur, held by a party of Germans with a machine-gun.

A platoon of D Company led by Lieutenant Sir Archibald Gibson-Craig charged the German position and captured it, but Gibson-Craig was killed in the rush (La Ferte-sous-Jouarre Memorial) and his platoon exacted a terrible revenge, bayoneting an estimated 50 Germans. Another machine-gun opened fire causing heavy casualties, but could not be located. The troops took cover where they could in ditches and behind haystacks. Seeing some figures moving in a small wood nearby, **Private George Wilson** thought he had located the gun position. He reported this to his officer who rose up to use his binoculars and was shot dead. Although unnamed the only other 2nd HLI officer killed that day was 2nd Lieutenant Rhys Campbell Folliot Powell (Vendresse British Cemetery – Special Memorial 2).

Wilson saw more movement and opened fire bringing down two Germans. He then sprang from cover before the enemy could recover and charged towards them crying out, "*Come on men charge*", as if a whole battalion was behind him. He reached a small hollow in which were eight Germans and two British prisoners. The ruse worked; thinking there were many more behind Wilson, the Germans surrendered.

The gravestone of 2nd Lieutenant Rhys Campbell Folliot Powell, believed to be buried in Vendresse British Cemetery.

The trees in the middle distance were part of a more substantial wood in 1914. George Wilson stalked the second machine-gun in this area, advancing from the left. The trees on the skyline mark the top of the Beaulne spur. On the right is a covered spring dedicated to French Sergeant Martin Monteil, 57th Infantry Regiment, killed there on 19th December 1914.

Having called for help to escort the prisoners away, Wilson turned his attention back to the machine-gun. He persuaded a rifleman from 1st KRRC to join him and began to stalk the gun position. The rifleman was killed by shellfire, but Wilson continued alone, making use of the available cover and moving as quickly as conditions allowed. He remained undetected and eventually reached a position from where he could see the machine-gun hidden in a heap of hay. Taking careful aim he shot the gunner. Another German immediately replaced him and suffered the same fate. Wilson shot four more of the team and then charged and captured the position. The officer commanding the gun sprang out from hiding and fired his pistol, but missed Wilson who bayoneted him. Wilson then turned the gun around and blazed away at the Germans. He was wounded and staggered back to his own lines where he fainted. On coming to he discovered the Maxim had not been retrieved so set off to get it, returning twice more for the ammunition boxes. His last action before going to the aid station was to recover the body of the KRRC soldier.

At 5.30 p.m., 5th Brigade advanced on Courtecon, while 2nd Oxfordshire & Buckinghamshire Light Infantry was detached to assist 4th (Guards) Brigade at Soupir. With 2nd Connaught Rangers already at Soupir, 5th Brigade consisted of only 2nd HLI and 2nd Worcestershire plus the half battalion of 1st KRRC from 6th Brigade on the flank. About 9.00 p.m., after a slow march across difficult country, the Chemin des Dames road just west of Point 163 (168 on modern maps) was reached and the two battalions deployed along it. The 1st KRRC companies reported some German outposts and reconnaissance patrols to east and west discovered the Germans in strength on both flanks. No contact was made with friendly troops

Contemporary interpretation of George Wilson's VC action.

and the Brigade commander decided to pull back to Verneuil, which was reached at 11.30 p.m.

While the main fighting on 14th September took place in the I Corps area, II and III Corps also fought actions to the west. During the crossing of the Aisne on 13th September, 5th Division seized the damaged bridge at Missy, which was re-taken by the Germans, but captured again that night. 4th Division had gained a bridgehead at Venizel to the west and 3rd Division had a bridgehead at Vailly to the east. Between the two, 5th Division's crossing stalled and it was imperative to link the two small bridgeheads. The Missy bridge was impassable so a reconnaissance of the river bank west as far as Venizel took place to find suitable crossing points until the bridge could be repaired.

It was impossible to move near the Missy bridge in daylight so 59th Field Company RE used the time to collect bridging stores and construct small rafts out of planks, straw and wagon covers. The sappers began working at Ciry station, but were driven out by shelling into the cutting to the west. Meanwhile 17th Field Company RE used the only two pontoons held by 5th Division to construct large rafts at Moulin des Roches, east of Venizel. These were in use by the afternoon and early evening to move most of 14th Brigade across to the north bank.

At nightfall at Missy, a sapper swam the river to recover a boat from the north bank, which was used to ferry small parties of 1st Royal West Kent (13th Brigade) across. Five rafts were brought into service, each capable of ferrying five soldiers. When 40 men had been carried over a German patrol intervened but was driven off. Crossings continued relatively uninterrupted throughout the night and by daybreak

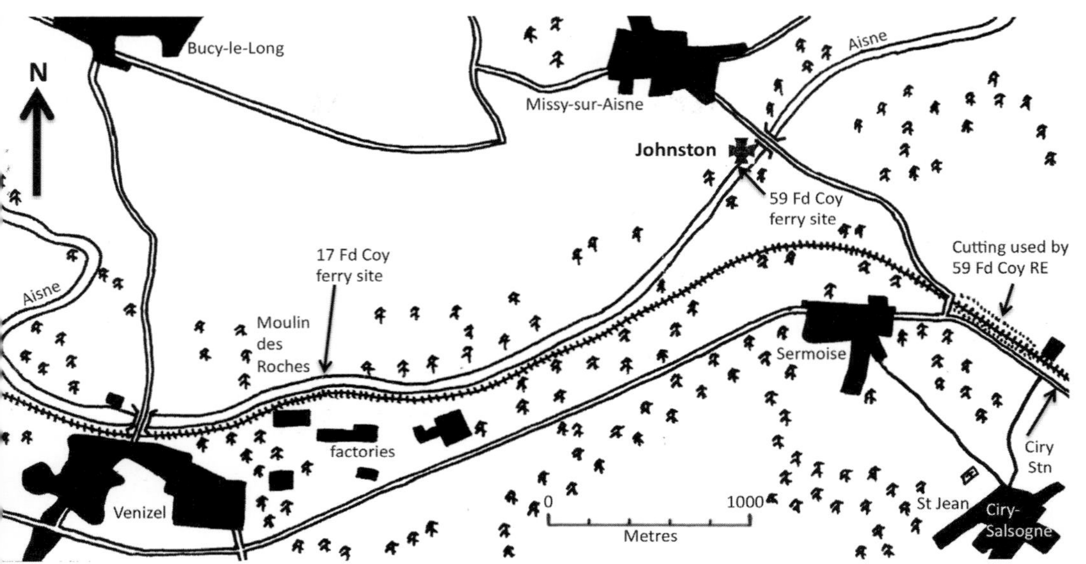

William Johnston earned his VC operating rafts under heavy fire close to the Missy bridge. Leave Missy-sur-Aisne southeast on the D101. Pass over the bridge, which replaced the original in 1921, and park on the right after 100m. The site of the ferry is downstream of the bridge. This area was under heavy fire from German positions on high ground on the north bank, but it is difficult to see now because of tree growth.

on 14th September, 1st Royal West Kent and 2nd KOSB were across. The rest of 13th Brigade had to remain on the south bank.

A day of confused fighting followed on the Chivres spur and around Fort de Condé, but little progress was made and 5th Division was pinned down by heavy fire. The ferry site at Missy was under direct rifle fire and the movement of troops was halted, but the sappers continued to ferry ammunition over the river and recover the wounded. This dangerous work was carried out by **Captain William Johnston** and Lieutenant R B Flint, who was awarded the DSO for this action, but was killed on 23rd January 1915 and is buried in Dranoutre Churchyard near

The ferry site from the south bank.

The ferry site just below the Missy bridge.

Kemmel, Belgium – II A 2). Johnston personally worked two rafts and ensured an adequate supply of ammunition reached the troops on the north bank. Without it they would not have been able to hang on to their precarious positions.

On the evening of the 14th the pontoons at Moulin des Roches were ordered to Missy to assist in moving the remainder of 13th Brigade across and were in position by 2.00 a.m. on the 15th. Later on the 15th, Missy bridge was opened for pedestrian traffic.

By the end of this day's fighting the momentum of the British offensive on the Aisne had been lost. The BEF was ordered to dig in where it stood, beginning the long period of trench warfare that characterised the war into 1918.

Actions on the Aisne Heights, 19-20th September 1914

22 Capt Harry Ranken RAMC, attached 1st KRRC (6th Brigade, 2nd Division), Soupir, France

Following the intense fighting for command of the Aisne Heights on 14th September, the opposing lines north of the river gradually settled into entrenched positions. Most of the construction work took place at night, when trenches were dug to link individual rifle pits, wire was put out and standing patrols deployed into no man's land to cover likely danger spots. The wet weather added to the miseries of the troops in this unfamiliar environment. Despite ferocious localised and sporadic fighting the front remained essentially unchanged.

On 14th September, 1st KRRC had crossed the Aisne over a pontoon bridge at Pont d'Arcy. C and B Companies were sent to the right to gain contact with 5th Brigade, while A and D Companies went to the west of Bois de la Bouvette, in the vicinity of La Cour Soupir Farm, north of Soupir, to gain contact with 4th (Guards) Brigade. The Battalion was thus split between the flanks of 6th Brigade. A and D Companies suffered heavily from snipers and reformed half way down Bois de la Bouvette, with 1st Irish Guards on the left. They advanced again, but suffered heavy casualties and, being very exposed, fell back to a slightly better position half way down the wood. Advanced posts were left out in front.

At dawn on 15th September the Battalion advanced again and dug in along the edge of the wood. The right flank was very exposed as there were insufficient troops to hold the frontage effectively, but early on 16th September, A Company, 1st Royal Berkshire prolonged the right and took over positions previously occupied

The track running along the north-western edge of Bois de la Bouvette passes through this small copse. Either side are former quarry workings. The ravine crossed by Harry Ranken is off to the right.

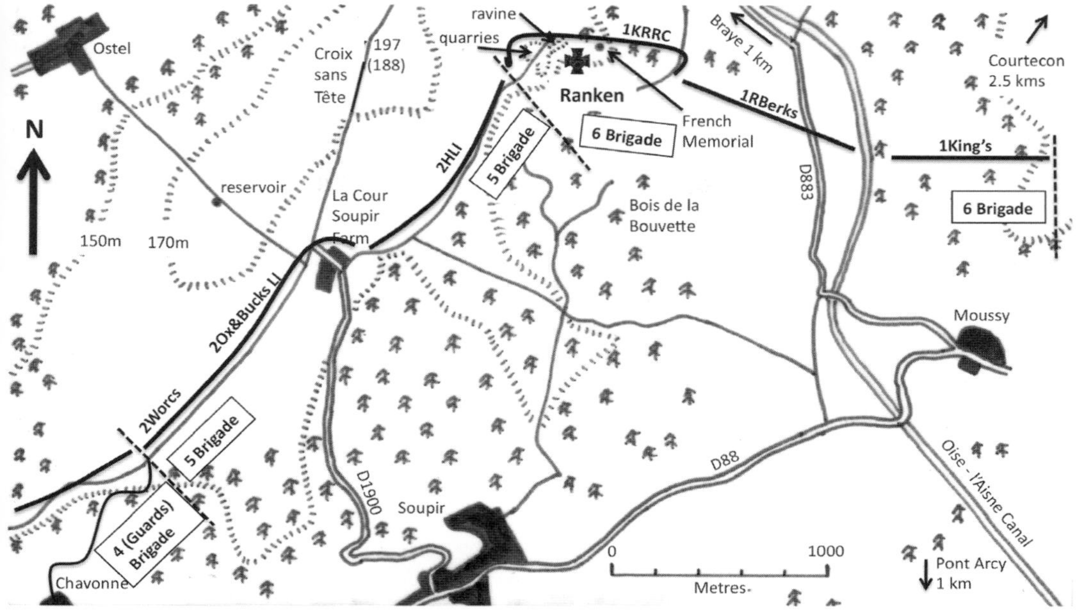

The site of Harry Ranken's VC action is best approached from the south on the D1900 running north from Soupir to la Cour Soupir Farm. Park at the southern end of the Farm and follow the track on the outside of the wood-line northeast towards the French Memorial. Keep the trees on the right and after about 1,200m the track passes through a small copse, with the quarries left and right. Enter the wood to the right to find the ravine, but take care on the steep slopes and unstable ground. Return to the track and continue eastwards to reach the French Memorial, with magnificent views over the Aisne valley.

by 1st KRRC in the quarries. During the day a single shell killed twelve men of 1st KRRC and wounded fifty-six others.

The next few days were very active with fighting patrols and sniping, but the front line did not alter. At 1.30 p.m. on 19th September a very heavy bombardment fell on 4th (Guards) Brigade near La Cour Soupir Farm. The barrage spread along the front to include 6th Brigade's trenches, particularly those occupied by 1st KRRC

From the French memorial overlooking the Aisne valley with the Oise - Aisne Canal in the distance. In the foreground are the remnants of trenches and other defensive works.

1st KRRC's front line ran along the edge of this wood. The German line ran through Croix sans Tête or Point 197 (188 on modern maps), marked by the lone tree on the skyline.

La Cour Soupir Farm from the covered reservoir on the track to Ostel. Bois de la Bouvette is beyond the Farm, with the Aisne valley in the right distance.

in the northeast corner of Bois de la Bouvette. The Germans attacked, but were repulsed. Another attack at 7.00 p.m. also met with little success, although neither was pressed home with great determination. The enemy then brought up machine-guns to engage the British lines.

Fighting continued all next day, during which the enemy launched another four attacks. Riflemen Bullock and Baker were noted in the war diary for continuing to observe from a treetop despite the heavy fire. A and D Companies were relieved by B and C Companies from Brigade reserve at Verneuil and went back to Soupir to rest. Later 2nd South Staffordshire relieved the whole Battalion.

From 1st KRRC's left flank looking southwest towards la Cour Soupir Farm along the front line held by 2nd HLI (5th Brigade). The covered reservoir is next to the lone tree on the right skyline.

Captain Harry Ranken, medical officer of 1st KRRC, distinguished himself throughout the fighting on both days. On one occasion he had to cross a ravine to reach the wounded. During one attack he was in the thick of the action attending to Lieutenant Alston, when he was seriously wounded in the leg by a British shell. Although the injured limb was only hanging on by a scrap of flesh, he arrested the bleeding and went back to work. By this selfless act he sacrificed whatever chance of survival he might have had. Eventually, when he was too weak to continue, he allowed himself to be carried to the rear. His leg was amputated and it was thought he might survive. Lieutenant H Robinson saw

This ravine in the quarries is probably the one crossed by Harry Ranken in his VC action. There are others in the area, but this seems the most likely due to its proximity to 1st KRRC's front line, along the edge of the trees a few metres to the left.

Ranken lying on a stretcher at Braine Station platform, *"When I saw him … he was smoking a cigarette and talking with animation. He had recently had his leg amputated somewhere above the knee and said he was in no pain and was quite comfortable and well. We were all horribly shocked to hear a day or two later that he had died* (on 25th September) *suddenly of an embolism."*

28th September 1914

23 Pte Frederick Dobson 2nd Coldstream Guards (4th (Guards) Brigade, 2nd Division), Chavonne, Aisne, France

Approach the site of Frederick Dobson's VC action from the south on the D1900 running north from Soupir to la Cour Soupir Farm. Park at the Farm and walk 1,500m southwest along the track towards Chavonne. The British front line was to the right of this track, which can be driven with care in dry conditions, but it becomes difficult in the wet. 4th (Guards) Brigade front line was as shown, but how it was divided between units is not entirely clear. On 28th September, 3rd Coldstream Guards was on the right close to Cour Soupir Farm and 2nd Coldstream Guards' was supposedly on the left, but 2nd Grenadier Guards' war diary indicates it was in the line north of Chavonne. It is known that the right of 2nd Coldstream Guards was in the open and the left was in thick woods. The only place that matches this description is the centre of the Brigade line. 2nd Coldstream Guards' war diary is imprecise about its location and inconveniently the Brigade war diary for this period is missing.

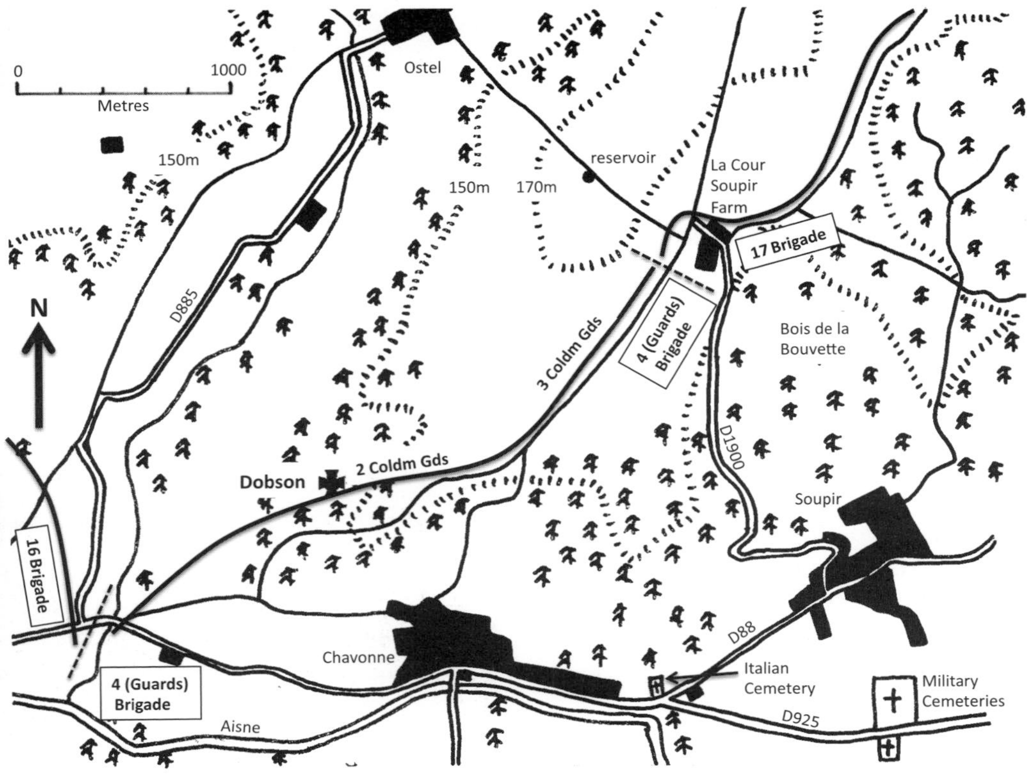

Looking west along the British front line in September 1914. The German lines were to the right of picture. The open ground on the right of 2nd Coldstream Guards is in the foreground and the thickly wooded area on the Battalion's left is in the background. The ground falls away sharply on the left towards Chavonne and the Aisne valley.

On 28th September, 2nd Coldstream Guards was on the left of 4th (Guards) Brigade's line near La Cour Soupir Farm. The right of the Battalion's sector was bare and open, with a gradual uphill slope towards the German trenches, which were 50-200m away. However, on the left the Battalion faced thick woods, in places only 15m from the German forward trenches. In this area was Tunnel Post, from where patrols were frequently sent into the woods to prevent the Germans launching surprise attacks. To increase the problems of visibility, the day dawned in thick mist.

Despite it being daylight and with the Germans only a few metres away, one of the company commanders, Captain Gilbert B S Follet MVO (died 27th September 1918 commanding 3rd Guards Brigade, buried in Beaumetz Cross Roads Cemetery, Beaumetz-les-Cambrai, France F 24), considered it safe enough to send three men on a reconnaissance into no man's land. Suddenly the mist lifted and the Germans opened fire, hitting two of the men, while the third managed to scamper back with only a graze.

Remnants of trench lines in the woods close to Tunnel Post.

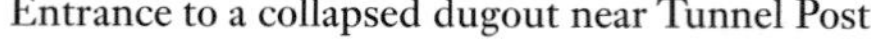

Entrance to a collapsed dugout near Tunnel Post

The grave of Albert Haldenby in Vailly British Cemetery. He died before Frederick Dobson could reach him.

The wounded men in no man's land could not be recovered until darkness fell some 14 hours later. Exposed to enemy fire and without medical attention, they were unlikely to survive that long. **Private Frederick Dobson** volunteered to bring them in straight away. The task seemed impossible, with the victims lying in full view of the enemy. However, he managed to crawl out and reached the wounded men, avoiding injury on the way.

Dobson discovered that 7317 Private Albert Haldenby was already dead (Vailly British Cemetery III A 4A). Private Butler, although wounded in three places, was still alive. Having bandaged Butler's wounds, Dobson realised he could not move him on his own, so he crawled back and persuaded Corporal Brown to help. Returning to the wounded man with a stretcher they managed to get Butler onto it and dragged him back. No one was hit, which in the circumstances was a miracle, although their movements were covered for short periods by the mist. Corporal Brown received the DCM for his part in the rescue.

Chapter Three

Operations in Flanders 1914

Battle of Armentières, 22nd October 1914

24 Pte Henry May, 1st Cameronians (19th Brigade, 6th Division) La Boutillerie, France

Soon after the fighting on the Aisne stagnated into trench warfare, both sides attempted to outflank the other in the 'Race to the Sea'. At the same time the British were anxious to re-establish themselves on the Allied left flank, close to their supply lines, Channel ports and home base. In early October the BEF began to disengage from the Aisne front one Corps at a time. By the middle of the month the British had been relieved by French troops and the move to Flanders was well advanced.

The 'Race to the Sea', during which the BEF detached itself from the Aisne front east of Soissons and moved to Flanders. En route it was engaged at La Bassée, Armentières and Messines before the First Battle of Ypres (Official History, France and Belgium 1914, Volume 1).

Before the war of movement finally ground to a halt, a number of small but intense engagements were fought in the second half of October at La Bassée, Messines and Armentières. For the sake of clarity, the VCs awarded in these battles will be covered

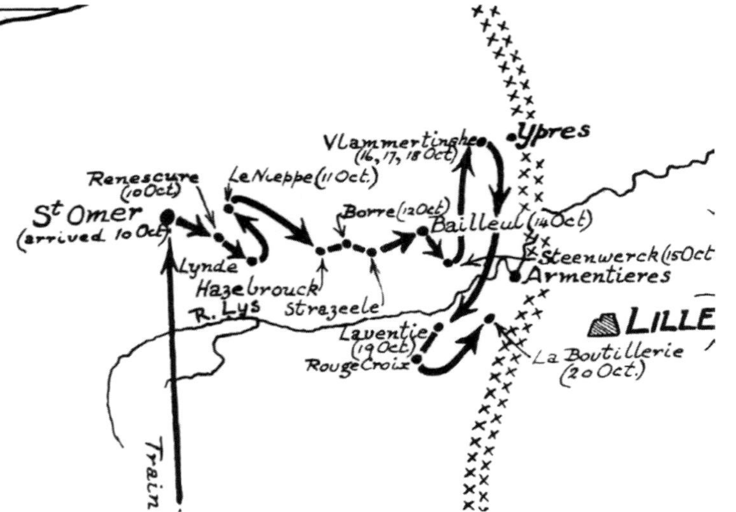

1st Cameronians made numerous moves after arriving at St Omer by train from the Aisne on 10th October (History of the Cameronians, Volume II).

geographically from south to north, rather than attempting to describe them strictly chronologically.

19th Brigade was formed from lines of communication units and joined 6th Division when that formation arrived at St Omer from the Aisne. On 19th October, the Brigade was in reserve to III Corps and at 2.00 p.m. it was ordered to move to Laventie. 1st Cameronians was resting at Vlamertinghe in Belgium, having just been relieved in France. The men were looking forward to their first meal of fresh meat, when orders were received to move back into France at once. London buses were provided for the 35 kms journey and the Battalion arrived at Laventie, 11 kms southwest of Armentières at 8.45 p.m.

A Company, 1st Cameronians aboard London buses bound for Laventie on 19th October 1914. This was the first time the Battalion ever moved by motor transport (History of the Cameronians, Volume II).

Shortly after dawn on the morning of 20th October, heavy firing broke out to the east and southeast, as 1st Cameronians and 2nd Royal Welsh Fusiliers were entrenching on the line Fauquissart – Croix Blanche. The right of III Corps was at Radinghem and the left of II Corps was about Aubers, with the gap between being covered by French cavalry. At noon, 19th Brigade was ordered to move on Fromelles, which was reached at 3.00 p.m. 2nd Royal Welch Fusiliers and 1st Middlesex were pushed forward to the line Fromelles – Pont de Pierre, slightly in rear of the French,

The situation just before 19th Brigade, with 1st Cameronians, arrived at Laventie on 19th October 1914. The left of II Corps' line, held by 3rd Division, is at the bottom and the right of III Corps is at Radinghem, held by 6th Division. In between are elements of Conneau's French Cavalry Corps (Official History, France and Belgium 1914, Volume 2).

who were engaging the Germans. 1st Cameronians and 2nd Argyll & Sutherland Highlanders bivouacked northwest of Fromelles.

During the night orders came from III Corps for 19th Brigade to fill the gap between the two Corps by occupying Fromelles and Le Maisnil. 2nd Argyll & Sutherland Highlanders moved at 4.00 a.m. to Le Maisnil, which was occupied by French cavalry and cyclists. 2nd Royal Welsh Fusiliers extended its front to hold a line from the southwest corner of Fromelles to Pont de Pierre. 1st Middlesex and 1st Cameronians moved at 7.00 a.m. to a central position behind Fromelles to form the Brigade reserve. 1st Cameronians occupied a ditch at Bas Maisnil between Fromelles and La Boutillerie, from where it could assist the units in front. The Battalion remained concealed while heavy artillery and small arms exchanges took place in front.

At 11.00 a.m. the Germans commenced shelling Le Maisnil and it continued for the rest of the day. About noon, half of 1st Middlesex was sent forward to support 2nd Argyll & Sutherland Highlanders. The Germans launched strong attacks against Le Maisnil in the afternoon and some of the French on the left flank gave way around 5.00 p.m. This caused some amusement initially as French cavalrymen, resplendent in baggy red breeches and armed with carbines and lances, passed by on bicycles. However, their withdrawal made the rest of the position untenable and 2nd Argyll & Sutherland Highlanders and half 1st Middlesex retired on Bas Maisnil. A line was taken up for the night astride the Fleurbaix – Le Maisnil road about la Boutillerie. 1st Cameronians was compelled to fall back at 9.00 p.m. to

Major Crofton Bury Vandeleur DSO, 1st Cameronians became the first British prisoner of war to escape from Germany. His son JOE Vandeleur, led the Irish Guards battlegroup spearheading the armoured thrust to relieve 1st Airborne Division at Arnhem in September 1944 (Cameronians).

conform. Such was the speed of the withdrawal that HQ 19th Brigade's war diary records six men killed, 49 wounded and 253 missing. No doubt many of the missing rejoined later, but some were taken prisoner.

By midnight 19th Brigade had established a new line from Rouge Bancs to the eastern side of La Boutillerie in contact with 16th Brigade on the left and French cavalry on the right. 1st Cameronians (left) and 1st Middlesex (centre) dug in overnight, with 2nd Argyll & Sutherland Highlanders in support. 2nd Royal Welsh Fusiliers was in Brigade reserve, but later joined the line on the right. Each of the three forward battalions then had a frontage of about 1000m.

Henry May's VC action took place in flat open farmland and the scene today is largely unchanged. The front line settled here for most of the rest of the war and there are a number of later German concrete pillboxes in the fields. Although the lanes are narrow there are places where cars can be parked off the road, but beware the deep roadside ditches in places. There are no facilities in the immediate area. For restaurants and hotels etc go to Laventie, La Bassée or Armentières.

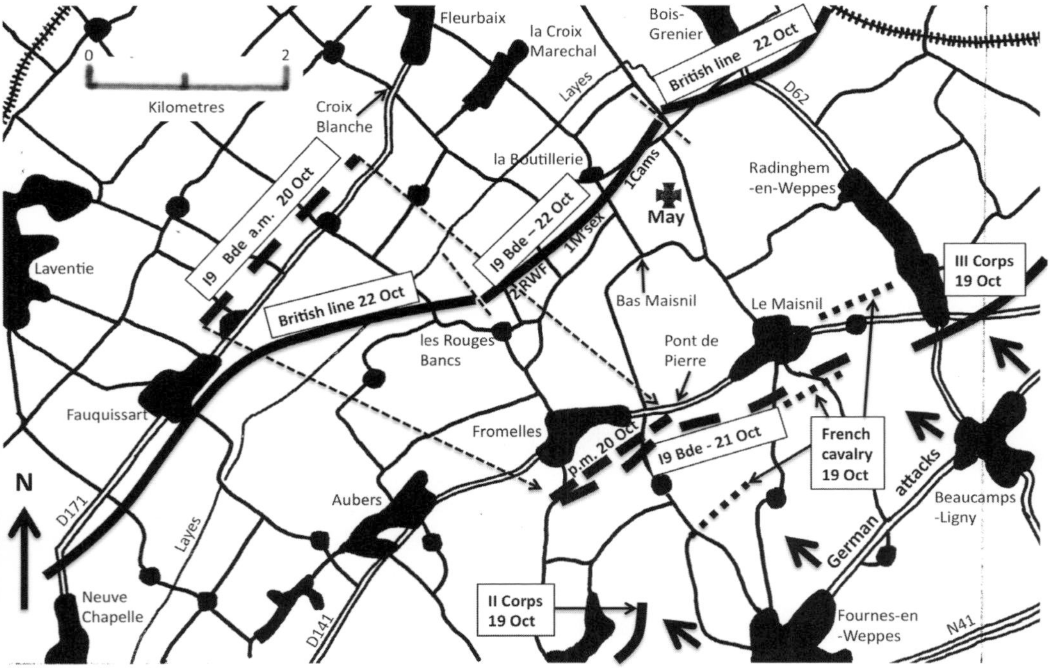

Dawn on 22nd October found 1st Cameronians digging in on the left of the Brigade line to the north and east of La Boutillerie. Half each of C (Captain RWH Rose) and D (Captain AR MacAllan) Companies were sent forward to cover the rest of the Battalion. The Germans allowed this party to advance 650-700m before opening close range fire from a flank. The half companies took cover in a ditch, where they remained under heavy fire. There was no artillery support and the Battalion Machine-Gun Section had neither the equipment nor the experience to provide overhead fire support. Although heavily outnumbered, the party continued to resist attacks in order to cover the diggers. They were eventually forced back having suffered seventy-two casualties (twenty killed, including Captain Rose, thirty-seven wounded and fifteen missing, who were recovered later). Most of those killed are commemorated on the Ploegsteert Memorial.

As **Private Henry May** fell back with the other survivors, he saw one of his comrades, 7300 Lance Corporal James Lawton, lying wounded about 100m away. He ran to where Lawton had fallen followed by his popular platoon commander, Lieutenant DAH Graham, and was joined by Lance Corporal McCall and Private Bell. May pulled off Lawton's equipment and got him to his feet. With McCall on one arm and May supporting the other, they began to fall back when Lawton was shot again and killed (Ploegsteert Memorial). McCall was knocked unconscious.

May was determined to fight back and took up a firing position. At that moment he saw his platoon commander, Lieutenant DAH Graham, go down wounded in the leg. May called on Bell for assistance. The two ran to the officer and managed to carry him some distance until Bell was hit in the hand and foot.

May continued to drag Graham as best he could and stripped off some of his equipment to lighten the load. Almost exhausted, about 300m from the British trenches, May was joined by his section commander, 8445 Corporal Thomas William Taylor (MID for this action) . Graham told them both to get away, but they declined and May lifted the wounded officer onto Taylor's shoulders. A few seconds

The buildings in the background are on the Rouge Bancs – Bois Grenier road at La Boutillerie. 1st Cameronians dug in to the right and rear of the hamlet. Half of C and D Companies advanced across this field to the left until coming under fire and being forced to take cover in a ditch. During the subsequent retirement to La Boutillerie, Henry May was involved in two rescue attempts that earned him the VC. The German pillbox was constructed later.

Officers of 1st Cameronians in billets on the Aisne front on 1st October 1914, before the move to Flanders. Lieutenant Graham is seated first from the left and Captain MacAllan is standing second left with a pipe and stick (History of the Cameronians, Volume II).

later Taylor was shot dead (Ploegsteert Memorial). Making a supreme effort, May dragged Graham into the cover of a ditch 40m from the British positions. Graham then insisted that May returned to the Battalion, which he did, but arranged for a rescue party to pick up the officer later. He survived to become Major General Douglas Graham CB CBE DSO & Bar MC.

1st-2nd November 1914

31 Dmr Spencer Bent, 1st Battalion, East Lancashire (11th Brigade, 4th Division), Le Gheer, Belgium

Late on 20th October 1914, 11th Brigade was ordered to form the reserve for 4th Division. 1st East Lancashire had been digging trenches at Wez Macquart when it moved to Chapelle d'Armentières and after a short rest in the market square was ordered to Ploegsteert. Arriving at dawn, it was learned that the Germans had attacked overnight and captured Le Gheer, driving a wedge into the front held by 12th Brigade. At 6.00 a.m., 1st East Lancashire and 1st Somerset Light Infantry were placed under 12th Brigade and ordered to attack through Ploegsteert Wood to reinforce 2nd Inniskilling Fusiliers (12th Brigade), which had been driven back 400m. Two platoons of 2nd Essex, also 12th Brigade, north of Le Gheer charged south through the Wood. One platoon took up a position facing Le Gheer as a block and the other lined the Ploegsteert road to enfilade Germans occupying a series of ditches in the open.

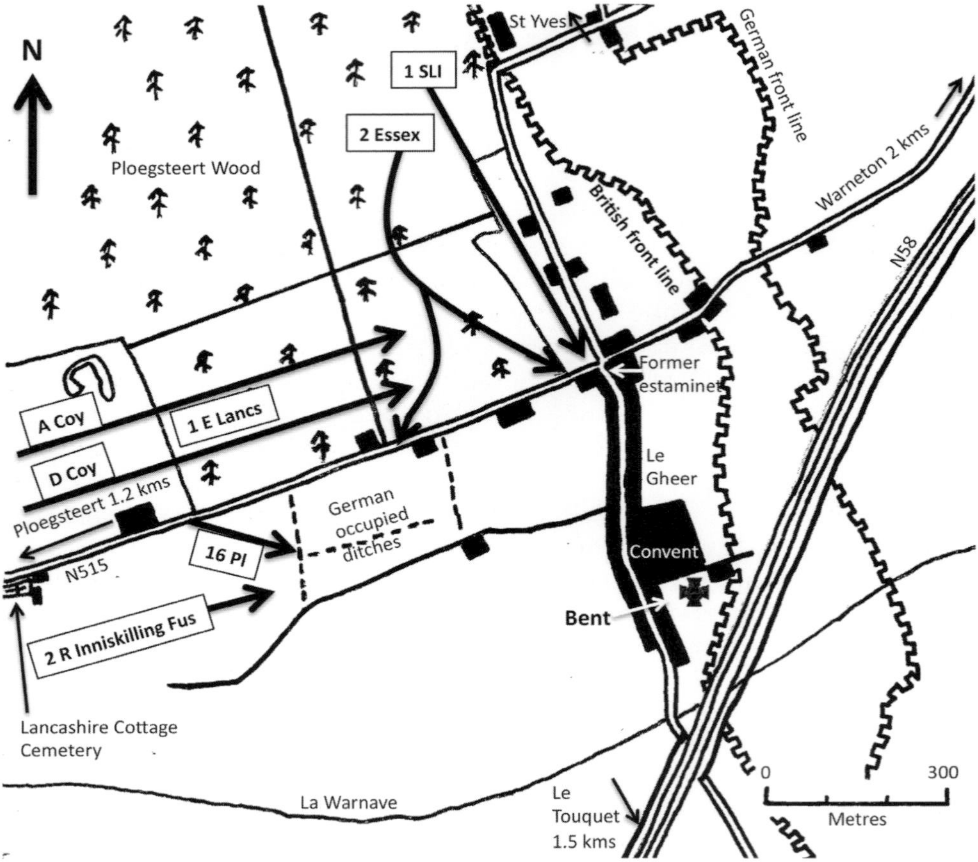

Le Gheer and the southeast corner of Ploegsteert Wood. Drummer Bent was active in this area 22nd October - 3rd November 1914. There are plenty of places to park, particularly along the road south of Le Gheer crossroads, near the former convent.

Le Gheer crossroads from the south. The British front line ran parallel with this road about 150m to the right. The Calvary is original, but the cover was added post-war. 1st Somerset Light Infantry charged the crossroads from straight ahead and one of the two 2nd Essex platoons emerged from Ploegsteert Wood in the left background.

In 1st East Lancashire, D and A Companies (right and left respectively) led in columns of extended platoons and the eastern edge of the Wood was reached without encountering any opposition. 1st Somerset Light Infantry advanced simultaneously along the northern edge of the Wood and swung south to take the Germans around Le Gheer crossroads in the rear and cut off the escape of those south of the Wood being pushed back by 2nd Inniskilling Fusiliers. Having cleared the Wood, D Company, 1st East Lancashire lined the southern edge and opened heavy fire on the Germans in the ditches to the south. 2nd Inniskilling Fusiliers also engaged the Germans, who suffered numerous casualties. They were then charged from the northwest by 16 Platoon under Lieutenant F D Hughes, who was killed (Ploegsteert Wood New Cemetery Memorial in Strand Military Cemetery, Ploegsteert). Many Germans were killed and wounded and shortly after the original line was restored and 45 Inniskilling prisoners were released. It is estimated the Germans suffered a thousand casualties, including about 130 prisoners. The recaptured ditches were held by C Company.

Orders were then issued to support a 2nd Essex (12th Brigade) attack against Le Touquet. B Company was already assisting the Essex, but patrols were unable to contact either the Essex or Germans. When this attack finished, one platoon each from A & D Companies remained to assist C Company, while the remainder took up supporting positions.

At 4.45 a.m. on 22nd October, a German attack supported by machine-guns on the line St Yves – Le Gheer – Le Touquet was repulsed. The rest of the day was relatively quiet except for hour-long bombardments at 9.00 a.m. and 5.00 p.m. Later in the day, 1st East Lancashire took over 1,000m of frontage from Le Gheer crossroads south to the crossroads north of Le Touquet, with A and B Companies in the front line and C and D Companies in reserve in Ploegsteert. On the left was 1st Somerset Light Infantry and on the right 1st Rifle Brigade, with 1st Hampshire in reserve.

23rd October was quiet and at dusk C and D Companies relieved A and B Companies in the front line. At 1.15 a.m. on the 24th, the Germans attacked again supported by artillery and machine-guns, but were repulsed with the assistance of the British artillery, which managed to silence the German guns within 15 minutes. Another attack next day was also beaten off.

The Le Gheer crossroads Calvary in 1915, looking west.

It was during this period that **Drummer Spencer Bent** first distinguished himself. On 22nd October he carried ammunition to a patrol cut off by the Germans.

Two days later he carried food and ammunition up to the front line under heavy rifle and shell fire. However, the main deeds for which he was awarded the VC took place a few days later.

The period 26th-28th October was characterised by shelling, reliefs of the front line and digging support trenches behind 1st Rifle Brigade. Some of this work was carried out by civilians. On 29th October heavy shelling broke out at 11.00 a.m. One shell wrecked the kitchen of Battalion Headquarters in the Estaminet du Commerce at the Le Gheer crossroads and as a result it was moved to the keeper's hut on the southern edge of Ploegsteert Wood, 225m west of the crossroads. There was more shelling in the afternoon and at 6.00 p.m. the Germans attacked all along the line, but were driven off.

At 7.15 a.m. on 30th October the shelling began again and continued with heavy machine-gun and rifle fire at intervals. Another attack seemed imminent, so three of C Company's platoons was sent up to support A and B Companies in the front line, while the fourth was held in support in trenches on the edge of Ploegsteert Wood. The Battalion was to be relieved by 1st Somerset Light Infantry, but this was cancelled until the situation was resolved. The Germans attacked at 3.00 p.m. but were once again forced back.

The 31st was similar, with shelling starting at 7.45 a.m. and continuing heavily all day. Battalion Headquarters in the keeper's cottage was hit and moved back another 700m to La Belle Promenade, on the Le Gheer – Ploegsteert road. Half a company was sent to support 1st Hampshire.

1st November brought no respite, with the Germans shelling the Battalion's positions, resulting in heavy casualties and some sections of trench being destroyed. The Germans were entrenched very close on the left near the crossroads and the reserve company was sent up to assist. The shelling continued sporadically into the night and at 4.00 a.m. on the 2nd a new weapon to the British made its battlefield debut; the German minenwerfer or trench mortar. A section of B Company's trench was destroyed and a number of men were buried alive. Requests were sent back to locate it by air and destroy it with artillery. At 5.00 a.m. the enemy attacked the left of the Battalion's line, but were cut to pieces by steady rifle and machine-gun fire.

Bent was in a dugout snatching a well-earned rest when the German attack began. He had just dropped off to sleep when he was woken by a commotion in the trench outside. Rising quickly, he discovered the rest of his platoon (4 Platoon, B Company) withdrawing in some haste. The platoon commander and platoon sergeant were absent, visiting advanced posts and word had been passed down the line for the Battalion to retire. It is possible that this was a ruse by a German disguised as a British officer.

At first Bent followed his comrades but, remembering a French trumpet he had found, went back for his souvenir in the dugout. When he reached the trench he saw a shadowy figure crawling towards him. Keeping perfectly still he waited until the man was close and then jabbed his rifle to the man's head, demanding to know who he was.

Modern buildings at the Le Gheer convent. The 1st East Lancashire front line ran parallel with the road in the foreground about 100m beyond it. Spencer Bent rescued Private McNulty in this area.

War time photograph of the convent at Le Gheer.

From the embankment of the N58 dual carriageway looking north along no man's land. The modern convent buildings are in the background, Bent rescued McNulty from in front of the buildings on the right and dragged him back towards the British lines on the left.

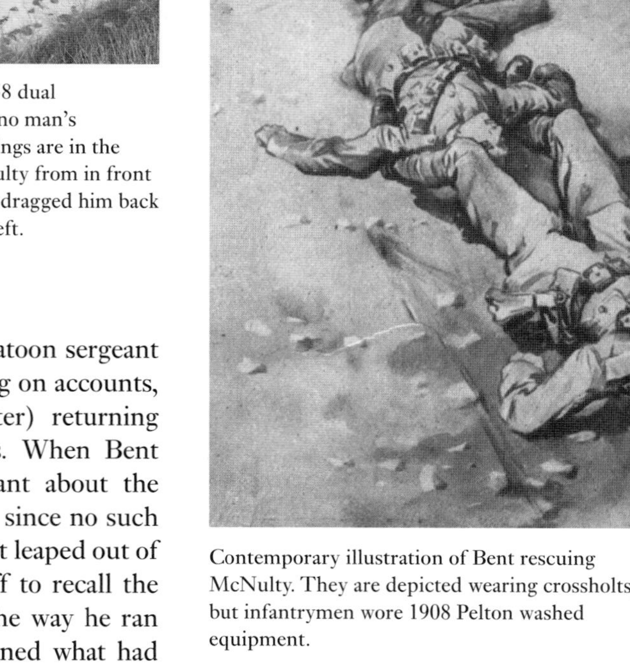

Contemporary illustration of Bent rescuing McNulty. They are depicted wearing crossholts, but infantrymen wore 1908 Pelton washed equipment.

It turned out to be the platoon sergeant (Jelks or Waller, depending on accounts, but more likely the latter) returning from the advanced posts. When Bent hurriedly told the sergeant about the retirement he was aghast, since no such order had been given. Bent leaped out of the trench and dashed off to recall the rest of the platoon. On the way he ran into an officer and explained what had happened. The officer went off to recall some other men and shortly afterwards the trench garrison was back in position.

Shelling in the early hours was followed by another attack. Holding their fire until the Germans were 350m away, they opened up with everything at their disposal, including a recently brought-up machine-gun. The German dead were left in heaps, but a retaliatory bombardment knocked out the platoon commander and 9126 Sergeant H Waller (died of wounds on 10th November and buried in Trois Arbres Cemetery, Steenwerck – II 1 3), together with several other men. Bent took command of the platoon and by keeping his head managed to beat off a number of attacks during the day until relieved.

At daybreak on 3rd November the minenwerfer opened fire again and destroyed the forward trench south of the Warneton road, burying 15 men, of whom only two were dug out alive. The survivors moved back 25m to occupy another trench. However, the British artillery got the range and at 9.00 a.m. knocked out the minenwerfer, which was positioned just south of the road.

The final act for which Bent was awarded the VC took place on 3rd November when he brought in several wounded men. One man in particular, Private McNulty, who had been shot through both legs, was rescued under very dangerous circumstances as he lay only 30m from the German front line trench near the walls of a ruined convent. Bent dashed out and was pulling McNulty onto his back when he lost his footing and fell over. This was fortuitous, since a second later a burst of fire whistled over him and slammed into the convent wall, showering plaster fragments into his eye. As long as Bent lay flat the Germans could not hit him, but if he raised himself up even a couple of inches he risked being shot to pieces. Shuffling around the wounded soldier, Bent hooked his feet under his armpits and slowly dragged him back to the shelter of the trench. Bent left McNulty in the care of another man while he went to find a surgeon to attend to him.

Prior to this incident, McNulty had taken great delight in disparaging drummers at any opportunity, but having been rescued by one, took back everything he had said previously. Bent merely commented, *"Any bloody fool can be a rifleman. It takes time to make a drummer!"* After dark on the 4th the Battalion was relieved by 1st Hampshire and went into reserve in three farms behind Ploegsteert.

Battle of La Bassée, 29th October 1914

II Corps was holding the Givenchy front at the end of October 1914 when plans to attack the Germans in cooperation with the French Tenth Army had to be shelved;

26 2nd Lt James Leach, 2nd Manchester (14th Brigade, 5th Division), La Quinque Rue, near Festubert, France

27 Sgt John Hogan, 2nd Manchester (14th Brigade, 5th Division), La Quinque Rue, near Festubert, France

the British were finding it difficult just to hold their ground. On 21st October, 2nd Manchester was attached to 13th Brigade to hold the line La Quinque Rue (further north in 1914 than marked on modern maps) to the main Festubert road on the left of 5th Division's front. The Battalion was in the thick of the fighting for some days thereafter. Heavy shelling and close range sniping made movement by day impossible.

On 25th October, 1st Manchester (Lahore Division) was also attached to 13th Brigade and next day relieved 1st Bedfordshire on the right of 2nd Manchester. This was the first time the two battalions had served together since 1882 in Alexandria.

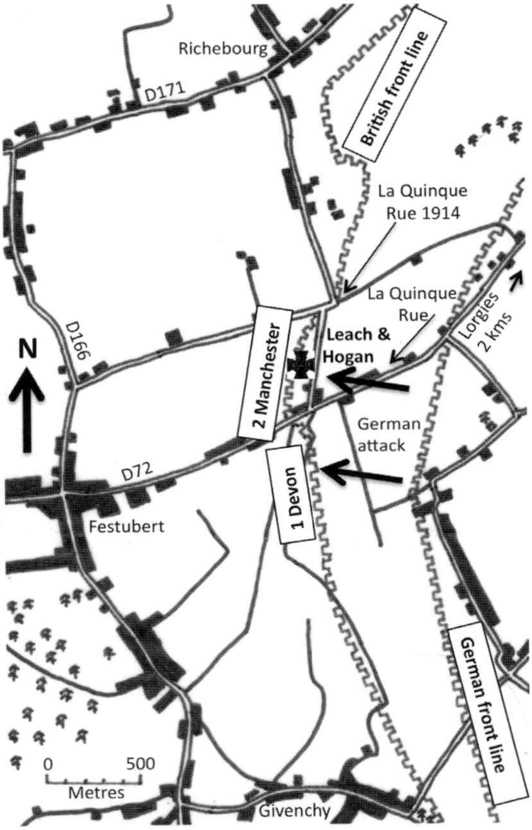

Early on 29th October, 2nd Manchester reported being fired upon by a mortar from 550m away; the shells were about the size of tennis balls. About 6.30 a.m. the British artillery opened fire, followed soon after by the German guns, which cut all communications with the front line. At 7.00 a.m. the Germans opened heavy rifle fire all along the front and launched a strong attack against the centre and left of 1st Devonshire (relieved 1st Manchester early that morning) and the centre and right of 2nd Manchester. **2nd Lieutenant James Leach** and 34 men of A Company held the centre of the 2nd Manchester forward trench. Despite putting up a gallant fight against 200–300 enemy, they were forced down a communications trench. About a dozen men were lost, but the rest of the line on the right, under Captain Evans, held and the Germans were halted 10m from the support trench.

The area in which 2nd Manchester fought off the German attack on 29th October 1914. From the crossroads at Festubert church head east on the D72 towards Lorgies. After 1,400m turn left towards Richebourg and stop after 250m. Leach and Hogan's VC action was about 100m to the left (west) of this minor road.

Leach and **Sergeant John Hogan** gathered their men and prevented the Germans from advancing any further. They then made two unsuccessful attempts to dislodge the enemy from the lost trench and two men were killed. Leach was determined to recapture the trench and went forward on his own to conduct a detailed and highly dangerous reconnaissance. The Germans initially had things their own way so Leach returned to await a more favourable moment. He went out again later and on returning called for Hogan and 10 volunteers. They moved forward carefully on their hands and knees along the communications trench and caught the Germans by surprise when they rushed into the middle of the lost stretch of trench.

The 2nd Manchester front line trench cleared by Leach and Hogan ran parallel with and to the right of this road. Looking south with Festubert out of view on the right.

Having retaken half the front line trench and with their rear secured, Leach and Hogan went on alone along the left section. As they approached the first traverse Leach fired his revolver around the corner to clear the immediate opposition. He could do this without showing himself, but the Germans had to be completely exposed in order to use their long rifles. Hogan kept a sharp lookout above ground to ensure the enemy did not climb out of the trench and attack them from the rear.

Coming to the next traverse Leach repeated the procedure, this time using the revolver in his left hand. To avoid running into their covering fire, Hogan exposed his hat above the parapet on the end of his rifle. At times they had to resort to hand to hand fighting as they rounded a traverse but, having the initiative, Leach and Hogan managed to keep the upper hand.

As they became bottled up into the end of the trench, the Germans sent one of their prisoners, taken in the morning's fighting, to offer their surrender. Leach was surprised to hear the voice of one of his own men shout out, *"Don't shoot, Sir."* As he and Hogan turned the final traverse the Germans fell to their knees and cried in unison, *"Mercy"*. Leach made them remove their equipment and double over the open ground to the British main line. Leach and Hogan had retaken the trench for no loss and in the process had killed eight of the enemy, wounded two more and captured 16 unwounded. Although he was unharmed, Leach's cap and scarf had been shredded by bullets.

Some accounts maintain this action took place after dark. However, the Battalion war diary records the event taking place at 2.00 p.m. and 13th Brigade's war diary supports this, putting it after 11 a.m. but before 3.30 p.m.

With the trench secure, reinforcements from 1st Bedfordshire (15th Brigade) and 2nd Royal Munster Fusiliers (Army Troops) came forward. The Bedfordshires managed to push along a communications trench to connect with 2nd Manchester. During the afternoon arrangements were made for 21st (Bareilly) Brigade (Meerut Division) to relieve the line. By 1.00 a.m. on 30th October, 2/8th Gurkhas had taken over and 2nd Manchester withdrew. The Germans broke into the line again next day and fierce fighting continued for some days after, resulting in a small retirement to a new line.

Chapter Four

First Battle of Ypres 1914

23rd October 1914

25 Dmr William Kenny, 2nd Gordon Highlanders (20th Brigade, 7th Division), Kruiseke and Zandvoorde, Ypres, Belgium

The First Battle of Ypres, 19th October - 22nd November 1914, saw some of the most desperate fighting of the war, during which the BEF was stretched to the limit. At times only a thin line of troops stood between the Germans and Ypres, but they failed to break through. The cost was enormous on both sides, but particularly for the BEF, with its regular divisions being reduced to the strength of weak brigades in some cases. The Salient was formed and its defenders faced almost three years being overlooked on three sides. Eight VCs were awarded for the Battle.

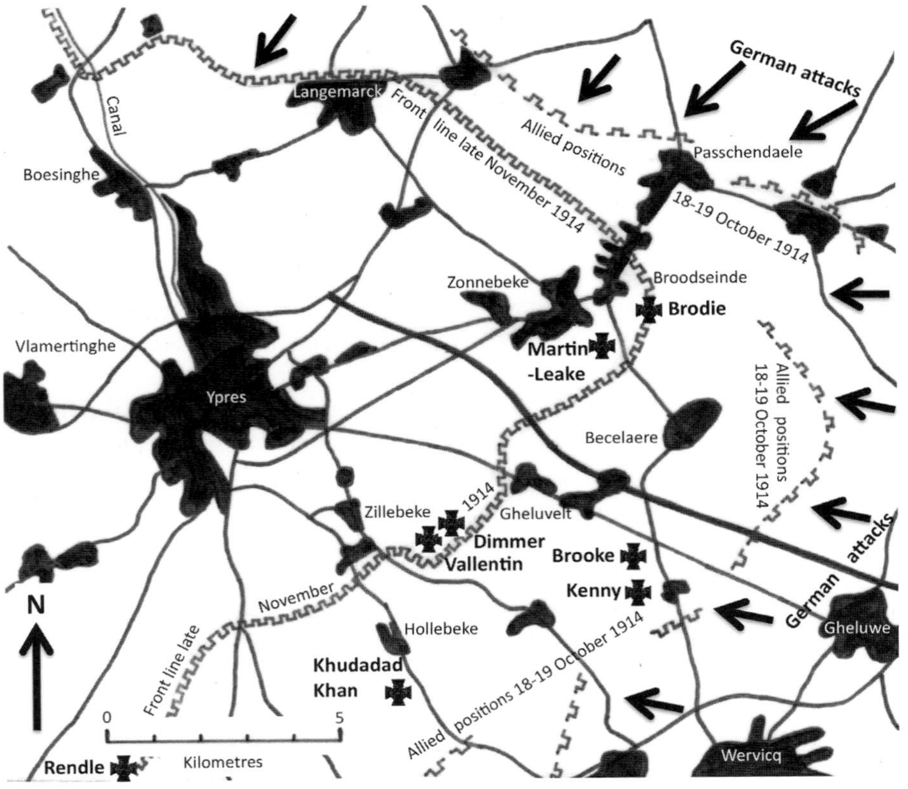

When war broke out, 2nd Gordon Highlanders was recalled from Egypt. With eight other battalions from overseas and the last of the home-based battalions it formed the new 7th Division. This formation landed at Zeebrugge on 6/7th October 1914, initially to attempt the relief of Antwerp, but this quickly changed to covering the retirement of the Belgian Army. Although well trained, most of the Division's soldiers were not in the best physical condition and they suffered on long marches. The Gordons also discovered that their boots had dried out in the Egyptian heat and shrank when exposed to the wet in Belgium.

On 14th October, 7th Division arrived in the Ypres area, where life continued relatively normally. However, this was about to change, as the Belgians prepared to defend the line of the Yser Canal and the BEF began to arrive from the south. On 18th October, 7th Division commenced a deliberate advance on Menin. 20th Brigade was ordered to occupy a ridge with the left resting on the crossroads at Kruiseik through America and bending back to Zandvoorde on the right. The line was held by 2nd Scots Guards on the left, in contact with 21st Brigade, then 2nd Gordon Highlanders to America and 2nd Border continuing to Zandvoorde. The frontage was too long for a brigade and there were insufficient reserves. The salient at America was a significant weakness and the area was also wooded, allowing the enemy to close unseen.

The position was adjusted on 19th October (the official commencement date of the First Battle of Ypres, which ran until 22nd November), to run from Zonnebeke – Gheluvelt – Kruiseik – Zandvoorde. Even then it was clear the position at America was too exposed, so the line was adjusted again from the 10 kms point on the Ypres – Menin road to the crossroads just south of Kruiseik and on to Zandvoorde. Two battalions were in the line (1st Grenadier Guards and 2nd Border) and two in reserve to the Division (2nd Scots Guards and 2nd Gordon Highlanders). 21st Brigade was on the left and 5th Cavalry Brigade on the right at Zandvoorde.

On 20th October, the reserve battalions were sent forward to reconnoitre Gheluwe. They were heavily shelled from Wervicq, but had few casualties. The battalions returned at 1.00 p.m., having ascertained that Gheluwe was held by the Germans. At 2.30 p.m., HQ 20th Brigade was informed that 5th Cavalry Brigade was withdrawing, leaving one regiment at Tenbrielen to cover for an hour or so while the rest pulled back. 3rd Cavalry Brigade was taking up positions from the canal near Houthem to Kortenwilde, but was not ready, leaving the right flank wide open. At 3.00 p.m. the Germans advanced against 1st Grenadier Guards and 2nd Border, but it was more of a reconnaissance in force than a serious attack. They occupied America and 2nd Scots Guards fell back into divisional reserve again.

On the 21st, 2nd Scots Guards was sent to Zandvoorde to fill the gap on the right until 3rd Cavalry Brigade was established at Kortewilde. 2nd Gordon Highlanders went back into the line east of Zandvoorde facing south, where it was attacked in the morning. Constant shelling and sniping made rest impossible, except in short snatches, and the fire swept roads made the carriage of ammunition and rations to the front hazardous. **Drummer William Kenny's** deeds are not well documented. It is known that on 21st October he went out and brought in the mortally wounded Corporal 'Cockney' Robertson of C Company and then helped carry in more wounded. Robertson has not been identified as there were a number of men of that name and a Robinson killed in this period, but none was a Corporal or had an obvious London connection.

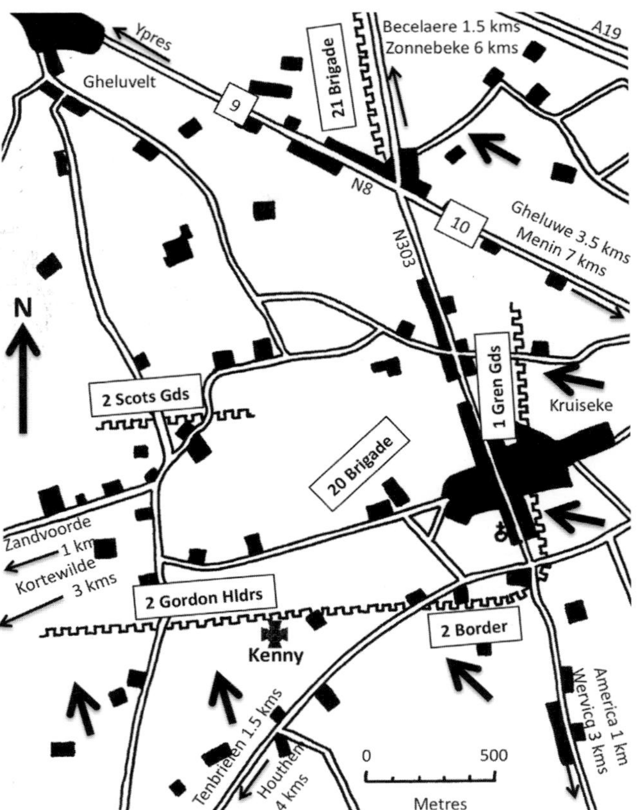

The line held by 2nd Gordon Highlanders was across almost featureless farmland to the west of Kruiseke. This shows the situation on 22nd October 1914.

Later on the morning of the 21st, large bodies of enemy were seen advancing towards Tenbrielen. Half of 2nd Scots Guards moved to Gheluvelt and the other half was attacked between Zandvoorde and Kortewilde around 10.30 a.m. At 11.00 a.m. it was clear that 21st Brigade on the left was under heavy attack and HQ 7th Division ordered 20th Brigade to send two companies of 1st Grenadier Guards to reinforce it.

22nd Brigade on the far left and 3rd Cavalry Brigade on the right were also engaged heavily. It was clear a major German attack was underway. A troop of the Northumberland Hussars and the Divisional Cyclists made contact with 3rd

The view northwest over 2nd Gordon Highlanders' positions from the German lines. These fields are frequently inundated and would have been most unpleasant to entrench in.

Looking southwest from the Kruiseke–Zandvoorde road over the line held by 2nd Gordon Highlander 20th–27th October 1914. The farm on the left is also in the previous picture.

Cavalry Brigade about 1.15 p.m, making the right flank more secure. 2nd Gordon Highlanders was much troubled by machine-guns in farms to its front and 2nd Border had its trenches blown in by shellfire. By 3.00 p.m., 1st Grenadier Guards was under heavy attack, as was the left of 21st Brigade. 2nd Border was attacked at 4.00 p.m., but the Germans held off and dug in so close that the British artillery was unable to engage them. At 10.00 p.m., 2nd Scots Guards was relieved by the cavalry at Zandvoorde.

Attacks continued in varying strength over the next few days. At times it seemed there would be a breakthrough but none occurred, despite being very hard pressed. On 23rd October, while returning to his Platoon after delivering a message, Kenny came under fire from a sniper, but succeeded in reaching the safety of his lines. He then rescued five wounded men under heavy fire. Next he organised a stretcher for 10556 Private Alexander 'Tim' McBain and helped move him to the dressing station. Despite these efforts, McBain died next day (Ypres Town Cemetery – A2 10). In the days before this, Kenny twice saved machine-guns from capture and on numerous occasions took urgent messages over fire swept ground; quite an achievement for a man of only 5'3".

Late on the 26th a raid was launched on a house in front of 2nd Gordon Highlanders by the Cyclists to destroy a troublesome machine-gun; it failed, with severe casualties. 20th Brigade's strength was gradually sapped with 150-200 casualties even on relatively quiet days. Eventually the pressure was too much and a withdrawal took place on the 27th, following which the Brigade was relieved and went into billets in Gheluvelt.

The final action which contributed to Kenny's VC award took place on the morning of 29th October. The Germans launched a furious attack (see the account of Lieutenant James Brooke's VC action) and 2nd Gordon Highlanders was driven back. Kenny spotted a machine-gun had been left behind, so sprinted across open ground, retrieved the weapon and then continued delivering urgent messages.

29th October 1914

28 Lt James Brooke, 2nd Gordon Highlanders (20th Brigade, 7th Division), near Gheluvelt, Belgium

After its baptism of fire in Flanders, 20th Brigade was withdrawn from the line on 27th October. However, an intelligence report indicated that the German XXVII Reserve Corps had been ordered to take the crossroads southeast of Gheluvelt, where the Kruiseke – Becelaere road crosses the Menin Road. This point was the junction between 1st and 7th Divisions. By 4.30 p.m. on the 28th, the weary troops

The Menin Road can be very busy, so it is best to get off it onto one of the roads to the south to view the battlefield of 29th October 1914. There is a café near the church in Gheluvelt and extensive facilities for the battlefield visitor in Ypres.

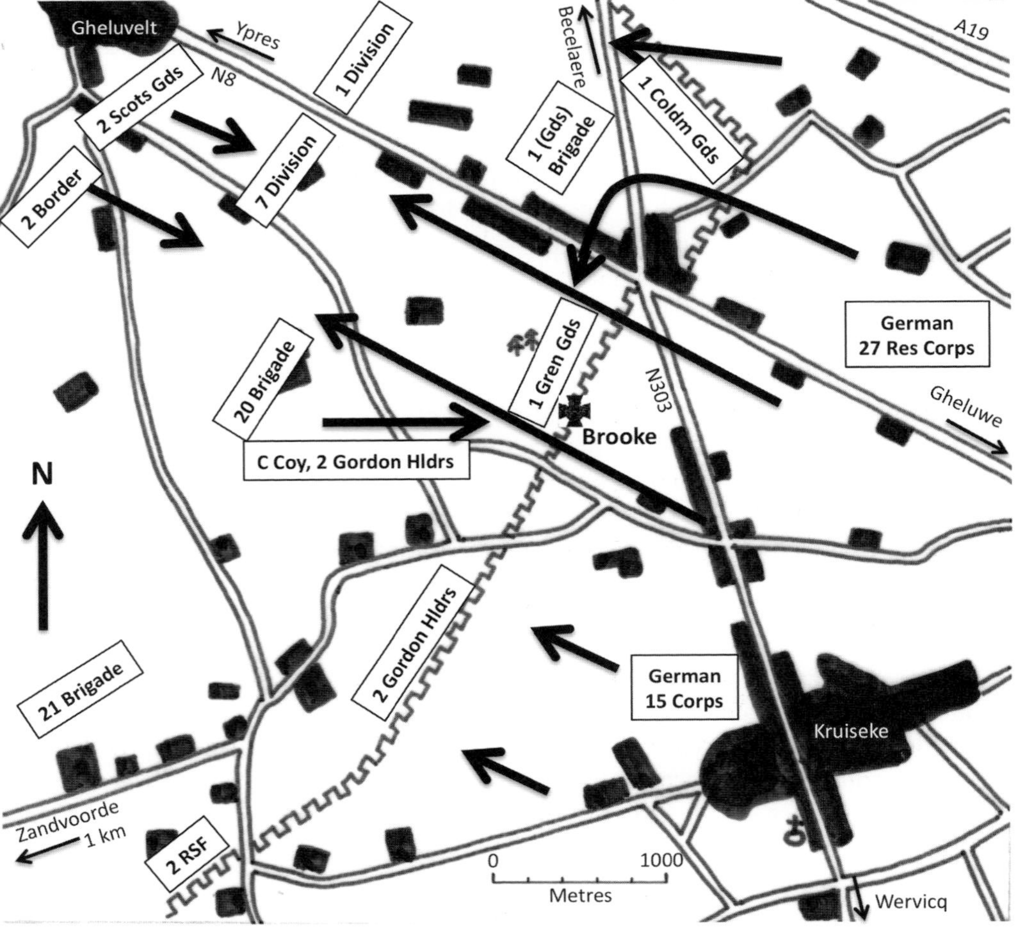

of 20th Brigade were marching back to the front, where they took up positions running southwest from the crossroads. On the left was 1st Grenadier Guards with 2nd Gordon Highlanders on the right and 2nd Scots Guards and 2nd Border in support. To the left of 1st Grenadier Guards, in 1st Division's area, was 1st Coldstream Guards reinforced by 1st Black Watch. To the right of 2nd Gordon Highlanders was 2nd Royal Scots Fusiliers in 21st Brigade.

There was no attack on the 28th and it was calm on the foggy morning of the 29th. Accordingly at 6.45 a.m., 2nd Scots Guards and 2nd Border pulled back to Veldhoek, to the rear of Gheluvelt to avoid being easy artillery targets as it grew light. At 7.30 a.m. the Germans opened a terrific bombardment, followed by an attack on the right flank of 1st Division north of the Menin Road. Most of 1st Coldstream Guards' position was wiped out, but there was no immediate attack on 7th Division. Because of the fog and the shape of the ground, 1st Grenadier Guards was initially unaware of what had befallen the Coldstream and Black Watch to the north. When the situation became known, two counter-attacks were launched into the German flank, but they were too strong and the attacks failed.

1st Grenadier Guards then came under heavy fire and was attacked all along its front. The Battalion was outflanked from the north and cut to pieces after a gallant fight to front and rear. 2nd Gordon Highlanders was also attacked from the front, but was not in danger of being overwhelmed. C Company in reserve went to assist 1st Grenadier Guards, which was pushed back to the high ground east of Gheluvelt. The German advance was checked there with assistance from 2nd Border. The Germans continued to attack, but suffered heavy casualties and gained no more ground. The situation was gradually brought under control. Reinforcements were gathered and pushed into the north of Gheluvelt.

C Company became isolated when 1st Grenadier Guards fell back. Led by Captain BGR Gordon, it hung on all day until relieved in a counter-attack about 4.00 p.m. by 2nd Scots Guards and 2nd Queens (1st Division). Two hundred and forty dead Germans were counted in front of one platoon alone.

Early in the fighting **Lieutenant James Brooke**, Assistant Adjutant, 2nd Gordon Highlanders, was sent by his CO to deliver a message, but on the way he became involved in C Company's attack and noticed the Germans breaking into part of the line. A Grenadier sergeant leapt to attention and saluted when Brooke appeared and they had one of those bizarre conversations that only take place in wartime. With bullets whizzing around them, Brooke remarked casually, *"Things not too good here Sergeant?"* The Sergeant replied indignantly, *"Them Jerries are in our trench"*. *"They won't be for long"*, Brooke replied. Moving along the trench he cracked jokes, raised morale and then addressed a group of Guardsmen, *"Are you gentlemen of the 1st Guards averse to going into action with humble Highlanders?"* One Guardsman replied, *"Not bloody likely Sir!"* *"Good man"*, responded Brooke, *"now then who's going to win the VC? Fix bayonets and give 'em hell!"* He led his force of about 100 Gordons and Grenadiers in two determined counter-attacks against heavy opposition and succeeded in regaining one of the lost Grenadier trenches.

Looking northwest with the Kruiseke (behind camera) - Becelaere road on the right leading to the junction with the Menin Road just after the slight corner. The 1st Grenadier Guards line ran from the junction across the middle ground to the left in front of the prominent copse. The counter-attack led by James Brooke came from the left towards, but not as far as, the camera position.

In order to hold the position he had just taken Brooke knew he must have support. On two occasions he left the cover of the trench and dashed to a nearby house from where he could send back messages detailing his requirements to hold the front line. He had 25m of open ground to cover to reach the house, with the Germans only 200m away, sniping at anything that moved. A Grenadier officer noted dozens of bullets ricocheting off the walls every time Brooke passed the house. Inevitably one eventually hit him and he was killed instantly. However, his bold action had restored the front and saved the situation.

By evening, 20th Brigade was more or less back in the same positions it held in the morning, but not all the lost ground was regained. The Brigade suffered about 900 casualties, over half in 1st Grenadier Guards. 2nd Gordon Highlanders had about 100. When the Brigade withdrew into reserve that night it was about the strength of a battalion.

29th October – 8th November 1914

29 Lt Arthur Martin-Leake 5th Field Ambulance RAMC (2nd Division), near Zonnebeke, Belgium

During the First Battle of Ypres, 2nd Division was frequently committed to the fighting piecemeal. Its brigades and battalions fought many individual actions, plugging gaps and strengthening weak spots in the line. Accounts of the fighting are therefore disjointed and confused.

5th Field Ambulance arrived in Ypres on 21st October 1914 and set up facilities in St Martin's cloisters for up to 250 lying casualties. There were no latrines of any kind. Within hours wounded men were streaming in for treatment. In the first

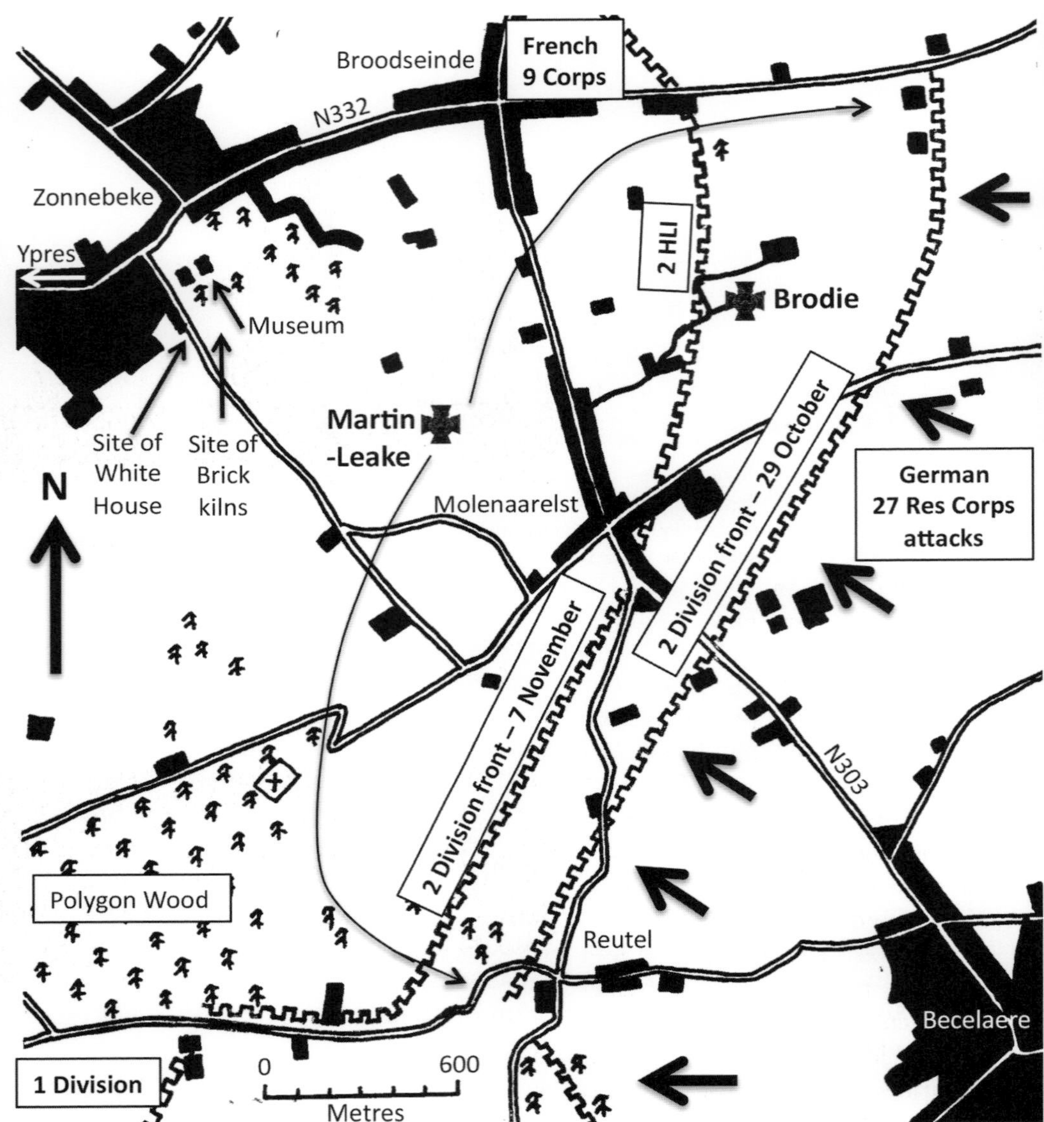

Arthur Martin-Leake performed the deeds for which he was awarded a Bar to his VC throughout the 2nd Division area; there is no particular site mentioned in the citation or accounts of his actions. The 'White House' was a prominent building in Zonnebeke at the time. Head towards the centre of Zonnebeke from Ypres along the N332. Turn right into Berten Pilstraat signed for "Memorial Museum Passchendaele", which is 150m on the left and worth a visit for the trench experience. Continue south on Berten Pilstraat for another 200m; the 'White House' was on the right.

Drive north along the N303 from Molenaarelst crossroads for 400m and turn right onto a minor road. Continue for 400m to the site of Walter Brodie's VC action.

two days alone, 188 casualties or sick were taken in of whom five died and most of the rest were evacuated in ambulance trains or motor ambulances, mostly at night.

A wartime photograph of the 'White House' taken in late 1915. In the background is one of the brick kilns in this area at the time. Today there is no trace of either.

On the 23rd the unit moved to the communal school at the junction of St Jean and St Nicholas streets, where there were latrines and water taps in the courtyard. On 26th October, the CO of 5th Field Ambulance recorded in the unit war diary that cases of self-inflicted wounds were being seen due to the appalling conditions being endured by the front line troops.

From 2nd Division's front line looking back over the British area, with Polygon Wood in the right background.

On 4th November, 5th Field Ambulance moved to a farm owned by M Jean Verbrugge about one mile northeast of Dickebusch and southwest of Ypres. Just after it left, a heavy shell hit the schools. Throughout this period there were also enormous logistical problems to overcome, including insufficient blankets and medical supplies. Often they had to resort to purchasing equipment locally, as the supply chain could not react quickly enough at that stage of the war.

During most of this period **Lieutenant Arthur Martin-Leake** was detached with the Bearer Division at an Advanced Dressing Station, which from 1st November was in the 'White House' near Zonnebeke, at one time only 450m behind the trenches. One bearer section was at Zonnebeke and two others at Wulvestraate, near St Jean. The casualty evacuation system was for lightly wounded men to make their way to the 'White House'. Badly wounded men were generally retained by their units in the trenches until nightfall, then stretchered back to the 'White House' and taken by horse ambulance to hospital in chateau on

The view north along 2nd Division's front line south of Broodseinde.

the Ypres – Vlamertinghe road. Heavy shelling of Ypres railway station had forced ambulance trains to stop at Vlamertinghe.

During the period 29th October–8th November, Martin-Leake distinguished himself on a number of occasions near Zonnebeke. He rescued a large number of men lying in no man's land close to the enemy trenches while under constant fire. It has proved impossible to pinpoint precisely any of the locations where his gallant deeds were performed. All that is known is that they took place in the 2nd Division area, which stretched from south of Polygon Wood northwards to the east of Broodseinde. He was continuously exposed while searching for the wounded under fire, which was so intense that on occasions he had to search crawling on his hands and knees. He managed to save many lives by getting wounded men away, even though it often took many hours of effort to achieve this. The ADS was bombarded on the 5th (and on the 9th and 12th, although outside the dates for the award), throughout which he was an inspiration to both the staff and the wounded.

31st October 1914

30 Sepoy Khudadad Khan, 129th (DCO) Baluchis, 7th (Ferozepore) Brigade, 3rd (Lahore) Division), Hollebeke, Belgium

On 19th October 1914, the Germans commenced their attacks on Ypres, marking the beginning of some of the most desperate fighting of the entire war during which the Regular Army suffered enormous losses. The Territorial Force had not yet begun to deploy en masse and the New Armies were still under training. The only viable reinforcements in the short term were from India.

The Lahore Division began arriving at Arques on 19th October and reached Bailleul on the 22nd. The Ferozepore Brigade joined 2nd Cavalry Division, while the rest of the Lahore Division and the Meerut Division reinforced II Corps. 1st Connaught Rangers was the first unit of the Indian Corps to enter the line on 23rd October. The honour of being the first Indian unit at the front fell to 57th Wilde's Rifles.

The Cavalry Corps was holding the line in front of Wytschaete as far south as Messines, where it joined III Corps. 2nd Cavalry Division held 3,000m of this front from the canal east of Hollebeke southeast towards Messines, with 3rd Cavalry Brigade (Brigadier General Vaughan) on the left and 5th Cavalry Brigade on the right. 129th Baluchis moved by bus to join 3rd Cavalry Brigade late on 22nd October. At 5.30 a.m. on 23rd October, Vaughan accompanied the Baluchis into the line to take over 2,000m of front from 16th and 5th Lancers and 4th Hussars.

The line was not continuous, more a series of posts without shelters under fire from artillery, machine-guns and snipers. The first officer to die was Jemadar Jafar Ali on 23rd October and the first soldiers were Signaller Naik Mazar Khan and Lance Naik Khan Bahadur on 25th October. Unless stated otherwise, all fatalities mentioned in this account are commemorated on the Ypres (Menin Gate) Memorial.

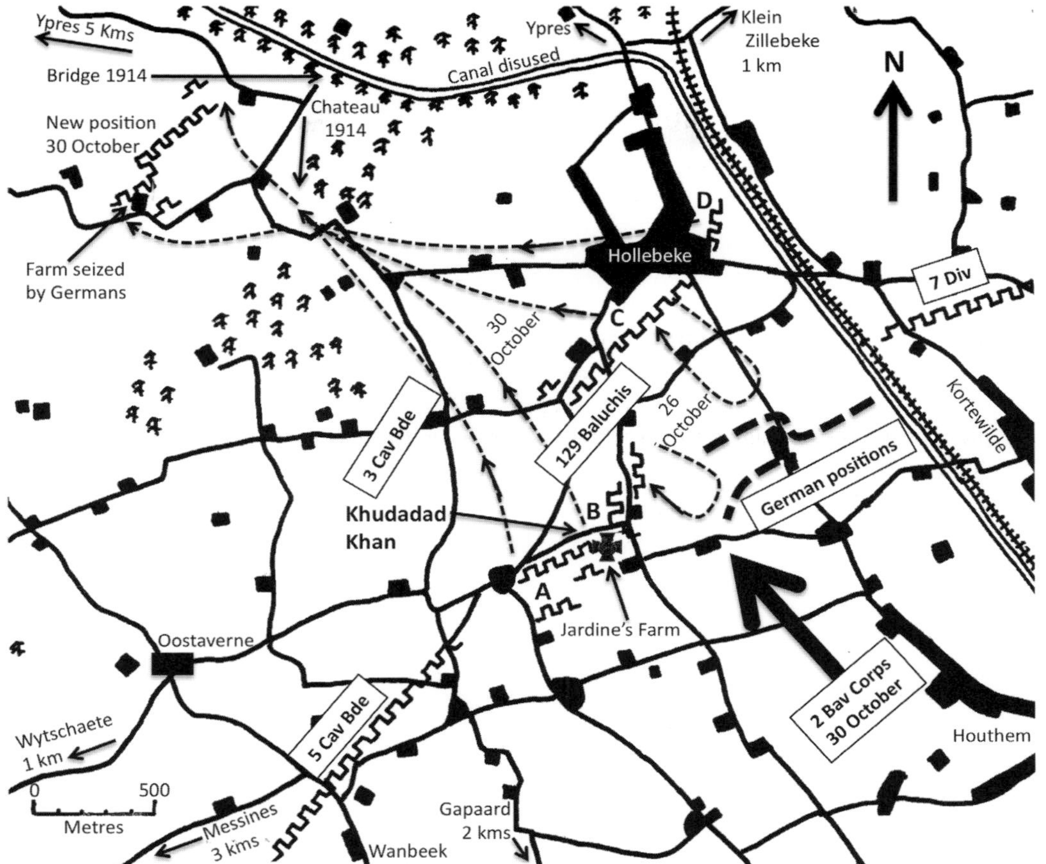

There are places to park along most of the roads in this area, which are rarely busy, but at some times of year the movement of large farm vehicles makes it imperative not to block passages. Having completed the tour of the battlefield, there is a café at Hill 60 at Zwarteleen, a few kilometres to the north. Alternatively, just north of the disused canal, is a large restaurant in a nature reserve. It is just above the Chateau on the map, but can only be reached by vehicle from the north, off the Hollebeke - Ypres road.

On the night of 25/26th October, the cavalry supports were withdrawn except for their machine-gun detachments. The weather turned wet and the Indians had gone into the line without blankets; 5th and 16th Lancers lent them some. Early on the afternoon of 26th October, 129th Baluchis was ordered to take part in an attack by the Cavalry Corps at 3.00 p.m. in conjunction with 7th Division on the left. 1st Cavalry Division was to hold Messines, while 1st Connaughts and 57th Wilde's Rifles (both attached from the Ferozepore Brigade) pivoted on it to attack the line Gapaard to west of Wanbeek. 2nd Cavalry Division was to continue the line of attack to Houthem.

Lieutenant Colonel WM Southey, commanding 129th Baluchis, was unable to assemble his company commanders until 2.00 p.m. By the time orders had been issued it was 2.30 p.m., leaving no time for preparations. The plan was for No 2 Company, occupying trenches in C Section about Hollebeke, to advance on a frontage of 550m with its left on the canal. When No 2 Company came up in line,

No 1 Company was to advance alongside on the right. Two platoons of No 3 Company and the Machine-Gun Section's two Maxims were to provide flanking fire from trenches near Jardine's Farm. The rest of No 3 Company and No 4 Company were in reserve.

At 3.00 p.m., a 10 minutes bombardment by four horse artillery guns commenced, but when the advance began it was supported by only one gun. The attack was halted 200-250m from the enemy line, despite support from No 3 Company and the Machine-Gun Section. No 1 Company lost direction and came in on the right of No 2 Company. Two platoons of No 4 Company were sent forward as reinforcements, but by that time it was getting dark and heavy fire was being received from numerous German machine-guns. Captain Hampe-Vincent was shot in the head; the first British officer serving with an Indian unit to be killed in Flanders. At 5.15 p.m. orders went out to fall back on the original trenches.

On the morning of 27th October the Battalion was relieved and went into billets at Hollebeke, but the men were soon digging a new position north of the Chateau. That evening, Nos 1 & 2 Companies under Major Hannyngton were back in the line in A and B Sections.

On 29th October, Nos 3 & 4 Companies were still digging when ordered at 11.15 a.m. to march to the bridge over the canal northwest of Hollebeke to support the cavalry in Hollebeke Chateau. At 1.10 p.m. they were ordered to Klein Zillebeke in reserve to I Corps, but marched back to billets about 7.00 p.m. This movement entitled the Battalion to the battle honour 'Ypres 1914'; the only Indian unit to gain it.

At 6.30 a.m. on 30th October, II Bavarian Corps attacked 3rd Cavalry Brigade's sector on the left of 2nd Cavalry Division. 129th Baluchis had two companies in the line, which were due to be relieved by 5th and 16th Lancers at 7.00 p.m. No 1 Company (Captain Adair) had just taken over No 3 Company's (Major Hannyngton) sector with No 2 Company (Major Humphreys) in reserve. No 4 Company (Major Potter) was withdrawn under heavy artillery fire and No 3 Company was forced to seek cover behind a farm in a wood. Both companies were ordered to concentrate at Brigade HQ at the Chateau, but only No 4 Company and a platoon of No 3 Company arrived.

Nos.1 and 2 Companies were subjected to heavy close range bombardment and bore the brunt of the enemy attack as their frontage formed a salient. Major Humphreys (attached from 127th Baluchis) was mortally wounded (Kemmel Churchyard Grave 2). Lieutenant Lewis took over No 2 Company and with Subadar Adam Khan's support hung on. Lewis brought up two support platoons, but the only positions they could occupy were in the open near Jardine's Farm, which the Machine-Gun Section was using to refill belts. The Farm was cut in half by a shell, set alight and the men inside burned to death. Lewis had numerous casualties and ran back to organise stretcher-bearers. On the way forward he encountered British, Indian and German troops falling back from the salient, fighting in small groups, to a position 550m behind.

Jardine's Farm from the west. In 1914 the farm buildings were in the foreground. Beyond the modern farm buildings, in the left distance, is Zandvoorde church. The German attack on 30th October 1914 overran this position from the right.

Captain Dill's machine-gunners distinguished themselves in this withdrawal. One gun was worked by Naik Sar Mir, Lance Naik Hobab Gul and Sepoy Redi Gul until it was blown to pieces by artillery fire ahead of the final German assault.. Dill was wounded later, but refused to leave his men until utterly exhausted (DSO for this action). The remaining machine-gun was kept in action until the German assault swept over it and every man was shot or bayoneted. Only one man survived, **Sepoy Khudadad Khan**, who continued firing until severely wounded and he fell unconscious. He was left for dead, but managed to crawl back after dark. Of the others in the section, Colour Havildar Gulam Muhamad was awarded the IOM and Sepoys Lal Shah, Sayid Ahmad, Qasim and Afsar Khan the IDSM, but all were killed.

No 1 Company, occupying C Section trenches was badly battered and shortly after noon was ordered to fall back via the bridge north of Hollebeke to hold the canal crossing, but it was cut off and only a few men got through. Captain WF Adair was mortally wounded and refused to allow his men to carry him back as it would have put them in more danger. Five soldiers managed to cross the Canal, joined a British unit and fought with it for some weeks before rejoining.

German pressure increased and at 12.30 p.m. all available men at the Chateau were ordered to reinforce the line. Battalion HQ, No 4 Company and a platoon of No 3 Company went forward and ran into the whole line falling back. The troops were rallied by Lieutenant Colonel Southey and took up positions in hedges and

From the site of Jardine's Farm looking north-northeast with Hollebeke in the right distance. This is the route taken by the troops defending A and B sectors as they fell back on 30th October. It was also over this ground that Khudadad Khan crawled away having been left for dead at the Farm. The Battalion eventually took up a new line in the left distance beyond the trees.

The new line dug north of the Chateau ran through here to the canal bank in the far distance marked by the line of trees. The buildings on the left are on the site of the farm taken by the Germans and retaken by 129th Baluchis on 31st October/1st November 1914.

Another view of the farm retaken by 129th Baluchis.

farms around the Chateau, while No 4 Company and the platoon of No 3 Company occupied a wood to protect the right flank. The Germans were held until 4.00 p.m. when orders from 3rd Cavalry Brigade were received to pull back to the new line dug over the previous two days north of the Chateau. No 4 Company occupied trenches for the night while the rest of the Battalion went into billets 800m to the rear close to the canal bank, where they came under fire from a French battery. Fortunately there were no casualties.

On the 31st, three French battalions and twelve guns moved forward towards Oosttaverne and Hollebeke and much of 3rd Cavalry Brigade's front was cleared. No 4 Company remained where it was while No 2 Company relieved 18th Hussars in the line at dusk, with No 3 Company in support and No 1 Company in reserve. Around 9.00 p.m. a German attack on the right was repulsed, but during the night they occupied a farm held by part of No 4 Company. They appeared to be French, who were holding the line either side, so no action was taken until too late. Major Potter pulled back 50m and at 4.00 a.m. he attacked on the right and the CO led another party on the left. The enemy was overcome in room-to-room fighting, losing 10 killed, three wounded and 14 prisoners. One of the Indian soldiers remarked, *"It was a very good game"*.

At 5.00 a.m. orders came to hand over the sector to the French and move back. It wasn't until 4th November that the Battalion rejoined the Ferozepore Brigade at Estaires. According to the Regimental history, the 10 days in the line cost five officers killed (Humphreys, Hampe-Vincent, Adair, Azad Gul and Jafar Ali), five officers wounded, 26 soldiers killed, 138 wounded, 67 missing and 11 sick. Of the 67 missing, it was assessed that most were dead. However, CWGC records show only 30 soldiers were killed or died of wounds in the period 22nd October – 10th November, indicating all but four of the missing eventually rejoined. Interestingly, Jemadar Azad Gul and Naik Mir Muhammed are commemorated on the Neuve Chapelle Memorial, whereas the other missing from this period are on the Ypres (Menin Gate) Memorial.

7th November 1914

32 Capt John Vallentin, 1st South Staffordshire (22nd Brigade, 7th Division) Zillebeke, Belgium

By early November 1914, 7th Division had been in continuous action for three weeks and was utterly exhausted. Having withstood the full force of the German onslaught during the First Battle of Ypres it was a mere shadow of the formation it had been a few weeks earlier. On 5th November it was withdrawn for rest around Ypres, but shelling of the town was so heavy that 22nd Brigade moved 3.5 kms to the southwest, near Dickebusch, to avoid it.

The area around Zwarteleen is much as it was prior to the war, with the exception of a few more buildings and the loss of some woods. The front lines depicted were not yet mature trench systems. At this stage of the war there were few quality maps available and war diaries are often difficult to follow. The representation shown here is the result of consulting the war diary of every unit involved, their superior HQs and flanking units and formations. The VC sites shown for Vallentin and Dimmer are the best estimate given the incomplete and often conflicting information. There is a café at Hill 60 in Zwarteleen.

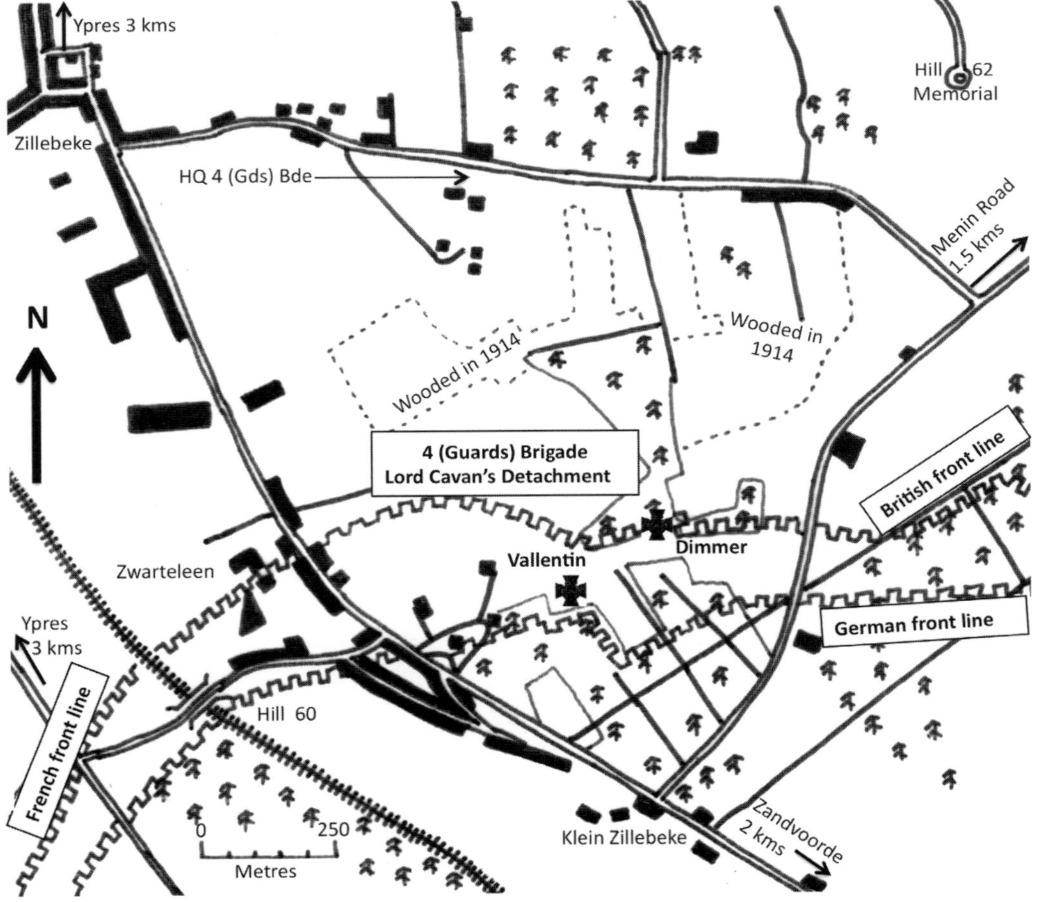

Next day the Germans launched a heavy attack on the front from the Menin Road south to the Comines Canal. The French line was breached at Zwarteleen, just south of the junction with the British, and the Germans were then only three kilometres from Ypres. Many British units also suffered heavily. 7th Cavalry Brigade was able to restore the situation somewhat, together with an ad hoc force of four battalions under Colonel Lovett, but after an abortive counter-attack further action was suspended until daylight.

At 4.00 p.m., 22nd Brigade was warned it may have to assist 4th (Guards) Brigade and at 5.30 p.m. the Brigade began moving forward. At about 10 p.m. it arrived at HQ 4th (Guards) Brigade, 1,500m east of Zillebeke. Some of its trenches had been lost in the attack and, following consultation between the two commanders, it was decided 22nd Brigade would attack to recover them.

The strength of 22nd Brigade at this time was 14 officers and 1,100 men; about the strength of a battalion. The Brigade was formed into two composite battalions;

Drive southeast from Zwarteleen into Klein Zillebeke and turn left to follow the road running northeast towards the Menin Road. After 200m park on the roadside and walk 250m northwest along the ride to reach the edge of the trees. This is where 2nd Queens broke into the captured German trenches. John Vallentin's VC action was to the left of this clearing.

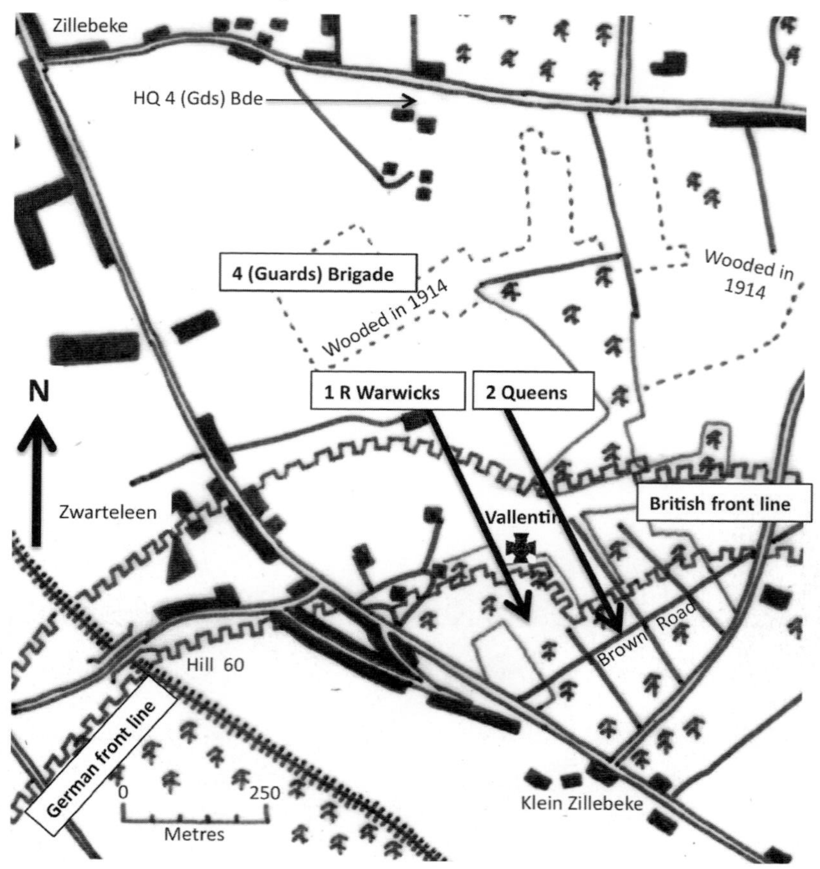

one consisting of 2nd Queen's (Royal West Surrey) and 1st RWF and the second of 1st South Staffordshire (about 20% strength) and 2nd Royal Warwickshire.

1st South Staffordshire was commanded by **Captain John Vallentin**, who was in hospital in Ypres having been wounded on 30th October at Zandvoorde. He was also suffering from dysentery and had a high fever, but knowing there was a desperate shortage of officers, rejoined his unit immediately.

7th November dawned cold, misty and damp. While it was still dark, 22nd Brigade moved forward 3.5 kms east of Zillebeke and assembled behind a slight rise in a narrow wooded clearing 300-400m from the German trenches. At 6.15 a.m. the order to attack was given, the objective being the 4th (Guards) Brigade trench lost the previous day. 2nd Queen's led the assault through Armagh Wood, supported by 1st South Staffordshire on the right with 2nd Royal Warwickshire in reserve.

In spite of the mist the troops were hit by heavy small arms fire as soon as they topped the rise. 2nd Queen's pressed on and in the initial charge took the enemy front line trench, which had been dug during the night. The impetus of the assault carried them forward to capture the lost 4th (Guards) Brigade trench about 100m further on.

During the attack, Captain Vallentin led an assault on an enemy trench. He was wounded, but managed to get up and continued the advance only to be shot down by a burst of machine-gun fire. He had inspired his men with such confidence that, despite his death, the attack was a complete success.

The main enemy line lay 125m beyond through the wood and over a road (Brown Road). Part of the wood was very thick and presented great difficulties to further advance, which was halted by enfilade fire. Once the Germans recovered they brought forward reserves and quickly retook the second trench. They then forced the British back to the edge of the wood and the trench dug by the Germans the previous night.

Elements of 3rd Brigade came up on the left and right of 22nd Brigade, but could make no impression. A company of 2nd Royal Warwickshire went forward

From the British front line looking in the direction of attack on 7th November 1914. John Vallentin led his combined battalion into the woods on the right.

The German view on 7th November 1914. The British attack started near the farm buildings. 2nd Queens attacked towards the camera with 2nd South Staffordshire on the left.

From Brown Road looking along one of the rides through the woods towards the front lines. This is the furthest point reached by 2nd Queens. The trees do not appear to be as thick as described in 1914. The woods are now a nature reserve and even the rides can be extremely boggy in wet weather.

to support 2nd Queens and this portion of the line was held all day. French troops were expected to come up on the right flank, but did not appear. With the flanks exposed, the position gained in the attack formed an exposed salient.

The Germans kept up relentless pressure on the British gains, working around 22nd Brigade's flanks. By nightfall there was no option other than to withdraw. Although no ground was gained permanently, the attack had relieved pressure on the front. 22nd Brigade pulled back into reserve at Zillebeke. Casualties were 44 killed, 166 wounded and 100 missing. It is sobering to note that of the 1,100 other ranks in 1st South Staffordshire at the outset of the fighting around Ypres, only 78 came out of the line on 11th November.

7th November 1914

33 Capt Walter Brodie 2nd Highland Light Infantry (5th Brigade, 2nd Division), near Becelaere, Belgium

On 6th November 1914, the Germans resumed their offensive against the Ypres Salient. 2nd Division was in poorly constructed trenches northeast of Polygon Wood and conditions became appalling as the weather turned increasingly cold and wet. Most of the action on 6th and 7th November took place to the south, but a number of isolated heavy attacks were made against 2nd Division. It was during one of these attacks on 7th November that **Captain Walter Brodie** won the VC and not 11th November as stated in the London Gazette. 5th Brigade's war diary makes no mention of 2nd HLI's action on 7th November, although it records the Battalion suffering 46 casualties. On 11th November the Brigade war diary records 2nd HLI having only a supporting role with no casualties.

2nd HLI was in trenches east of the Becelaere – Passchendaele road on the extreme left of 2nd Division's line. Both sides had become wary of making long assaults over open ground and to overcome this the Germans sapped forward to within 50m of the British positions. 2nd HLI devised a plan to counter this in the event of an attack; troops in the front line were to clamber out, take cover behind the parados and when the enemy entered the trench fall upon them.

Apart from continuous sniping and shelling, 6th November was a comparatively quiet day for 2nd HLI. However, at 4.40 a.m. on the 7th a party of 300 Germans launched a very determined attack against the centre of the Battalion's front, held by B Company. In a few locations the Germans sapped to within 15m of the British trenches and because of this and the early morning mist 2nd HLI was unable to resist the initial rush, but was quick to recover.

East of the main Becelaere–Broodseinde road, looking northeast. Moorslede church tower is faintly visible on the skyline above the road. Captain Brodie's VC action was in the field right of the road.

The front line was only lightly held and the men took up positions behind the parados as planned. When the Germans entered the trench the Highlanders jumped down onto them and fierce hand-to-hand fighting followed. Captain Brodie's machine-guns were overrun in the first rush but undaunted he grabbed a rifle and personally bayoneted four of the enemy in the melee. He was then set upon by four Germans and forced to feign death, but when they moved on he managed to crawl back in the half-light to rejoin the fight. He shot five more Germans before helping his men bring a machine-gun back into action, clearing the Germans as far as the next traverse.

As the fighting died down a party of Germans was trapped. When a prisoner was sent to ask for their surrender the Germans shot him. A second prisoner was sent (his enthusiasm for the task is not recorded), but this time the Germans gave up after one of the officers committed suicide. 2nd HLI suffered 46 casualties in this action, including 20 killed. The Germans lost 80 dead and a further 54 were taken prisoner, but the result was not a total failure for them. They held a section of the HLI line and the two sides were only separated by a barricade across the trench.

12th November 1914

34 Lt John Dimmer 2nd King's Royal Rifle Corps (2nd Brigade, 1st Division), Klein Zillebeke, Belgium

Although fighting in the First Battle of Ypres continued, the Germans realised by the end of 11th November that they had failed to break through and began to transfer troops to the Russian front. This was fortunate for the BEF, which had almost ceased to exist. 1st Division, for example, mustered only 2,844 all ranks, about one seventh of its establishment, and this grave situation was reflected throughout the BEF.

The British were not assaulted directly on 12th November. However, to the north the French were heavily attacked and to the south they were shelled out of Zwarteleen. This left Lord Cavan's ad hoc detachment, based upon 4th (Guards) Brigade, with a dangerously exposed flank. 2nd KRRC (less two platoons) was

John Dimmer won his VC close to John Vallentin a few days previously. Park in the same place on the road running northeast from Klein Zillebeke and walk through the woods to overlook the gap in the trees where the action was fought. Please respect private land.

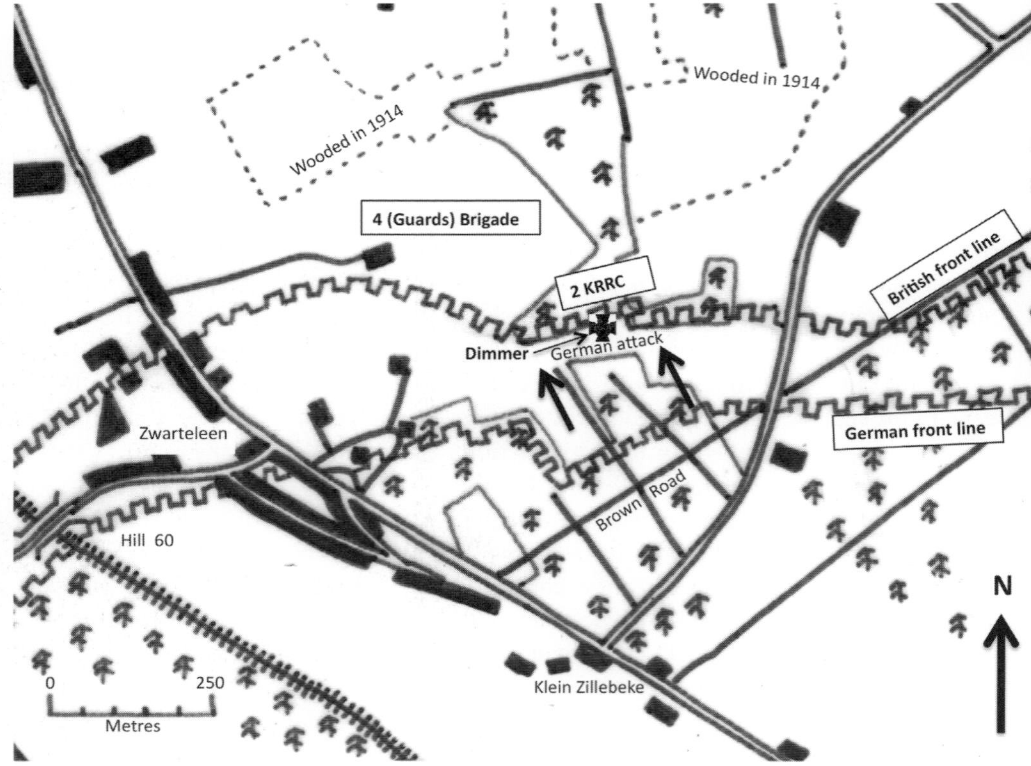

attached to 4th (Guards) Brigade and sent to fill the gap that opened at Brown Road Wood, east of Zwarteleen. Two companies were posted in the firing line along with the battalion machine-guns, commanded by **Lieutenant John Dimmer**.

The Prussian Guards advanced out of this wood and attacked across the open towards 2nd KRRC's positions in the wood on the far side.

Around noon the Germans shelled the British positions for about half an hour and then poured machine-gun fire into gaps in the parapet caused by the shellfire. At 1.00 p.m. the massed ranks of the Prussian Guards advanced out of the wood only 100m in front of 2nd KRRC's position. The Battalion opened fire, cutting the enemy down in swathes.

Whatever the Germans lacked in finesse they made up for in courage. Despite horrific casualties they came on regardless. Dimmer's machine-guns were quickly into action, but one was destroyed by shellfire almost immediately; only Dimmer and three men remained. He was wounded in the face and almost fainted, but recovered when one of his men gave him some brandy. A shell then killed one man and wounded the other two, leaving Dimmer on his own. He manned the remaining gun and fired it continuously until a wet belt caused it to jam. Disregarding the enemy he climbed onto the emplacement to clear the stoppage and was hit by a bullet in the right jaw as he completed the repair.

A later German pillbox with John Dimmer's machine-gun position in the wood beyond.

Despite this wound, Dimmer got back behind the gun and opened fire, but it jammed again. He got up once more to effect repairs and as he did so was shot through the right shoulder. Having repaired the gun he opened fire again, but a shell burst above his emplacement and three shrapnel balls hit him in the right shoulder. Draining the rest of the brandy he went back to serve the gun, firing for all he was worth until, when the Germans were only 50m from his position, they broke and ran.

The enemy retreat was covered by accurate artillery fire and one shell hit

Dimmer's gun, spattering his face with tiny fragments. He described the incident in a letter to his mother, "*We were suddenly attacked by the Prussian Guard – they shelled us unmercifully and poured in a perfect hail of bullets at a range of about 100 yards. I got my guns going, but they smashed one up almost immediately and then turned their attention on the gun I was with, and succeeded in smashing that too, but before they completed the job I had been twice wounded, and was finally knocked out with the gun.*"

As the attack petered out the gun jammed and Dimmer lapsed into unconsciousness from loss of blood. When he came to, he insisted on reporting in person to Lord Cavan, commanding 4th (Guards) Brigade. Having done this he collapsed and was taken to a dressing station.

20th November 1914

35 Bdsmn Thomas Rendle 1st Duke of Cornwall's Light Infantry (14th Brigade, 5th Division), Wulverghem, Belgium

By 20th November the serious fighting in the First Battle of Ypres had all but petered out. The Germans had failed to break through and both sides resigned themselves to a winter of deadlock in the trenches. During the battle troops had plugged gaps in the line as and when they occurred. As a result the British and French were intermingled, making command and control confusing and difficult. It was decided to rationalise the situation and give the British a continuous front of 21 miles from Givenchy to Wytschaete.

14th Brigade began marching north from south of the Lys on 14th November. On the night of 16/17th November the Brigade took over the front line trenches from the French facing Messines Ridge between the Wulverghem – Messines road on the right and the Kemmel – Wytschaete road on the left. All four battalions were in the line; from left to right these were – 1st East Surrey, 1st DCLI, 1st Devonshire and 2nd Manchester. 1st DCLI had a frontage of only 225m. The move into the line was slow as the French allocated insufficient and inexperienced guides and it was not until 3.40 a.m. that 1st DCLI completed its takeover.

The French trenches were little more than isolated shallow ditches, each able to hold a section. There were few communication trenches or telephone lines between them. Movement in daylight was impossible, with the Germans only 40-50m away, but by the end of the first night considerable progress had been made with the shovel. This continued the following night, during which all Battalion HQs were connected with Brigade HQ by telephone.

The weather was very cold and snow covered the ground, but at least the hard frost froze the mud. At 9.00 a.m. on 20th November, the German artillery opened fire for most of the day. Observers were amused to see the first salvo land on the German front line trench, but the error was quickly corrected. Hits were scored on 1st DCLI's

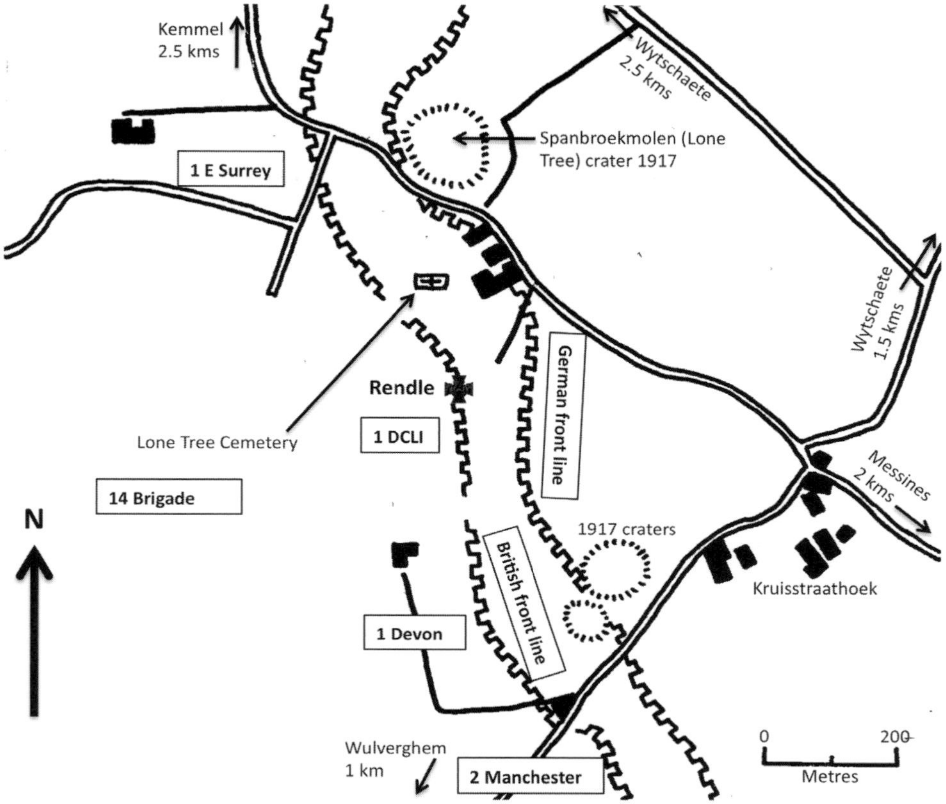

Kemmel 2.5 kms
Wytschaete 2.5 kms
Spanbroekmolen (Lone Tree) crater 1917
1 E Surrey
Wytschaete 1.5 kms
German front line
Rendle
Lone Tree Cemetery
1 DCLI
Messines 2 kms
14 Brigade
N
1917 craters
British front line
Kruisstraathoek
1 Devon
Wulverghem 1 km
2 Manchester
0 200 Metres

The site of Thomas Rendle's VC action is a few hundred metres south of Spanbroekmolen (Lone Tree) mine crater (Pool of Peace), created at the opening of the Battle of Messines in June 1917. The simultaneous explosion of this mine and 18 others was heard in London. There are a few places to park safely along the road around the rim of the crater, but as this is a favourite stop for battlefield tours it can get busy. Cross the road to Lone Tree Cemetery behind the farm, to look over the area held by 1st DCLI on 20th November 1914. Most of the burials here are from the 1917 battle.

From Lone Tree Cemetery looking south down the length of 1st DCLI's front line on 20th November 1914, with Wulverghem church on the right. Beyond it on the far horizon, Vimy Ridge can just be seen.

front line, the worst affected sector being that held by the left centre of A Company, where six heavy howitzer shells landed. One shell landed close to the parapet, burying 15 men alive and killing many others, according to some accounts. The CWGC record only two fatalities for this battalion on 20th November 1914. Another 10 died the next day, all but one of whom has no known grave and is commemorated on the Ypres (Menin Gate) Memorial.

Bandsman Thomas Rendle helped to dig out the survivors. Realising many would die unless they were evacuated quickly, he calmly took them to the rear one by one. This was a very hazardous undertaking under heavy artillery and small arms fire. With 40m of the front line trench blown-in, cover was limited or non-existent. In complete contrast, while this action was going on, the Prince of Wales was visiting Brigade HQ at Dranoutre, six kilometres to the rear.

At 4.30 p.m. the Germans resumed the bombardment with the assistance of a spotter plane. At about the same time, second Lieutenant RM Colebrook (attached from 3rd Royal Hampshire), was hit by a ricochet in the knee. Between where he lay and where the trench joined the communication trench to the rear was a blown-in section, five or six metres wide. The Germans could see into this gap and covered it with a machine-gun.

Lieutenant Wingate and Rendle crawled across the gap and Rendle bandaged the severed artery in Colebrook's leg. Having decided they could not get back until darkness fell, Wingate sat chatting with Colebrook until a fresh salvo of shells landed very close. Wingate decided they must accept the risk and get away as soon as possible, but was then called away to the other end of the trench. Rendle set about scraping a burrow across the gap. Every time he threw up a handful of earth he momentarily exposed himself and the Germans took pot shots at his head. Although there were a number of near misses, he was not hit.

The barrage continued unabated, with shells landing very close and Rendle decided they could wait no longer. He carried and dragged Colebrook on his back across the gap to the comparative shelter of the undamaged portion of the trench. Rendle later took Colebrook to the rear and, although not hit, was evacuated sick shortly afterwards.

Chapter Five

Winter Operations 1914-1915

Festubert, 23rd – 24th November 1914

36 Naik Darwan Sing Negi, 39th Garwhal Rifles (20th Garhwal Brigade, 7th Meerut Division)
37 Lt Frank de Pass, 34th Poona Horse (9th Secunderabad Cavalry Brigade, 1st Indian Cavalry Division)

At the end of October 1914, the Indian Corps relieved the battered British II Corps by taking over 13 kms of the line between Givenchy and Fromelles. On 21st and 22nd November the Germans bombarded the Corps front, causing many casualties and destroying some trenches. On the morning of the 23rd the Lahore Division began relieving the Meerut Division, resulting in a mixture of units from both formations holding the line. In the south were half of 2nd Black Watch and 58th Rifles of the Bareilly Brigade (Meerut Division). The other half of 2nd Black Watch and 41st Dogras were moving back to billets and 2/8th Gurkhas was at Gorre with 107th Pioneers. To the north was 9th Bhopal, 34th Sikh Pioneers, a company of 1st Connaught Rangers, 57th Rifles and 129th Baluchis, all of the Ferozepore Brigade (Lahore Division) except 34th Pioneers, a divisional unit. 6th Jats of the Dehra Dun Brigade (Meerut Division) was in reserve at Festubert.

During the night of 23rd/24th November the Germans dug saps to within five metres of 34th Pioneers' front line. As dawn broke, the line was showered with bombs, particularly at the junction with 1st Connaught Rangers on the left. An attack followed at 7.45 a.m., and the centre of the line was broken. By 9.00 a.m. the attack was slackening, but a large part of 34th Pioneers had been driven from its trenches and pushed into 1st Connaught Rangers' trench. A counter-attack came to nothing due to enfilade machine-gun fire. As a result the right of 1st Connaught Rangers was exposed and it had to move left into the section of line held by 57th Rifles and 129th Baluchis. A barricade was built at Point N (refer to map) and the German advance was halted. By 9.30 a.m. it was known that part of 58th Rifles on the left of the right section had also been driven back.

At 10.00 a.m. the division commanders agreed that the Lahore troops taking over should move up in support at once. A counter-attack by the Ferozepore Brigade was arranged with 2/8th Gurkhas and 107th Pioneers attached. By noon the situation was more serious with 34th Pioneers and 9th Bhopal being driven out of their

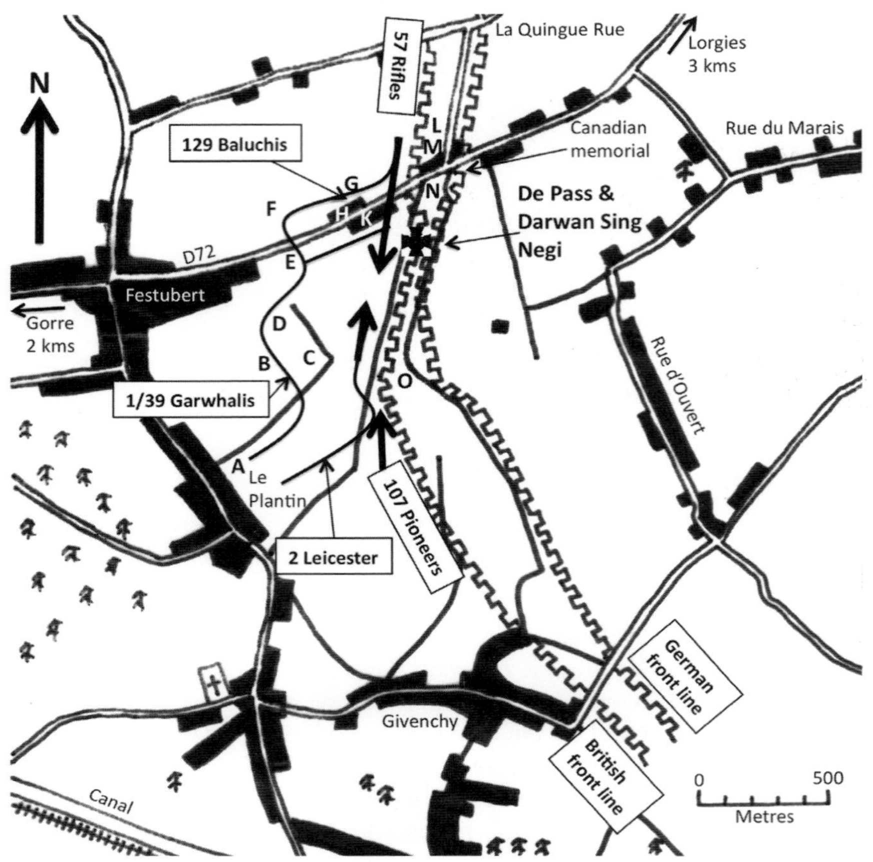

Leave Festubert church eastwards on the D72 towards Lorgies. After 1,300m, in la Quingue Rue, stop on the right at the Canadian memorial to the 1915 Battle of Festubert. Walk back 125m. This is where the lost British trench crossed the road. Turn left along the track heading south. The ditch on the left is the one used by Captain Lane's company. The trench retaken by 1/39th Garwhalis ran parallel with the ditch through the field on the left. This is where Darwan Sing Negi led the advance and where Frank de Pass was in action later.

trenches. 6th Jats attempted to get back, but was checked by machine-guns. The British artillery ensured the Germans were held, but a long section of front line trench had been lost.

1/39th Garwhalis (Garwhal Brigade) under Lieutenant Colonel ERR Swiney arrived at La Couture from Le Touret at 3.40 p.m. It was ordered to Gorre immediately and an officer was sent ahead for orders. 2nd Leicestershire and 2/3rd Gurkhas prepared to move from La Couture.

Brigadier-General RG Egerton (Ferozepore Brigade) arrived to direct the counter-attack. He found the left section of the front held by 57th Rifles and 129th Baluchis was standing fast and the 1st Connaught Rangers company was also able to hold its own. By occupying some houses to the rear of the exposed flank, 129th Baluchis stopped the enemy advancing further, but the whole of the centre sector, formerly held by 34th Pioneers, 9th Bhopal and most of 58th Rifles, was in

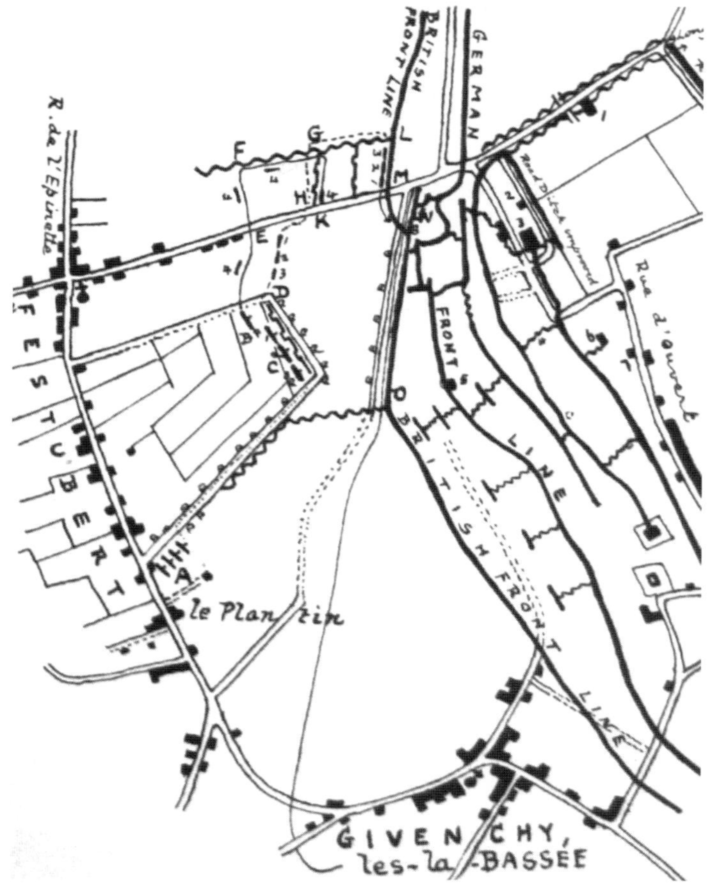

A contemporary map showing more details of the trenches. The main features are readily identifiable today (With the Royal Garhwal Rifles in the Great War).

Most of the 1/39th Garwhalis officers mentioned are pictured at Marseilles shortly after they landed in France. Back row, 4th from left is Captain JTH Lane. Front row from the left - Capt FGE Lumb, Major K Henderson, Major WH Wardell and Lieutenant Colonel ERR Swiney (Historical Record of the 39th Garhwal Rifles).

German hands (Points N to O). The remainder of 58th Rifles and 2nd Black Watch held on to the right. Orders from Corps HQ were to restore the line before dawn. The Secunderabad Cavalry Brigade (1st Indian Cavalry Division) was ordered to Wessars from where it could reinforce the line as necessary.

The plan was for 2/8th Gurkhas to take the trenches lost by 9th Bhopal, while 6th Jats with a detachment of 34th Pioneers was to reoccupy the latter's trenches, supported by 1st Connaught Rangers. 107th Pioneers was to occupy the trenches vacated while 58th Rifles reoccupied its own lost trench.

At 4.30 p.m. the counter-attack was launched, supported by British and French artillery. The barrage damaged the enemy held trenches severely and caused many casualties. By 8.30 p.m., 2/8th Gurkhas had reoccupied the trenches on the right by attacking from both flanks inwards. 58th Rifles, supported by a party of 2nd Black Watch on the right, reoccupied part of its lost line. 107th Pioneers was held temporarily by furious bombing, but was directed to get on and gain touch with 58th Rifles. 9th Bhopal recovered another portion of trench, but the Germans still held a large section.

1/39th Garwhalis arrived at Gorre at 5.30 p.m. and was ordered to halt until 2nd Leicestershire closed up. The Battalion moved off again at 6.00 p.m. and reached Le Plantin at 7.30 p.m. Egerton directed 1/39th Garwhalis to move to the left of the centre section and clear the Germans occupying the trenches to the right. A simultaneous attack was to be made from the right by 2nd Leicestershire and 107th Pioneers, with the two forces meeting in the middle of the lost section.

Swiney went to Point A with Lieutenant Colonel Grant of 2/8th Gurkhas, who commanded the centre section. Grant told Swiney to replace 107th Pioneers in the support trench at Point C then, keeping his left on a road, advance 550m and attack frontally 300m of the lost trench, with 107th Pioneers prolonging the right. Swiney realised this meant attacking with a thin line and no depth.

While the Battalion moved up to Point A, Swiney made a reconnaissance. The ground was flat, open and covered in snow; men could be seen 300m away, even at night. Swiney met Lieutenant Orchard of 2/8th Gurkhas, who was holding a ditch halfway towards the lost trench. Egerton had told Swiney that the enemy had left the captured trench, but Orchard was adamant they were there in force with several machine-guns. A frontal attack was very risky and he recommended oblique attacks from left and right.

From the track near Point C, looking northeast towards the captured trench, which ran just inside the trees on the right beyond the pylon. 1/39th Garwhalis' attack was launched from the area of the white buildings on the left, alongside the D72 Festubert - Lorgies road at la Quingue Rue.

Grant went to consult with Egerton, but returned with the order to attack immediately. The Battalion moved up to the start line with three companies in Trench C and one in support in Ditch B. There was another delay while the support company went back to Festubert, where the Battalion's carts had just arrived, to draw two entrenching tools per man. On its return Swiney ordered the support company to the left of Point C to follow the attack on the right of the road on which the Battalion's left was to rest. However, reconnaissance found the road ended at Point D and did not reach the enemy held trench as expected. The Battalion was in the wrong place and clarification was sought from Egerton as there was a danger of attacking friendly troops instead of the lost trench.

Grant and Swiney set off to find the correct road, which they struck at Point E. The Battalion moved along a ditch on the right of this road, while the support company moved up a communications trench to Point M. The company, under Major Henderson, struck the communications trench at Point F and moved to Point G, where it found the reserve company and Battalion HQ of 129th Baluchis. Its CO, Lieutenant Colonel Southey, commanding the left section, believed a frontal attack was unlikely to succeed. At 1.30 a.m. Grant went to consult Brigade HQ about the Battalion attacking from Point M instead of frontally.

While Grant was away the Battalion was placed in the ditch to the right of the road with the head at Point K. Grant returned at 2.30 a.m. The order stood to attack immediately, but Swiney had discretion to decide how to carry it out. He decided to attack from Point M along the lost trench rather than frontally and the move into new positions took some time. The support company moved to Point H, ready to move up to the line of the road, which was being held by 57th Rifles and 129th Baluchis. The rest of the Battalion moved via Points H, G, L and M.

Major W H Wardells' company attacked along the captured trench from north to south, while Captain Lumb led one and a half sections of his company along a parallel shallow ditch about 20m behind it. Wardell's company was led by a bombing party consisting of Lieutenant RGG Robson RE (killed 23rd December – Estaires Communal Cemetery & Extension – I E 14), Captain DH Acworth and a small party of soldiers. **Naik Darwan Sing Negi**, supported by Lance Naik Sankaru Gusain and Rifleman Ghantu Rawat, was first in the rush round each traverse, although wounded in the arm and twice in the head. He refused to go back and continued to face the volleys of grenades.

They cleared 50m of the trench and took 30-40 prisoners before the supply of primitive bombs ran out and the attack had to be continued

Contemporary impression of Darwan Sing Negi's VC action (Historical Record of the 39th Garhwal Rifles).

by bayonet alone. At a barricade, Robson called on the Garwhalis to charge and the leading men jumped over it and continued down the trench "like tigers". They cleared another 30m, but the Germans had plenty of bombs. Wardell's attack ran out of steam due to casualties and the clogged trench, just as Lumb's shallow ditch was ending and the head of his column came under cross fire. Lumb's party wheeled left and rushed into the enemy held trench to support Wardell. They cleared a traverse with the bayonet and took more prisoners. Their impetus was unstoppable and traverse after traverse was retaken, but a gap opened behind Lumb as Wardell's party, weakened by having to escort prisoners was unable to keep up. Lieutenant J C St G Welchman arrived with the rest of Lumb's men, who had been blocked in the communications trench by Wardell's prisoners going to the rear, and the gap was soon filled. Lumb pressed on and at 6.00 a.m. joined hands with 107th Pioneers advancing from the right. By the end of the action Darwan Sing Negi was covered in blood from head to foot.

The captured trench ran across this field from left to right parallel with the ditch in the foreground, which was used by Captain Lumb's party.

Captain Lane brought up reinforcements to occupy the left of the recaptured trench and came under enfilade fire at Point O, where the left of the trench was still held by the Germans. A number of men were hit, but Lane built another barricade close to Point N with debris and held it until relieved.

The simultaneous attack from the right by 2nd Leicestershire (right) and 107th Pioneers (left) started in some confusion as the left crowded in on the right. 2nd Leicestershire advanced into heavy machine-gun fire and, although a hold was gained in the enemy held trench, the Battalion was hard pressed to hang on. 107th Pioneers was forced back, but their attack assisted 1/39th Garwhalis coming along the trench from the opposite direction.

1/39th Garwhalis captured a trench mortar, two machine-guns and 105 prisoners. Thirty-two enemy dead were found in the trench, with many more outside. The Battalion's own losses were 20 killed, 36 wounded and Major Wardell was missing, later confirmed killed (he and other named fatalities are commemorated on the Neuve Chapelle Memorial unless otherwise stated). The recaptured trench was held until the night of 25/26th November, when the Battalion was relieved by 2/39th Garwhalis. In addition to Darwan Singh Negi's VC, the Battalion received seven IOMs 2nd Class (including Sankaru Gusain and Ghantu Rawat), four MCs (Lumb, Acworth, Lane and Dhan Sing Negi), and an

OBI 2nd Class. Swiney was made Brevet Colonel; he was killed when SS *Persia* was torpedoed in the Mediterranean on the way to India on 30th December 1915 (Chatby Memorial, Alexandria, Egypt).

While the counter-attack was in progress, detachments of the Secunderabad Cavalry Brigade were sent to reinforce the Ferozepore Brigade. 7th Dragoon Guards, 34th Poona Horse and 20th Deccan Horse provided 150 men each and 50 more came from the Jodhpur Lancers. They moved to Gorre, where the Jodhpur Lancers remained as Brigade reserve, while the other 450 went forward to Festubert to hold the newly regained line; 300 went into the front and support trenches and 150 into local reserve, later joined by the 50 at Gorre.

Captain Grimshaw, commanding D Squadron, with Captain Alderson and **Lieutenant Frank De Pass**, led the 34th Poona Horse detachment into the trenches at 4.00 a.m. A German sap had been dug up to the British parapet and a breach of 2.5m had been blown, exposing it to fire. The junction was held by the troop under De Pass with orders to construct a traverse to provide some protection. At dawn Grimshaw inspected it and 3027 Sowar Abdullah Khan volunteered to conduct a reconnaissance. He reported the sap turned after 10m and beyond was a sandbagged loop-holed traverse. Khan was fired upon by the German sentry but returned unharmed.

At 8.00 a.m. the Germans began throwing grenades into the British trench from behind the traverse and carried on all day, causing several casualties. De Pass had nothing with which to reply, so he and his men had to sit it out. At dawn on 25th November, De Pass decided something had to be done. With 3154 Sowar Fateh Khan and 3250 Sowar Firman Shah he crawled along the sap and placed a gun cotton charge against the loophole. The explosion wrecked the traverse, rounded off the bend in the sap and exposed 30m of it to fire from the British line. The Germans threw a grenade at De Pass, but it exploded behind him and the three made their escape unscathed. Fateh Khan was killed shortly afterwards, trying to subdue enemy rifle fire from the end of the sap. For the next 24 hours the Germans were quiet while they replaced the traverse.

On 25th November, De Pass visited the neighbouring trenches occupied by 7th Dragoon Guards. He observed a wounded sepoy of 58th Rifles lying 180m away in the open and, accompanied by Private C Cook, went out in broad daylight to rescue the man under heavy fire. Later that day De Pass volunteered to enter the sap and blow up the traverse again, but permission was denied.

German bombing increased and at 3.00 p.m. on 26th November, De Pass went to the saphead to supervise the repair of the parapet. He saw a sniper behind the loophole and tried to shoot him, but the sniper shot him through the head and he died instantly. Shortly after the cavalry detachments were rotated in the line. In addition to De Pass's VC, Abdullah Khan, Firman Shah and Fateh Khan received the IDSM and Cook the DCM.

Attack on Wytschaete, 14th December 1914

38 Pte Henry Robson, 2nd Royal Scots (8th Brigade, 3rd Division) Near Wytschaete, Belgium

Following the end of the First Battle of Ypres, the Germans thinned out their troops in Flanders to send to the Eastern Front. The French saw an opportunity to regain some lost ground and the British agreed to cooperate in an offensive, which was to take place in three phases. In the first phase, 3rd Division was to attack alongside the French 32nd Division to capture Wytschaete and Petit Bois. Later phases to the south were to capture Spanbroekmolen, followed by Messines.

Some preparations were woefully inadequate; the artillery did not undertake any wire cutting and the assault troops were left to improvise methods of penetrating it

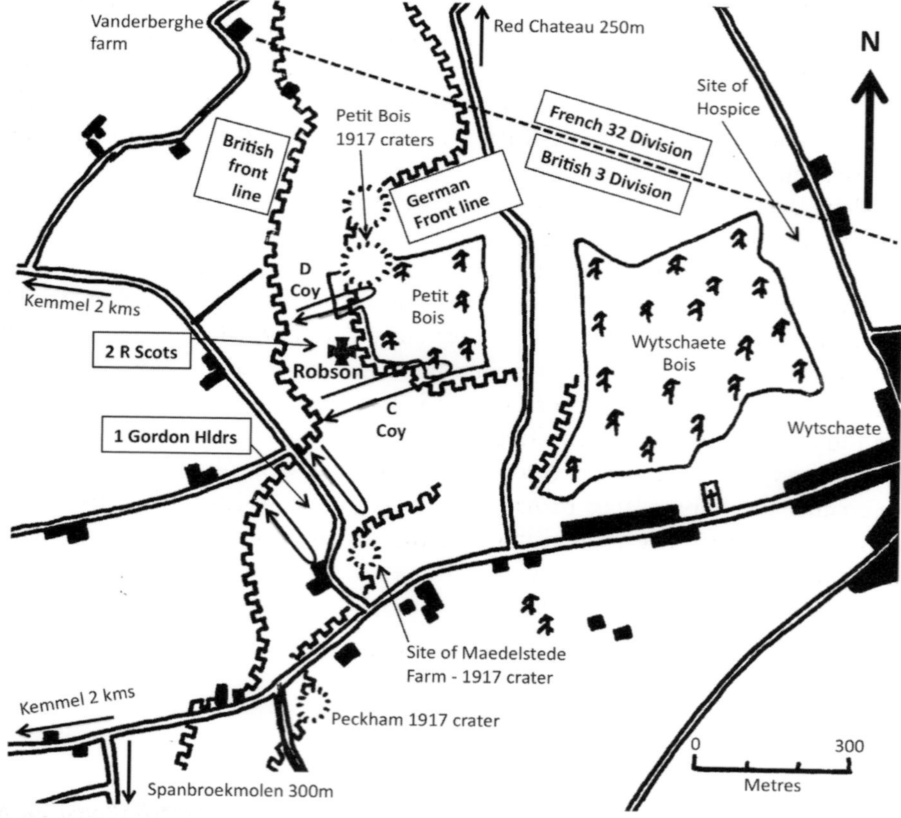

Leave Wytschaete westwards on the Kemmel road and after a kilometre turn right at Oosthoeve Farm (Maedelstede in 1914). The road doglegs right and left to pass around the Maedelstede Farm mine crater on the right, created in June 1917 in the Battle of Messines; it contained 94,000 lbs (42.6 metric tons) of explosives. The modern farm is on the left. A little further on, Petit Bois is on the right and there are plenty of places where a car can be parked temporarily. Just north of Petit Bois are two more 1917 mine craters, each formed by 30,000 lbs of explosives (13.6 metric tons).

with cutters and mattresses. However, efforts were made to ensure rapid exit from the front line trench and new support trenches were dug. Battalion and company commanders went into the trenches on 12th December to observe the ground over which they would attack.

In 8th Brigade, 1st Gordon Highlanders on the right was to attack Maedelstede Farm and on the left 2nd Royal Scots was to take Petit Bois. 2nd Suffolk and 4th Middlesex were in reserve. The French were to the left of 2nd Royal Scots, with the boundary running from Ferme Vandenberghe – Hospice – northwest of Wytschaete – Wambeek. On the evening of 13th December the assault battalions moved forward from Locre, initially to Kemmel Chateau's grounds. Around 5.30 a.m. they took up their assault positions in the trenches held by 9th Brigade.

On the right, 1st Gordon Highlanders was halted at the uncut wire 50m from the German front line. In the afternoon another bombardment was arranged, but the Battalion was still unable to get into the German trenches. The French on the left reached the Red Chateau in front of Croonaert Wood (Bois 40 to the French and Bayernwald to the Germans) and the Wytschaetebeek, but then faltered. HQ 8th Brigade's war diary states that the French reached Hollebeke Chateau, which is a further three kilometres to the east; an example of the understandable mistakes frequently encountered in war diaries written up by tired men working under pressure in the heat of battle.

At Petit Bois, C and D Companies, 2nd Royal Scots, right and left respectively, made the initial attack, with B Company in support and A Company in reserve. The first objective was the German trench in front of the wood. The preliminary bombardment at 7.00 a.m., although heavy, had little effect on the defenders. The attack commenced at 7.45 a.m. and the men struggled forward over muddy ground into a hail of bullets. 7th Brigade's machine-guns in support ceased firing at a critical time in the assault. It was only momentarily, but the Germans took advantage of the error and many casualties were suffered.

D Company was channelled through a gateway in a thick hedge just short of the German line. Some men managed to get through to make the final assault alongside C Company. A 200m section of the enemy trench was taken, together with 42 prisoners and two machine-guns, but 50 men had been lost, including one of the company commanders, Captain The Hon Henry Lyndhurst Bruce, killed in the act of capturing a machine-gun (Ypres (Menin Gate) Memorial). A patrol from D Company pressed on and occupied an unmanned trench deep in the wood but when C Company tried to make further progress, it was repulsed with heavy

From behind 2nd Royal Scots' right flank, with Petit Bois in the background. The German front line was just in front of the trees.

The section of Petit Bois penetrated by C Company, 2nd Royal Scots. The German front line ran along the forward edge of the trees.

Looking over no man's land from the German front line towards 2nd Royal Scots' start position. This field is where Henry Robson rescued the wounded and was eventually hit twice. The trees on the left are at Maedelstede Farm (now Oosthoeve), the objective of 1st Gordon Highlanders.

casualties. Throughout the day British shells fell amongst the forward troops despite messages being sent to lengthen the range.

Due to the failure of the attacks on either side, 2nd Royal Scots was stuck with both flanks in the air. The Germans were able to concentrate on this salient in their line and the small gains had to be given up. Efforts were made to recover the wounded at this time. **Private Henry Robson** of C Company succeeded in crawling over open ground to assist a wounded NCO and brought him back into the trench. When he went to recover another wounded man he was hit, but pressed on until he was hit again. This second wound brought his valiant rescue attempt to an end.

By nightfall the situation had not changed materially and the assault battalions were relieved. Even with the assistance of the support battalions, many wounded were still lying in the open. That night 2nd Royal Scots moved back behind the reserve trenches. Having been relieved there by 1/10th King's Liverpool, it marched back to its old billets. Immediately after the attack it was known that the cost to the Battalion was 26 killed, 52 wounded and 28 missing. However, the CWGC record 53 men of 2nd Royal Scots killed on 14th December 1914, meaning only one of the missing survived. They are commemorated on the Ypres (Menin Road) Memorial, except for two buried in Loker (formerly Locre) Churchyard. Fighting in the area continued for a few days, but no further progress was made.

Operations in Support of the French, 18th-21st December 1914

39 Lt Philip Neame, 15th Field Company RE (8th Division) Neuve Chapelle
40 Pte James Mackenzie, 2nd Scots Guards (20th Brigade, 7th Division) Rouges Bancs
41 Pte James Smith, 2nd Border (20th Brigade, 7th Division) Rouges Bancs
42 Pte Abraham Acton, 2nd Border (20th Brigade, 7th Division) Rouges Bancs
43 Lt William Macrae Bruce, 59th Scinde Rifles (Jullundur Brigade, Lahore Division) Givenchy

The Anglo-French offensive south of Ypres on 14th December failed and the French switched their attention to the Arras area, where the ground was less waterlogged. General Joffre requested British assistance and Sir John French ordered attacks to be made along the whole front on 18th December. However, British aspirations were limited because of the paltry artillery ammunition allocation of only 40 rounds per gun.

8th Division was ordered to make one attack near Neuve Chapelle. It was carried out at 4.30 p.m. from 'C' Lines by 2nd Devonshire (23rd Brigade) and a section of 15th Field Company RE. Fire support was provided by troops on the flanks. Two companies of 2nd West Yorkshire were in support as digging parties to help consolidate the gains. The attack was late starting. The right assault company never got out of its trenches and the left company was held up by thick wire entanglements. However, the centre company (Captain Lafone) appears to have surprised the defenders, passed over an advanced trench and through the Moated Grange (Ferme

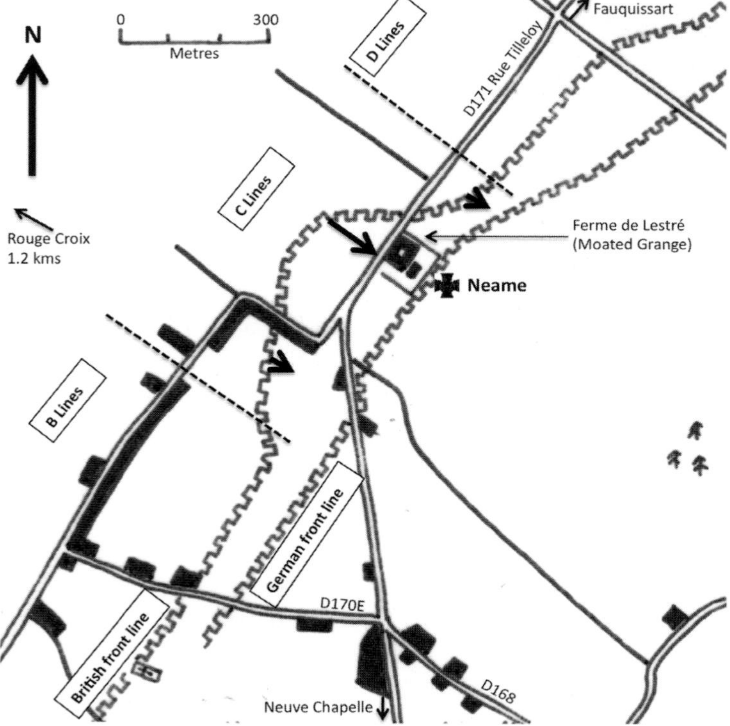

Leave Neuve Chapelle northwards on the D171 Fauquissart road. The 'Moated Grange' (Ferme de Lestré) is on the right after 800m, but stopping on the roadside here is not recommended. 200m before the 'Grange' is a sharp left turn with space to park a car on the left, just before the next bend. Take care walking along the D171 as it is a fast road and there is no pavement, just a grass verge. The moat surrounding the 'Grange' is most prominent on the southwest side.

de Lestré) on Rue Tilleloy to gain a 135m long foothold in the German trenches. A party of 2nd West Yorkshire under Lieutenant Harrington came up to assist bombing a stretch of enemy held trench. Twenty-four prisoners were taken and an estimated 100 killed. 2nd West Yorkshire relieved 2nd Devonshire (140 casualties) after midnight. Consolidation work continued.

From late on the afternoon of the 18th, No 1 Section, 15th Field Company RE, commanded by **Lieutenant Philip Neame**, was held in reserve in case of an advance against Neuve Chapelle. At midnight Neame received orders to relieve No 3 Section at dawn. The task was to improve and consolidate the forward trenches, which had been taken over by 2nd West Yorkshire and, more importantly, to join the captured trench to the British lines.

At 5.00 a.m. on the 19th, Neame and his men arrived at Brigade HQ at the Red Barn, just north of Rouge Croix, where he was briefed on the situation before proceeding to relieve No 3 Section at the Moated Grange. The situation was not good; the enemy had commenced strong bombing attacks on the northeast of the line at 7.30 a.m. and water had got into the trenches from the moat. The 2nd West Yorkshire's CO told Neame that his bombers were having trouble resisting German counter-attacks. Leaving his Section to get on with their work, Neame went forward to investigate with Sergeant Hales. Crawling along a ditch he dashed the last 10m over open ground into the former German trench, arriving there at about 9.00 a.m. He contacted the West Yorkshire company commander and discovered the bombers had been reduced to a sergeant and two other ranks. The rest, including the bombing officer, were either dead or badly wounded. Neame went to investigate and found the surviving bombers in the most forward traverse of the captured trench, with German grenades raining down on them from two directions. The sergeant told Neame that the fuses of their improvised jam tin bombs were damp and would not light.

Neame asked for a knife and a box of matches. Just then another shower of bombs arrived wounding a soldier and blowing Neame's hat off. Realising they had little time, Neame ordered the rest back to the next traverse, which was already crowded with sheltering West Yorkshire soldiers. Then cutting a fuse considerably shorter than the usual four seconds, he held a match head against it and struck the matchbox across it. As soon as it lit he stood up and threw the bomb, which exploded instantaneously amongst the enemy bombers. Neame quickly prepared and threw another six bombs, stopping the enemy advance, although he had to give up a traverse in the process. A German bomb killed and wounded several of the West

Ferme de Lestré from the turning off the D171 where it is possible to park.

A closer view of Ferme de Lestré from the west. The broad white strip in front of the buildings is the frozen moat.

Yorkshires and the survivors pulled back a little further.

Neame then played a cat and mouse game with the Germans. Every time they recommenced bombing he returned a well-placed bomb, which dissuaded them from further action for a few minutes. He had a number of close shaves, as the German bombers just missed hitting him on a number of occasions and a machine-gunner and some riflemen opened fire every time he stood up to throw. Fortunately the gunner was slow and the West Yorkshires kept his head down with covering fire.

During a lull, Neame ordered more bombs brought forward and set the men behind him to dig two new traverses and a trench block. Two men with fixed bayonets were stood by to assist if the enemy attempted to rush him. When the order was eventually received, the West Yorkshires were able to withdraw in good order due to Neame's gallant stand. He was down to seven or eight bombs and pulled back after his two bayonet men had got away. Having crossed the road at the gap in the trench, he assisted in pulling the wounded in and with a West Yorkshire subaltern, dragged them back along a ditch on a greatcoat. He also assisted in fighting off some enemy who looked as if they were about to attack again. After about three-quarters of an hour the Germans gave up and Neame rejoined his Section. By nightfall all the work was completed and at 5.00 p.m. the Section reported back to the Company. 2nd West Yorkshire sustained over 120 casualties, mainly in the retirement.

7th Division was ordered to make an attack on the Rouges Bancs – La Boutillerie front on 18th December. A number of troop movements had to take place in daylight in preparation and this, together with unusual artillery activity, was not lost on the Germans; they knew the attack was coming. 22nd Brigade was to attack at 4.30 p.m. following a bombardment by all the guns of the Division. At 6.00 p.m., 20th Brigade was to attack on a frontage of 450m eastwards from the Sailly – Fromelles road with two half battalions. 21st Brigade was moving to rejoin

Ferme de Lestré looking towards Neuve Chapelle from the northeast, with the D171 on the right. Philip Neame's bombing action was near the prominent tree on the left. He eventually withdrew over the road close to the walls of the Ferme.

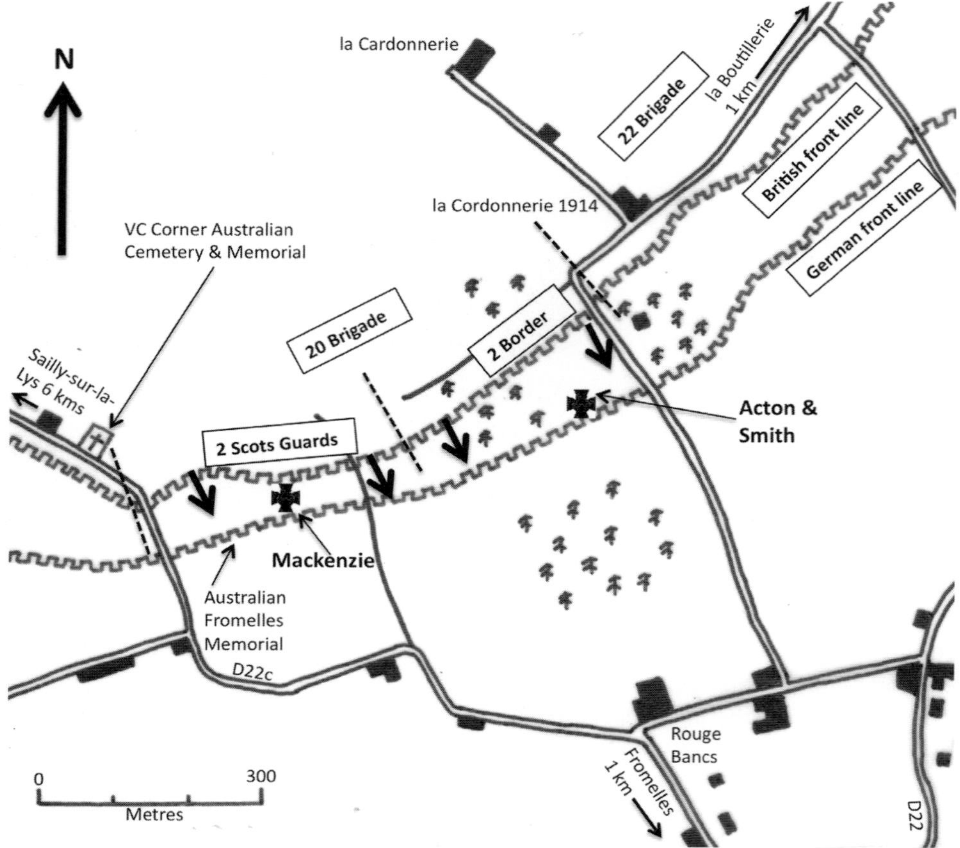

The area of 20th Brigade's attack on 18th December 1914 was fought over a number of times during the war. There is plenty of room to park at the Fromelles Australian Memorial (Cobbers Memorial) on the east side of the D22c Fromelles - Sailly-sur-la-Lys road to see where James Mackenzie won his VC. The German front line ran generally east to west through here and later German concrete pillboxes can be seen near the Memorial. To see the site of Acton's and Smith's VC action, park on the corner 125m southwest of the 1914 la Cordonnerie Farm where the road turns southeast.

the Division and on arrival was to take over its old line held by two companies each of 2nd Border and 2nd and 6th Gordon Highlanders.

By 5.30 p.m. it was clear the 22nd Brigade attack had failed. F and Left Flank Companies, 2nd Scots Guards led 20th Brigade's attack on the right with its right boundary being the Sailly – Fromelles road. G Company was in support. A and C Companies, 2nd Border were on the left, with the left boundary on the road running southeast of La Cordonnerie Farm. The leading 2nd Scots Guards companies were led by Captain Loder and his whistle blast was the signal for both battalions to attack.

At 6.00 p.m., under cover of darkness, the assault troops filtered out into no man's land and lay down behind the British wire. The whole affair went wrong from the beginning. Although there was no preliminary bombardment for this phase of the operation there was a lot of noise from other sectors. Many men, particularly

From the German front line looking northwest towards 2nd Scots Guards' trenches, which ran across this field in front of VC Corner Australian Cemetery and Memorial in the background. James Mackenzie rescued the wounded from this field before being killed. The impressive Fromelles Australian Memorial on the right commemorates the action fought here on 19th July 1916, resulting in 5,533 Australian and 1,547 British casualties. Four hundred and ten unknown Australians are buried in VC Corner Cemetery without individual headstones. The Cemetery also includes a memorial to 1,186 missing from the battle; its layout is unique. Many dead from the 1916 battle were buried by the Germans close to Pheasant Wood at Fromelles. The burial pits were excavated in 2009 and the remains of 250 soldiers were recovered and reburied in Fromelles (Pheasant Wood) Military Cemetery in 2010, the first CWGC cemetery for over fifty years.

in the 2nd Border companies, did not hear the whistle and their attack was delayed until about 6.30 p.m. As a consequence the assault lacked cohesion.

The left of 2nd Scots Guards advanced as silently as possible and found little German wire in the way. The lack of artillery preparation ensured the Germans were surprised and the attackers reached the enemy trench before they could react. Resistance on the left was subdued quickly, but despite this the right of 2nd Scots Guards and 2nd Border had less success. Held up by thick wire entanglements and engaged by a machine-gun on the right flank, very few managed to penetrate the enemy lines.

Those who managed to get into the German trench found they could not see over the parados to engage the Germans further back. Some men climbed out and took up positions in the open where they came under fire from the machine-gun on the right. Strong German reinforcements arrived from the second line and by 11.30 p.m. they had retaken some of their lost trench.

The 2nd Border companies were held up in no man's land for an hour by heavy German fire and British shells falling short. Captain HA Askew, a veteran of the South African War, led another attack. Although he was killed on the enemy parapet (Ploegsteert Memorial), a few men did get into the trench, but were quickly evicted by a counter-attack. Another attack broke on the enemy wire and the survivors withdrew.

Because of the lack of success and the vigour of the German counter-attacks, the reserve companies were not sent over. However, the centre of the line taken in the first rush was retained and an attempt was made to sap across no man's land to join the 2nd Scots Guards' gains with the British front line. It was a hopeless venture to dig 160m of trench under heavy fire, and it was given up as daylight approached. Just before dawn the survivors retreated, dragging back their wounded as best they could. The whole affair cost 20th Brigade 322 casualties for absolutely no gain; the CWGC record three men in 2nd Border and 28 men in 2nd Scots Guards killed or died of wounds up to 21st December.

Looking east along the German front line from 2nd Scots Guards' right boundary. 2nd Scots Guards attacked from the left on 18th December 1914. The trees in the background behind the Cobbers Memorial mark 2nd Border's left boundary.

It was during the withdrawal that **Private James Mackenzie** of Left Flank Company, 2nd Scots Guards, saw a stretcher party give up an attempt to bring in a wounded man from close to the enemy front line. Under very heavy fire, Mackenzie went out alone and brought the man in. At about 2.00 p.m. he returned to the trenches after helping two stretcher-bearers carry a wounded man back to the dressing station. He then attempted to rescue another man with the stretcher party. Passing a dangerous spot in the line the bearers made it across, but their movement alerted the Germans. As Mackenzie attempted to cross he was shot through the heart and died almost immediately.

Once the attackers had returned to their lines and the front settled again, the Germans allowed the Scots Guards into no man's land to collect the other wounded, but this did not occur opposite 2nd Border. The weather turned very wet and the communications trenches were flooded to waist height. Ration parties and stretcher-bearers faced wading through the mud or moving in the open with all the dangers that entailed.

In 20th Brigade's area a party of 35 men came in from no man's land on 20th December, having sheltered in a ditch since the attack failed. However, at least two wounded men were still lying out in no man's land as late as 21st December in the sector where 2nd Border had attacked. It was a miracle they

From the German front line looking west. The line ran between the left of the trees and the first telegraph pole. 2nd Border's front line ran parallel with the overhead cables through the copse in the centre. Acton and Smith rescued David Ross and another man from this field on 21st December 1914.

survived so long in the winter cold. **Privates Abraham Acton** and **James Smith** of B Company volunteered to bring them in. The first man they rescued was Private David Ross, who coincidentally came from Acton's hometown of Whitehaven. He was lying close to the German front line and was seen waving his hand weakly. Reaching him was an extremely hazardous venture. Under fire all the way, they crawled out to Ross, who had a thigh wound and could not walk or help them in any way. By crawling with the wounded man between them they managed to inch him back to the front line. Smith and Acton were in no man's land and exposed to heavy fire for over an hour. Undaunted, they later went out and rescued a second man; a remarkable feat of courage and endurance in the circumstances. One of those recovered was "off his head", but the other reported that any movement brought German fire and he had seen many wounded shot dead before he was rescued. He had survived by drinking water in a muddy puddle at night.

In the Indian Corps, the Lahore Division attacked the German line northeast of Givenchy on the morning of 19th December with the right of the Sirhind Brigade

Reverse view of the previous picture taken in the summer looking east from the centre of no man's land in December 1914. The house surrounded by trees is midway between the German lines on the right and the British front line, which ran in front of the buildings on the far left on the site of the 1914 la Cordonnerie Farm.

(1st HLI and 1/4th Gurkhas) and the left of the Ferozepore Brigade. However, in the Ferozepore Brigade, 129th Baluchis had been involved in a hard fight for the same ground on 16th December, suffering 19 killed and 67 wounded and was not fit for another attack so soon afterwards. The Jullundur Brigade had just been relieved in the line when one of its units, 59th Scinde Rifles, was sent back and attached to the Ferozepore Brigade to replace 129th Baluchis.

The Sirhind Brigade attack went in at 5.34 a.m. after a short bombardment. Two lines of trenches about 180m long were captured with very few casualties and about 70 prisoners were taken. Unusually the German trenches had no traverses and the men were soon under enfilade fire. The gains were held all day, but there was no

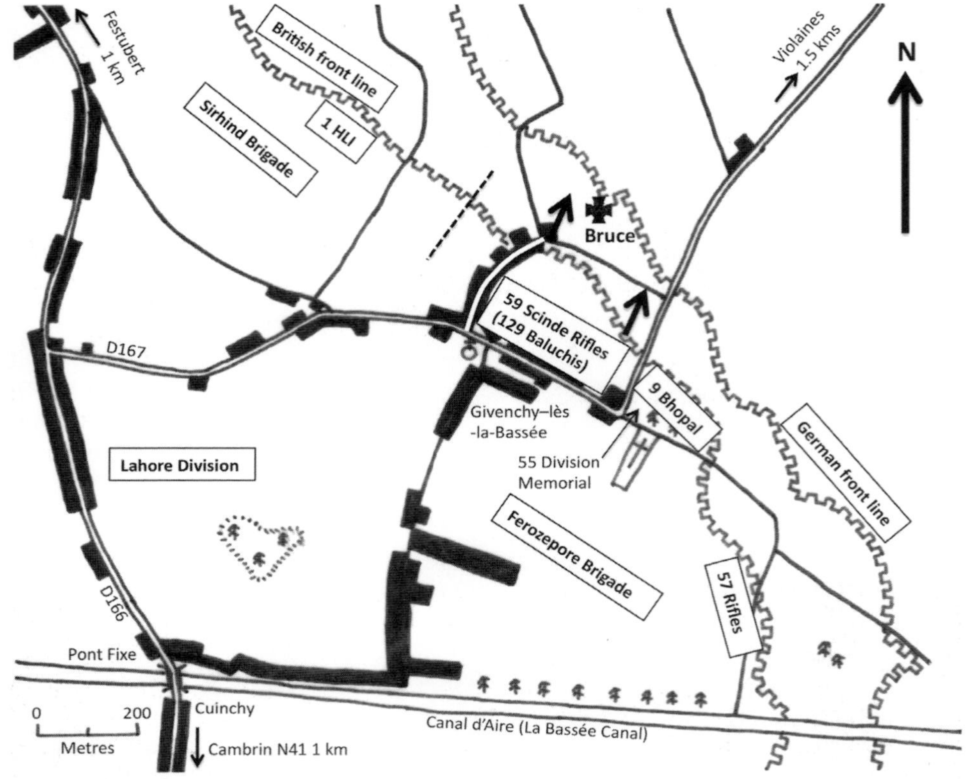

From Givenchy church drive north along an unclassified road for 250m. Park carefully where it forks and take the right track heading east through the former no man's land. It is possible to drive along this track, which is metalled, but it is narrow and if you stop you may block access for others. Walk 200m to the highest point to consider the action fought by 59th Rifles on 19th December 1914. The British front line was roughly parallel with and 50-100m south of this track and the German line was about the same distance to the north. There are no facilities in the immediate area, but there are a number of options along the main Béthune - La Bassee N41 road, particularly in the shopping centre at Auchy-les-Mines.

prospect of digging trenches to connect them with the British front line. After dark they were abandoned and the wounded were withdrawn.

In the Ferozepore Brigade, 59th Scinde Rifles moved back into the line on the dark and stormy night of 18th December. The Battalion was guided from Pont Fixe to the HQ of 129th Baluchis, holding the left section of the Ferozepore Brigade's front. Arriving at 4.00 a.m., it was guided forward into its assault positions, where 129th Baluchis had evacuated 180m of their front and support lines to make space for the attackers. Nos.1 and 4 Companies were to lead from the front line and Nos.2 and 3 Companies were in the support line. As soon as 59th Scinde Rifles had gone forward the trenches were to be reoccupied by 129th Baluchis.

The assault troops had only just got into position at 5.30 a.m. when a four-minute bombardment by a single battery commenced; this was the signal to attack. The front line trench was overcrowded and the troops found it very difficult to struggle out of it in the deep mud. No-one had seen the ground over which they were to attack and in the advance over no man's land many men went in the wrong direction.

A platoon of No 1 Company on the right under Jemadar Mangal Singh captured an offshoot of a German sap and held it all day, also capturing a German officer.

Givenchy on the right from the Sirhind Brigade's area. The Ferozepore Brigade attack by 59th Rifles was to the right of the small copse in the centre on top of the slight rise, which dominates the Sirhind Brigade's front.

Looking along no man's land in the Ferozepore Brigade's area, with Givenchy on the left and Festubert church in the centre distance. 59th Scinde Rifles attacked over this field from left to right. The small copse slightly right of centre is seen from the opposite direction in the previous picture. Right of the copse, where the snow is thicker, is the area of the later mine craters.

The platoon was relieved at dawn on the 20th when the Sappers and Miners pushed through a sap to reach it. Two other platoons under the company commander, Captain Scales, seized 30m of the German front line, but were forced out again with heavy casualties.

The fourth platoon, under **Lieutenant William Bruce,** lost direction in the dark, crossed the front of the attack and got into the German line on the left. As the platoon approached the German trench, the occupants said they would surrender and held up their rifles, but anyone looking over the parapet into the trench was shot. Bruce was first into the trench and ordered 3191 Havildar Dost Mahommad to fortify the left and hold it. Many rifles were jammed with mud and they came under fire from a mortar. Casualties were heavy on both sides and bodies piled up. Bruce was wounded in the neck, but continued moving about encouraging his men. He was killed soon afterwards having repelled a number of counter-attacks. Eventually Dost Mahommad realised the situation was hopeless and ordered the remnants to retire, but they refused, telling him they had been ordered to fight to the end by

Lieutenant Bruce. Only two men came back, the rest being killed or captured. It was not until officers were repatriated after the war that Bruce's gallantry came to light and he was recommended for the VC.

Some of the men were able to join up with No 4 Company, which had missed the German saphead in the dark, but managed to get into the main trench. Men from the support companies and some Sappers and Miners passed along another sap on the left, but there were numerous casualties in doing so. Eventually a barricade was erected across the sap and it was held until the Battalion was relieved at 9.30 p.m.

About 25 men of No 4. Company advanced 225m and joined with 1st HLI on their left. In the confusion there were numerous instances of troops firing on their own men in the dark. At daybreak it was clear the attack had been a failure. A few sections of German front line were still held, but reinforcements suffered casualties trying to get across no man's land using a sap. The CO of 59th Scinde Rifles was less than flattering in his report about the support received from 129th Baluchis and was scathing about the futility of these local attacks. After a very trying day the survivors of 59th Scinde Rifles were withdrawn at 10.00 p.m. and returned to their billets at 11.35 p.m., utterly exhausted. Casualties were twenty-nine killed, forty-three wounded and thirty-seven missing. The CWGC record forty-nine men killed or died of wounds on 19-20th December 1914, indicating twenty of the missing and wounded were also killed or died of wounds. Only two of the forty-nine dead have a known grave; the rest are commemorated on the Neuve Chapelle Memorial.

On 21st December the Germans exploded two mines under the trench held by 1st HLI and 1/4th Gurkhas, obliterating the position they held in the German front line.

Affairs of Cuinchy, France, 1st February 1915

44 LCpl Michael O'Leary, 1st Irish Guards (4th (Guards) Brigade, 2nd Division)

Although the Western Front was never inactive, January 1915 was one of the quietest times of the whole war. One exception was the Brickstacks area at Cuinchy, at the southern extreme of the BEF front. Here the British line formed a salient running from the La Bassée Canal on the left eastwards towards the Triangle formed by the Béthune – La Bassée railway joining the line from Vermelles, and then south to the La Bassée – Béthune road.

The Brickstacks at Cuinchy in 1915. Nothing remains today.

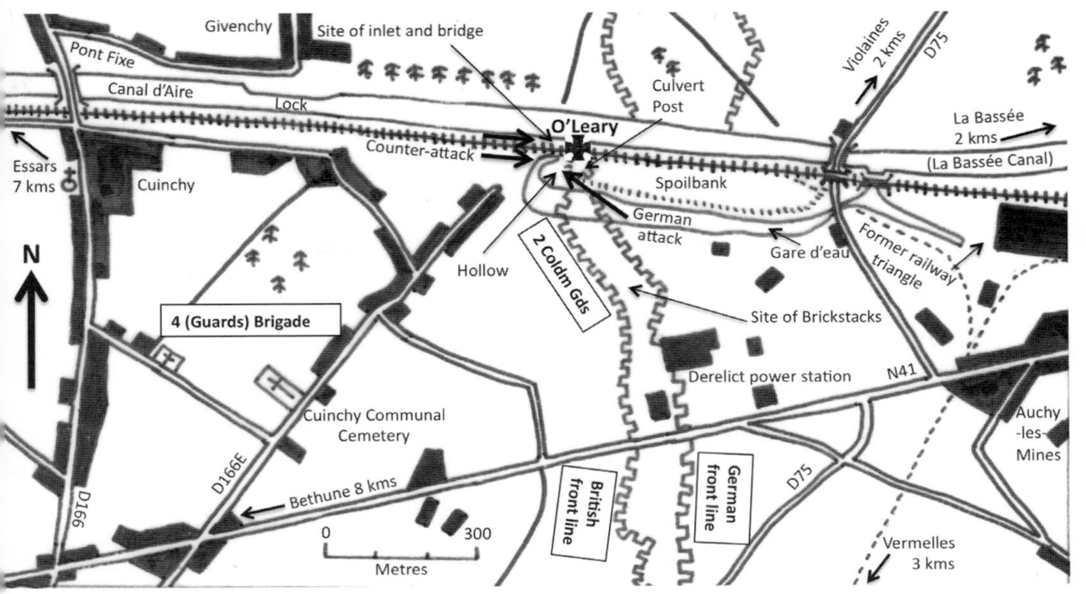

The area where O'Leary's VC action took place was altered extensively when a power station was constructed on the site of the Brickstacks after the war. It has since been demolished and the site is derelict, full of hazards and is consequently fenced off; entering it is not advisable. Leave the N41 Cambrin - La Bassée road on the D166E (not the D166). Keep going straight ahead to the northeast for almost a kilometre, passing Cuinchy Communal Cemetery on the left (contains 27 dead from the action on 1st February 1915), until the road runs out and there is a small area for parking beyond the last houses. Ahead is the railway embankment with the Canal beyond. On the right is the power station's coolant reservoir (Gare d'eau). The ground here has been altered so extensively that it bears little resemblance to the scene in February 1915.

There were two groups of brickstacks, known as Keeps, separated by 50m, one group held by the British and the other by the Germans. Each was an enormous structure up to 10m high, connected to its neighbour by saps and communications trenches. All around the ground was flat, interrupted only by railway embankments and a few houses.

The Germans captured some British posts on 1st January 1915, which were retaken on the 10th, only to be taken again by the Germans on the 12th. On 25th January a strong German attack on both sides of the Canal succeeded in penetrating to strong-points behind the support line. 1st Scots Guards and 1st Coldstream Guards were forced back to partially prepared positions 450m west of the Railway Triangle. North of the Canal a quickly organised counter-attack regained the lost ground, but to the south it was delayed and the Germans could not be dislodged, resulting in a dangerous salient in the British line. 4th (Guards) Brigade was rushed forward, but was not required and

From the parking area looking northeast. Beyond the fence on the right, the old power station coolant reservoir is just visible. Straight ahead is the railway embankment and the section in the middle of the picture is where the iron girder bridge stood. The Canal is out of sight beyond the embankment.

spent the next few days around Essars with its battalions at short notice to move.

The Germans renewed their attacks on 29th January, but made no further progress and on the 30th, 4th (Guards) Brigade took over the line south of the Canal from 2nd Brigade. 2nd Coldstream Guards was in the front line, 1st Irish Guards in support and the remaining three battalions were in reserve at varying distances from the front – 3rd Coldstream Guards at Annequin, 1/1st Hertfordshire at Beuvry and 2nd Grenadier Guards at Béthune.

At 2.10 a.m. on 1st February a strong German bombing party used an old communication trench as an approach to attack 2nd Coldstream Guards, close to where the railway line crossed

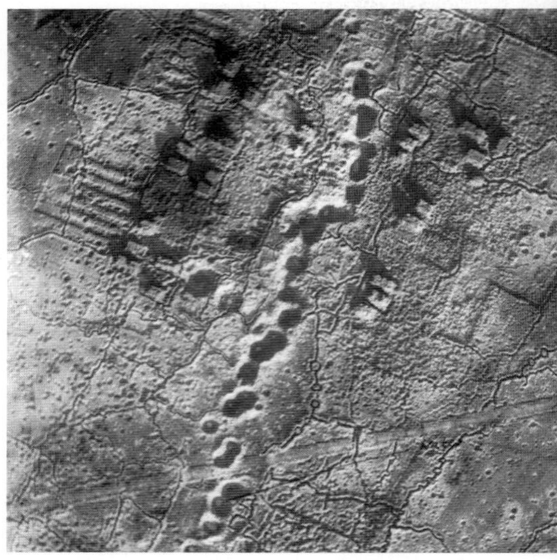

Air photograph from December 1916 with the Brickstacks separated by a line of small mine craters. The Canal is off the top of the picture and the Cambrin - La Bassée road crosses diagonally towards the bottom. Five more VCs were awarded for fighting in this area later in 1915.

Contemporary map of the Cuinchy area; most of the features are recognisable today. The area marked 'Brickstacks' is now covered by the derelict power station.

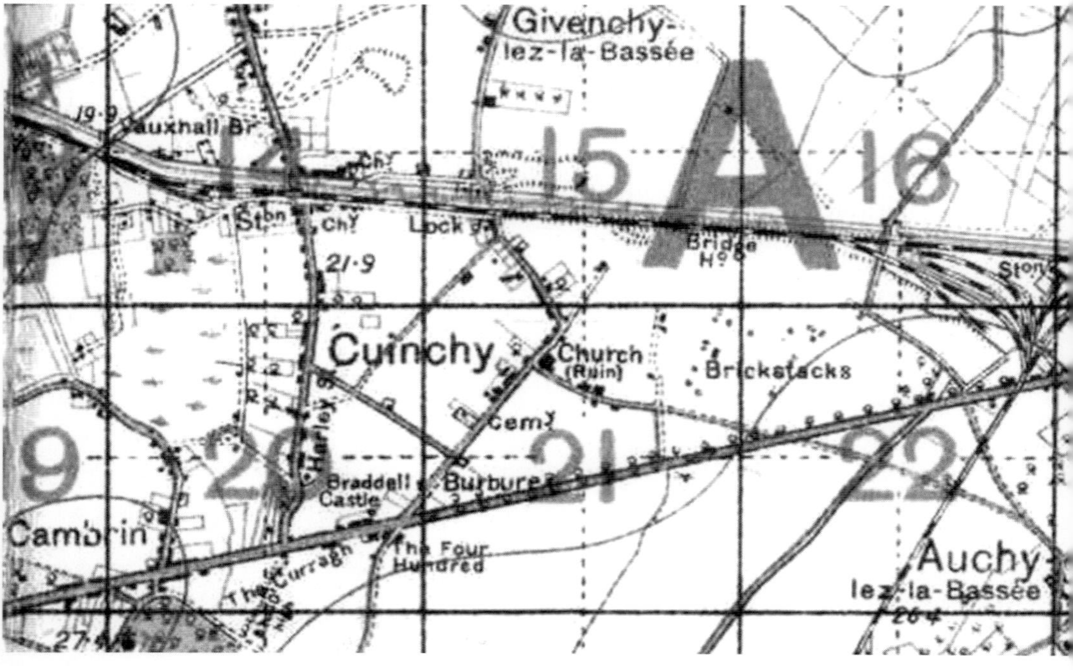

In the early hours of 1st February 1915 a strong German bombing party used an old communication trench to approach 2nd Coldstream Guards' positions in the Hollow, which was on the right of this railway embankment. Bottom right is the inlet, which connects with the Canal on the left via a culvert. In 1915 an iron girder bridge crossed the inlet in the foreground. This is where 2nd Coldstream Guards fell back to a sandbag barricade and held the German attack. In the subsequent counter-attack, O'Leary advanced from here along the railway embankment and also down in the Hollow. The railway is electrified and climbing the embankment for a better view should not be attempted.

a culvert leading to the Canal. After a flurry of trench mortar bombs, the trenches in the Hollow east of the culvert were rushed with grenade and bayonet. 2nd Coldstream Guards fell back to a sandbag barricade in front of where the railway embankment crossed an inlet on the Canal by an iron girder bridge. From there they prevented the enemy advancing along the towpath. Due to telephone lines being cut and runners killed, it took a long time for Battalion and Brigade HQs to work out what had happened.

No 1 Company, 1st Irish Guards was brought up to reinforce 2nd Coldstream Guards and 3rd Coldstream Guards was ordered to Pont Fixe. A counter-attack was launched in moonlight on Culvert Post at 4.00 a.m. by 2nd Coldstream Guards, with two platoons of No 4 Company, 1st Irish Guards in support. It failed to retake the lost ground although pressed with great determination to within 15m of the enemy position. By daylight (around 6.30 a.m.) it was clear the Germans were well established and bombs and rifles alone would be insufficient to remove them. The survivors of the counter-attack were withdrawn, but on the left they had regained the canal bank covering the iron girder bridge and thus prevented further German advances.

The commander of 1st Division, Major General Richard Haking, went forward to HQ 4th (Guards) Brigade to see the situation for himself and ordered another attack. A barrage was arranged and 3rd Brigade on the north bank of the Canal was asked to cooperate by sniping the Germans around the culvert. The attack was delayed when it was discovered 2nd Coldstream Guards was too weak and elements of 1st Irish Guards needed to be positioned to help.

At 10.05 a.m. there was an accurate and heavy bombardment lasting for 10 minutes, during which bodies were seen blasted into the air, with one landing in the Canal. A second attack by fifty men of 2nd Coldstream Guards, was made at 10.15 a.m., covered by the fire of No 2 Company, 1st Irish Guards. Ten Coldstream soldiers were directed on the towpath and forty on the Hollow, with four bombers following behind. Then came 30 Irish Guardsmen of No 1 Company, led by 2nd Lieutenant Innes, with some sappers to consolidate the position once it had been

Contemporary artist's (believed to be Fortunino Matania) impression of O'Leary's VC action.

Another artist's impression of O'Leary winning his VC. This version shows one of the brickstacks.

From the railway embankment looking southwest with Cuinchy and the parking area in the background. The construction of the power station altered the site significantly after the war. Bottom left is a culvert under the embankment to the Canal, on the site of the inlet and iron girder bridge.

recaptured. They carried filled sandbags, spades and boxes of grenades. Amongst this party was Innes' orderly, **Lance Corporal Michael O'Leary**.

The initial surge succeeded in overcoming the first barricade and the Coldstream officer commanding the attack, Captain A Leigh-Bennett, decided to press on to the apex of the Hollow. The line secured was beyond that lost in the morning, with about 60m of the enemy front line being captured.

During the preparations for the attack, O'Leary noticed that a machine-gun position some way behind the enemy forward outposts. He realised if the Germans got this gun into action the attack would fail and many of his comrades would die. So, as soon as the attack commenced, O'Leary rushed onto the railway embankment and made his way quickly to the corner of a trench blocked by a barricade and defended by five Germans. He shot all five of them and moved on. There was a second barricade 50m further on, behind which five more Germans were desperately trying to set up another machine-gun. A patch of boggy ground blocked the direct approach so O'Leary was forced to divert onto the railway embankment

From the spoilbank overlooking the railway and Canal with Givenchy in the background. The spoilbank is considerably larger than it was in 1915. O'Leary attacked along the railway from left to right. The iron girder bridge stood where the overhead electric cable gantry straddles the railway line. The Hollow was to the left.

again. Getting closer he opened fire, killing three and taking prisoner the remaining two. O'Leary returned triumphantly with his prisoners while the attack swept on. Throughout the whole engagement he moved about at a leisurely pace, visible to all around.

In addition to two machine-guns, eight unwounded and 24 wounded prisoners of the 112th Regiment were taken. The whole affair cost 111 casualties, including 46 killed. Work to consolidate the position started immediately and three batteries registered on the culvert position in case of a repeat attack. Later in the day, 1st Irish Guards was withdrawn from the line. As a result of the action it was decided to divide the brigade frontage into two battalion sectors; A1 covered by the two Coldstream battalions and A2 by 2nd Grenadiers and 1st Irish Guards.

The British counter-attack reached this point on 1st February 1915. Looking back over the British lines with Cuinchy in the background. The Brickstacks were on the extreme left.

Chapter Six

Summer Operations 1915

Battle of Neuve Chapelle, 10th – 12th March 1915

45 Rfn Gobar Sing Negi, 2/39th Garhwal Rifles (20th (Garhwal) Brigade, 7th (Meerut) Division)
46 Pte William Buckingham, 2nd Leicestershire (20th (Garhwal) Brigade, 7th (Meerut) Division)
47 CSM Harry Daniels, 2nd Rifle Brigade (25th Brigade, 8th Division)
48 Cpl Cecil Noble, 2nd Rifle Brigade (25th Brigade, 8th Division)
49 Pte Jacob Rivers, 1st Nottinghamshire & Derbyshire (Sherwood Foresters) (24th Brigade, 8th Division)
50 LCpl Wilfred D Fuller, 1st Grenadier Guards (20th Brigade, 7th Division)
51 Pte Edward Barber, 1st Grenadier Guards (20th Brigade, 7th Division)
52 Cpl William Anderson, 2nd Yorkshire (Green Howards) (21st Brigade, 7th Division)
53 Capt Charles Foss, 2nd Bedfordshire (21st Brigade, 7th Division)

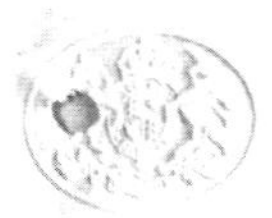

Special Order.

To the 1st Army.

We are about to engage the enemy under very favourable conditions. Until now in the present campaign, the British Army has, by its pluck and determination, gained victories against an enemy greatly superior both in men and guns. Reinforcements have made us stronger than the enemy in our front. Our guns are now both more numerous than the enemy's are, and also larger than any hitherto used by any army in the field. Our Flying Corps has driven the Germans from the air.

On the Eastern Front, and to South of us, our Allies have made marked progress and caused enormous losses to the Germans, who are, moreover, harassed by internal troubles and shortage of supplies, so that there is little prospect at present of big reinforcements being sent against us here.

In front of us we have only one German Corps, spread out on a front as large as that occupied by the whole of our Army (the First).

We are now about to attack with about 48 battalions a locality in that front which is held by some three German battalions. It seems probable, also, that for the first day of the operations the Germans will not have more than four battalions available as reinforcements for the counter attack. Quickness of movement is therefore of first importance to enable us to forestall the enemy and thereby gain success without severe loss.

At no time in this war has there been a more favourable moment for us, and I feel confident of success. The extent of that success must depend on the rapidity and determination with which we advance.

Although fighting in France, let us remember that we are fighting to preserve the British Empire and to protect our homes against the organized savagery of the German Army. To ensure success, each one of us must play his part, and fight like men for the Honour of Old England.

(Sd.) D. HAIG, General,
Commanding 1st Army.

9th March, 1915.

1st Printing Co., R.E. G.H.Q. 673.

General Douglas Haig's eve of battle message.

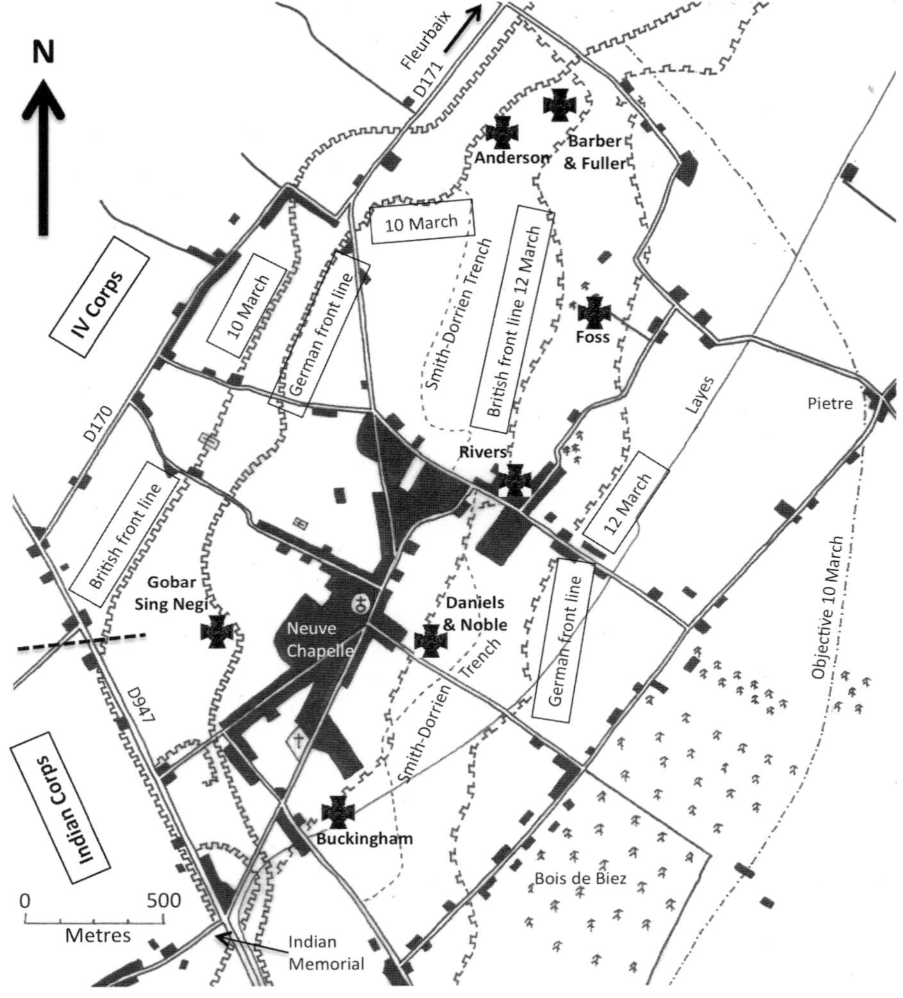

The main features of the Neuve Chapelle battlefield, including the front lines before the offensive and where they came to rest on 12th March.

In March 1915 the British went over to the offensive at Neuve Chapelle. The strategic intentions were to assist the Russians by holding enemy forces in the west, support French attacks at Arras and in Champagne and to foster offensive spirit after a long winter holding the line. The tactical aim was to gain advantageous positions east of the village in order to seize the high ground from Aubers to Ligny le Grand. This would deny the Germans observation over the British rear areas and allow the British to watch over Lille, Roubaix and Tourcoing. The ultimate intention was to cut off enemy forces down to the La Bassée Canal.

The attack was split into two areas, with IV Corps north of the village and the Indian Corps to the south, while I Corps attacked northeast of Givenchy. The ground was flat, wet and crossed by many ditches and hedges. The main obstacle was the Layes brook, some 2-3m wide and 1-1.5m deep. The opening bombardment, lasting only 35 minutes, consumed more shells than were fired in the whole of the Boer War.

The Indian Corps assault on 10th March 1915 was made by the Garhwal Brigade (Brigadier-General CG Blackader DSO) of the Meerut Division. The Bareilly Brigade held the line prior to the assault and was to provide fire support. Once the Garhwal Brigade had secured the enemy forward defences, the Dehra Dun Brigade would pass through to seize Bois du Biez. The attack was launched from breastworks along the La Bassée – Estaires road held by 6th Jats (Bareilly Brigade). The Garhwal Brigade had four battalions in line, from the right – 1/39th Garhwal Rifles, 2nd Leicestershire, 2/3rd Gurkha Rifles and 2/39th Garhwal Rifles. 3rd London was in reserve. To assist artillery observers, the forward troops of the flank battalions carried pink flags and the inner battalions light and dark blue flags.

The objective was to seize the German forward trenches and press on beyond Neuve Chapelle to the old Smith-Dorien Trench. In the nights before the attack, two new breastwork lines were constructed behind the front line along the La Bassée – Estaires road, 108 bridges were positioned over ditches, ladders were installed in trenches and gaps cut in the British wire.

Head north from the Indian Memorial at La Bombe Corner (Port Arthur) on the D947 La Bassée - Estaires road. The left of this road was the Indian Corps front line. Continue for 700m and turn right into a farmyard to park. If the farmyard is in use turn left instead and park on the roadside. This is just north of the IV/Indian Corps boundary and from here almost all of the Indian Corps assault area can be viewed.

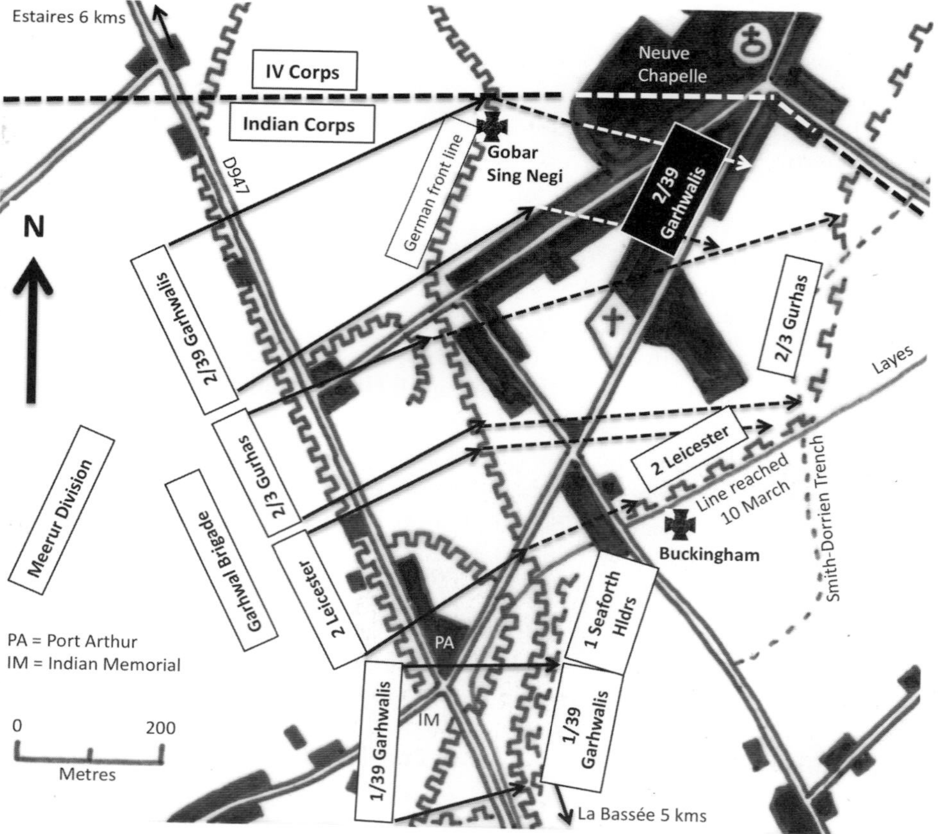

Prior to the attack the leading troops of 2nd Leicestershire, under Lieutenant Colonel Gordon left their trenches and lay down in a shallow forward trench constructed for the purpose on the east side of the La Bassée – Estaires road. The most forward German troops realised something was afoot, but more senior commanders failed to react. It was not until a German aircraft flew low over Port Arthur at 7.00 a.m. and saw the assault troops crammed into the trenches that the German artillery opened fire. 1/39th Garhwal Rifles and 2nd Leicestershire suffered some casualties as a result.

The barrage by the guns of the Meerut and Lahore Divisions opened at 7.30 a.m. The troops were impressed with its accuracy, although a few shells dropped short. The first 10 minutes concentrated on cutting the enemy wire. For the final 25 minutes the field guns switched onto likely enemy reinforcement routes while the howitzers engaged the enemy trenches. In the rear areas the RFC bombed railway junctions to disrupt the movement of German reserves. The Germans were quick to respond with their own artillery.

At 8.05 a.m. the barrage lifted onto the village and the assault troops rushed forward with hardly a check. 2nd Leicestershire attacked north of Port Arthur and by 8.30 a.m. the leading companies (B and C), had reached their objectives beyond the village in the vicinity of Smith-Dorien Trench. However, as 2nd Leicestershire advanced, a gap opened between its right and the left of 1/39th Garhwal Rifles. Two companies of 1st Seaforth Highlanders (Dehra Dun Brigade) attacked from the left flank, while two companies of 3rd London and one of 1/39th Garhwal Rifles cleared the enemy trenches in a dashing frontal assault.

Further north, at 5.15 a.m., 2/39th Garhwal Rifles, under Lieutenant Colonel D H Drake-Brockman, had been able to move forward of the front line breastworks without interference due to the shape of the ground. The troops lay down to await the attack in the bitter cold, covering themselves with their great coats and waterproof sheets, which were shrugged off and abandoned as the assault started. The bombardment was so intense that the assault troops were able to stand in the open with impunity. Nos 1 & 2 Companies (right and left respectively) advanced at the double with their second platoons 50m behind. The wire was well cut and there was little resistance, except on

An accurate artist's depiction (believed to be Frederic Villiers) of the scene as 2/39th Garwhal Rifles started its attack across the La Bassée - Estaires road on 12th March 1915. Note the breastworks on the right of the road and the bridges laid over the ditch on the left (The Royal Garwhal Rifles in the Great War).

the left of No 1 Company, which was overcome by No 2 Company after some casualties had been incurred.

Bombing and bayonet parties were soon working along the trenches. Amongst them was **Rifleman Gobar Sing Negi,** the leading bayonet man in a bombing party on the left, as they worked along a trench to join up with 8th Division in IV Corps. He was first to rush around each traverse and bayoneted several Germans. When the NCO was killed, Gobar Sing Negi took command and carried on, driving back many more Germans, who eventually surrendered to 8th Division troops attacking the other way. He was killed later.

A similar view today, looking south from the farmyard east of the La Bassée - Estaires road. Neuve Chapelle is on the left. 2/39th Garwhal Rifles started from the foreground and 2nd Leicestershire further down the road.

About 190 prisoners and three machine-guns were taken, firm contact was made with the right of IV Corps and the first objective was reached. No 3 Company came forward and the three companies then advanced through Neuve Chapelle to Smith-Dorien Trench, where contact was made with 2nd Rifle Brigade (8th Division) on the left. The front was then taken over by 2/3rd Gurkha Rifles, with 2/39th Garhwal Rifles in support and German trench stores found in a house in Neuve Chapelle were put to good use.

2/39th Garhwal Rifles suffered 128 casualties (twenty-eight killed, seventy-eight wounded and twenty-two missing – CWGC record forty-one dead for 10-11th

The area of 2/39th Garwhal Rifles' attack from the farmyard. Gobar Sing Negi's action was about halfway between here and Neuve Chapelle church. He led a bombing party from the right towards the centre of the picture to join up with 8th Division in IV Corps.

View from the German front line towards the La Bassée - Estaires road. The farmyard is on the extreme right of picture.

March). 1/39th Garhwal Rifles on the right flank had even more casualties, including the CO, wounded in the leg. Lieutenant Colonel Drake-Brockman was ordered to take command of both battalions and secure the right flank. While 2/39th Garhwal Rifles began moving from its support position to Port Arthur, Drake-Brockman went ahead, but fell into a shell hole and was unable to move quickly. He sent Major HM MacTier on and shortly after he was appointed to command 1/39th Garhwal Rifles (killed on 12th March – Laventie Military Cemetery – IV G 4). Drake-Brockman turned his own Battalion around and returned to where it had started.

At 5.00 p.m. the Dehra Dun Brigade, less 1st Seaforth Highlanders, passed through the Garhwal Brigade, using eight portable bridges to cross the Layes. Around 6.30 p.m. elements reached the northwest edge of Bois du Biez in darkness, guided by the light of a burning house. However, there was no support on either flank and the troops had to fall back during the night to the line of the Layes. 2/39th Garhwal Rifles was then attached to the Dehra Dun Brigade.

The offensive was to continue on 11th March in conjunction with 8th Division on the left, but there were numerous delays. 2/39th Garhwal Rifles moved to various positions and suffering a number of casualties during the day, but the attack never took place and that night it went into billets at La Couture. The rest of the Garhwal Brigade held the line gained on the first day. The intention was to attack on the 12th with the Sirhind Brigade (Lahore Division).

At 5.00 a.m. on 12th March the Germans launched a major counter-attack. Listening posts reported the enemy advancing through the early morning mist, and all was ready to receive them when they emerged out of the gloom. The Germans attacked 2nd Leicestershire for an hour before withdrawing to Bois du Biez, leaving hundreds of dead behind, but some remained in the abandoned Smith-Dorien and Dehra Dun Trenches. Another attack at 9.00 a.m. also failed with heavy losses.

About 11.30 a.m. some of the Germans in the abandoned trenches indicated they wished to surrender. A company of the Sirhind Brigade to the left of 2nd Leicestershire rushed forward to take advantage of the situation, taking about 100 prisoners and killing another 50 as they tried to escape. A company of 2nd Leicestershire advanced and reoccupied Dehra Dun Trench at the Layes.

The Sirhind and Jullundur Brigades attacked at 1.00 p.m., but 8th Division on the left was held up, allowing the Germans to enfilade the Indians. Some progress was made, but when a second attack was attempted at 6.05 p.m., the enemy fire was so intense that the men could not get out of their trench. Further advances were cancelled. Total casualties in the two Garhwal Rifles battalions were 452. They were amalgamated on 1st April and remained so for the remainder of their time in France.

Private William Buckingham of 2nd Leicestershire was active throughout the actions described. On the 10th and 12th he risked his life on a number of occasions to rescue and help the wounded, many of whom would have died otherwise. Amongst those he saved was 16152 Corporal W Tarry of A Company, who he carried out of the firing line under heavy fire. Tarry survived and was discharged unfit for further service on 4th June 1916. Buckingham went on to rescue 20532 Private Michael Lane; he died at King George's Hospital, London on 3rd October 1916 of wounds received in another action on 14th July (Leicester (Gilroes) Cemetery – NN 72).

While in no man's land, Buckingham came across a badly wounded German soldier exposed to the fire of both sides. One of his legs had been blown off and Buckingham administered aid as best he could before putting the German in a place of safety. On 12th March he jumped over a parapet with a message for the CO and was shot in the chest. However, the bullet was deflected by his pay book and 49 field postcards in his breast pocket through one of his ammunition pouches and embedded in his upper right arm. He was evacuated to England, one of 343 casualties (including 96 killed or died of wounds up to 14th March 1915) suffered by 2nd Leicestershire.

Neuve Chapelle from the south. Right of centre in the distance is the church. The line held by 2nd Leicestershire was just beyond the Layes, which runs across the picture in a deep ditch in line with the car on the road on the left. William Buckingham performed many rescues in this field.

The IV Corps attack north of Neuve Chapelle on 10th March commenced at 8.35 a.m. and was led by 8th Division. 23rd Brigade was on the left and 25th Brigade on the right. 2nd Rifle Brigade in 25th Brigade began the day in support, but later passed through the leading troops to take part in the capture of Neuve Chapelle and suffered 116 casualties.

The German counter-attack on the morning of the 12th was detected by listening posts and the main line was fully manned by the time the enemy reached it. The Germans emerged out of the mist when about 100m away and were met by rapid fire. They pressed home their attacks courageously for an hour before retreating, leaving hundreds of dead behind. As a result of the German action, a British attack timed for 7.30 a.m. was delayed to 10.30 a.m. and then by another two hours.

The British attack resumed at 12.30 p.m. Lack of coordination between IV Corps and the Indian Corps meant the Indians on the right of 25th Brigade attacked half an hour later. In 25th Brigade, A and B Companies, 2nd Rifle Brigade set off towards the enemy lines with 1st Royal Irish Rifles on the left. The preparatory bombardment was ineffective, leaving the enemy trenches almost intact. The Layes

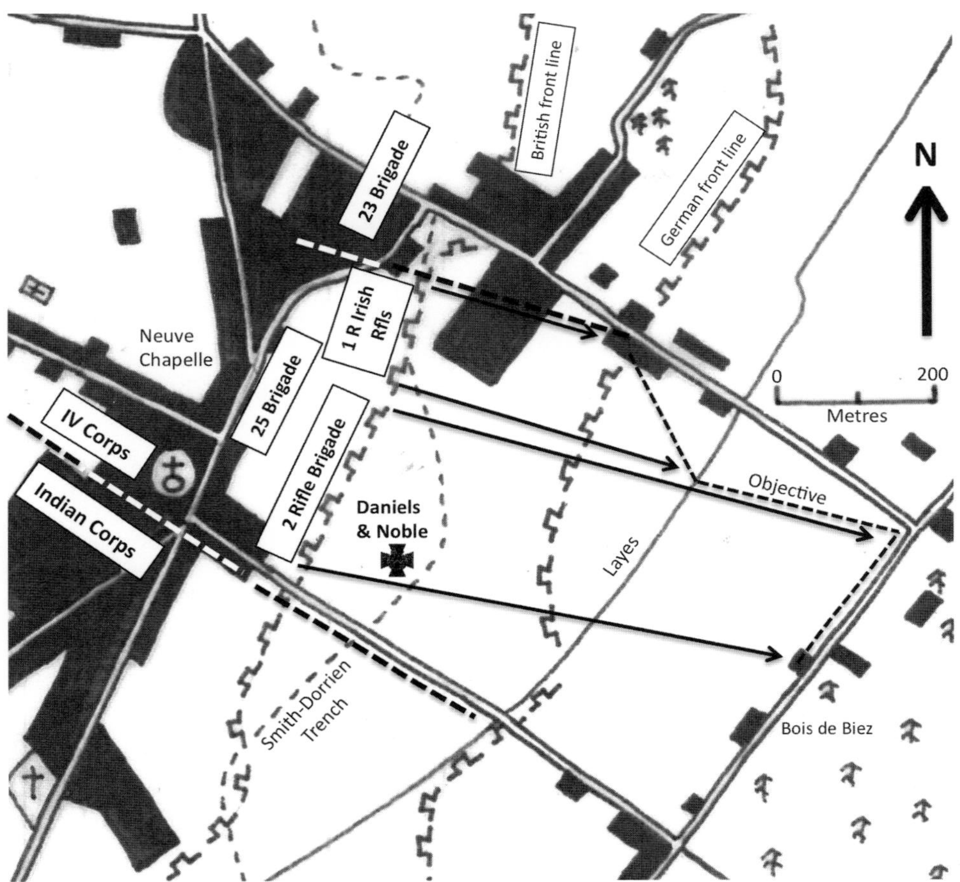

Drive southeast from Neuve Chapelle church towards Bois de Biez. Stop after 150m at the football ground to overlook the scene of 2nd Rifle Brigade's attack on 12th March 1915.

Brook Redoubt was hardly touched and the wire before it was uncut. At least 15 machine-guns were identified, particularly on the left flank and from a new German trench in front of Bois de Biez. To add to the difficulties, the advance had to cross deeply ploughed ground and a series of ditches leading from the Layes to the village.

The troops were met by a devastating crossfire as they advanced into a salient in the enemy line. The survivors of 2nd Rifle Brigade took cover in Smith-Dorrien Trench, only half way to the objective. Lieutenant Mansel was hit in the head and **CSM Harry Daniels** of D Company went to assist him, but Mansel refused help to avoid risk to others. He shook hands with Daniels and sent him back. Mansel survived and was eventually evacuated to London.

The Brigade Commander realised another attack in daylight was pointless, but he was overruled by Division. At 4.45 p.m. orders were received for the Battalion to attack again at 5.15 p.m., allowing little time for preparation. C and D Companies, left and right respectively, were to pass through the survivors of the first attack and continue the assault. It was an impossible task and the artillery support was ineffective. In C Company only the commander and five men made it to Smith-

Neuve Chapelle church in the background and the Layes in the foreground. 2nd Rifle Brigade attacked towards the camera.

Reverse view of the last picture from 2nd Rifle Brigade's front line. The wire cut by Harry Daniels and Cecil Noble under heavy fire ran across this football pitch. Smith-Dorien Trench was just beyond the goal.

Dorrien Trench. D Company did not get beyond its own wire, which had no gaps in it, and was covered by heavy enemy machine-gun fire.

The survivors were concerned about being able to meet a counter-attack, when they received the order to attack again. Daniels realised that, with the wire not being cut, the attack would be suicidal. He protested to his acting company commander, but Lieutenant Pennyfather ordered Daniels to detail a party to cut the wire. Rather than risk others on such a hazardous mission he sent for **Corporal Cecil Noble**, an old friend. Daniels said, "*Come on Tom, get some nippers*". Noble nodded, "*Right! I reckon we'll get something if we do*", which was prophetic, but Daniels thought he meant that they would probably catch a German bullet.

They shook hands and rushed forward in full view of the enemy into a hail of fire. Lying on their backs, with the enemy blazing away at their arms and bullets pinging off the wire, they cut the lower strands. They then had to get onto their knees to cut the breast high wire and seemed to bear a charmed life with bullets flying around them without finding the target. However, as they were finishing, Daniels was shot through the left thigh and Noble through the chest. Despite their wounds they carried on until a gap had been cleared. Noble was eventually too weak to continue and lapsed into unconsciousness. Daniels was unable to reach him.

Shortly after, the CO called off the attack to avoid further unnecessary casualties. Daniels rolled into a shell hole for cover and improvised a tourniquet using two hard tack biscuits and a field dressing. It stopped the bleeding and speaks volumes for Army biscuits. He was stuck in no man's land for four hours until it was dark enough to crawl back. The days fighting cost the Battalion another 222 casualties, making a total of 442, including 125 killed or died of wounds between 10th and 20th March.

During the initial assault by 8th Division on 10th March, 24th Brigade had been in reserve. Late in the afternoon it continued the advance, attacking from north

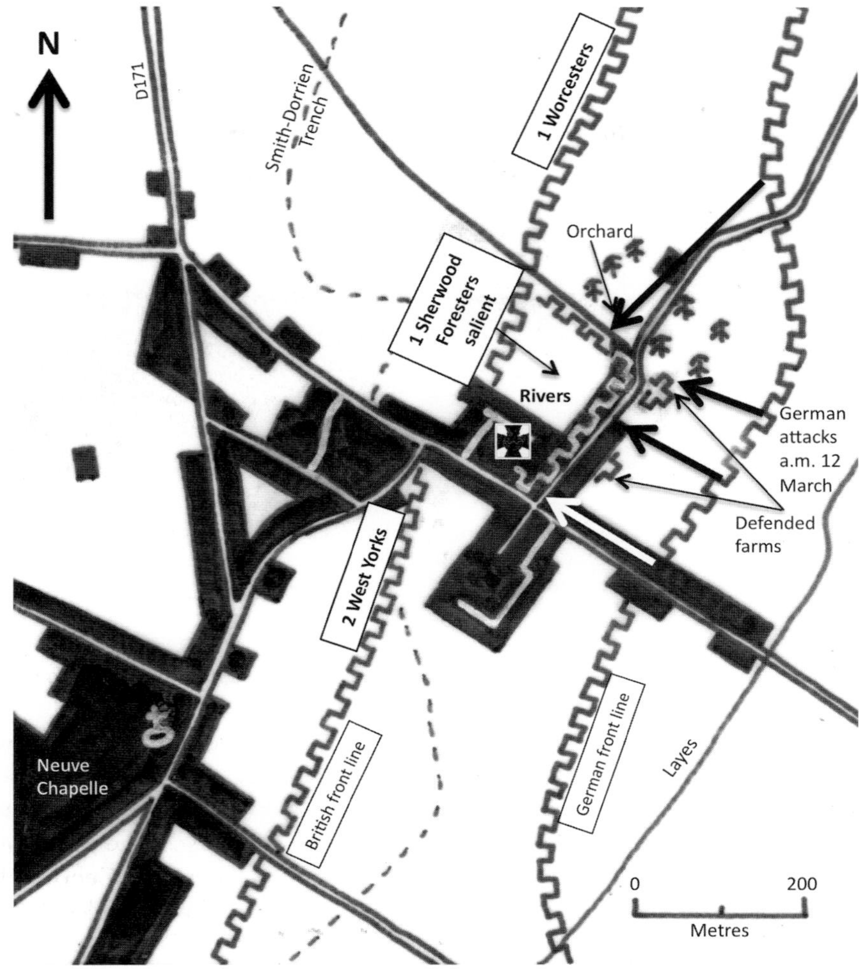

From Neuve Chapelle church head north on the D171 Fleurbaix road. After 100m branch right onto Rue Jacquet. After 350m turn right at the T-junction onto Rue des Boulans and left after 150m into Rue de Mauquissart, which was 1st Sherwood Foresters' front line on the morning of 12th March 1915. The German breastworks were off to the right. Park where convenient.

of the village. In the dark units became mixed up, ammunition ran short and no contact was made with 7th Division on the left. The right flank was open and under heavy fire from a strongly held breastwork. The attack was called off until dawn to allow units time to reorganise.

The advance on the morning of the 11th was disjointed; the artillery barrage was ineffective and the troops ran into heavy crossfire and faltered. However, there was some progress. At 10.00 a.m., C Company, 1st Sherwood Foresters, advanced through an orchard on the left of the Battalion's line and occupied two broken down farmhouses, with the German lines 100-200m away. At 4.00 p.m., D Company rushed the breastwork, but after three attempts suffering heavy losses from machine-guns, it had to give up. Reorganisation took place during the night in preparation for the Brigade to attack again next morning.

1st Sherwood Foresters' front line ran along this road (Rue de Mauquissart). The left farm was in the small copse. The German breastworks ran across the field in the middle distance, where a later concrete pillbox can just be made out.

Another view along 1st Sherwood Foresters' front line, looking east. Apart from the two broken down farms, of which there is no trace today, there were no buildings in this area in 1915. The left farm was amongst the trees at the end of the road and the right farm was at the road sign.

On the misty morning of 12th March, 1st Sherwood Foresters was occupying a salient 100m in front of the rest of 24th Brigade. To the left was 1st Worcestershire and on the right and to the rear was 2nd West Yorkshire (25th Brigade). When the Germans attacked at 5.00 a.m., all the company commanders were at the Battalion HQ farm on the left of the line for a conference.

The Germans rushed the position in four places and very soon after most officers had been lost. The troops on the left mistook the enemy advancing from the north for a returning listening patrol. This area was quickly overrun and the attackers went on to the left farm, in conjunction with another party attacking from the east. The platoons holding the north face were surrounded and the Germans bombed the farm buildings before rushing in. Hand-to-hand fighting room by room and in the courtyard followed. Only eight survivors managed to fight their way out.

The main attack fell on the right and it was feared the Battalion might be outflanked due to the gap on that flank. Many of the attackers here were cut down by a machine-gun in the right farm, but they still managed to take the front line trench. A confused tangle of Germans and retreating Sherwood Foresters were carried back another 160m to the support line, which held firm.

Another German party advanced between the two farms against the centre company. With the enemy already past its right flank it was forced to pull back, but by 6.30 a.m. small arms fire had stemmed the German rush and counter-attacks were being organised. A company of 1st Worcestershire came up in support and with one and a half companies of the Battalion, counter-attacked on the left and retook the lost trenches on that flank. However, the Germans still held a three-sided pocket in 1st Sherwood Foresters' line.

An estimated 1,000 Germans massed on the right and right centre for another attack on the support line. **Private Jacob Rivers**, a bomber in C Company, crept

This road (Rue des Boulans) was 1st Sherwood Foresters' right flank. The first turning on the left marks the support line, where the German onslaught was halted. About 200m down the main road just before a car parked on the roadside is another left turn into Rue de Mauquissart, which was the front line. The junction in the foreground was 2nd West Yorkshire's left flank. The area between these two junctions was 1st Sherwood Foresters' open right flank. Jacob Rivers' VC action was amongst the houses on the left.

forward on his own initiative to within a few metres of the enemy. He hurled bombs with such rapidity and accuracy that the surprised Germans were sent scurrying back. This was followed by a determined charge by 1st Sherwood Foresters and the Germans left behind over 600 dead. During this later phase of the battle, Rivers repeated his earlier bombing feat, accompanied by 11588 Private Jesse Stanbury Draycott of HQ Company (DCM for this action). They dislodged another concentration of the enemy, but Rivers was killed. Although his body was found and buried, it was not identified after the war.

By 7.30 a.m. the Battalion had regained all its losses and had taken up to 50 prisoners. That night 1st Sherwood Foresters pulled back into support and next day moved into the reserve trenches at Sign Post Corner on Rue de Tilleloy. It had suffered 458 casualties since the fighting started on the 10th, including 198 killed or died of wounds up to 20th March.

The left of 24th Brigade seized part of the objective on 11th March, but later all the gains were lost. 23rd Brigade took 24th Brigade under command for a joint attack in the early hours, but it was half-hearted and unsuccessful. Early on 13th March, 8th Division consolidated its positions. 23rd Brigade took over from 24th Brigade, which withdrew into reserve. The Brigade commander, Brigadier General Francis Charles Carter, had been recalled from retirement and asked for authority to resign on the grounds of ill health. He was replaced on 17th March.

On 10th March, 20th Brigade (7th Division) started in Corps reserve south of Estaires. Early on the 11th, it pushed forward to cover a gap between 21st Brigade and 8th Division and was then ordered to take part in an attack from northeast of Ferme de Lestré towards Aubers, in cooperation with 8th Division on the right. Moving to the start line, the troops found the trenches occupied by 8th Division's reserves and much pushing and shoving took place to find shelter; some had to resort to lying down three deep. The attack commenced at 7.00 a.m. with 1st Grenadier Guards right and 2nd Gordon Highlanders left. They came under heavy enfilade fire from the left. 1st Grenadier Guards reported it was on the Layes, but had mistaken another ditch for it, and on the left, 21st Brigade was also not as far forward as reported.

Another attack was ordered for the 12th by 2nd Scots Guards right and 2nd Border left, to seize a line of redoubts just west of the Piètre road. It was postponed

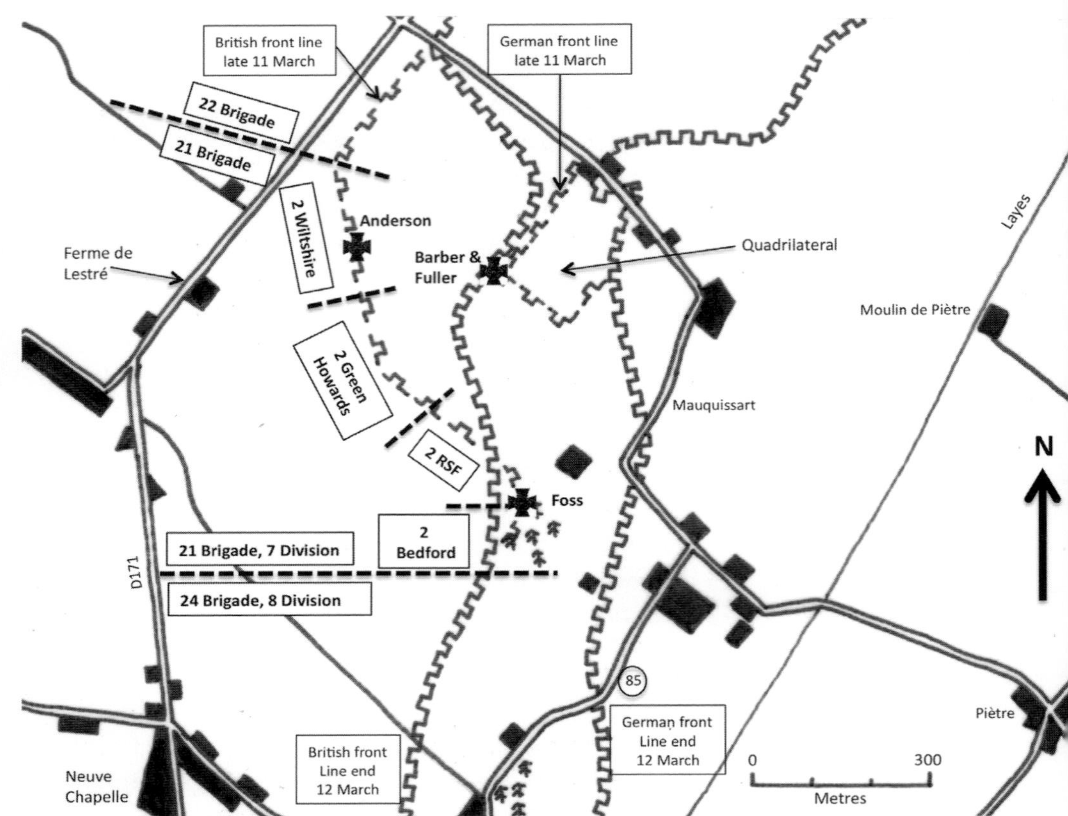

Leave Neuve Chapelle northwards on the D171 Fleurbaix road. About 550m after Ferme de Lestré turn right onto Rue des Lurons and park on the roadside. The VC actions of Edward Barber, Wilfred Fuller and William Anderson took place in the fields on the right, looking southwest back towards Neuve Chapelle. Continue for just over a kilometre around a right then a left bend. Turn next right and stop after 200m (Point 85) to look over the fields to the right towards Ferme de Lestré. Foss' VC action was in the small copse.

due to mist until 8.00 a.m., then 10.30 a.m and finally 12.30 p.m. This order did not reach the forward troops, who advanced under heavy fire from the Quadrilateral and took cover in no man's land. The artillery preparation, when it came at 11.50 a.m., was accurate and heavy. There was little resistance and the objectives west of the Piètre road were taken quickly, along with 400 prisoners.

At 12.30 p.m. 1st Grenadier Guards was ordered to continue this attack by advancing on Moulin de Piètre on the right. Moving forward at 1.30 p.m., 3 and 4 Companies came under very heavy shellfire. Progress was slow and the CO, Lieutenant Colonel L Fisher-Rowe, was killed about 4.00 p.m. (Estaires Communal Cemetery and Extension – II F 9). The Battalion lost its way in unfamiliar trenches, but eventually found the old British line. During the attack the acting CO, Major GW Duberly, was killed (Le Touret Memorial – Panel 2), and the troops were held up by their own artillery. Captain Hon R Lygon MVO took command and decided to hold where he was.

The intention was to continue on the 13th with an attack by 1st Grenadier Guards and 2nd and 1/6th Gordon Highlanders, following a night attack by 23rd

Brigade to seize houses around Point 85. This necessitated a major reorganisation and movement was very difficult. The 23rd Brigade attack failed. At daybreak only one company of 1st Grenadier Guards was in position. Other units attempted to advance, but it soon petered out. 20th Brigade was relieved during the night of 14th/15th March. The four days fighting resulted in 342 casualties for 1st Grenadier Guards, including 89 killed or died of wounds up to 17th March.

At the northern end of the offensive on 10th March, 21st Brigade (7th Division) followed 23rd Brigade (8th Division) to pass through and continue the advance to Piètre. Some progress was made, but a gap opened on the right and until it was filled further advance was not possible. Early on the 11th the Brigade was ordered to complete the advance to seize Piètre, with the left resting on Ferme de Lestré. The advance was to be conducted by three battalions in line, while 2nd Bedfordshire on the right connected with 20th Brigade. The barrage was ineffective and caused some casualties amongst 2nd Green Howards. A few minor gains were made, but the line was not advanced significantly. Units of 20th and 21st Brigades became mixed up, necessitating reorganisation during the night.

At dawn on 12th March, 2nd Green Howards was facing northeast towards Mauquissart, flanked on the left by 2nd Wiltshire and on the right by 2nd Royal Scots Fusiliers, with 2nd Bedfordshire in support on the right. After the initial attack on 10th March, nine bombers in D Company, 2nd Green Howards, led by **Corporal William Anderson**, succeeded in capturing a trench on the left of the position, taking 62 prisoners in the process. However, it was not for this action that he was awarded the VC.

The German counter-attack at dawn on the 12th failed completely against 2nd Green Howards, leaving 400-500 dead in front of the trenches. However, 2nd Royal Scots Fusiliers had a salient overrun on the right and 2nd Wiltshire was pushed back on the left. The enemy on the left were ejected at 9.30 a.m., but at 9.45 a.m. they made an attempt to infiltrate 2nd Wiltshire's front line by crawling forward through

Looking southwest from the Rue des Lurons on the northern edge of the Neuve Chapelle battlefield. The D171 Neuve Chapelle - Fleurbaix road is on the right, Ferme de Lestré is in the centre and the Quadrilateral was in the area of the trees on the left. The line held by 2nd Wiltshire on 12th March ran in front of Ferme de Lestré but beyond the trees on the left. William Anderson was in action between here and Ferme de Lestré. The 20th Brigade bombers, including Edward Barber and Wilfred Fuller fought in the area close to the trees on the left.

old communication trenches. In 2nd Green Howards, D Company's bombers and some riflemen led by Anderson went to assist, together with 20 bombers from 20th Brigade under Captain Nichol of the Grenadiers.

Anderson threw himself into the attack fearlessly. Standing on the parapet, he directed the fire of some supporting riflemen, also using his own rifle to good effect. He then jumped down into the trench and bombed along it with three of his men, all of whom were eventually wounded. As he used up the bombs he found fresh supplies from wounded comrades and threw back German stick grenades. When all the bombs were expended he used his rifle again until the Germans had been driven off. He cleared the enemy from Ferme de Lestré almost single-handed and took 60 prisoners in the process before setting off to bomb the enemy again.

The 20th Brigade bombers infiltrated forward before the bombardment ended and crossed no man's land via a disused communication trench towards the Quadrilateral. **Private Edward Barber**, a Grenadier, dashed ahead of the main body with a bag of bombs. A sniper hit the bag, igniting one of the fuses and he just managed to throw it away seconds before it exploded. Snatching another bag from a dead comrade he rushed forward again, bombing as he went. His throwing was so accurate that the enemy began surrendering in considerable numbers. By the time the rest of the attackers caught up with him, Barber had pushed forward 100m and was surrounded by over 100 prisoners; an outstanding achievement for one man. He was killed later by a sniper.

As **Lance Corporal Wilfred Fuller**, another Grenadier, advanced, he spotted a large party of Germans fleeing down a communications trench from their front line. Dashing forward he threw a bomb, killing the leading enemy soldier. The remainder immediately surrendered to Fuller, although he was alone. The Germans were taken by surprise by the bombing attack and a 40m stretch of their front line was captured. 2nd Wiltshire pushed forward two companies with a few platoons of 2nd Green Howards to expand the captured section of front line, but the attack ground to a halt 120m from the objective.

At about 10.30 a.m., 21st Brigade began a general advance following a heavy bombardment. 2nd Green Howards took one of the two redoubts still held by the Germans along with 300 prisoners. However, the advance by the rest of the Brigade made no significant progress. 2nd Green Howards suffered 311 casualties over four days, including 117 killed or died of wounds up to 20th March. William Anderson was amongst the dead and his body was never recovered.

Meanwhile, on 12th March, on the right of 21st Brigade a party of A Company, 2nd Bedfordshire tried to recover the salient lost by 2nd Royal Scots Fusiliers, which had only been taken the previous night. They rushed 135m over open ground and although a few reached the lost trench, they failed to recapture the lodgement. The Brigade Commander wanted the trench retaken and gave this order personally to **Captain Charles Foss** who, as Adjutant of 2nd Bedfordshire, had been sent to Brigade HQ to report British shells falling short and causing casualties. Foss thought he could do it with bombers. On his way back he took a section from D Company and reported to the CO (Major Onslow) to discuss his idea. Onslow agreed and told him to use his bombers to support B Company's counter-attack.

At 9.30 a.m. Foss led his party of eight bombers and a rifle platoon from B Company in single file over open ground. They started from the left flank of 2nd Northamptonshire's (8th Division) line on the right, with Foss acting as leading bayonet man for the bombers. They had a wide ditch to cross and no-one was inclined to get their feet wet. The men covered Foss while he jumped over the ditch and he then covered them as they crossed. They closed with the enemy and threw percussion grenades. It was the first time Foss had used these devices in anger. The Germans were surprised and, after a short bombing fight, 49 surrendered. Another 100 Germans sheltering in ditches and shell holes in no man's land then stood up in confusion, not sure what was going on. About 60 surrendered, but the rest retreated, many being killed in the attempt. A Company moved into the recovered trench to consolidate and during the night two machine-guns were brought into the position. The leading bomber with Foss, Private Eade, received the DCM for his part in this action. When 2nd Bedfordshire was relieved on 14th March it had sustained 198 casualties, including 44 killed or died of wounds up to 18th March.

The attack resumed early on the 13th, but the artillery was ineffective and enemy small arms fire stopped all attempts to advance. During the night, 21st Brigade was relieved, having suffered 1,144 casualties. Enemy casualties in the Brigade area were estimated at 900–1,000 killed and 450 prisoners.

At 10.05 p.m. on 12th March, Haig's orders came through to shut down the offensive. The British suffered 12,811 casualties at Neuve Chapelle (2,527 killed, 8,533 wounded and 1,751 missing). German losses may have been up to 12,000, including 1,687 prisoners. The line had been advanced 900m, the difficult salient at Port Arthur had been eradicated and the Germans had received a nasty surprise, but there had been no major success. The Germans resolved not to be caught out again and strengthened their defences all along the front. The enormous expenditure of shells by the British led to shortages later in attacks at Aubers and Festubert, where the stronger German defences required greater quantities of explosives to reduce them.

From the south, with Ferme de Lestré in the background. Charles Foss led the bombing attack across this field from the left towards the small copse on the right.

Spanbroekmolen, 12th March 1915

54 Lt Cyril Martin, 56th Field Company RE (3rd Division)

At Neuve Chapelle the British took a number of prisoners from 6th Bavarian Reserve Division. Intelligence reports placed this formation in the Ypres area and GHQ concluded the Germans were transferring reserves to reinforce the Neuve Chapelle front. Second Army was ordered to attack to prevent more troops being moved.

7th Brigade (3rd Division) was ordered to attack through the line held by 85th Brigade at Spanbroekmolen at 8.40 a.m. on 12th March, in cooperation with 5th Division on the right. This was intended as a preliminary to a further advance. Two battalions were detailed for the assault, 3rd Worcestershire (right) and 1st Wiltshire (left) with 2nd South Lancashire in support. Each assault battalion attacked with two companies. Little time was allowed for preparation. 3rd Worcestershire allocated A and C Companies for the assault, with D Company following behind to dig a new communication trench to link the British front line to the gains and B Company to consolidate the new line.

57th Field Company was responsible for positioning a number of 5m long trench bridges and cutting gaps in the British barbed wire. It was also to bring forward 450m of knife rest barbed wire entanglements and commence digging communications trenches from the front line to link up with the captured German trenches.

56th Field Company RE initially acted as guides to the battalions as they moved up from billets around Locre. A rendezvous was made at Kemmel crossroads at 3.05 a.m. by 3 and 4 Sections, who attached themselves to 1st Wiltshire, while 1 and 2 Sections guided 3rd Worcestershire from Lindenhoek. The newly dug, shallow and waterlogged assembly trenches behind the front line were occupied by 5.45 a.m. Mist interfered with the British artillery programme, so the attack was delayed until 4.10 p.m., with the artillery recommencing at 2.20 p.m. The assault troops sheltered as best they could from the enemy artillery, which became more accurate as the mist cleared. **Lieutenant Cyril Martin**, commanding 2 Section, was to accompany 3rd Worcestershire to improve gaps cut in the enemy wire by the artillery, block communication trenches to the front and flanks against counter-attacks, assist the infantry in reversing captured trenches and ready them for defence.

The attack took place over muddy ground and the leading companies were hit by heavy fire. Many men were shot down crossing flying bridges over the front line opposite gaps cut in the British wire the previous night. Very few managed to get through the enemy wire, which the artillery had failed to cut. 3rd Worcestershire was particularly troubled by a machine-gun at the pond on the right (near the CWGC cemetery), but a party under 2nd Lieutenant Holland (Dorsetshire Regiment attached 3rd Worcestershire) took a short stretch of trench and held it with 40 men.

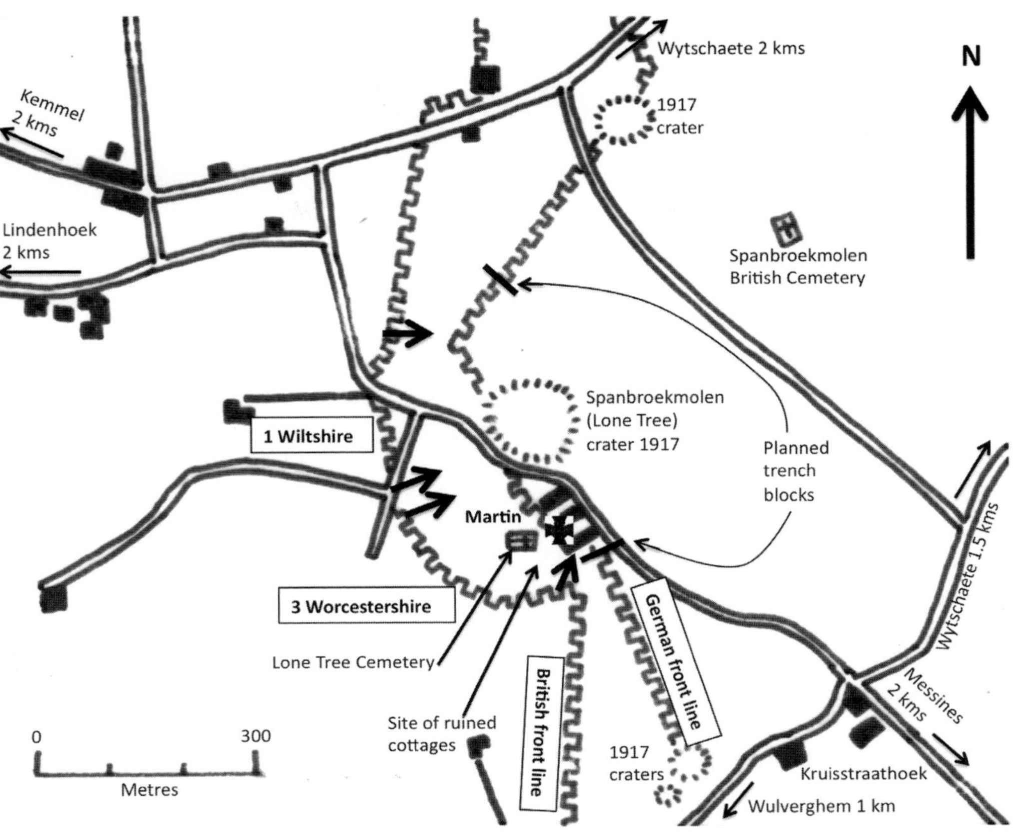

The area of the 7th Brigade attack on 12th March 1915 is largely unchanged except for the enormous Spanbroekmolen mine crater (Pool of Peace) created on 7th June 1917. The mine completely obliterated the top of the hill and the mill. There are a few places to park along the roadside around the crater, but this favourite stop for battlefield tours can get busy.

Martin was wounded early on, but made light of it and led his party of sixteen sappers with 2nd Corporal Skinner against a section of trench, routing the enemy by skilful bomb throwing. They joined up with Holland's party and Martin set his men to work reversing the parapet and strengthening the captured position. A little further to the right another party of about 25 men of 3rd Worcestershire broke into the enemy lines and seized a group of ruined houses. However, the remainder of the two assault companies were halted in no man's land with heavy casualties. 1st Wiltshire's attack on the left failed completely and the survivors were back in their own lines at 5.25 p.m.

Very quickly the Germans launched counter-attacks against the two Worcestershire parties. The situation was not improved by being shelled by the British artillery, which wiped out the party in the ruined houses. Corporal Mansell of 3rd Worcestershire was awarded a Bar to his DCM for crossing no man's land with a message to stop the British artillery fire. He was wounded three times but, having delivered his message, insisted on returning. The Germans came on against

From 3rd Worcestershire's left boundary with 1st Wiltshire. Spanbroekmolen (Lone Tree) Crater dominates the skyline surrounded by bushes and trees. 3rd Worcestershire attacked up this slope from right to left on 12th March 1915. The section of trench held by Cyril Martin was amongst the farm buildings to the right of which is Lone Tree Cemetery. The pond from where the German machine-gun caused heavy casualties to 3rd Worcestershire is amongst the trees in front of the cemetery.

Message from CO 3rd Worcestershire to HQ 7th Brigade requesting authority to withdraw the party in the German trenches that included Cyril Martin.

"A" Form. Army Form C. 21

MESSAGES AND SIGNALS. No. of Message

Prefix Code m. Words Charge

Office of Origin and Service Instructions.

Sent At m. To By

This message is on a/c of: Service.

(Signature of "Franking Officer.")

Recd. at 6.57P Date 12.3.15 From WO By JHR.

TO 7th Bde

Sender's Number	Day of Month	In reply to Number	AAA
* XXX B.	12th		

I have 40 men and 3 officers 2 of them wounded in German trenches just to left front of E 2 AAA Germans established on both sides Shall I withdraw them if possible AAA They are in an untenable position I understand

the remaining party in what appeared to be overwhelming numbers. However, they held the position for another two and a half hours.

As darkness fell, Sergeant Ince and Private Wootton of 3rd Worcestershire went back with a report on the situation. As a result the Brigade Commander ordered the support battalion to remain where it was and a little later the 3rd Worcestershire party was withdrawn rather than risk more unnecessary casualties. Having removed the wounded, the survivors pulled back at 6.30 p.m. In addition to Martin's VC and Mansell's DCM, five other members of the party received the DCM. The raid cost 3rd Worcestershire 180 casualties, including 83 killed. 56th Field Company lost nine men killed.

Messines, 12th April 1915

55 Pte Robert Morrow, 1st Royal Irish Fusiliers (10th Infantry Brigade, 4th Division)

In early April 1915 the Germans were preparing a major offensive in Flanders (Second Battle of Ypres). Although there was little fighting at this time, the Germans used their artillery superiority to make life as miserable as possible for the British. Their guns were active on 12th April while 1st Royal Irish Fusiliers was preparing to be relieved by 5th Royal Warwickshire (143rd Brigade, 48th Division). At 5.00 p.m. a heavy bombardment opened, with the first salvo falling harmlessly northwest of Dead Cow Farm. The Germans had excellent observation positions on Messines Ridge and the range was shortened until shells were falling into D Company's trenches immediately south of the River Douve.

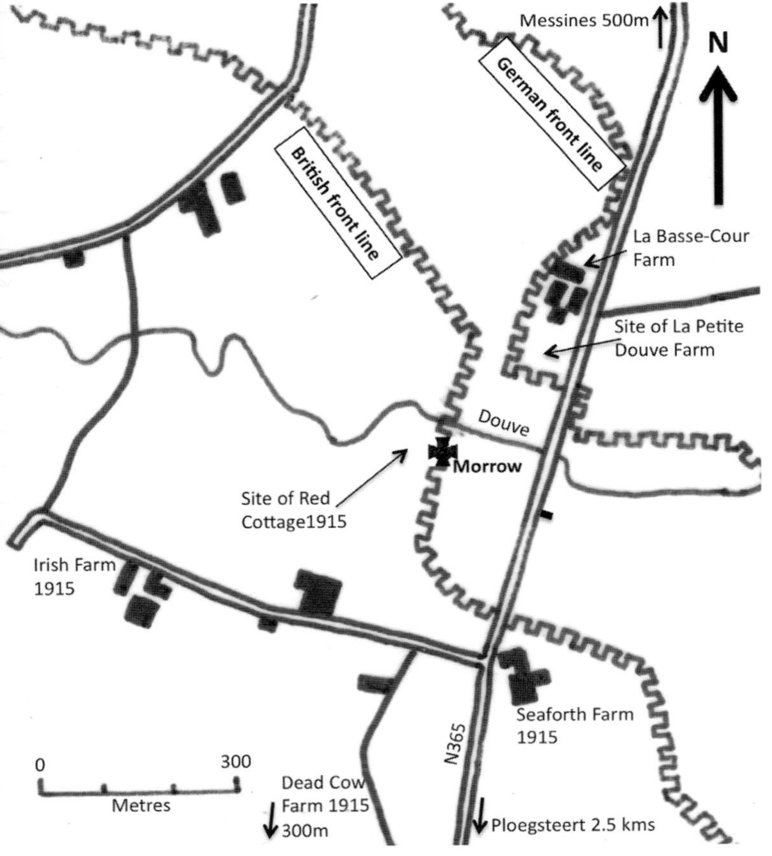

The site of Robert Morrow's VC action should be approached from the N365 Ploegsteert - Messines road. From the north (Messines) cross the Douve and after 300m turn right opposite a farm on the left. Morrow's action took place in the field on the right. There is no exit straight on, but plenty of turning places along this road. There are a number of restaurants and cafes in Ploegsteert three kilometres to the south. You can see the names of the six men killed in the shelling on 12th April on the Ploegsteert Memorial – Privates John Jackson, William Watson, Bernard Gray, Frank Alderman, James Murphy and Christopher Whelehan.

The Fusiliers pulled back to the comparative safety of the support line, but five men had been killed and others were trapped under the debris of the collapsed front line trench. Despite the shelling, **Private Robert Morrow** in D Company went forward to assist the injured and free those buried alive. He reached the destroyed trench, dragged one of his comrades out of the earth and then took him to the support line. Morrow returned to the front line trench again and again, rescuing a man on each occasion and bringing him back to safety. The Battalion was relieved later the same day.

Looking north from the area of 1st Royal Irish Fusiliers' support line on 12th April 1915. On the right is the tree lined N365 Ploegsteert - Messines road, descending to the crossing over the Douve in front of La Basse-Cour Farm in the centre, where an unexploded mine from 1917 still lies. La Petit Douve Farm in 1915 was between La Basse-Cour and the Douve. The road rises to Messines, with its church prominent on the skyline. Adolf Hitler was treated in the crypt when wounded in late 1914. Above the left of Petit Douve Farm is the Island of Ireland Peace Park with its distinctive tower. Slightly right of the leftmost prominent tree on the banks of the Douve is the New Zealand Division Memorial. Robert Morrow rescued his buried and wounded comrades in front of these trees and carried them back towards the camera position.

Morrow already had a reputation for bravery. On a previous occasion he took an empty rum jar to a farm behind the front line to fill it with water. He avoided injury, although under fire all the way there and back. Just as he got back to the trench a bullet shattered the rum jar. Undeterred he collected a number of water bottles and went back to fill them instead. Some time after his VC action, he again went for water at the farm on a very windy day. The only structure of the farmhouse remaining was the brick chimney. As he was passing it, the stack collapsed due to the force of the wind and missed him by a few inches.

Morrow never knew of his award. He was mortally wounded by a shell splinter in the head at St Julien on 25th April while carrying the wounded to safety.

Petit Douve Farm in October 1915 from the British front line about where Robert Morrow rescued his comrades the previous April. The line of the road to Messines can be seen left of the farm ruins. Barbed wire stakes are in the foreground and the trees, which mark the line of the Douve, are related to those in the previous picture.

Capture of Hill 60, Zwarteleen, near Ypres, 20th – 21st April 1915

56 Pte Edward Dwyer, 1st East Surrey (14th Brigade, 5th Division)
57 2nd Lt Benjamin Geary, 1st East Surrey (14th Brigade, 5th Division)
58 Lt George Roupell, 1st East Surrey (14th Brigade, 5th Division)
59 2nd Lt Geoffrey Woolley, 9th London (Queen Victoria's Rifles) (13th Brigade, 5th Division)

The spoil from the 19th century construction of the Ypres – Comines railway cutting near Zwarteleen formed three artificial hillocks; Hill 60 north of the cutting and the Caterpillar and the Dump to the south. Only the Dump was in British hands. The importance of these features, particularly Hill 60, lay in the all round observation they

It is difficult to believe that 3,000 casualties were suffered by the British alone in an area barely 200m square. Hill 60 is cared for by the CWGC and the Caterpillar on the other side of the railway cutting was taken over by the Province of West Flanders in 2001. If possible, use the car park at the 14th (Light) Division Memorial (moved from Railway Wood in 1978), but it can become very busy here with coach parties. Close by are two other memorials – 1st Australian Tunnelling Company, which shows shrapnel damage from WW2 and by the bridge to two resistance fighters killed in October 1944. The Queen Victoria's Rifles memorial on top of the Hill was damaged deliberately by the Germans in WW2 and the original stone mounting lost. From it can be seen most of the area fought over in April 1915. The café across the road opens daily 1030-1900, except Monday 1500-1900.

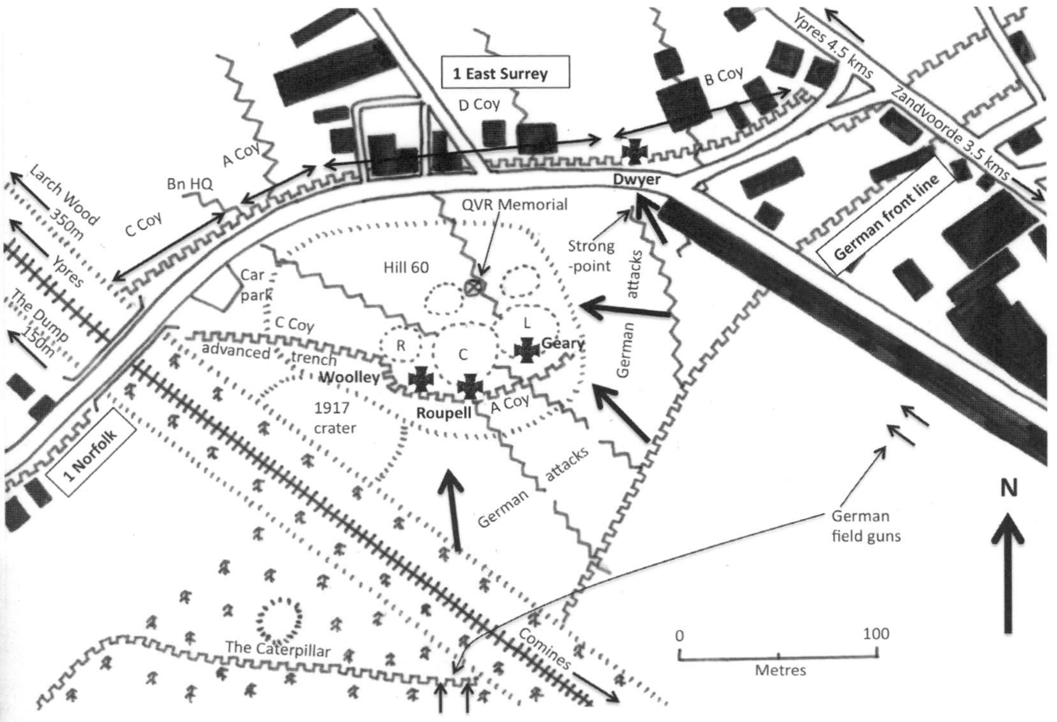

afforded over the flat Flanders plain, allowing German artillery observers to dominate the Ypres salient. Ironically before the war Hill 60 was known as 'Cote des Amants' (Lovers' Knoll). Planning to regain the Hill from the Germans began as soon as the British took over the sector from the French in early 1915.

The view from the 14th (Light) Division Memorial gives an idea of the importance of Hill 60, with its uninterrupted views over Ypres. Elsewhere around Hill 60 buildings and trees now obscure the view.

Mining under the Hill was fraught with difficulties, as it consisted of a mixture of soil, sand, clay and quicksand, but the British persevered. On 17th February 1915 the first British mine of the war was fired, using tunnels started by French. Major mining operations commenced in March, with the construction of three tunnels (M1-M3). The miners faced numerous hazards including heat, tunnel collapses, countermining, camouflet charges and gas, as well as the unpleasant business of uncovering numerous bodies. By 15th April, five chambers had been charged with guncotton blocks as follows:

Rear pair – 2000 lbs each.
Forward pair – 2700 lbs each.
Right – only 500 lbs to avoid detection as it was close to German workings.

On 16th April, 13th Brigade took over the line. 1st Royal West Kent was to seize Hill 60 and 2nd King's Own Scottish Borderers was also in the front line, with 2nd Duke of Wellingtons in support near Zillebeke Lake and 2nd King's Own Yorkshire Light Infantry in reserve.

17th April was quiet until 7.05 p.m. when over ten seconds the five mines were exploded. Debris was thrown up 100m and out to 300m, shattering the defences of 172nd Infantry Regiment, killing 150 German soldiers and altering the shape of the ground. Two British sappers were also killed. A massive bombardment by 15th and

Hill 60 on the left and the Caterpillar on the right from the Dump, behind the British front line in 1915. The bridge over the railway cutting in the centre has been replaced, but is in the same position.

The northern slope of Hill 60, falling away to the road, which was the front line in April 1915. The Queen Victoria's Rifles memorial is on the extreme right. The attack swept up this slope following the mine explosions on the evening of 17th April 1915.

27th Field Artillery Brigades, 9th Heavy Artillery Brigade, plus two French and three Belgian batteries followed.

Under cover of the bombardment, C Company, 1st Royal West Kent and 1/2nd Home Counties Field Company RE attacked with bugles playing. Complete surprise was achieved and 50-60 German survivors were bayoneted, shot or captured. Within 15 minutes the position was being consolidated for the loss of just seven casualties. B Company, 1st Royal West Kent, two companies of 2nd King's Own Scottish Borderers and the Machine Gun Section of Queen Victoria's Rifles (9th London) followed.

There is evidence that the survivors of the mines fled from ruptured chlorine gas cylinders, positioned for a German attack some days later. Over the next few days British units reported asphyxiating gas on a number of occasions, probably from cylinders cracked by the mine explosions and shelling, rather than deliberate German use. The first acknowledged use of gas by the Germans was eight days away.

From 10.00 p.m. the German artillery grew in intensity, with fifty-four gun positions firing on Hill 60. By 2.30 a.m. a new trench had been dug, connecting old trenches on the flanks. Early next morning the German artillery lifted onto the support lines and a series of counterattacks began. The defenders had few flares and had to fight in the dark with bombs and bayonets. When 2nd King's Own Scottish Borderers went to relieve 1st Royal West Kent, it coincided with another German attack. The main pressure was on the two large craters, which were held, but the battle swayed back and forth all day.

At 8.30 a.m., 2nd Duke of Wellingtons arrived to relieve the remnants of 1st Royal West Kent (50% casualties) and 2nd King's Own Scottish Borderers. All movement was extremely hazardous. The Germans regained the sector on the right near the railway cutting, leaving the British holding a small salient on the summit. At 6.00 p.m. two companies each of 2nd Duke of Wellington's and 2nd King's Own Scottish Borderers attacked. They suffered heavy losses, but an enemy trench was seized and an hour later another charge recovered the whole of the top of the Hill, which 59th Field Company RE helped to consolidate. Hand to hand fighting continued, with grenades being exchanged from a few metres. The men were exhausted, but the Germans had been broken temporarily.

On the night of 18/19th April, 15th Brigade (with 1st East Surrey attached from 14th Brigade), relieved 13th Brigade (less Queen Victoria's Rifles) in the forward trenches. The relieving troops found a shocking scene of devastation. A spade could not be put into the earth anywhere without uncovering human remains. They found the mine craters arranged in two rows. In the front row were two large and slightly overlapping craters, with a smaller one on the right. In the second row two small craters lay directly behind the large ones in the front row. An advanced trench (previously the German support line) ran along the southern edge of the front row, but did not connect with the unit on the left and consequently this flank was dangerously exposed. The front line ran behind the craters, following the line of the road from Zwarteleen over the railway cutting.

During the 19th, 1st East Surrey cleared the trenches and improved the defences. There was a German strongpoint with steel loopholes only 20m away on the left; anyone who popped up was instantly shot at. The Germans shelled all day, but at 5.00 p.m. this intensified and more damage was caused. A and C Companies, left and right respectively, each had two platoons in the advanced trench, with the remainder in the front line. The rest of the front line on the left was occupied by D Company and three platoons of B Company. The Queen Victoria's Rifles moved up in close support.

By dawn most of the damage from the previous evening had been repaired, but continuous pressure was applied, particularly on the left, from the German strongpoint. At about 3.00 p.m. an attack developed against B Company's right from the strongpoint. During this action **Private Edward Dwyer** found himself alone with the Germans, so close he could hear them speaking. He realised that if the trench fell the whole position might be lost. Collecting all the bombs he could find and disregarding the enemy fire, he climbed onto the parapet and flung bomb after bomb into the German strongpoint. Showers of grenades were returned, but the enemy was so unnerved by Dwyer's steadiness that their throwing was inaccurate. The brief respite allowed Dwyer's comrades to get back into the trench, man the parapet and drive off the attackers. Dwyer had already distinguished himself earlier in the day by leaving the trench to attend to the wounded under heavy shellfire.

From behind the British front line. Edward Dwyer's position was at the bus shelter at the end of the fence on the left, with the German strongpoint on the far side of the road. Hill 60 is in the centre background.

At 4.00 p.m. the Germans began a furious bombardment, causing many casualties and smashing the defences again. To add to the confusion, all telephone cables were cut, Battalion Headquarters was hit and the CO, Lieutenant Colonel Walter Paterson was killed (Bedford House Cemetery – Encl2 VA39). The Battalion War Diary records that some of the shells gave off lachrymatory gas.

The two A Company platoons, commanded by **Lieutenant George Roupell,** in the advanced trench were very badly shaken, particularly on the right, and had to be reinforced by another A Company platoon. Many men were buried and the trench was all but destroyed. During a lull in the bombardment, Roupell went to the rear to have his wounds dressed. Although the MO tried to persuade him to go to hospital, he insisted on going back to his men.

At 5.00 p.m. the German artillery lifted onto the support lines and an attack emerged from the railway cutting near the Caterpillar. It was halted by heavy artillery and machine-gun fire from both sides of the cutting. A Company in the advanced trench was also attacked from the German sap on the left. The situation there was so desperate that the defenders resorted to throwing back German grenades before they exploded. Another attack behind the open left flank against the left crater threatened to isolate A Company from D Company in the front line, before it too was halted.

At 5.45 p.m. Major Allason (1st Bedfordshire) arrived at the foot of the Hill with reinforcements and assumed local command of all troops, including 1st East Surrey. He sent a party to reinforce Roupell, but it couldn't get through. In the left crater a platoon of C Company, led by **2nd Lieutenant Benjamin Geary,** was joined by some of 1st Bedfordshire and he took command of the composite force. More reinforcements arrived from A and D Companies, but the Germans kept up the pressure, pouring rifle fire and grenades into the advanced positions. Desperate fighting followed, during which Corporal Frederick Adams fought his machine-gun alone for 30 minutes with part of his jaw shot away, until he was shot through the head and killed (Menin Gate Memorial).

The two left craters were between here and the Queen Victoria's Rifles memorial in the left distance. There is nothing of them to see today. Benjamin Geary was particularly active in this area. Edward Dwyer saved his section of trench falling into German hands in the low ground behind the tallest tree in the centre.

A Company in the advanced trench was being weakened by the minute, but managed to hold on. The Germans attacked continuously, preceding each rush with a shower of grenades, but each attempt was driven off by rapid rifle fire inspired by Roupell's determination to hang on. As darkness fell and the intensity of the fighting slackened slightly, Roupell went back to explain the situation to Lieutenant Colonel Griffiths, CO 1st Bedfordshire. He had his eight wounds dressed again before returning to the advanced trench. Meanwhile the Germans continued to attack and gained entry into the left of the A Company advanced trench. However, most of this trench continued to be held by the combined force of Bedfordshires and East Surreys.

From the area of the forward left crater looking west over where the forward middle and right craters were in 1915. This is where George Roupell and Geoffrey Woolley earned their VCs. A veteran of WW2 (the author's father-in-law) contemplates the devastation of a previous world conflict.

Throughout the night attacks were also made against the left crater by Germans using old communications trenches to close with the British positions. On each occasion Geary rallied his men and drove off the attackers, exposing himself throughout the action in order to gain a better view of the enemy. When not organising the defence, he used a rifle and grenades to good effect. For an hour, with the Germans only 10m away, he poured rapid fire down one of the communication trenches while Private White loaded rifles for him. As the night progressed the left crater filled with dead and wounded.

Later in the evening Geary went along the line to check how the men were faring. He met the officers in the advanced trench and they agreed to hang on for as long as possible. On the way back he ran into a party of A Company, Queen Victoria's Rifles, led by Major Thomas P Lees, on their way to rush the portion of the advanced trench occupied by the Germans. Arrangements were made for the men in the left crater to cooperate in this attack. Geary then organised the digging of a new trench behind the centre crater to neutralise the Germans who had penetrated into this crater and were firing into the backs of the defenders of the left crater.

While in this position a flare revealed to Geary the Germans holding part of the British advanced trench. Taking a rifle he shot a number of them and, with other men joining him, they soon cleared the trench. Geary made his way back towards his own position and met a Queen Victoria's Rifles party bringing forward ammunition, but they did not know where to take it. Having led them into the left crater, where supplies were required urgently, he went to find out what had happened to the Queen Victoria's Rifles attack, as he had not seen the agreed signal. The fire directed by Geary had already cleared the objective of the enemy, although they were still close in the communications trench, throwing grenades. Returning to the left crater, Geary discovered that matters were getting worse and shortly before dawn he went back for reinforcements. On the way he was severely wounded, losing his left eye, and could not return to the firing line.

The Queen Victoria's Rifles party met by Geary was one of two companies sent forward at 9.30 p.m. to reinforce the top of the Hill. They took two hours to cover 200m because of the heavy crossfire on the exposed hillside. The company was ordered to dig in near the large craters to support the troops in the advanced trench. Around midnight, 17 men were ordered to charge over the remaining 20m to the top of Hill 60 to fill a gap that had opened due to casualties in the advanced trench; only six made it. They hung on for a few minutes, but their position was hopeless and they were forced to withdraw.

Only one third of the two Queen Victoria's Rifles companies remained, but they hung on, resisting all efforts to shift them. Just before dawn the 30 survivors were surprised to see **2nd Lieutenant Geoffrey Woolley** making his way calmly up the Hill towards them. Almost by a miracle he avoided the fearful fire sweeping the slope and jumped into the trench. It was known that supplies on the Hill were short, so Woolley had been ordered to take the support platoons (7 and 8) forward with ammunition boxes from Larch Wood dugouts. Having handed over the ammunition. Woolley went to get a report from Major Lees of A Company and then took advantage of a lull in the fighting to set off back. In the support line a heavy barrage was falling prior to another counter-attack. Major Allason ordered Woolley to take the support platoons forward again, but cancelled this when he realised the carrying party had no rifles and sent them back to Larch Wood.

However, Woolley went back to the craters where he discovered that Major Lees was dead (Menin Gate Memorial). He found plenty of jam tin bombs but no-one was using them. Borrowing a box of matches from Lieutenant Summerhays, he commenced lobbing bombs over the parapet while others spotted for him. Soon he was the only officer left in both craters. Runners brought up more bombs and the fight continued. They were hit by enfilade machine-gun fire, including one slightly in their rear, trench mortars, grenade throwers and field guns only 300m away, blasting the parapet to pieces. The line wavered, but 20 men of 1st Bedfordshire in support charged and the line held. British guns came forward to silence the Germans for a while. Woolley was ordered to pull the survivors out, but refused to do so until properly relieved. A grenade hit him on the head and exploded, but the main force seems to have gone upwards and, although stunned, he was not seriously injured. Throughout the enemy artillery continued to fire at point blank range from across the railway cutting.

Attacks against Roupell's men in A Company also continued throughout the night. About 11.00 p.m. he went back to bring up a party of reinforcements from 1st Bedfordshire. The situation eased somewhat when the Germans were pushed out of the left end of the advanced trench, but the hard-pressed defenders still had to endure three or four more attacks in as many hours. After midnight a message was received from Brigade HQ concerned that the Battalion was withdrawing. The response went back, "*We have not budged a yard, and have no intention whatever of doing so*".

At 6.00 a.m. on 21st April, 1st East Surrey handed over to 1st Devonshire and withdrew singing ragtime songs, to Kruisstraat, southwest of Ypres; the Battalion had suffered 279 casualties. Woolley's party was also relieved by 1st Devonshire. With 14 other survivors of the four officers and 150 men who had gone up the Hill the previous evening, Woolley went back to Larch Wood, where he slept for 24 hours. Fighting gradually subsided on Hill 60 during the afternoon. By then it was unrecognisable. Trenches had disappeared in a mass of craters and shell holes with corpses lying everywhere.

On 1st May, chlorine gas was released against the Hill causing 204 casualties, but there was no attack. Early on the morning of 5th May, gas was released again and the British were forced to give up Hill 60 in the subsequent German attack. By then it had cost 5th Division over 3,000 casualties. It would be 7th June 1917, during the Battle of Messines, before British soldiers stood on Hill 60 again.

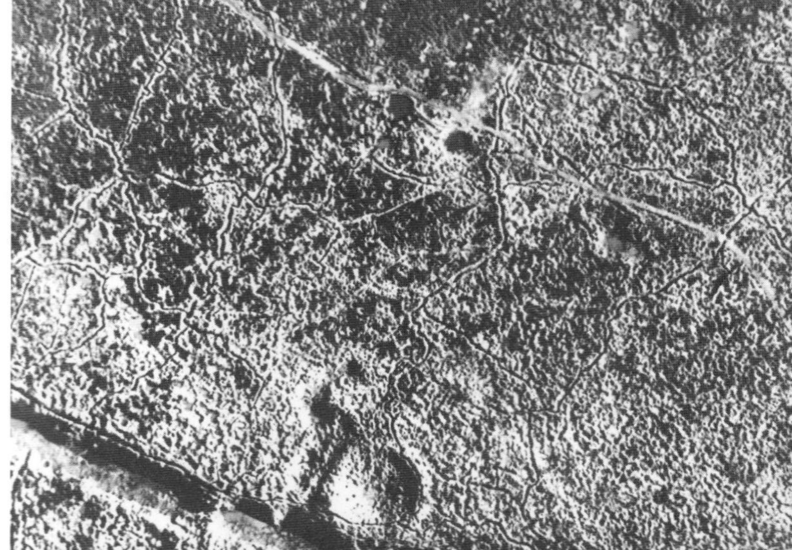

Aerial photograph taken in late 1917. The 7th June 1917 mine crater is alongside the railway cutting with the remains of the bridge to the left. Shelling has obliterated the 1915 craters.

Biographies

10694 PRIVATE ABRAHAM ACTON
2nd Battalion, The Border Regiment

Abraham Acton was born at 2 Tyson's Court, behind Roper Street, Whitehaven, Cumberland on 17th December 1892. His father was Robert Acton (1865-1940), a fisherman and mariner (Second Class Certificate No 7686), who served in the Royal Engineers (Inland Waterways and Docks) from 28th February 1917 (No 258839 and later WR/300579 or 310579). He was promoted Lance Corporal on 6th May, Acting Corporal the following day, Acting Sergeant on 9th May and Acting CSM on 1st July 1917. He was discharged on 22nd March 1918 unfit for further service. Abraham's mother was Elizabeth Eleanor née Armstrong (1868-1944). Robert and Elizabeth were married at Holy Trinity, Whitehaven on 23rd July 1890. Abraham had five brothers, six sisters and a half sister. His paternal grandparents came from Ireland.

Abraham was educated at Crosthwaite Memorial School 10th May 1899 – April 1906 and also attended West Strand Mission Sunday School. He was then employed as a general labourer by United Steel at No 10 Colliery, Lowca, Whitehaven. Abraham was a member of the Juvenile Orange Lodge of England and became the first Orangeman to win the VC in the War.

He enlisted in 5th Border (TF), transferred to Regular service with the 2nd Battalion on 17th January 1914 and went to France with his unit on 25th November. **Awarded the VC for his actions at Rouges Bancs, France on 21st December 1914, LG 18th February 1915.** 2nd Border was involved in the 1914 Christmas truce. **Mentioned in Sir John French's Despatch dated 14th January 1915, LG 17th February 1915.** Sir John French presented the VC ribbon to him in France, but the date is not known. Before the VC could be presented, Abraham was killed in action at Festubert, France on 16th May 1915 and is commemorated on the Le Touret Memorial, France.

Abraham never married, but is understood to have been engaged to Kitty, who waited seven years in vain for him to return. The VC was presented to his parents by the King at Buckingham Palace on 29th November 1916. They moved to the Isle of Man in 1932. Abraham is commemorated in a number of places:

- St James's Church War Memorial, Whitehaven.
- Plaque on Roper Street, Whitehaven, dedicated on 21st September 1994.
- Crosthwaite School Memorial, Whitehaven.
- St Matthew's Church, Douglas, Isle of Man.
- Douglas War Memorial, Isle of Man.
- Acton Court, Whitehaven, completed in March 2006 on the site of Whitehaven Castle.
- A portrait by John Dalzell Kenworthy, painted in 1916, hangs in The Beacon, Whitehaven.

In addition to the VC, Abraham Acton was awarded the 1914 Star, British War Medal 1914-20 and Victory Medal 1914-19 with Mentioned-in-Despatches oak-leaf. The medals were donated by his brother Charles to Whitehaven in October 1951 and they are held at The Beacon, West Strand, Whitehaven. Other members of Abraham's family also served in the military:

Brother Charles Lister Acton served in 42nd Battery, 15th (Isle of Man) Light Anti-Aircraft Regiment, Royal Artillery (Manx Regiment) in the Second World War. He is reputed to have married Agnes Ross, the sister of one of the two men rescued by Abraham Acton and James Smith, but the family say there is no truth in this; Ross is a common local name. Charles presented a trophy for piano to the Manx Music Festival.

Brother Harold Armstrong Acton also served in the Royal Artillery.

Nephew Abraham Acton Parr served in the Royal Navy as an Ordinary Telegraphist (P/JX232112) and was awarded the DSM for bravery and resource while in forward observation posts in Italy under heavy fire, LG 8th February 1944.

Abraham Acton's cousins George (left) and William Acton were two of the 37 men lost when SS *Empire Leopard* was torpedoed and sunk in the North Atlantic on 2nd November 1942 (Mrs Enid McConnell née Acton).

Cousins Able Seamen George and William Acton were lost when SS *Empire Leopard* was torpedoed and sunk by *U-402* on 2nd November 1942. They are commemorated on the Tower Hill Memorial, London.

MAJOR ERNEST WRIGHT ALEXANDER
119th Battery, Royal Field Artillery

Ernest Alexander was born at 4 Devonshire Road, Toxteth Park, Liverpool, Lancashire on 2nd October 1870. His father Robert (c.1837-1911) was from Belfast and moved to Liverpool in the 1850s to become a shipbroker and manager with Young, Liston & Co of Castle Street. He established his own shipping company, Robert Alexander & Co, at 19 Tower Buildings, North Water Street, Liverpool and by 1870 had bought or leased over 20 vessels for passenger and cargo services to Australia and India. In 1868 he founded the Sun Shipping Company for the India trade at 17 Tower Buildings. All his vessels were named after stately homes ending with Hall and in 1899 he changed the group's name to Hall Line. On 1st September 1901 he sold Hall Line to John R Ellerman for £434,000 and it became the Ellerman Hall Line. Robert was also a director of the Suez Canal Company. He lived at The Hayes, Woolton, Liverpool and later at 13 Abercromby Square, Liverpool, close to where the parents of Theodore Wright VC and Noel Chavasse VC & Bar lived at various times. Ernest's mother was Annie née Gregg from Ireland. She was born c.1841 and died in the period 1901-11. Ernest had four brothers and a sister.

Ernest was educated at Cherbourg House Preparatory School at Malvern 1876–81, privately at home 1881-84 and at Harrow 1884-87, where he was a member of the Rifle Corps. He entered the Royal Military Academy Woolwich in January 1888 and was commissioned on 27th July 1889. Posted to 9th Battery RFA at Fort Bovisand, Plymouth and later to Pembroke Dock. Promoted Lieutenant 27th July 1892. He served in India 1892-1900 with 60th Battery at Barrackpore, Rawalpindi, Mooltan, Allahabad and Kamptee. Promoted Captain on 26th December 1899. Posted to No 1 Depot, Aldershot, Hampshire.

Ernest married Rose née Newcome (1883-1935) on 1st September 1903 at her family home, Aldershot Manor. Rose was the daughter of Major Henry George Newcome RA (1846-95), who served in Egypt in 1882 and was a member of HM Bodyguard to the Royal Household. She was first cousin once removed to Ross Lowis Mangles VC. One of her brothers was in the Royal Navy and two brothers served in the Army:

> Major General Henry William Newcome CB CMG DSO was Brigadier-General Royal Artillery 21st Division May 1917 – November 1918. He was first

Commandant of the School of Artillery at Larkhill 1918-22, where Newcome Hall was named after him, and Colonel-Commandant Royal Artillery 1938-45.

Major George Newcome, 130th (King George's Own) Baluchis (Jacob's Rifles), who died on 11th March 1916 and is buried in Taveta Military Cemetery, Kenya (IX A 3).

Ernest and Rose lived initially at Chichester House, Chichester Place, Kemptown, Brighton, Sussex. They had four children – Annie and Robert born in India on 22nd May 1904 and 7th June 1905 respectively, George William born in Ireland on 30th June 1911 (died in Ireland 2nd June 1914) and Mary, whose birth on 15th February 1918 was registered at Farnham, Hampshire.

The family returned to India, where Ernest served with 79th Battery at Cawnpore, Barrackpore and Umballa 1st October 1903 – 25th June 1906. Promoted Major 25th April 1906 and served at No 6 and then No 3 Depot, Seaforth, Lancashire. He took command of 119th Battery, XXVII Brigade RFA at Ballincollig, Co Cork, Ireland in 1911 and was attached to Newbridge Artillery Barracks in Co Kildare; the family lived at Martinstown, near the Curragh.

Ernest embarked with his Battery at Dublin on 4th August 1914 and disembarked in France on 20th August 1914. **He was awarded the VC for his actions at Elouges, Belgium on 24th August 1914, LG 18th February 1915. Mentioned in Field Marshal Sir John French's Despatch dated 8th October 1914, LG 19th October 1914 (duplicated 20th October and reissued 9th December 1914).** Appointed Commander XXII Brigade RFA in 7th Division on 5th October and promoted Lieutenant Colonel on 30th October 1914. He later commanded XXVII Brigade RFA in 5th Division. **Awarded CMG 3rd June 1915, LG 23rd June 1915.** His VC was presented by the King at Buckingham Palace on 12th July 1915. Promoted Temporary Brigadier-General and appointed BGRA 15th Division on 25th August 1915. Appointed BGRA XV Corps 22nd April 1916 – 11th March 1917. Brevet Colonel 1st January 1917. Appointed BGRA XI Corps 31st May 1917 – 8th April 1918. Promoted Temporary Major General and GOC 38th Division on 23rd October 1917. Reverted to BGRA XI Corps 16th November 1917 – 1st April 1918 as Temporary Brigadier-General. Promoted Temporary Major General and appointed MGRA First Army 9th April 1918 – 23rd March 1919.

Major General Ernest Alexander summer 1918 (Jean Crichton).

During the war he received a number of other honours and awards – CB, LG 1st January 1919; Croix de Guerre (France), LG 21st August 1919; Cavalier of the Military Order of Savoy 5th Class (Italy), LG 12th September 1918 and Grand Officer of the Military Order of Aviz 2nd Class (Portugal), LG 21st August 1919. He was Mentioned another 10 times in:

Sir John French's Despatches dated:

> 14th January 1915 (XXVII Brigade RFA), LG 17th February 1915; 31st May 1915 (XXII Brigade RFA), LG 22nd June 1915; 30th November 1915 (twice), LG 1st January 1916.

Sir Douglas Haig's Despatches dated:

> 30th April 1916, LG 15th June 1916; 13th November 1916, LG 4th January 1917; 8th November 1918, LG 20th December 1918; 16th March 1919, LG 5th July 1919; 21st March 1919, LG 10th April 1919.

Sir Herbert Plumer's Despatch dated:

> 18th April 1918, LG 30th May 1918.

Despite his seniority, Ernest had to revert to Lieutenant Colonel on 24th March 1919. Promoted Colonel 2nd June 1919 with seniority from 30th October 1918. Half-pay 2nd-7th June 1919. Promoted Temporary Brigadier-General 8th June 1919 and appointed to command Royal Artillery 2nd Division, Southern Area, Aldershot Command. His wife, Rose Alexander, was awarded the OBE as Chairman and Honorary Organiser of the Aldershot War Hospital Supply Depot, LG 30th March 1920.

Ernest retired on 1st October 1920 as Honorary Major General. He settled at Horswell House, South Milton, Kingsbridge, Devon where he employed three men on the estate who were with him at Elouges. He became a JP in 1922. Having attained the age limit he ceased to belong to the Reserve of Officers on 2nd October 1925. Appointed Deputy Lieutenant Devon 17th July 1931.

Ernest Alexander died following an operation at The South Hams Hospital, Kingsbridge on 25th August 1934. He was cremated at Putney Vale, London and his ashes placed in the family grave at Putney Vale Cemetery (AB 149), where Alexander Way was named after him. His batman of 28 years, Gunner T Williams, attended the funeral. In his will he left £91,815/17/1 with net personalty £86,425 on which estate duty of £27,194 was paid.

In addition to the decorations already mentioned he was awarded the 1914 Star with 'Mons' clasp, British War Medal 1914-20, Victory Medal 1914-19 with

Mentioned-in-Despatches oak-leaf and King Edward VII Coronation Medal 1902. His medals passed to his son Robert on the understanding he would donate them to the Royal Artillery Institution in his will. This did not happen and on Robert's death someone outside the family claimed the VC had been promised to them. The claim failed legally and the medals were sold, but the vender is not known. His medals were sold at auction by Dix Noonan Webb on 25th February 1999 for £92,000 and are held by the Lord Ashcroft VC Collection in the Lord Ashcroft Gallery of the Imperial War Museum.

Ernest's brother Austin served as a subaltern in the Lancashire Artillery Militia 1893-95. His brother Frederick was awarded the OBE, LG 3rd June 1918, while Commandant of No 3 Motor Ambulance Convoy, British Red Cross Commission, Italy. His daughter Annie married William Philip Jopp Akerman (1889-1972) CB DSO & Bar MC RA, who served in India, Mesopotamia and on the Western Front from 1908 and rose to Major General before retiring in 1942. Ernest's son Robert served in the Royal Navy 1923-50 and was awarded the DSO (LG 23rd May 1943) in command of HMS *Vivacious* during the torpedo attack on the German battlecruisers *Scharnhorst* and *Gneisenau* on 12th February 1942 and the DSC for his part in the Normandy landings in June 1944 (LG 14th November 1944). Ernest Alexander is commemorated in various places:

- Harrow School Speech Room, along with the other 18 Harrow VCs.
- Portrait at South Milton Parish Hall in Devon.
- Name inscribed on the Royal Artillery VC Memorial in the ruins of St George's Chapel, the former Garrison Church at Woolwich, which was reduced to a roofless shell by a V1 in 1944.
- Royal Military Academy Woolwich VC Memorial Board in the Royal Military Academy Sandhurst library.
- In July 2008 a memorial to Captain Noel Chavasse VC & Bar was unveiled in Abercromby Square, Liverpool; the memorial also carries the names of Ernest Alexander and 14 other VCs associated with Liverpool.

8191 CORPORAL WILLIAM ANDERSON
2nd Battalion, Alexandra, Princess of Wales's Own (Yorkshire Regiment)

William Anderson was born at Dallas, Elgin, Morayshire, Scotland on 28th December 1882. His father was Alexander Anderson (1851-1913), a general labourer and his mother was Isabella née Anderson (1846-1900). Alexander and Isabella married on 26th November 1880 at Dallas and they lived at 23rd House there. Despite having the same surname, they were not previously related. Before she married, Isabella had six illegitimate children, two sons and four daughters. William also had one full younger brother.

Having been educated at Forres Academy, Moray, William was employed by Glasgow Tramways Depot as a conductor. He moved to Newcastle-upon-Tyne, where his half brother James Watt Anderson was serving with the Yorkshire Regiment, usually referred to as the Green Howards. William enlisted in 1905 and served in India, Egypt and South Africa before being discharged to the Reserve in 1912. He was then employed at Elder Hospital in Govan, Glasgow.

When war broke out he was recalled on 4th August 1914 and instead of joining a battalion straight away, was sent to Middlesbrough to help with recruiting. He met Lucy Dudley there, a St John's Ambulance British Red Cross Society nurse from Port Clarence, near Middlesbrough. She asked him jokingly if he would have her as a recruit and when he said he would they got talking, had tea and went for a motor ride to West Hartlepool. A few days later he proposed to her and she accepted. Lucy called him Jock.

William was sent to France on 14th November to join the 2nd Battalion. **He was awarded the VC for his actions at Neuve Chapelle, France on 12th March 1915, LG 22nd May 1915.** He was wounded soon after his VC action and is believed to have died on 13th March 1915. Although his pay book was found and returned to the unit, his body was not recovered and he is commemorated on the Le Touret Memorial (Panel 12). In August 1915 a Forres Gazette reporter interviewed Lucy Dudley:

> "... *I can't believe that he is dead. He is either a prisoner of war or wounded and won't tell me for fear of upsetting me... When he went away on 11 November he*

William Anderson, 2nd right, in a pre-war military gymnastics team photograph.

The banqueting hall of Edinburgh Castle where William Anderson's brother Alexander, received his VC from Lieutenant General Sir Francis Davies, GOC Scottish Command, on 19th May 1920.

> *said to me,* "Look here kiddie. Never mind me. I'll do all right. I am going to come back with a commission."*… I begged and prayed him not to do anything rash, as I knew he was brave enough to do anything to get an honour that he could share with me. I told him to come back alive, as that was all I wanted… and I am not going to give up hope that he will return after the war…"*

The VC was presented to his brother Alexander (born 1887), by Lieutenant General Sir Francis Davies, GOC Scottish Command, in the banqueting hall of Edinburgh Castle on 19th May 1920. Alexander had been unable to attend a Buckingham Palace investiture because of his own war service as a Lance Corporal (8767) in the Highland Light Infantry (MID, LG 15th August 1917) and an acute attack of malaria. Alexander donated the medals to the Green Howards in March 1969 at a small ceremony at his home at Inverlochy, Fort William, Inverness-shire. The VC is held by the Green Howards Regimental Museum, Trinity Church Square, Richmond, Yorkshire.

William's half brother, James Watt Anderson (born 1871), enlisted in the Yorkshire Regiment on 23rd November 1892. He reached the rank of Corporal in 1896 and 1905 before being reduced to Private on both occasions. Having served in the 4th and 2nd Battalions in Gibraltar 1898, South Africa during the Boer War 1899-1902, Egypt 1908, India 1912 and Britain in 1899, 1902 and 1913, he was discharged on 26th December 1913. He served in the Regiment again from 28th October 1914 and was promoted Sergeant on 8th November. From 12th November 1916 he served in 2nd Garrison Battalion until transferring to the National Reserve on 10th October 1918, from which he was discharged on 3rd February 1919.

15518 PRIVATE EDWARD BARBER
1st Battalion, Grenadier Guards

Edward Barber was born at 40 King Street, Tring, Hertfordshire on 10th June 1893. His father was William Barber (1860-1937), a blacksmith and his mother was Sarah Ann née Davis (1861–1943). William and Sarah were married at Berkhampstead, Hertfordshire in December 1882. The family later lived at 22 Miswell Lane, Tring. Before Edward was born his parents had another son named Edward (1890-91). There were four other brothers. Edward was educated at Tring National Schools and was a member of the Tring Company No 196, Church Lads' Brigade at St Peter & St Paul Church. He was employed as a bricklayer's labourer until he enlisted in October 1911.

Edward went to France with his Battalion on 6th October 1914. **Awarded the VC for his actions at Neuve Chapelle, France on 12th March 1915, LG 19th April 1915.** He was shot through the head by a German sniper and killed later on 12th March. He has no known grave and is commemorated on the Le Touret Memorial (Panel 2). He never married.

The VC was sent to his mother on 13th March 1916 and was presented to her formally by the King at Buckingham Palace on 16th November. In addition to the VC, Edward was awarded the 1914 Star with 'Mons' clasp, British War Medal 1914-20 and Victory Medal 1914-19. The VC is held by the Grenadier Guards, Wellington Barracks, London. He is commemorated in a number of places:

- Tring War Memorial in front of St Peter & St Paul Church.
- Barber's Walk, Tring, named after him in 1965.

St Peter & St Paul Church, Tring, where Edward Barber was a member of the Tring Company No 196, Church Lads' Brigade.

- Church Lads & Church Girls Brigade Memorial Plot at the National Memorial Arboretum, Alrewas, Staffordshire includes 22 Berberis shrubs representing the 22 members of the Church Lads' Brigade who were awarded the VC.

Three of his bothers also served:

Alfred in the RAMC.
William Charles in 1/1st Hertfordshire.
Ernest trained with 2/1st Hertfordshire (266355), transferred to 1/1st Battalion and was posted missing in September 1917. He had been taken prisoner and was repatriated in 1918 with arm injuries and partial paralysis. He died on 18th September 1920 as a result of his wounds and the effect of mustard gas. He is buried in Tring Cemetery (F 90).

8581 DRUMMER SPENCER JOHN BENT
1st Battalion, The East Lancashire Regiment

Spencer John Bent was born at Spikes Farm, Spikes Lane, off Bury Road, Stowmarket, Suffolk on 19th March 1891. His father, William Bent (1863-1926), was born in Worcestershire and was employed as a groom in London in 1881. He served as a Driver in the Royal Engineers (No.22932), enlisting at Exeter on 27th December 1888 and transferring to the 1st Class Army Reserve on 26th December 1891. He was recalled under a Special Army Order on 2nd December 1899 and served in South Africa from 20th December 1899 until being discharged on 30th December 1901. Spencer's mother was Gertrude Mary Ann née Baker (1867-1943). William and Gertrude's marriage took place on 23rd November 1889 at Paddington; William did not have leave from the Army to marry. Spencer's early childhood was spent in Spikes Lane, where his mother's parents, John and Caroline Baker, had a market garden. From 1898 he lived with his uncle and aunt, William and Ellen Baker, at Verandah Cottage, Upper Street, Witnesham near Ipswich. William Baker was a wheelwright and Ellen was a dressmaker. Spencer had two sisters and a brother and the rest of his family lived together in Chatham and then at College Gardens, Farnham, Surrey while his father was serving in the Army. It is not known why they were split up. At the time of the 1901 Census he was recorded incorrectly as Spencer Bentley. It is likely that he attended the local school in Witnesham for only half days.

Spencer enlisted aged 14 on 19th July 1905 at Ipswich as a Drummer. He was known as 'Joe' in the Army, a corruption of the name of a famous northern boxer, 'Chow' Bent. Joe represented his Battalion in the Army Championships as a lightweight. He served at the Curragh 1905-08, Woking until 1912 and Colchester until war broke out.

Joe Bent went to France with the Battalion, sailing from Southampton aboard SS *Braemar Castle* on 22nd August 1914. He took part in the Retreat from Mons, Battle of Le Cateau, advance to the Marne, Battle of the Aisne and First Battle of Ypres. **Awarded the VC for his actions near Le Gheer, Belgium 22nd October – 3rd November 1914, LG 9th December 1914.** He was wounded in the right leg and head and evacuated to England on 10th November 1914, where he was in hospital in Oxfordshire before being transferred to 15 Northern General Hospital in Leicester. Promoted Corporal 1st January 1915 and was involved in recruiting while convalescing. His VC was presented by the King at Buckingham Palace on 13th January 1915. He was presented with a cheque for £50, in a casket made from material salvaged from Queen Victoria's yacht *Osborne*, by the mayor of Ipswich. **Awarded the Cross of the Order of St George 3rd Class (No.16682) (Russia), LG 25th August 1915.** Promoted Sergeant and attached to the Reserve (Training) Battalion at Laira, Plymouth and Plympton, Devon.

Joe returned to France in 1916, took part in the Somme battles and was evacuated with rheumatic fever in November 1916. He married Alice Helena née Powell (c.1894 -1984) on 16th January 1917 at St Andrew's parish church, Plymouth, Devon. She was a nurse known as 'Chum' in the family. Her father was Chief Boilermaker at the RN Dockyard, Plymouth. They had three children – Spencer Powell Bent born on 18th June 1920 at Plymouth (he later stood as the Communist Party candidate in Southwark), Beryl Helena Bent born on 13th November 1922 in Jamaica and Pauline Patricia Bent born on 5th September 1929 at Greenwich, London.

Joe returned to France in the spring of 1917 and served with 7th Battalion. At Messines he was promoted CSM on 7th June 1917 and also took part in the Third Battle of Ypres. He rejoined the 1st Battalion on 7th February 1918 when 7th Battalion disbanded and took part in the Second Battle of Cambrai in October 1918. **Awarded the MM for his actions north of Semperies on the far bank of the river Rhonelle on 29th October 1918 – he led two patrols to gain touch with the enemy following intelligence reports from aircraft that the enemy had withdrawn from the high ground in front of the bridgehead. This was found not to be the case and the patrols made very little headway and had to withdraw under cover of a smoke barrage, LG 17th June 1919.**

Joe left France in December 1918 and was based at Blackdown, Surrey. He became a recruiting officer in Blackburn, Lancashire in March 1920 operating from the Territorial Army Barracks in Canterbury Street with an office in Ainsworth Street. He was a member of the VC Guard at the Interment of the Unknown Warrior on 11th November 1920. While serving in the West Indies with the Battalion he carried the medals of Sergeant W J Gordon VC, West India Regiment at his funeral in August 1922. Awarded the Long Service and Good Conduct Medal in 1923 and was discharged from Malta in July 1925. In a letter to Canon Lummis on 16th November 1949, Major C Y Cant, Secretary of the East Lancashires, mentioned, *"Bent left us after 18 years service when the battalion was at Malta. He was not a clever man, and I think would have been made to relinquish his rank of CSM had he not retired on pension for he was not fit to hold it in peace time."*

Joe Bent in later life.

Joe became a school keeper at Paragon School, New Kent Road, London, a commissionaire with Mond Nickel Council in 1956 and a Courage Brewery commissionaire at Tower Bridge Road, London from 1962 until he retired in 1976. He served for a time in the East Lancashire Regiment in the Second World War in the rank of Warrant Officer Class II.

Joe was Initiated as a Freemason into the Aldershot Camp Lodge (No.1331) on 8th December 1920, while stationed at Blackdown Camp, Surrey. He was Passed to the second degree on 9th February 1921 and Raised on 20th May 1921. Harry Daniels VC and Padre William Addison VC were also members of this Lodge. On 8th March 1958, he became a Joining Member of the Cyclists Lodge (No.2246), meeting at Surbiton, Surrey and was appointed a Provincial Grand Standard Bearer for Surrey. In August 1968 he opened a new public house in Chatham, Kent, named 'The Victoria Cross'.

Joe Bent died at his home in Hackney, London on 3rd May 1977 and was cremated at West Norwood, where his ashes were scattered on Rose Bed 41. In addition to the VC, he was awarded the Military Medal, 1914 Star with 'Mons' clasp, British War Medal 1914-20, Victory Medal 1914-19, Defence Medal, George VI Coronation Medal 1937, Elizabeth II Coronation Medal 1953, Army Long Service & Good Conduct Medal and the Russian Cross of St George 3rd Class. His VC was displayed in the Imperial War Museum until being sold for £11,000 at Sotheby's on 27th June 1985. It was purchased by Michael Ashcroft's VC Trust at Dix Noonan Webb for £80,000 on 28th June 2000 and is on display in the Lord Ashcroft Gallery at the Imperial War Museum.

CAPTAIN EDWARD KINDER BRADBURY
L Battery, Royal Horse Artillery

Edward Kinder Bradbury was born at Parkfield, Altrincham, Cheshire on 16th August 1881. His father was the Hon James Kinder Bradbury MA JP (1847-1913), a barrister and later a Judge of the Lancashire County Court Circuit No 5 (Bolton, Oldham, Wigan, Bury and Rochdale). His mother was Grace née Dowling (1856-1924), whose father was Vicar of Christ Church, Timperley, Cheshire. Their marriage was registered at Altrincham in the 3rd quarter of 1878. Edward had two sisters. He was educated at St Ninian's Moffat, Marlborough College and the Royal Military Academy Woolwich.

Edward was commissioned into the Royal Artillery on 2nd May 1900 and posted to 125th Brigade in Ireland. Promoted Lieutenant 3rd April 1901. He served in the Imperial Yeomanry (Fincastle's Horse) in the South African War 23rd January – 18th October 1902 before returning to Ireland. An attachment to 4th (Uganda) Battalion, King's African Rifles followed on 8th February 1905, but in August 1906 he was invalided home with fever, although he remained on strength until 4th March 1907. Promoted Captain 4th February 1910. Appointed Adjutant 1st February – 17th November 1912. He also served in India before the war and spent his leave in Co Cork, fishing and hunting.

Edward disembarked with L Battery in France on 16th August 1914. **Awarded the VC for his actions at Néry, France on 1st September 1914, LG 25th November 1914. Mentioned in Field Marshal Sir John French's Despatch dated 8th October 1914, LG 19th October 1914 (duplicated 20th October and reissued 9th December 1914).** He was killed during his VC action at Néry on 1st September 1914 and is buried in Néry Communal Cemetery. He never married. Edward is commemorated at:

- Royal Artillery VC Memorial in the ruins of St George's Chapel, the former Garrison Church at Woolwich, which was reduced to a roofless shell by a V1 in 1944.
- Royal Military Academy Woolwich VC Memorial Board in the Royal Military Academy Sandhurst library.

In addition to the VC, he was awarded the Queen's South Africa Medal 1899-1902 with two clasps (Cape Colony & South Africa 1901), 1914 Star with 'Mons' clasp, British War Medal 1914-20 and Victory Medal 1914-19 with Mentioned-in-Despatches oak-leaf. His VC was presented to his mother by the King at Buckingham Palace on 29th November 1916 and was one of those displayed at the VC Centenary Exhibition, Marlborough House, London 15th June – 7th July 1956. It was bequeathed to L (Néry) Battery RHA by his nephew, Major A J Crewdson MC, and handed over on his behalf by George Dorrell VC during a Néry Day parade at Hildesheim, West Germany in November 1956. It is on loan to the Imperial War Museum, Lambeth, London. Edward's Memorial Plaque was sold by Spink in London on 19th April 2007 for the hammer price of £4,600.

CAPTAIN WALTER LORRAIN BRODIE
2nd Battalion, The Highland Light Infantry

Walter Brodie was born at 13 Belgrave Crescent, Edinburgh on 28th July 1884. His father, John Wilson Brodie (1851-1934), was a partner in Edinburgh stockbrokers, Torrie, Brodie & Maclagan. He was a member of the Society of Accountants in Edinburgh from 1875, President of the Speculative Society 1877 and director of the Scottish-American Trust Company. In 1893 he and William Hugh Murray were appointed directors of the Scottish-American Investment Company; Murray's brother-in-law was David Reginald Younger VC. Walter's mother was Grace Mary née Lorrain (1854-1938). John and Grace married at her home, 53 Northumberland Street, Edinburgh on 27th August 1879. Walter had a brother and two sisters and the family lived at 6 Lynedoch Place, 23 Belgrave Crescent and 13 Belgrave Place, Edinburgh at various times. Walter was educated at Edinburgh Academy 1892-98, where he was a member of the OTC; the Academy was attended by Robert Louis Stevenson 1861-63. Walter was later tutored by a private coach.

His paternal grandfather was Patrick Brodie (1817-67). He was Secretary of the National Fire & Life Insurance Company in Edinburgh until 1846, then joint Agent of the British Linen Bank in Glasgow. He became sole Agent from 1851 and was Manager 1860-67. His maternal grandfather was Walter Scott Lorrain (1807-71), an East India Merchant.

Walter trained at the Royal Military College Sandhurst and was commissioned on 2nd March 1904. He served with the 2nd Battalion in Jersey, at Edinburgh Castle and Fort George near Inverness. He was a Freemason, Lodge Canongate Kilwinning No 2 from 7th February 1906. Promoted Lieutenant 19th June 1908.

The years 1909-13 were spent in Ireland with the Battalion at Cork and Mullingar, where he was a keen follower of the hounds. Walter attended Mounted Infantry, Signaling and Machine-Gun courses.

When war broke he was Battalion Machine-Gun officer based in Aldershot and disembarked in France on 14th August 1914. Promoted Captain on 10th September. **Awarded the VC for his actions near Becelaere, Belgium on 7th November 1914, LG 12th December 1914. Mentioned in Field Marshal Sir John French's Despatch dated 14th January 1915, LG 17th February 1915.** His VC was presented by the King at Windsor Castle on 17th July 1915.

Walter returned to the front and took part in operations at Richebourg, Givenchy and Festubert in 1915. He became an intelligence staff officer (GSO3) on 1st March 1916 until being appointed Brigade Major of 63rd Brigade from 25th April 1916 until 9th December 1917. He took part in the Battles of the Somme and Arras. **Awarded the MC, LG 1st January 1917. Mentioned in Field Marshal Sir Douglas Haig's Despatch dated 7th November 1917, LG 11th December 1917.** Appointed Acting Lieutenant Colonel to command 2/10th King's (Liverpool) on 23rd December 1917. Brevet Major 1st January 1918. Appointed to command 2nd HLI on 25th April 1918. He was killed in action leading an attack near Behagnies, France on 23rd August 1918 and is buried in Bienvillers Military Cemetery (XVIII F 15).

In addition to the VC and MC, he was awarded the 1914 Star with 'Mons' clasp, British War Medal 1914-20 and Victory Medal 1914-19 with Mentioned-in-Despatches oak-leaf. His VC is held privately. Walter never married.

His sister's niece by marriage, Ivry Perronelle Katherine Guild, married Paul Richard Freyberg, son of Bernard Freyberg VC. His aunt, Helen Lorrain, married Reverend George Cook, cousin of John Cook VC.

LIEUTENANT JAMES ANSON OTHO BROOKE
2nd Battalion, The Gordon Highlanders

James Brooke was born at Fairley House, Newhills, Counteswells, near Aberdeen on 3rd February 1884. His father was Sir Henry 'Harry' Vesey Brooke (1845-1921) KBE JP DL, former Captain 92nd Highlanders 1864-79 who served in India 1868-71 and 1873-76. His mother was Patricia Byres née Moir (1859-1951). They married in London on 9th December 1879 and were living at 82 Eccleston Square, London in 1881, but had moved to Fairley House, Newhills by 1884. James had four brothers and two sisters.

His paternal grandfather was Sir Arthur Brinsley Brooke (1797-1854) Bt, MP for Colebrook, Co Fermanagh, who also served in the 92nd Regiment. His paternal grandmother was Hon Julia Henrietta Brooke née Anson (1819-86), a Maid of Honour to Queen Victoria 1839-42 and daughter of General Sir George Anson GCB KT MP, Colonel 4th Dragoon Guards, who served in the Peninsula War and was Groom of the Bedchamber to Albert, Prince Consort. James' great uncle was Augustus Henry Archibald Anson VC. His maternal grandfather was James Gregory Moir (1803-81), a surgeon. James was educated at Winton House Winchester and Wellington College.

At the Royal Military College Sandhurst he was a good academic student, Senior Colour-Sergeant of the College, Captain of the Shooting Eight and a member of the Riding Club and Football team. He won the big obstacle race, tied for the Saddle and was awarded the Sword of Honour. James was commissioned on 11th October 1905. He served in Cork, Ireland from November with the 1st Battalion and transferred to the 2nd Battalion in India in 1907, where he won several trophies for Markhor, Ibex, Sambur and Boar shooting. Promoted Lieutenant on 5th August 1907. He received the Battalion's Colours from King George V at the Dehli Durbar in 1911 and went with the Battalion to Egypt in 1913. Promoted Captain on 1st September 1914, but the notification arrived posthumously.

He disembarked with the Battalion at Zeebrugge, Belgium on 7th October 1914 and was appointed Assistant Adjutant on 29th October. **Awarded the VC for his**

2nd Gordon Highlanders and 2nd Scots Guards aboard the troopship SS *Lake Michigan* heading for Zeebrugge on 6th October 1914.

actions near Gheluvelt, Belgium on 29th October 1914, LG 18th February 1915. Mentioned in Sir John French's Despatch dated 14th January 1915, LG 17th February 1915.

James Brooke was killed in action near Gheluvelt, Belgium on 29th October 1914 and is buried in Zantvoorde British Cemetery (VI E 2). He is also commemorated on a memorial in Springbank Cemetery, Aberdeen. He never married. His VC was originally sent to his father on 9th March 1915 and was presented to him formally by the King at Buckingham Palace on 29th November 1916. In addition to the VC, he was awarded the 1914 Star with 'Mons' clasp, British War Medal 1914-20, Victory Medal 1914-19 with Mentioned-in-Despatches oak-leaf and the 1911 Delhi Durbar Medal. His VC is held by the Gordon Highlanders Museum, Aberdeen, along with his original wooden grave marker and revolver.

His father was awarded the KBE, LG 1st January 1920 for services while Chairman of the Aberdeenshire Local Emergency Committee. Three of James' brothers (the fourth and youngest died aged 10) also served:

Arthur Brooke (1886-1952) was a Captain in the 18th (King George's Own) Lancers attached to 4th (Queen's Own) Hussars. He was present at the Dehli Durbar in 1911 and was severely wounded by a shot through the thigh during the First World War. He was later a Colonel in the Indian Army, Zone Commander Home Guard 1940-43, DL and JP.

Henry Brian Brooke (1889-1916) spent seven years as a settler and big game hunter in British East Africa. He was severely wounded in Jubaland, Somalia with serving with local forces and evacuated to Britain. He was later commissioned from the Special Reserve into 2nd Gordon Highlanders on 5th January 1916. As a Captain at Mametz on 1st July 1916 he was shot twice, but continued fighting until a third bullet struck him in the neck. He was admitted to the Base Hospital and evacuated to the Empire Hospital, Vincent Square, London on 7th July, where he died on 24th July. He is buried in Aberdeen (Springbank) Cemetery (N 19). Mentioned in Despatches, LG 4th January 1917.

Patrick Harry Brooke (1895-1917) served in the Royal Navy – Midshipman 15th May 1913, Acting Sub Lieutenant 15th May 1915 and Sub Lieutenant 15th January 1916. He was aboard HMS *Indomitable* at the Dardanelles in November 1914 and at the Battle of the Dogger Bank in January 1915, when she was involved in sinking SMS *Blucher*. He was serving on HMS *Courageous* when he died of enteric fever on 24th May 1917 and is buried with his brother Henry in Aberdeen (Springbank) Cemetery.

James' two sisters married into military families:

Constance Geraldine (1887-1973) married Captain Napier Charles Gordon Cameron, 1st Gordon Highlanders, son of General Sir William Gordon Cameron GCB and nephew of Aylmer Cameron VC CB. Napier had previously served in the Scottish Horse and Northumberland Fusiliers. He was killed in action on 28th September 1914 and is buried in Bourg-et-Comin Communal Cemetery, Aisne, France (Grave 1).

Alice Irene (born 1897) married Lieutenant (later Lieutenant Colonel) Richard Gilbert Lees, Gordon Highlanders.

James Brooke's cousin was Field Marshal Viscount Alanbrooke.

James's uncle, Sir Victor Alexander Brooke (1843-91), was so named due to the wish of Queen Victoria; her names were Alexandrina Victoria. One of Victor's sons was Alan Francis Brooke (1883-1963), later Field Marshal Viscount Alanbrooke, CIGS during the Second World War and Lord High Constable of England.

LIEUTENANT WILLIAM ARTHUR MCCRAE BRUCE
59th Scinde Rifles (Frontier Force)

William Bruce was born on 15th June 1890 at 5 Warrender Park Crescent, Edinburgh, Midlothian, Scotland. His father was Colonel Andrew Murison McCrae Bruce (1842-1920), who was commissioned on 4th November 1860 and served with 2nd Bengal Fusiliers, 1st Gurkhas and 4th Punjab Infantry, before commanding at Bangalore as a local Brigadier-General. He saw active service in Bhootan 1864-66, Miranzai 1869, Jowaki 1877-78, Afghanistan 1879-80 (MID), Zhob Valley 1884, Hazara 1888 and on the 1st Miranzai Expedition 1891 (MID). He retired on 5th January 1899 and was created CB, LG 23rd May 1900. He was awarded the India General Service Medal 1854-95 with clasps 'Bhootan', 'Jowaki 1877-78' and 'Hazara 1888' and the Afghanistan Medal 1878-80. William's mother was Margaret née Hay (born 1856). Andrew and Margaret were married at Portsea, Hampshire on 6th July 1889. William had a younger sister. Amongst his many uncles were:

Farquhar McCrae Bruce, commissioned as a Cornet in 1st Dragoons on 24th December 1870. He transferred to 77th Foot on 23rd April 1873, 36th Foot on 4th February 1874 and 66th Foot on 23rd October 1875. He was promoted Captain while serving with 2nd Battalion, The Berkshire Regiment on 28th July 1880 at Chatham and retired on 19th February 1890.

George Ward Cole Bruce, commissioned as a Sub-Lieutenant in 2nd Foot on 19th June 1872. Promoted Lieutenant 19th June 1873. Having transferred to the Bengal Staff Corps on 17th June 1879 he was promoted Captain on 8th January 1885 and Major on 19th June 1893, before retiring on 19th June 1894.

The Bruce family traces its ancestry back to James V of Scotland. The family acquired Whalsay in the Shetland Islands in the 1600s and oppressed the residents for the next three centuries. Their decline was largely caused by the 6th Robert Bruce of Symbister building Symbister House in 1823 at a cost of £30,000 (c.£3M in 2013). It is alleged he did this more to ensure his heirs would not inherit his fortune than to build somewhere to live. The last resident laird died in 1944 and since the 1960s the house has been a school.

On returning from India the family settled at 'La Fontaine', Pontac, Jersey, Channel Islands. William was educated at Victoria College in St Helier 1904-08 and was a member of the Cricket XI in 1907-08. Another future VC, Allastair Malcolm Cluny McReady-Diarmid (then Arthur Malcolm Drew) was at Victoria College in 1904 and the two must have known each other.

William entered the Royal Military College Sandhurst (King's Indian Cadet) in 1908. When he was commissioned on 29th January 1910, he was initially attached tto a British battalion in India for a year, which was the practice for all officers before joining an Indian Army regiment. William's attached was to the Northumberland Fusiliers. He learned Urdu in this time and transferred to 59th Scinde Rifles on 8th March 1911. Promoted Lieutenant 29th April 1912. He was in England on leave in 1914 when war broke out and began the journey back to India immediately, but was ordered instead to meet his unit in Cairo, Egypt. The Battalion sailed from Karachi on HMT *Takada* on 29th August, disembarked at Port Tewfik and continued to Cairo, where it stayed for two days. It re-embarked at Alexandria on HMT *Takada* and arrived at Marseilles on 26th September. Its first action was at La Bassée at the end of October.

He was awarded the VC for his actions near Givenchy, France on 19th December 1914, LG 4th September 1919. What he did during this action was not known until captured officers returned after the war and made their recommendations. William was killed in action at Givenchy during his VC action. His body was not identified after the war and he is commemorated on the Neuve-Chapelle Memorial, Pas de Calais, France (Panel 25). His father was not well enough to attend an investiture at Buckingham Palace. William's VC was presented to his mother at a private ceremony by the Lieutenant Governor of Jersey, Major General Sir Alexander Wilson KCB. William Bruce is commemorated in a number of places:

- Bruce House at Victoria College was named after him in 1919.
- 59th Scinde Rifles officers' memorial, Garrison Church, Kohat, India.
- St Clement's Church, Jersey.
- Jersey Militia Museum, Elizabeth Castle, Jersey.

In addition to the VC, he was awarded the 1914 Star with 'Mons' clasp, British War Medal 1914-20 and Victory Medal 1914-19. When the VC came up for auction at Christie's on 10th November 1992, former Victoria College teacher, Dixie Landick, launched an appeal and raised the £19,000 needed to purchase it. It is displayed at the Jersey Museum, The Weighbridge, St Helier.

6276 PRIVATE WILLIAM BUCKINGHAM
2nd Battalion, The Leicestershire Regiment

William Buckingham was born at 51 St John Street, Bedford on 29th March 1886 as William Henry Billington. His father was William John Billington (1868-88), a market gardener and greengrocer. His mother was Annie Susan née Bennett (1867-1943). William and Annie were married at St Cuthbert's Church, Bedford on 1st February 1886. When William died of tuberculosis on 5th March 1888, Annie struggled to bring up her young family. They were living at Howbury Street, Bedford and she received relief from the local Board of Guardians. William entered the Bedford Union Workhouse on 17th May 1889. His younger brother, Frederick Ernest Billington (born 1887), went to live with his grandparents, Joab and Flora Bennett at 14 Bower Street, Bedford.

Annie went to Leicester to work as a shoe fitter, met Thomas Henry Buckingham (born 1873), a shoe riveter, and they were married at Holy Trinity Parish Church, Leicester on 3rd August 1891. They lived at 9 Court C, Upper Charles Street and a son, Joseph Henry Buckingham, was born on 19th November 1891. Joseph was admitted to the Leicester Union Workhouse on 21st April 1892, but was taken out by his parents on 14th May. The return to normal life did not last long, as Annie and Joseph were admitted to the Leicester Union Workhouse on 20th June 1892 due to being neglected by her husband, who was not heard of again for years. Annie and Joseph were joined by William and Frederick on 27th June from the Bedford

One of the Countesthorpe Cottage Homes around the end of the 19th Century. Each cottage had a House Mother and the whole establishment was overseen by a Superintendent and Matron.

Workhouse; they were admitted under the surname Buckingham, which they used thereafter. After the death of Joseph on 4th September 1892, aged nine months, Annie took her discharge on 26th October. Her whereabouts were unknown until William died in 1916, when she was discovered working as a shoe binder living at 35 York Street, St Cuthbert's, Bedford.

William and Frederick were brought up at Countesthorpe Cottage Homes (as was Robert Gee VC) from 15th July 1892. William was admitted to Cottage No 6. The Cottage Homes were a progressive way of looking after orphans and poor children, providing parental care, stability, education and preparation for work. From 1896 William's upbringing was supervised by Mr and Mrs William Harrison, the Superintendent and Matron of the Homes. They had an enormously positive influence on him.

The Countesthorpe Cottage Homes School 2009 (Derek Seaton).

William was educated within the Cottage Homes until aged 11, when the children attended Bassett Street School in South Wigston. He trained for employment as a tailor, but instead enlisted at the Leicestershire Regiment Depot at Glen Parva Barracks on 29th November 1901, aged 15 years and eight months. He stated he had no knowledge where his father was and appears not to have known he died some years before. On enlistment he was recorded as a tailor's boy and was just 5' 2⅛" tall and weighed only 98 lbs.

William transferred to the 2nd Battalion on 12th May and joined it in Alexandria, Egypt on 26th May 1902. He served with the Battalion in Guernsey from 15th December 1902 and Colchester from 29th September 1904. He underwent ten days hard labour for misconduct on 2nd October 1905. On 28th February 1906 he transferred to the 1st Battalion at Belgaum, India and also served at Madras, Bellary and Bareilly. When the 2nd Battalion arrived on 16th October 1906 to replace the 1st Battalion, William transferred to it to remain in India. He forfeited his Good Conduct Badge on 16th November 1907, but was allowed to re-engage to complete 21 years at Madras on 11th December 1912. The Battalion departed India on SS *Elephanta* on 21st September 1914 and disembarked at Marseilles, France on 12th October.

The 2nd Battalion went into the line for the first time on 29th October 1914. William was noted for great gallantry at Givenchy on 18th December by the Indian Corps Commander, Lieutenant General Sir James Willcocks. At the end of his leave in Leicestershire during February 1915 his prophetic leaving remark to William Harrison at the Cottage Homes was, *"Well, goodbye sir. I'll win the VC or get killed!"*

Awarded the VC for his actions at Neuve Chapelle, France on 10-12th March 1915, LG 28th April 1915. He was wounded in the VC action and evacuated to England where he was treated at South Manchester Hospital. The bullet lodged in his arm was removed without anaesthetic at his own request. While recovering he was transferred to the strength of the Depot on 15th March and 3rd (Reserve) Battalion on 1st April. He returned to Countesthorpe on 7th April while convalescing. William Harrison saw the VC notification in his morning paper on 29th April and asked William to verify his number – this was the first he knew of the award. William was a rather shy, modest man and William Harrison helped him deal with press interest and adulation.

The VC was presented by the King at Buckingham Palace on 4th June. Returning to Countesthorpe that evening, he was greeted by a guard of 120 boys and the school band. Next day he was presented with a gold mounted walking stick by the staff of the Homes and at the annual sports day on 15th July the town of Leicester presented him with a War Loan Bond for £100 and a purse of 10 guineas in cash. At an event for wounded soldiers at Coleorton Hall, near Ashby-de-la-Zouch, he met Corporal W Tarry, one of the men he saved at Neuve Chapelle.

On recovering from his wounds William helped with recruiting, based at Glen Parva, where the Depot CO, Lieutenant Colonel John Mosse, was impressed with

William Buckingham with some of the boys at the Cottage Homes, just after receiving news of the award of the VC.

his unassuming manner and professionalism. On 19th February 1916, William and Lance Corporals Thomas Newcombe and AG Robinson were honoured with a reception at Hinckley. Newcombe was awarded the DCM for his actions on 15/16th May 1915 and he and Robinson were also awarded the Russian Cross of St George, the latter for rescuing a wounded Gurkha under heavy fire.

William was promoted Lance Corporal on 8th April 1916 and returned to France on 12th April, joining 6th Infantry Base Depot next day. He transferred to 8th Entrenching Battalion on 23rd April and was promoted Acting Corporal on 28th April. Rejoining the 2nd Battalion he reverted to Unpaid Lance Corporal on 15th May. He reverted to Private at his own request on 21st May in order to join the 1st Battalion. He became orderly to Captain J W E Mosse, son of the Depot CO who collapsed and died on 17th June.

William Buckingham was killed in action by a burst of machine-gun fire near Ginchy, Somme on 15th September 1916. Characteristically, he was going to the aid of another soldier during an attack. He was one of 424 casualties suffered by the Battalion in two days. Captain Mosse was awarded the MC for his part in this action. William is commemorated on the Thiepval Memorial. The executors to his will were Herbert Mansfield (Clerk to the Board of Guardians of the Leicester Poor Law Guardians) and William Harrison (Superintendent of the Cottage Homes); he left £129/7/11.

The VC, seated second right, with medical staff at what appears to be a first aid post at a London & North Western Railway station.

A recruiting rally at Barwell on 18th March 1916. From left to right – Pte Sidney 'Togo' Bolesworth DCM (killed 1st October 1917 – Tyne Cot Memorial), Pte William Buckingham VC, LCpl T Newcombe DCM, an unnamed local dignitary, Sgt Payne of the Leicestershire Regiment Depot and LCpl A G Robinson of Hinckley who was awarded the Russian Cross of St George. (Mrs K Best)

In addition to the VC, William Buckingham was awarded the 1914 Star with 'Mons' clasp, British War Medal 1914-20 and Victory Medal 1914-19. His medals were held by the Countesthorpe Cottage Homes until 1958 when they closed and passed to the Children's Committee of the Child Welfare Department, Leicester, where they remained until 1966. They are now on loan to the Royal Leicestershire Regiment Museum, Newarke Houses Museum, Leicester. William is also commemorated in a number of places:

- Leicester War Memorial.
- Buckingham Road in Countesthorpe was named after him in 1961 – a granite boulder with bronze plaque was unveiled in the road on 18th November 1986 and the ceremony was attended by Eric Holmes, who was present when William visited Bassett Street School to show his VC to the children.
- Countesthorpe War Memorial, unveiled by HRH Duke of York on 21st November 1921 and attended by Captain Robert Gee VC. When the memorial was moved to St Andrew's churchyard in 1986, it was noticed that William's name was not on it; it was added subsequently.

The Buckingham VC Memorial Fund of £600 was set up by the Leicester Board of Guardians to benefit children who had been, *"under the care, nurture or control of the Guardians of the Poor of the Parish of Leicester and their successors"*. Responsibility for the fund passed to Leicester City Council in 1932 and it continues to help young people who have been in the care of the local Social Services Department.

William's brother Frederick took his discharge from Countesthorpe Cottage Homes on 11th September 1902 to join the Royal Navy, but did not enlist at Chatham until 14th January 1907, signing on for twelve years. His previous employment was as a baker. He served at HMS *Pembroke*, a shore establishment, on probation, then as a 2nd Clerk's Mate and later as a Clerk's Mate. He then served on the battleships HMS *Victorious* and *Albemarle*, *Pembroke I* again and *Wildfire*, a shore establishment at Sheerness until 24th September 1910 when he was discharged 'Services No Longer Required' as a result of careless in performance of duty and conviction for theft. He subsequently enlisted in 16th Lancers (10290) and served in France from 12th October 1915. Later he transferred to the Royal Warwickshire Regiment (34185) and was promoted Lance Corporal.

9665 COMPANY SERGEANT MAJOR HARRY DANIELS
2nd Battalion, The Rifle Brigade

Harry Daniels was born at Market Street, Wymondham, Norfolk on 13th December 1884. His father was William Daniels (1844-94), a baker and confectioner. His mother was Elizabeth née Snelling, known as Eliza (1848-93). William and Elizabeth's marriage was registered during the 4th quarter of 1866 at Norwich, Norfolk. The family lived in Wymondham for six years before returning to Norwich and they lived at Eagle Walk, Newmarket Road and by 1891 were at 13 Esdelle Street, St Augustine. He is known to have had at least four

Market Street, Wymondham, Norfolk, where Harry Daniels was born.

brothers and five sisters and was reputedly the thirteenth of sixteen children. By the time he was 10 both parents were dead and he and one of his brothers were brought up in the Norwich Board of Guardians Boys Home on St Faith's Lane, Norwich.

Harry was educated at Thorpe Hamlet Boy's School, Norwich. He earned the nickname 'Spitfire' as he frequently went missing – on the second occasion he worked as a cabin boy on a fishing smack for two months. He was eventually apprenticed as a carpenter and joiner to Duke's Palace Steam Joinery Works, but did not finish.

Harry's eldest brother, 1596 Private William Daniels, died of disease at Pretoria on 24th June 1900 while serving with 1st Coldstream Guards during the South African War. Harry enlisted in the Rifle Brigade on 31st January 1903 and trained at Gosport and Chatham. He served in India with the 2nd Battalion from 1905 and was in the band for a period. Harry was a keen sportsman, winning the regimental lightweight and welterweight boxing tournaments. He also attended a gymnastics course in Lucknow. Promoted Corporal 19th July 1909 and Sergeant 21st December 1910. At a Christmas dance in 1912 he met Kathleen Mary née Perry (1895-1949), the daughter of a Warrant Officer in the Manchester Regiment. They were married on 21st January 1914 in Calcutta. It is understood they did not have any children.

The Battalion sailed from Bombay on 20th September 1914, landed at Liverpool on 22nd October and moved to Hursley Park, Winchester, where it joined the newly formed 25th Brigade, 8th Division. Appointed CQMS on 10th October and he landed at Le Havre, France with the Battalion on 7th November. Appointed CSM on 12th December. **Awarded the VC for his actions at Neuve Chapelle,**

France on 12th March 1915, LG 28th April 1915. Following his VC action he was evacuated to England and treated at the Military Orthopaedic Hospital, Hammersmith, where he learned of the award of the VC from a newspaper. Promoted substantive WO2, 29th January 1915. The VC was presented by the King at Buckingham Palace on 15th May.

Harry Daniels between being commissioned in July 1915 and before he was awarded the MC in March 1916.

Harry returned to Norwich with his wife on 10th June and while there was presented with a purse of gold by the Sheriff, Mr Frances Horner. Harry was commissioned on 23rd July and returned to France soon after. In September the Lord Mayor of Norwich received a telegram stating Harry Daniels had been killed in action. It was not until his relatives received field postcards from him that the error was realised and a contradiction was issued by the Press Association on 1st October. **Awarded the MC for consistent and conspicuous gallantry on patrol at Fromelles, France on 2nd March 1916. He rescued a wounded man from the edge of the enemy wire and carried him 300 yards to safety. On another occasion, when two patrols failed to find a wounded corporal, he took out a third patrol and brought back the body, LG 30th March 1916.**

Harry was wounded on 3rd July 1916 and his arm was fractured. Promoted Lieutenant 22nd August. Appointed Assistant Superintendent Physical and Bayonet Training 8th June 1917 – 18th July 1918. Temporary Major while an Instructor with the British Military Mission to USA 19th July – 23rd November 1918. Appointed Adjutant Aldershot HQ Gymnastic Staff 26th February 1919. Appointed Assistant Superintendent Physical and Bayonet Training and Assistant Superintendent Physical Training 7th April 1919 – 20th July 1921. Harry is reputed to have been a member of the 1920 British Olympic Boxing Team in Antwerp, but his name does not appear on the team list. He became a Freemason in the Aldershot Camp Lodge No 1331 in 1920. Promoted Captain 9th April 1921.

Harry transferred to the Loyal North Lancashire Regiment on 11th November 1922, but reverted to the Rifle Brigade and was appointed Assistant Provost Marshal Aldershot Command 28th September 1921 – 27th September 1925. Appointed Administrative Officer and later Company Commander at the Army Technical School (Boys), Chepstow 3rd October 1925 – 30th December 1929. Brevet Major 1st July 1929 (11288).

Harry retired from the Army on 26th April 1930 and managed hotels at Dovercourt, Abergavenny and Chester until being re-employed by the Army as Chief Recruiting Officer North Western Division in the rank of Captain from 11th November 1932. He was granted the local rank of Lieutenant Colonel on 4th December 1934 while

Chief Recruiting Officer East Lancashire Area. He ceased to be employed on 10th December 1942 and was granted the rank of Honorary Lieutenant Colonel.

Grand Theatre and Opera House Leeds in the 1940s.

Harry managed the Crown Hotel at Woodbridge, Suffolk until becoming the resident manager of the Grand Theatre and Opera House in Leeds in 1943. His wife became terminally ill in 1949 and Harry turned to Renée Martz, the then nine-year child preacher for assistance, but Kathleen died at home in West Park, Leeds later that year.

Harry Daniels died at Ida and Robert Arthington Hospital, Leeds on 13th December 1953. He was cremated at Lawns Wood Crematorium, Adel, Leeds and his ashes were scattered on the fields of the Aldershot Cricket Club. His nephew, Ernest Charles Fairhead, applied for the cremation, which indicates Harry had no children.

In addition to the VC and MC, Harry was awarded the 1914 Star with 'Mons clasp', British War Medal 1914-20, Victory Medal 1914-19, George VI Coronation Medal 1937, 1939-45 Defence Medal and Elizabeth II Coronation Medal 1953. His VC is held by the Royal Green Jackets (Rifles) Museum, Winchester. A plaque at Victoria Gardens, The Headrow, Leeds commemorates 17 VCs born or buried in the city; Harry's name appears on it although he was neither born nor buried there. Harry Daniels Close in Wymondham, Norfolk was named after him.

1909 NAIK (CORPORAL) DARWAN SING NEGI
1/39th Garhwal Rifles

Darwan Sing Negi was born on 4th March 1883 at Kafaditir Pauri, Badhan, Garhwal, Uttar Pradesh, India. His father was Kalam Sing Negi, a landowner and cultivator. Little more is known of his family. He was educated at the local Regimental School and became a goatherd and shepherd working for his father in the glacier valleys of northern India. He stayed out for weeks at a time and became very hardy, having to endure extremes of temperature and weather.

Darwan enlisted on 4th March 1902. Mobilisation orders were received on 9th August 1914 and the unit left its headquarters at Lansdowne, a hill station near Nagina, Bharat, Uttar Pradesh on 20th August, arriving at Karachi on 3rd

September. The unit disembarked at Marseilles, France as part of the Indian Expeditionary Force on 14th October. It travelled to Orléans on 21st October, reached Lillers on 27th October and marched to Rue de l'Epinette, where arrangements were made to take over trenches from British II Corps.

Awarded the VC for his actions near Festubert, France on 23rd/24th November 1914, LG 7th December 1914. He received the VC from King George V at General Headquarters, St Omer, France on 5th December 1914, two days before it was promulgated in the London Gazette. Although not the first native-born Indian to be awarded the VC, he was the first to actually receive it; the first was awarded to Sepoy Khudadad Khan.

Darwan was commissioned Jemadar (Lieutenant), backdated to 23rd November 1914 and returned to India on recruiting duties from January 1915. Promoted Subadar (Captain) 9th August 1915. He transferred to 1/18th Garhwal Rifles and saw active service in Iraq and Kurdistan. He retired with a pension on 1st February 1920 and was granted land by Lord Gort VC on 8th July 1920. In recognition of his work on behalf of wounded soldiers and war widows and also for motivating the youth of his nation to join the Army, he was honoured with the title Bahadur in 1926.

Darwan Sing Negi married Chandpur Garhwal, daughter of Ratan Sing Rawat, a cultivator and landowner, and lived at Kafarteer, Tharali sub-division, Chamoli District, Lower Garhwal. They had a son, B S Negi, who served as a Lieutenant Colonel in the Indian Army. Darwan lived in a remote area and petitioned for a 125 km railway line to be constructed from Rishikesh. The Viceroy agreed and a survey was carried out during 1924-26, but the cost of construction was so high the project did not proceed. It was resurrected in 1996 and on 9th November 2011 Sonia Gandhi laid a foundation stone. Darwan died at his home on 24th June 1950 and was buried locally. The Darwan Singh Sangrahalaya (Museum), opened in 1986 at Lansdowne, Northern India, is named after him.

In addition to the VC, he received the 1914 Star, British War Medal 1914-20, Victory Medal 1914-19, General Service Medal 1918-62 with clasps 'Kurdistan' & 'Iraq' and George VI Coronation Medal 1937. He presented his VC to his Regiment and wore a duplicate. The original is held by 39th Garhwal Rifles Officers Mess, GRRC Lansdowne, District Pauri Garhwal, India.

LIEUTENANT FRANK ALEXANDER DE PASS
34th Prince Albert Victor's Own Poona Horse

Frank de Pass was born on 26th April 1887 at his parents' home, 2 Kensington Garden Terrace, Paddington, London. The family was Sephardic-Jewish (Spanish/Portuguese) in origin and came to England in the 1660s. The original surname was Shalom, peace in Hebrew, but during the Inquisition some families changed it to the Spanish for peace 'De Paz'. When those families moved to England the name was anglicised to de Pass. His father was Sir Eliot Arthur de Pass KBE (1851-1937), founder of EA de Pass & Co, West India Merchants, trading in Jamaican sugar and coffee. He was a Special Commissioner and Attorney of the Windsor and Annapolis Railway in Nova Scotia 1873-78, Chairman of the West India Committee 1928-36 and President 1936, Governor of Imperial College Tropical Agriculture, Vice-President of British Empire Producers Organisation and Vice-President of the West Indian Club. Frank's mother was Beatrice (Trixie) née de Mercado (1866-1939), born at Kingston, Jamaica. Eliot and Beatrice married on 29th August 1883 at Kingston. The family lived at various other addresses in London (Lancaster Gate Terrace, 91 Lexham Gardens, 23 Queen's Gate Terrace and 54 Albert Court on Prince's Gate) and Bembridge, Isle of Wight. Frank had four brothers and a sister.

Frank was educated at Abbey School in Beckenham, Kent and Rugby School in Warwickshire, where he was a contemporary of Rupert Brooke. He entered the Royal Military Academy Woolwich in 1904, having been placed third on the list of successful candidates. Commissioned in the Royal Field Artillery on 20th December 1906, he was posted to India. Promoted Lieutenant 20th March 1909.

Transferred to 34th Prince Albert Victor's Own Poona Horse on 1st August 1909. He learnt Hindustani and studied Persian. Frank was an accomplished rider on the flat and cross-country, played a great deal of polo and was also a fine shot. Appointed Orderly Officer to Sir Percy Lake, Chief of General Staff in India, with the local rank of Captain in November 1913. He rejoined the Regiment in September 1914 and arrived at Marseilles on 15th October 1914; the first Indian cavalry regiment to serve in the war. The Regiment saw its first action at Neuve Chapelle on 2nd November and for the next few weeks served dismounted, providing work parties and acting as a mobile reserve.

Awarded the VC for his actions near Festubert, France on 24/25th November 1914, LG 18th February 1915. Frank de Pass was killed by a sniper during his VC action and is buried in Béthune Town Cemetery, France (I A 24).

Frank de Pass' grave in Béthune Town Cemetery, France, flanked by another Jewish officer, Captain CDW Bamberger Royal Engineers, and an Indian Christian, Captain Kanwar Indarjit Singh MC, Indian Medical Service attached 57th Wilde's Rifles. (Mike Cox)

His gravestone carries the words from Rupert Brooke's war sonnet 'IV. The Dead', "...... *loved; gone proudly friended*". Frank de Pass was the first Jew to be awarded the VC in the war. **Mentioned in Sir John French's Despatches dated 14 January 1915, LG 17 February 1915, and 31 May 1915, LG 22nd June 1915.** The VC was posted to his father, because he was not well enough to receive it from the King personally.

In addition to the VC, he received the 1914 Star with 'Mons' clasp, British War Medal 1914-20 and Victory Medal 1914-19 with Mentioned-in-Despatches oak-leaf. His VC was sold at Spinks on 28th March 1995 for £25,000 and is held by the National Army Museum, Chelsea, London. Frank is commemorated on the Royal Military Academy Woolwich VC Memorial Board in the Royal Military Academy Sandhurst library.

Frank's sister Marjorie (1891-1983) married Vice Admiral Henry Karslake Kitson KBE CB RN (1877-1952). Henry joined the Royal Navy in 1891 aged 13. By 1927 he was Captain of HMS *Rodney* and commanded the 3rd Battle Squadron in the Atlantic Fleet 1929-30. In 1931 he became Admiral Superintendent of Portsmouth Dockyard and helped set up what is now the National Maritime Museum at Greenwich. He was knighted in 1935 and organised the fleet review for George V's Silver Jubilee. He retired soon afterwards, but was recalled in 1940 to become Flag Officer-in-Charge Falmouth Sub Command of Western Approaches and retired for the second time in 1942. He was a talented naval artist and his sketches and paintings were published in '*When Britannia Ruled the Waves*' in 2008.

One of Marjorie's and Henry's sons was General Sir Frank Edward Kitson GBE KCB MC & Bar, born 1926. He served in Kenya during the Mau Mau rebellion, in Malaya during the Emergency, commanded 39th Airportable (later retitled Infantry) Brigade in Northern Ireland 1970-72, commanded 2nd Division 1976-78 and was Commander-in-Chief of UK Land Forces 1982-85. He published a number of books including, '*Gangs and Counter-Gangs*' 1960, '*Low Intensity Operations: Subversion, Insurgency and Peacekeeping*' 1971 and '*Bunch of Five*' 1977. He was called to give evidence in the Saville Inquiry (1998-2010) into Bloody Sunday, 30th January 1972, in Northern Ireland.

Frank de Pass' nephew, General Sir Frank Kitson, gained huge experience in low intensity conflicts in Kenya, Malaya and Northern Ireland before becoming Commander-in-Chief of UK Land Forces.

LIEUTENANT MAURICE JAMES DEASE
4th Battalion, The Royal Fusiliers (City of London Regiment)

Maurice Dease was born at Ballynagall, Coole, Co Westmeath, Ireland on 28th September 1889, although his place of birth is often seen as Gaulstown, Coole. His father was Edmund FitzLaurence Dease (1856-1934) JP DL, Vice-Lieutenant of Cavan. His mother was Katherine (Kate) Mary née Murray (1860-1944). They married on 15th November 1888 at St Patrick's, Cork, Ireland. Maurice had a sister, Maud Mary Dease (1890-1974), who married the Hon Bertram Leo French BA, ninth son of the 4th Baron de Freyne.

Maurice was educated at St Basil's and Frognal Park Preparatory Schools, both in Hampstead, before attending Stonyhurst College in Clitheroe, Lancashire 1903-07. At Stonyhurst he was a keen ornithologist and was appointed Aviary Boy and also became a Cadet in the OTC. He attended the Army Department of Wimbledon College (RC) September 1907 – December 1908, followed by the Royal Military College Sandhurst. Although not sporting by nature or an academic, he was determined, deeply religious and loved by those who knew him.

4th Royal Fusiliers officers at Parkhurst on 11th August 1914 – 13 of the 31 officers in this picture did not survive the war. Officers who feature in the Nimy story are:

Rear row from left – 2nd Dease, 4th Mead.

Middle row from left – 3rd Steele, 6th Smith, far right Ashburner.

Front row from left – 6th McMahon, 9th Bowden-Smith.

Maurice Dease's grave (front row centre) in St Symphorien Military Cemetery (V B 2), near Mons. To the right is the grave of Joseph Mead, the platoon commander who attempted to reinforce the railway bridge. Behind Mead is the grave of Canadian Private George Lawrence Price, the last Commonwealth soldier to be killed in the war on 11th November 1918. Elsewhere in the cemetery is the first British casualty of the war, Private John Parr, who is buried within a few metres of Private G E Ellison, the last British fatality on 11th November 1918. It is a fitting and tranquil place to end a visit to the Mons battlefield.

He was commissioned into the Royal Fusiliers on 20th April 1910 and that October took part in special mountainous warfare training in North Wales run by an Indian Army officer. Promoted Lieutenant 24th April 1912. The 4th Battalion was stationed at Parkhurst, Isle of Wight at the outbreak of war. It mobilised on 7th August 1914 and disembarked at Le Havre, France on 13th August, with Maurice Dease as the Machine-Gun Officer.

Awarded the first VC of the war for his actions at Nimy, near Mons, Belgium on 23rd August 1914, LG 16th November 1914. Mentioned in Field Marshal Sir John French's Despatch dated 8th October 1914, LG 19th October 1914 (duplicated 20th October and reissued 9th December 1914). Maurice was killed during his VC action at Nimy on 23rd August 1914 and is buried in St Symphorien Military Cemetery, Belgium (V B 2).

His father was executor of his will – effects £516/3/-, sealed London on 28th April 1915. The VC was sent to his father by post on 11th January 1915; this was before investitures were held for posthumous awards. In addition to the VC, Maurice was awarded the 1914 Star with 'Mons' clasp, British War Medal 1914-20 and Victory Medal 1914-19 with Mentioned-in-Despatches oak-leaf. The medals eventually passed to Dease's nephew, Major Maurice Aloysius French, who sold them to pay for his grandchildren's education. He offered first refusal to the Regiment for the valuation of £18,000. The Victoria and Albert Museum paid half and the Regiment found the remainder. The medals are held by the Royal Fusiliers Museum in the Tower of London.

Maurice is commemorated on the Stonyhurst College war memorial, on the Wayside Cross at Woodchester, Stroud, Gloucestershire where his aunt lived, and on the Catholic Officers' Association Roll of Honour in Westminster Cathedral. An uncle, Major Gerald Dease, also served in the Royal Fusiliers. A cousin on his mother's side, Lieutenant Percival Victor Alban Radcliffe, 5th Green Howards attached Machine Gun Corps (Cavalry), died on 25th November 1917 and is buried in Anneux British Cemetery, France (III F 22). Dease is related to John Aidan Liddell VC MC RAF, through his aunt's (Madeline Mary Dease) marriage to Charles Liddell, uncle of the VC.

LIEUTENANT JOHN HENRY STEPHEN DIMMER
2nd Battalion, The King's Royal Rifle Corps

John Dimmer was born at 37 Gloster Street, South Lambeth, London on 9th October 1883. His father, also John Dimmer (1849-99), enlisted as a Boy in the Royal Navy on 18th January 1866, giving his date of birth as 3rd July 1851. He served on HMS *Irresistible*, *Hector*, *Royal George*, *Pallas*, *Inconstant*, *Excellent*, *Volage* and *Duke of Wellington* and was discharged as an Able Seaman on 21st July 1879. In civilian life at various times he worked on the railways and as an engineer,

labourer and driller. His mother was Ellen née Busby (1852–1932), a domestic servant. John and Ellen were married in the 4th quarter of 1882 at Lambeth.

John junior had two younger brothers (a sister died shortly after birth) and the family lived at 36 Herbert Road, Wimbledon, Surrey. John was educated at Melrose Road School and Rutlish Science School, Merton 1896–98. George Edward Cates VC and John Major, who was Prime Minister 1990–97, later attended Rutlish Science School. John Dimmer was very active in youth organisations being a Sergeant in 1st Cadet Battalion KRRC 1900–01, a member of 1st Wimbledon Company and later 1st Barnet Company Boys' Brigade as a Sergeant Instructor until 1902 and a Boy Scout Worker in Southend. After leaving school he was employed for four years in the office of a civil engineer, Mr G H Hughes, of Queen Victoria Street in Westminster.

John enlisted into the KRRC on 1st July 1902, giving his date of birth as 1st June 1884, which appears in the Army List, and was posted to Cork on 3rd July. He won prizes for drill, shooting and other military activities. He served with 4th KRRC in South Africa 4th November 1902 – June 1904. Promoted Lance Corporal in 1902 and Corporal in 1903 for excellent reconnaissance and signalling work serving with the Mounted Infantry in Orange River Colony. He was commended by General Sir Ian Hamilton and General Neville Lyttelton for military sketching and served for some time as a sergeant instructor. Promoted Lance Sergeant in 1905. John studied the military systems of France and Germany in 1906 at his own expense and at the end of that year sat an examination to determine his qualities for commissioned service. He passed with high marks and also gained the First Class Army School Certificate in March 1907. In November 1907 the Army Council commended him for his work abroad on behalf of the Intelligence Department.

The Commanding Officer of 4th KRRC recommended John for a commission based upon his professional qualities, but not socially because he was unable to afford the lifestyle. On 26th March 1908, Mr HC Lea (MP for St Pancras and a former 43rd Regiment officer) approached Secretary of State for War, Lord Haldane, to represent John Dimmer's case. On 15th April the King approved a commission in the KRRC with the agreement that he was not required to purchase the uniform, as he was to be detached immediately. John was commissioned into 4th KRRC on 6th May 1908 and attached to the West African Regiment as a Local Lieutenant from 20th June 1908. While in Africa he became a Freemason; 1st Battalion West India Regiment Lodge No 390 (now Lodge South Carolina, Kingston, Jamaica) from 8th August 1908 and West African Regiment Lodge No 157 as a founding member on 2nd October 1908 (now Anniversary Lodge, Accra, Ghana). Promoted Lieutenant KRRC on 27th July 1911.

While home on leave from Africa (9th December 1912 – 8th April 1913) he sought another appointment, as he could no longer afford to live as a regimental officer. He wanted to be a staff officer with local forces, adjutant of a Territorial unit or work with the Boundary and Delineation Commission (he held a special pass at the School of Military Engineering at Chatham in Trigonometrical & Topographical Surveying). The War Office rejected all options; he had insufficient experience for a staff appointment, he could not be an adjutant because he had never served with the parent regiment and there was no boundary work at that time. Instead he was recommended for another tour with the West African Regiment. John applied to resign, but later withdrew it and took up the appointment.

John was home on leave when war broke out in Europe. His tour in Africa was cut short and he went to France with 2nd KRRC on 13th August 1914. At 5 a.m. on 29th October the Battalion moved out of Polygon Wood to Herenthage Chateau and with 1st Loyal North Lancashire reinforced 3rd Brigade in the afternoon. Before dawn on 31st October the enemy attacked and forced the left of the position. A and B Companies were almost surrounded, but held up the enemy and the force withdrew gradually to a less advanced position. The enemy attacked again early on 1st November, but were held. Throughout this difficult period John Dimmer and displayed great devotion to duty. **He was awarded the MC for his actions on 29th-31st October 1914 at Herenthage Chateau, LG 1st January 1915.** His name was on the first list for the award of the MC, making him the first VC and MC combination. **Awarded the VC for his actions at Klein Zillebeke, Belgium on 12th November 1914, LG 19th November 1914. Mentioned in Field Marshal Sir John French's Despatch dated 8th October 1914, LG 19th October 1914 (duplicated 20th October and reissued 9th December 1914).**

Having been wounded in the VC action, John was treated in hospital at the Bellevue Hotel at Wimereux, near Boulogne. During convalescence he and another officer bought English newspapers while having lunch in a restaurant. Suddenly John turned pale and fell back in his chair. The other officer rushed to help, asking if he was ill. John answered in a weak voice, "*It is nothing, but I have just read that I've got the Victoria Cross.*" Returning to England, he was appointed Brigade Major of 4th (Reserve) Brigade on 7th December 1914. Appointed Temporary Captain on 23rd December 1914. The VC was presented by the King at Buckingham Palace on 13th January 1915.

A medical board at Westcliff-on-Sea on 2nd February 1915 decided he had recovered from his wounds and there had been no recurrence of malaria resulting from service in Africa since the previous December; he was declared fit for general service. The same month he addressed the boys of Harrow School OTC. The Borough of Wimbledon offered him the honorary freedom in April 1915, but he declined, "*Too much publicity has been given to my name already, and caused me a great deal of worry and annoyance*". Promoted Captain 30th April 1915. The MC was presented by the King at Buckingham Palace on 10th May 1915.

John suffered from nervous strain and was apt to drink excessively, but was in denial about it. He was offered a Court of Inquiry to clear his name, but denied the charge, refused the inquiry and agreed to resign his appointment and return to his unit. He was replaced as Brigade Major of 4th (Reserve) Brigade on 9th September 1915. On 26th September he took command of the 6th (Reserve) Battalion training camp at Sheerness. Next day a medical board at Caxton Hall, London declared him fit for full service following nervous strain. He was sent to Salonika where he served as a brigade machine-gun officer in 10th Division (10th May – 4th November 1916), a company commander in 3rd KRRC and as an Observer with the RFC. He suffered a recurrence of malaria and refused to be evacuated, but when he fell ill again he was sent back to Britain. Having rejoined 2nd KRRC on 5th February 1917, he contracted blood poisoning. Appointed Acting Lieutenant Colonel on 22nd October 1917 to command 2/4th Royal Berkshire. Promoted Temporary Lieutenant Colonel 9th January 1918 with seniority from 22nd October 1917.

John Dimmer married Gladys Dora May née Bayley-Parker (1895-1982) on 19th January 1918 at Moseley Parish Church. They had no children. John was killed in action at Marteville, France on 21st March 1918 while leading a counter-attack on horseback. **Mentioned in Field Marshal Sir Douglas Haig's Despatch dated 7th April 1918, LG 24th May 1918.** His body was missing until March 1920 when it was discovered about 600m south of Maissemy and was reburied in Vadencourt British Cemetery, Maissemy (II B 46).

In addition to the VC and MC, John Dimmer was awarded the 1914 Star with 'Mons' clasp, British War Medal 1914-20 and Victory Medal 1914-19 with Mentioned-in-Despatches oak-leaf. His VC is held by the Royal Green Jackets (Rifles) Museum, Winchester. He is commemorated in a number of places:

- KRRC memorial in Winchester Cathedral.
- Grand Lodge of Ireland Masonic Roll of Honour for the Great War 1914-19.
- Kingston Vale War Memorial.
- Crown House Civic Offices, Borough of Morden.

Gladys married Leopold Ernest Stratford George Canning, 4th Baron Garvagh (1878-1956) on 1st January 1919 at St Mathew's, Bayswater. Leopold's previous marriage had been annulled in 1909. Their son, Victor Stratford de Redcliffe Canning (1924-44), served as a Lieutenant (262098) with 5th Grenadier Guards and was killed in action at Cassino, Italy on 6th May 1944; he is commemorated on the Cassino Memorial (MID). Their daughter, Dora Valerie Patricia Canning (1919-2002), married Philip Anthony Wellesley-Clark, who was killed in action in Normandy serving as a Lieutenant (R72223) in the Royal Artillery and No 4 Commando on 6th June 1944; he is buried in Bayeux War Cemetery, Normandy (X H 26).

6840 PRIVATE FREDERICK WILLIAM DOBSON
2nd Battalion, Coldstream Guards

Frederick William Dobson (known as Billy) was born at Nafferton Farm, Ovingham, near Newcastle-on-Tyne, Northumberland on 9th November 1886. The farm is now managed by Newcastle University. His father was Thomas Dobson (c.1867-1915), a groom in 1891, a stationary engineer in 1901 and a machine man in 1911. His mother was Elizabeth née Holt (1865-1909), a cook for the Reverend John Bee, Rector of Christ Church, Jarrow. Their marriage was registered at Gateshead in the 2nd quarter of 1885. Billy had three brothers and six sisters and was educated at Collingwood Junior School near Willington, North Shields, Northumberland. In 1901 the family was living at 38 Orde Avenue, Willington, Northumberland and at 25 Hopper Street, North Shields in 1911.

Billy was employed as a painter's apprentice until enlisting in the Coldstream Guards on 7th July 1906. He transferred to the Reserve on 7th July 1909 and was employed as an apprentice signwriter. By April 1911 he was a horsekeeper underground, boarding with the Brougham family at 14 Wood Terrace, Hooker Gate, Rowlands Gill, Co Durham. Billy Dobson married Rebecca Cutbell née Dobson (1889-1958) on 30th September 1911 at Gateshead. Despite the same surname it is understood they were not related; Dobson is a common name in the northeast. They had two sons – Robert born on 30th May 1912 and Thomas born on 17th November 1913, both registered at Newcastle-upon-Tyne.

Billy was recalled on 6th August 1914 and disembarked in France on 12th August. **Awarded the VC for his actions at Chavonne, Aisne, France on 28th September 1914, LG 9th December 1914.** Promoted Lance Corporal later on 28th November 1914. Although the recommendation was strongly supported by Lieutenant Colonel V Peretia, commanding 2nd Coldstream Guards, and Brigade and Divisional commanders, the Corps commander, Haig, acknowledged Dobson's bravery but was not in favour of the VC for rescuing the wounded and recommended the DCM; the King overruled him. His VC was presented by the King at Buckingham Palace on 3rd February 1915. **Awarded the Russian Cross of the Order of St George 4th Class (No.127163), LG 25th August 1915. Mentioned in Field Marshal Sir John French's Despatch dated 8th October 1914, LG 19th October 1914 (duplicated 20th October and reissued 9th December 1914).** Billy received a number of wounds during the war and was hospitalised at 3rd Southern General Hospital, High Street, Oxford where he was cared for by Staff Nurses Isabel Mace (MID France 1918), Soper, Hawker and

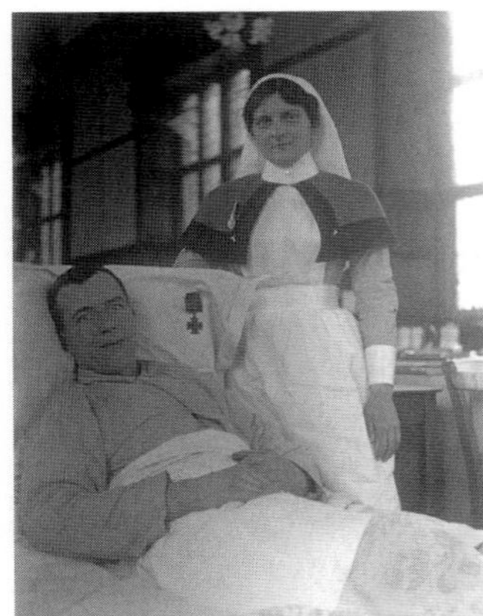

Billy Dobson in 3rd Southern General Hospital in Oxford with one of the Staff Nurses who cared for him.

Hughes. He was discharged from the Army on 1st July 1917, being medically unfit for further service. His wounds affected him for the rest of his life.

Billy worked in the mines for a while and later became a cinema commissionaire, but considered the VC a hindrance when seeking employment as his colleagues claimed he received special treatment. He lived in Leeds for a while at Abbey Terrace, Hunslet. He spent long periods in hospital as a result of his war wounds and was in constant pain from his injuries. Billy Dobson's address was 20 Mount Pleasant, Mickley, Northumberland when he died at 418 Westgate Road, Newcastle-upon-Tyne on 13th November 1935. The causes of death were congestion of the lungs, myocardial degeneration and syphilitic aortitis. He was buried in Ryton and Crawcrook Cemetery, Co Durham and the grave (A 234) was unmarked until the Newcastle Branch of the Coldstream Guards Association dedicated a headstone on 15 March 1986.

Billy is commemorated at High Spen Primary School, Co Durham, as he lived in the village just prior to the war, along with Thomas Young VC, who is buried there. In addition to the VC and Russian Order of St George, he received the 1914 Star with 'Mons' clasp, British War Medal 1914-20 and Victory Medal 1914-19 with Mentioned-in-Despatches oak-leaf. His VC, 1914 Star and Order of St George were found in a Newcastle pawnbroker's shop in 1936; the family donated them to the Regiment. His British War Medal and Victory Medal were donated to the Regiment in August 1988 by Mrs Florence Dobson, wife of Billy's eldest son Robert, who died in May 1988. His VC is held by the Coldstream Guards at the Guards Museum, Wellington Barracks, Birdcage Walk, London.

12343 BATTERY SERGEANT MAJOR GEORGE THOMAS DORRELL
L Battery, Royal Horse Artillery

George Dorrell was born at 23 G Street (later Galton Street), Queen's Park Estate, Paddington, London on 7th July 1880. His father was Thomas Richard Dorrell (1859-1931), a cab driver. His mother was Emma née Butcher (c.1857-1914). Their marriage was registered at Kensington in the 3rd quarter of 1878. George had two brothers and five sisters. In 1901 the family was living at 203 Kilburn Lane, Willesden, Middlesex, in 1911 at 12 Ashmore Road, Paddington and they also lived at 70 Kilburn Park Road, Carlton Vale, London at some time. George was educated at Campbell Street School, Maida Vale, London, which became Paddington Green Primary School in 1962.

He enlisted underage on 2nd December 1895, giving his date of birth as 2nd July 1876. He served in South Africa 27th October 1899 – 6th November 1902 and then in India until 7th March 1906, when he returned to England. Promoted Bombardier 2nd January, Corporal 31st May and Sergeant 18th June 1900. Promoted Battery Quartermaster Sergeant 2nd December 1908 and Battery Sergeant Major 29th November 1911. George Dorrell married Lucy née Frost (1884-1969), an elementary school teacher from Manchester, at Chorlton, Lancashire on 17th October 1914. They had three children – Lucy Joyce Dorrell born in the 1st quarter of 1917 and twins Pamela and George Thomas Edwin Dorrell born in the 2nd quarter of 1920; all three were registered at Chorlton. The family lived at Avington Park, Winchester, Hampshire at some time.

George disembarked in France with L Battery on 16th August 1914. **Awarded the VC for his actions at Néry, France on 1st September 1914, LG 16th November 1914. Mentioned in Field Marshal Sir John French's Despatch dated 8th October 1914, LG 4th December 1914 (reissued 9th December 1914).** His VC was presented by the King at Buckingham Palace on 13th January 1915. George Dorrell was commissioned on 1st October 1914. Promoted Temporary Lieutenant 7th March, Temporary Captain 2nd May and Lieutenant 9th June 1915. Promoted Acting Major and appointed Commander A/122 Battery RFA 25th September – 28th November 1916. Promoted Acting Major and appointed Commander B/190 Battery RFA 19th March 1917 – 24th July 1919. Promoted Captain 18th May 1918. **Mentioned in Sir Douglas Haig's Despatch dated 9th April 1917, LG 18th May 1917.** Appointed Adjutant 90th (1st London) Field Brigade RFA TF 2nd March 1920. He retired from the Regular Army on 23rd September 1921 with the rank of Major and seniority from 14th March 1919. The same day he was granted a commission in the TF as a Captain and continued as Adjutant of 90th (1st London) Field Brigade at Handel Street, London, until 16th September 1926. Promoted Major 25th December 1924. **Awarded the MBE, LG 3rd June 1925 for services with 90th (1st London) Field Brigade RA.** The MBE was presented by the King at Buckingham Palace on 4th July 1925. Having attained the age limit of liability to recall he ceased to belong to the Reserve of Officers on 2nd July 1926. George relinquished his TA commission on attaining the age limit on 17th October 1928 and transferred to the Regular Army Reserve of Officers with seniority from 14th March 1919. Promoted Brevet Lieutenant Colonel 1st January 1929.

In the Second World War he served in the Home Guard from May 1940 and was promoted Major and appointed Company Commander in 27th County of London (Roehampton) Battalion on 1st February 1941. James Leach VC served in the same unit. By 1950 he and Lucy were living at 5 Oakfield Court, Queen's Road, Weybridge, Surrey and by 1966 they had moved to Green End, Surrey Gardens, Effingham Junction, Surrey. They also lived at 146 Palewell Park, Sheen, London at some time. George was present at the Néry Day celebrations at Hildesheim, West Germany in 1956, during which he handed over Edward Bradbury's VC to L (Néry) Battery RHA on behalf of Bradbury's nephew, Major A J Crewdson MC, who was unable to attend.

George Dorrell died at his home at 30 Bray Road, Cobham, Surrey on 7th January 1971. He was cremated at Randall's Park Crematorium, Leatherhead, Surrey and his ashes scattered there. He is commemorated on the Royal Artillery VC Memorial in the ruins of St George's Garrison Church at Woolwich, which was reduced to a roofless shell by a V1 in 1944.

In addition to the VC and MBE, he was awarded the Queen's South Africa Medal 1899-1902 with six clasps (Relief of Kimberley, Paardeberg, Driefontein, Johannesburg, Diamond Hill & Belfast), King's South Africa Medal 1901-02 with two clasps (South Africa 1901 & South Africa 1902), 1914 Star with 'Mons' clasp, British War Medal 1914-20, Victory Medal 1914-19 with Mentioned-in-Despatches oak-leaf, Defence Medal 1939-45, Army Long Service & Good Conduct Medal, George VI Coronation Medal 1937 and Elizabeth II Coronation Medal 1953. His VC is owned by L (Néry) Battery RHA and is loaned to the Imperial War Museum, Lambeth, London.

69960 DRIVER JOB HENRY CHARLES DRAIN
37 (Howitzer) Battery, VIII (Howitzer) Brigade, Royal Field Artillery

Job Drain was born at 16 Parson's Buildings, Axe Street, Barking, Essex on 15th October 1895. His father, also Job (1867-1916), served in the ASC during the South African War and First World War. In civilian life he was a labourer at a chemical works. His mother was Susan née Stokes (1863-1900) a domestic servant. Their marriage was registered at Romford in the 1st quarter of 1894. Job had two brothers and a sister; all died young.

Having been educated at the Church of England School in Barking, Job was employed as a factory hand until he enlisted at Stratford on 27th August 1912. He disembarked in France on 19th August 1914. **Awarded the VC for his actions at Le Cateau on 26th August 1914, LG 25th November 1914. Mentioned in Field Marshal Sir John French's Despatch dated 8th October 1914, LG 19th October 1914 (duplicated 20th**

October and reissued 9th December 1914). His VC was presented by the King at Locon, near Béthune, France on 1st December 1914. The first Job knew about it was in the trenches near Béthune when a field officer informed him that the King wanted to see him. There was no time to clean up before he was in the King's inspection line at Locon and only then was he informed he was to receive the VC.

Job's cousin, G34043 Private Albert George Sun Drain 19th Middlesex, was killed in action on 24th March 1918 and is commemorated on the Arras Memorial, France. Job was demobilised in 1919 and discharged from the Reserve on 28th August 1924 as a Sergeant. In a ceremony at the municipal buildings and park he was formally welcomed back to Barking with a purse of gold, an illuminated address and a watch. He was a member of the VC Guard at the interment of the Unknown Warrior on 11th November 1920.

At various times he was employed as a Whitehall messenger, fish-porter at Billingsgate, London Passenger Transport Board bus driver and by London Electricity Board. His marriage to Patricia Cecilia née Murray (1899-1981) was registered at Poplar in the 4th quarter of 1919. They lived at 42 Greatfields Road, Dagenham, Essex and had two children – Patricia Winifred Drain born 28th June 1920 at Mile End (died 1986) and Job HG Drain, whose birth was registered in the 4th quarter of 1921 at Poplar.

On 28th October 1929, Job was defended by Brett Cloutman VC at West Ham Police Court, accused of blocking a tramway at Plaistow with his bus; he claimed he could not pull over due to the way being blocked by cyclists – the case was dismissed and Job was awarded two guineas costs. On 5th October 1931 during Barking's Charter Day celebrations, he was presented to Prince George, the future King George VI.

Job Drain died at his home on 26th July 1975 and is buried in Rippleside Cemetery, Barking (U 158). He is commemorated in various places:

- Royal Artillery VC Memorial in the ruins of St George's Chapel, the former Garrison Church at Woolwich, which was reduced to a roofless shell by a V1 in 1944.
- On 10th November 2009 two of his grandsons unveiled a statue of him in front of the Broadway Theatre in Barking.
- In November 2009 a blue plaque was unveiled on his former home at 42 Greatfields Road, Barking.
- 93 (Le Cateau) Battery, successor to 37 (Howitzer) Battery, comprises Drain, Luke and Reynolds Troops.

In addition to the VC, he was awarded the 1914 Star with 'Mons' clasp, British War Medal 1914-20, Victory Medal 1914-19 with Mentioned-in-Despatches oak-leaf, George VI Coronation Medal 1937 and Elizabeth II Coronation Medal 1953. His VC is held by the Lord Ashcroft VC Collection in the Lord Ashcroft Gallery of the Imperial War Museum, having been purchased in a private sale in 2008.

L/10523 PRIVATE EDWARD DWYER
1st Battalion, The East Surrey Regiment

Edward Dwyer was born at 4 Cassidy Road, Fulham, London on 25th November 1895. He was registered as Edwin at birth. His paternal grandparents came from Ireland. His father, James Dwyer (1863-1930), was variously a greengrocer, labourer and housepainter. He enlisted in the Army Service Corps on 6th October 1915 (No.SS18144) and served at Mudros with 27th Labour Company from 7th November 1915, at ANZAC later in November and Helles before being evacuated from the Gallipoli peninsula. He went to France via Egypt, but his health broke down with general weakness and failing eyesight and he was invalided out of the Army on 1st September 1916. Edwin's mother was Mary Ann née Felstead (1861-1941) known as Sally. She married Arthur Willis Inglis on 8th January 1880 at Camden Town and had a daughter. The marriage failed and Arthur remarried in 1890. James Dwyer and Mary Ann Inglis lived together and had six children before they married in the 3rd quarter of 1912 at Fulham. One daughter was born in the Chelsea Workhouse in 1888 indicating the family suffered hard times. They lived at various times at 25 Molton Street, 40 Walham Avenue and 83 Sherbrooke Road in Fulham.

Edward was educated at St Thomas of Canterbury Church School, Fulham (now St Thomas of Canterbury Roman Catholic Primary School) and was employed as a greengrocer's assistant in Knightsbridge. He enlisted in 4th East Surrey (Special Reserve) on 12th July 1912 giving his age as 17 years and 10 months (No.6686) and his first name as Edward. It is said he ran away from home to enlist in shame at his parents' marriage banns being read in church. Edward, as he was thereafter, transferred to Regular service on 6th September 1912 and was posted to the 1st Battalion on 6th October. He had a number of disciplinary problems in 1913:

- 18th April – confined to barracks for five days for attempting to sell another soldier's boots.
- 22nd June – confined to barracks for three days for being absent from church parade.
- 30th June – confined to barracks for five days for being improperly dressed on parade and disobeying an order.

He was based in Dublin, recovering from venereal disease, when war broke out and went across to France on 13th August 1914. He developed a septic heel on 24th October 1914. **Awarded the VC for his actions at Hill 60, near Ypres,**

Belgium on 20th – 21st April 1915, LG 22nd May 1915. He was the youngest winner of the VC until Boy Cornwell in May 1916. Promoted Lance Corporal 24th April 1915. Wounded by a gun shot to the head on 27th April 1915 and was treated at No 1 General Hospital at Étretat before being moved back to Britain. His VC was presented by the King at Buckingham Palace on 28th June 1915.

On recovering from his wounds he was posted to 3rd (Reserve) Battalion on 22nd September 1915 and carried out recruiting duties for six months. During this time he made a recording of his experiences ('With our boys at the front'), which can be heard via the internet. **Awarded the Cross of the Order of St George 3rd Class (Russia), LG 25th August 1915.**

Edward Dwyer married Maude 'Billie' née Barrett-Freeman at St Thomas' Catholic Church, Rylston Road, Fulham on 20th December 1915. She was a Red Cross nurse who tended him in hospital in France. The priest who married them, Father D Browne, was a long time friend of Dwyer's. The marriage was kept a secret and he didn't tell his mother until the following day. Edward and Maude had no children.

Appointed Acting Corporal 27th December 1915. Returning to duty, Edward was reprimanded on 29th January 1916 for being absent while on escort duty at Dover. He returned to the 1st Battalion on 29th March 1916 and was promoted Corporal on 27th July 1916. He was killed in action at Guillemont, France on 3rd September 1916 by a chance shell near Battalion HQ while guarding a prisoner who was also killed. He is buried in Flat Iron Copse Cemetery (III J 3).

Edward left his VC in the care of Father Browne who eventually became a Canon and died in 1962. The VC was found by the parish priest who contacted the War Office and it subsequently went to the Regiment in March 1962. It is held by the Queen's Royal Surrey Regiment Museum, Clandon Park, Guildford. In addition to the VC, Edward was awarded the 1914 Star with 'Mons' clasp, British War Medal 1914-20, Victory Medal 1914-19 and the Russian Cross of St George 3rd Class. He is commemorated in a number of places:

- Regimental Memorial at All Saints Parish Church, Kingston-Upon-Thames, Surrey.
- Bust in Fulham Library.
- St Thomas's Roman Catholic Church, Rylston Road, Fulham.

His brother James (born 1898) served in the Royal Naval Division. His other brother, 12887 Sergeant Charles Dwyer (1894-1917) 11th Worcestershire, was killed at Salonika on 7th January 1917 and is buried in Karasouli Military Cemetery, Greece (F 1308).

CAPTAIN CHARLES CALVELEY FOSS
2nd Battalion, The Bedfordshire Regiment

Charles Foss was born at 'The Firs', Kobe, Japan on 9th March 1885. His father was the Right Reverend Hugh James Foss DD (1848-1932), a SPG Missionary to Japan 1876-99 and Bishop of Osaka 1899-1923. His mother was Janet née McEwen (1855-94), who started Shoin High School, an Anglican girls' school in Kobe. Their marriage was registered during the 3rd quarter of 1880 at Chester. She died in 1894 and on 24th July 1901 Hugh married Lina Janet née Ovans (1870-1942) at Hiogo, Japan. Charles had a brother and four sisters.

Charles' paternal grandfather was Edward Foss (1787-1870), a solicitor, biographer, author of '*Judges of England*', director of Law Life Assurance Society, president of the Incorporated Law Society 1842-43, original member of the Archaeological Institute, Fellow of the Society of Antiquaries, Council of the Camden Society, member of the Royal Society of Literature and DL Kent. His maternal grandfather was Dr William McEwen MD FRCS (1812-82), originally from Dumfries-shire, who settled at Chester.

Charles Foss' father, the Right Reverend Hugh James Foss, Bishop of Osaka 1899-1923.

Charles was educated at Marlborough College 1899-1902 (OTC). He trained at the Royal Military College Sandhurst and was commissioned on 2nd March 1904. Promoted Lieutenant 22nd July 1906, appointed Adjutant 11th February 1912 – 14th August 1915 and promoted Captain 20th November 1912. The Battalion was in South Africa when war broke out. Having returned to Britain it landed at Zeebrugge on 4th October 1914.

On 18th October the Battalion went into action for the first time between Becelaere and Gheluvelt, digging in that night with its right on the Menin Road at the 10 kilometre post from Ypres. The CO was killed on 31st October and Charles was the senior officer remaining. When the Battalion came out of the line on 5th November, he was the only combatant officer left and only 350 men came out of the 900 who started. **Awarded the DSO for his services in the period 18th October – 5th November 1914, LG 18th February and 24th March 1915. Awarded the VC for his actions at Neuve Chapelle, France on 12th March 1915, LG 23rd August 1915.** The VC was presented by the King on 28th October

1915 at a parade on open ground near Hesdigneul, northwest of the La Buissierre – Hesdigneul road.

Charles married Vere Katherine née Ovans (1873-1947) on 6th June 1915 at St Thomas, Devon. Vere was the sister of Charles' father's second wife. She was the widow of Captain John Marshall Molesworth Collard (1870-1904), who was commissioned in the Northamptonshire Regiment in 1890, transferred to 90th Punjabis in 1895 and was shot dead by a Havildar of his Regiment at Mandalay, Burma on 13th December 1904; the Havildar also killed two Indian officers before committing suicide. Vere's brother, Captain Edward Hornby Ovans (1882-1915), was commissioned in the Liverpool Regiment from the Militia on 29th November 1905, transferred to 125th Napier's Rifles in 1908 and was killed on 23rd March 1915; he is commemorated on the Neuve Chapelle Memorial (Panel 14). Charles and Vere did not have any children.

Charles was appointed Brigade Major 20th Brigade, 15th August 1915 – 27th October 1916. **Mentioned in Sir John French's Despatches dated 14th February 1915, LG 17th February 1915 and 30th November 1915, LG 1st January 1916 (twice).** Brevet Major 1st January 1916. Appointed Temporary Major 28th October 1916 – 10th November 1918. Three GSO2 appointments followed with the Canadians – HQ 2nd Canadian Division 28th October 1916, HQ 1st Canadian Division 20th January 1917 and HQ Canadian Army Corps 5th July – 10th December 1917. He returned to England as GSO2 at the Staff School, Cambridge 11th December 1917 – 10th October 1918. He went back to France as GSO2, HQ XXII Corps 11th October – 10th November 1918. Appointed Temporary Lieutenant Colonel and GSO1, HQ 57th Division 11th November 1918 – 15th January 1920. **Mentioned in Sir Douglas Haig's Despatches dated 13th November 1916, LG 4th January 1917 and 7th November 1917, LG 11th December 1917. Awarded the Order of Danilo 4th Class (Montenegro), LG 9th March 1917.**

Brevet Lieutenant Colonel 1st January 1919. Attended Staff College from 1st April 1919, along with fellow VCs Gort, Freyberg, Hansen and Pearkes. After graduating in January 1920 he was appointed Brigade Major, Small Arms School, Hythe 26th January 1920 – 25th January 1925. Charles was a member of the VC Guard at the Interment of the Unknown Warrior on 11th November 1920. Promoted Major 1st January 1921. Appointed GSO2, Military Operations, War Office 1st March 1925 – 6th March 1929. Promoted Lieutenant Colonel and appointed CO 2nd Battalion, The King's Regiment 25th October 1930 – 1933. Promoted Colonel and appointed Temporary Brigadier and Commander Rangoon Brigade Area at Mingaladon 29th October 1933 – 1937 (seniority from 1st January 1923). Appointed ADC to the King 1st January 1935 – 8th December 1937. **Created CB, LG 1st February 1937 while Commander Rangoon Brigade Area.** Half pay 29th October 1937 and retired on 8th December, being granted the rank of Honorary Brigadier.

He was not long out of uniform before being appointed Area Organiser Bedfordshire, Local Defence Volunteers 1940. Appointed Lieutenant Colonel to command 3rd Bedfordshire Battalion, Home Guard 1st February 1941. Promoted Colonel and appointed Commander Bedfordshire Group Home Guard 18th April 1942, but reverted to Captain in 3rd Bedfordshire Battalion on 30th September 1943. Commandant Bedfordshire County Cadet Force 1942–47.

Appointed JP Bedfordshire 1942 and DL Bedfordshire 19th June 1943. He ceased to belong to the Reserve of Officers on 9th March 1945 on attaining the age limit. He took an active part in the Bedfordshire Boy Scouts, serving as a Scout and Cub master at Rushmore School and was later Assistant County Commissioner of the Rover Scouts. His wife died on 13th December 1947 and his second marriage to Phyllis Ruth Howie (née Bendyshe Crowther) (c.1888–1968) took place on 9th June 1950 at St Andrew's, Boscombe, Dorset. Phyllis was the widow of Arthur F Howie of Ceylon.

Charles Foss died at St Mary's Hospital, Paddington, London on 9th April 1953 and is buried in Westhill Cemetery, Winchester, Hampshire (2162/5-8). In addition to the VC, CB and DSO he was awarded the 1914 Star with 'Mons' clasp, British War Medal 1914–20, Victory Medal 1914–19 with Mentioned-in-Despatches oakleaf, 1939–45 Defence Medal, War Medal 1939–45, George V Jubilee Medal 1935, George VI Coronation Medal 1937 and the Order of Danilo 4th Class (Montenegro). His VC is held by the Bedfordshire and Hertfordshire Regiment Museum, Wardown Park Museum, Luton, Bedfordshire. Charles had a number of notable siblings:

Eleanor Foss (born 1908) was a CMS missionary in Japan 1936–41 and 1947–70. She became the first Principal of Poole Junior College when it opened in 1950, organized the administration of Poole Gakuin University in Osaka for 34 years, taught English in the Junior High School and Kindergarten and was also on the staff of Sei Ai Church. She wrote '*Seven Meet a Typhoon*', '*Spotlight on Japan*' and '*How They Came*', published between 1953 and 1963. For her work towards women's education in Japan she was awarded the Order of the Sacred Treasure 4th Class by the Emperor.

Charles' brother Hugh. With Oliver Strachey he broke the Japanese Naval Attaché's cipher in 1934 and headed the Japanese Naval Section at Bletchley Park 1942–43.

Hugh Rose Foss (1902–71) was fluent in Japanese and joined the Government Code and Cipher School in 1924. With Oliver Strachey (1874–1960) he broke the Japanese Naval Attaché's cipher in September 1934 and headed the Japanese Naval

Section (Hut 7) at Bletchley Park 1942-43. He was posted to Washington in December 1944 to work with US Navy cryptographers on Japanese ciphers. He was nicknamed 'Lend-lease Jesus' as he always wore sandals. He wrote '*Reminiscences on Enigma*' in 1949 and devised a number of Scottish country-dances including '*Fugal Fergus*', '*John McAlpin*', '*Polharrow Burn*' and '*The Wee Cooper O'Fife*'.

Charles' cousin, Hubert James Foss (1899-1953), was a musician, broadcaster, writer and the first Musical Editor of Oxford University Press. He served in 5th Middlesex in the First World War. His second marriage was to the singer Dora Maria Stevens.

7753 LANCE CORPORAL WILLIAM CHARLES FULLER
2nd Battalion, The Welsh Regiment

William Fuller was born at Newbridge, Laugharne, Carmarthenshire, Wales on 24th March 1884. His father was William Fuller (1850-98), a sailor and later a butcher. His mother was Mary née Fleming (1853-1942). Their marriage was registered at Carmarthen in the 1st quarter of 1873. William had three brothers and four sisters. The family moved to Swansea when he was about four and lived at 47 Orchard Street. He was educated at Rutland Street School and the Swansea Truant School at Bonymaen before being employed as a dock labourer.

William enlisted on 31st December 1902 and served in South Africa and India until transferring to the Reserve in 1909. He was then employed by timber merchants John Lewis & Sons and later as the caretaker of the Elysium Cinema in High Street, Swansea. William Fuller's marriage to Mary Elizabeth née Phillips (1888-1969) was registered in the 3rd quarter of 1909 at Swansea. They had five children – Mary E Fuller born 4th quarter 1910, William Charles Fuller born 4th quarter 1913, Caroline L Fuller born 3rd quarter 1916, Doris May Fuller born 16th January 1920 and Muriel Fuller born 1st quarter 1924; all were registered at Swansea. The family lived at 1 Charles Court and later at Jones Terrace, Swansea.

William was recalled on 4th August 1914 and disembarked in France on 13th August 1914. **Awarded the VC for his actions near Chivy-sur-Aisne, France on 14th September 1914, LG 23rd November 1914.** Promoted Lance Corporal later on 14th September 1914. **Mentioned in Field Marshal Sir John French's Despatch dated 8th October 1914, LG 19th October 1914 (duplicated**

20th October and reissued 9th December 1914). While tending a wounded comrade (Private Tagge) near Gheluvelt, Belgium on 29th October 1914, he was hit by shrapnel in both legs and as he bent over a shrapnel ball entered his right side, travelled up under the shoulder blade and came to rest against his spine close to the right lung. Having been evacuated to England, he was treated at Manchester and in Swansea, where a bullet was removed from his neck. Captain Mark Haggard's widow presented Fuller with a solid gold hunter watch with the bullet taken from Fuller's back moulded to the watch chain. Sir Rider Haggard called on Fuller at his home on 6th January 1915. His VC was presented by the King at Buckingham Palace on 13th January 1915. Unfit for further active service, he became a recruiter in Wales, being appointed Acting Corporal in mid-1915 and later Sergeant. At Fishguard on 19th July 1915 he was invited to enter the lion's cage of Bostock & Wombwell's Circus and calmly stroked the animals while chatting with the tamer. He was discharged unfit for further service on 30th December 1915.

William received Exchequer Bonds at Tenby, Pembrokeshire in 1916 bought by the inhabitants of West Wales. For employment he ran a horse drawn fish cart and bred canaries and greyhounds as a pastime; he also raced the dogs. The family lived at Evans Terrace then West Cross, Mumbles and later 55 Westbury Street, Swansea. On 7th June 1938 he saved two boys from drowning at Tenby Slip and was reputedly awarded the Royal Humane Society Medal, but the Society has no record of it. In the Second World War he was an ARP warden in Swansea.

William Fuller died at his home at 55 Westbury Street, Swansea on 29th December 1974 and was buried in an unmarked grave (R 373) in Oystermouth Cemetery, Mumbles, Swansea. The grave was marked with a headstone in 2005. He is commemorated at:

- Regimental Chapel at Llandaff Cathedral.
- Portrait hangs in the Regimental Museum at Cardiff Castle.
- Named on a silver candlestick in Laugharne Church.

William Fuller pictured with CSM Frederick Barter, who was awarded the VC for his actions at Festubert, France on 16th May 1915. The medal on Fuller's left breast cannot be identified.

In addition to the VC, he received the 1914 Star with 'Mons' clasp, British War Medal 1914-20, Victory Medal 1914-19 with Mentioned-in-Despatches oak-leaf, George VI Coronation Medal 1937 and Elizabeth II Coronation Medal 1953. His VC is held privately.

15624 LANCE CORPORAL WILFRED DOLBY FULLER
1st Battalion, Grenadier Guards

Wilfred Fuller was born at East Kirkby (Kirkby-in-Ashfield), Nottinghamshire on 28th July 1893. His father was Walter Frederick Fuller (1864-1931), a coal miner and later a night pit deputy. His mother was Sarah Ann E née Dolby (1866-1920), a servant. Their marriage was registered during the 2nd quarter of 1883 at Basford, Nottinghamshire. Wilfred had three brothers and two sisters. The family lived on Station Street, Kirkby in Ashfield then moved to Shirebrook and Warsop Vale. In 1907 they moved to 9 Skerry Hill, Mansfield, Nottinghamshire.

Wilfred was educated at local schools. He was a keen footballer, a bugler in the Mansfield Cadet Corps, a member of the Warsop Vale Church Choir and the Mansfield St Lawrence Bible Class. He was teetotal and did not smoke. He was employed as a pony driver at Warsop Vale Colliery and later at Crown Farm Colliery, Mansfield.

Wilfred enlisted on 30th December 1911 and was on the Regimental Police staff at Wellington Barracks, London in 1914. He went to France on 8th November to join the 1st Battalion. Promoted Lance Corporal in December. **Awarded the VC for his actions at Neuve Chapelle, France on 12th March 1915, LG 19th April 1915.** He received a public reception in Mansfield on 20th April and was presented with a gold watch and an illuminated address by the Mayor on 3rd June. His VC was presented by the King at Buckingham Palace on 4th June. **Awarded the Cross of the Order of St George 3rd Class (Russia) (No.16666), LG 25th August 1915.** It was presented by the King at No 3 Northern General Hospital, Sheffield on 29th September.

Wilfred married Helena May née Wheeler (1894-1989) on 13th March 1916 in London. She was a nurse at the Military Orthopaedic Hospital, Hammersmith and gained his attention by packing him with a hatpin from behind at Victoria Palace Music Hall. They had two daughters – Doris M M Fuller, birth registered in the 3rd quarter of 1917 at Mansfield and Beatrice M Fuller, birth registered in the 3rd quarter of 1919 at Axbridge, Somerset. They later adopted a son.

Crown Farm Colliery, Mansfield where Wilfred Fuller worked before he enlisted in the Grenadier Guards.

Wilfred was appointed Acting Corporal in mid-1916, but was discharged on 31st October unfit for further service. He returned to work in the colliery, but could not continue due to his health. From the autumn of 1917 he became a checker in the yard of the tramway company at Weston-super-Mare, but as men were demobilised and returned after the war he lost his job. In 1919 he became a Somerset policemen and served at Milverton, Ilminster, Clevedon and Nunney. His last post was at Rodden Road Police Station, near Frome. His pay was reduced by 2/- per week in 1929 for using a key to open a drawer without authority. He retired due to ill health on 2nd July 1940.

Wilfred Fuller died at 'Far End', Styles Hill, Rodden, near Frome, Somerset on 22nd November 1947 and is buried in Christ Church churchyard. In addition to the VC, he was awarded the 1914 Star with 'Mons' clasp, British War Medal 1914-20, Victory Medal 1914-19, George VI Coronation Medal 1937 and the Russian Cross of the Order of St George, 3rd Class. His medals were sold to benefit his children and grandchildren at Glendining's on 20th March 1974, raising £2,600. They were sold again at Sotheby's on 18th December 1991 and are held by the Guards Museum, Wellington Barracks, London.

Fuller Close in Mansfield was named after him in 1987. He is also named on a memorial in the grounds of Nottingham Castle unveiled on 7th May 2010, commemorating twenty Nottingham and Nottinghamshire VCs.

7368 CORPORAL CHARLES ERNEST GARFORTH
A Squadron, 15th The King's Hussars

Charles Garforth was born at 19 Chaplin Road, Willesden Green, London on 23rd October 1891. His father was John Edwin Garforth (1864-1928) who served in the Rifle Brigade before becoming a paperhanger and decorator. His mother was Hannah (Annie) née Dyer (1867-1904) who came from Great Wolford, Warwickshire. John and Hannah married at Hampstead in the 1st quarter of 1888. By 1901 the family had moved to Victor Cottage, St Kilda's Road, Harrow and in 1906 was living at 1 Willow Cottages, Fairholme Road, Greenhill, Harrow having lived at 32 Tudor Road, Southsea in between. After Hannah died, John Garforth married Kate Cole in Hendon in the 2nd quarter of 1909. Charles had five brothers and four sisters, but two brothers and a sister did not survive infancy. All surviving brothers served in the Army; two were wounded and one served in 9th Middlesex in India.

Charles was educated at three schools in Harrow – Greenhill Infant School 1897-99, Greenhill Boy's School 1899-1902 and Roxeth School 1902–05, then Bridge School at Wealdstone 1906-07. He worked as an apprentice at John Joiner's boot shop on St Anne's Road, Harrow 1907-1911 and was a member of Roxeth and Harrow Company London Diocesan Church Lads' Brigade before enlisting in 9th Middlesex (TF) in November 1909.

He transferred to the Regular Army (15th Hussars) on 19th May 1911, training at Aldershot before serving at Potchefstroom in South Africa. The Regiment returned to England in 1913 and Charles was promoted Corporal in 1914. He disembarked in France with the Regiment on 17th August 1914 and went to Rouen before moving up to Mons in Belgium. **Awarded the VC for his actions at Harmignies, Belgium on 23rd August 1914, at Dammartin near Meaux on 6th September 1914 and also the next day, LG 16th November 1914. Mentioned in Field Marshal Sir John French's Despatch dated 8th October 1914, LG 19th October 1914 (duplicated 20th October and reissued 9th December 1914).**

On 13th October 1914 at Laventie he was a member of a patrol of thirteen men commanded by Captain AE Bradshaw. They were surrounded, but fought for three hours until the officer and nine men had been hit. Charles Garforth was taken prisoner when his ammunition was spent. Some accounts suggest Captain Bradshaw and nine soldiers were killed, but records indicate no officers and only five soldiers of 15th Hussars were killed that day (Corporal Alan Tumley and Privates Robert Baker, Harold Doughty, William George Gardner and Albert Ernest Parsons). It is possible the survivors assumed the worst and reported them all killed. Charles was held at Hameln and Brohmte. He escaped three times, but was recaptured on each occasion on the Dutch/German border, weak from lack of food. He then faced three weeks' solitary confinement on bread and water. He was held in the Netherlands from 19th March 1918 and repatriated with other internees, arriving at Hull on 18th November 1918 on the *Arbroath*.

The VC was presented by King George V at Buckingham Palace on 19th December 1918 and he was then in great demand for a few months. On 21st January 1919 he was presented with £110 by Southend Council and was Master of Ceremonies at a Military Ball at the Municipal Hall, Tottenham, London on 30th January. He received a silver cigarette case at St Peter's Church, West Harrow on 8th March, £160 of War Savings Certificates and an illuminated scroll from the people of Harrow at Harrow School Speech Rooms on 10th March and a clock from the London Diocesan Church Lads' Brigade at the Guildhall, London on 31st March.

Charles Garforth married Lilian née Hay (1902–84) on 7th April 1919 at St. Mary's Church, Prittlewell, Southend, Essex. They had four children – Victor Charles born on 20th March 1920 at Kilkenny, Ireland, Walter Douglas born on 30th March 1922 at Tidworth, Hampshire, Valerie born on 24th November 1923 at Long Eaton, Derbyshire and Sylvia born on 17th February 1928 at Shardlow, Derbyshire.

Charles took part in the Allied Victory Parade in London on 19th July 1919 before rejoining 15th Hussars at Kerpen, Cologne, Germany on 4th August 1919 as part of the Occupation forces; he had been on the held strength of 3rd Reserve Cavalry Regiment. A month later the Regiment moved to Ireland where he served at Kilkenny as a Sergeant until March 1922 and was discharged on 1st June 1922 from Tidworth, Hampshire. He was present at the burial of the Unknown Warrior on 11th November 1920.

The family moved to 283 Curzon Street, Long Eaton Road, Chilwell, in Nottinghamshire where he took a job as a clerk at the Ordnance Depot. In 1924 he joined Ericson's Telephones (later Plessey), but returned to the Ordnance

Charles Garforth's discharge certificate.

al No. Cav/5367 Army Form B. 2079.
TE—This Certificate is to be issued without any alterations in the manuscript.

ertificate of discharge of No. 536751 Rank Sergeant
Name Garforth Charles Ernest V.C
Surname. Christian Names in full.
Unit* and Corps from which discharged: 15th Hussars
The unit of the Corps such as Field Co. R.E., H.T., or M.T., R.A.S.C., etc., is invariably to be stated.

orps to which first appointed 15th Hussars
During the engagement from which he is now being discharged he has served in the following Corps :—

Only Corps in which the soldier served since August 4th, 1914, are to be stated.
If inapplicable this space is to be ruled through in ink and initialled.

Specialist Qualifications (Military) Rifle & Bayonet Course. Inst. ommand School of Musketry (Distinguished)

Medals, Clasps, Decorations and Mentions in despatches: NIL Wound Stripes* NIL
To be inserted in words.

as served Overseas on Active Service†

Enlisted at Aldershot on 7th March 1919
* Each space is to be filled in and the word "nil" inserted where necessary.
† To be struck out in ink if not applicable.

He is discharged in consequence of his services being no longer required on reduction of establishment. Para 392 (XXV) Kings Regulations

after having served * THREE years* 87 days with the Colours, and
* nil years* nil days in the Army Reserve ~~or Territorial Army~~† (Strike out whichever inapplicable.)
* Each space is to be filled in and the word "nil" inserted where necessary; number of years to be written in words.
† Service with Territorial Army to be shown only in cases of soldiers serving on a T.A. attestation.

Date of discharge 1st June 1922

[illegible] Capt for Col. (Signature and Rank)
Officer i/c Cavalry Records.
Canterbury (Place).

Description of the above-named soldier when he left the Colours.
Year of Birth 1891 Marks or Scars
Height 5 ft. 4½ in.
Complexion Fresh
Eyes Brown Hair Brown

(8402-P450) Wt.W2032/P4599 100,000 10/21 Sch. 44 D. D. & L. P.T.O.
Forms/B2079/26

Depot Chilwell in 1926 as a security policemen, living at 10 Married Quarters, Ordnance Depot. His son Victor was killed in a road accident on 16th October 1926 at Nottingham. In 1935 he became a security policeman at British Celanese, Spondon, Derbyshire and was also an ARP instructor there in the Second World War, living at Clovelly, 229 By-Pass Road, Chilwell, Nottingham. He attended the Coronations of George VI in 1937 and Elizabeth II in 1953. His final employment was as a warehouse manager from 1945 until retiring in 1956. He was an active man throughout his life, enjoying cycling, gardening and walking. He maintained close contact with his Regiment after it amalgamated to become 15/19th King's Hussars and attended a number of ceremonies, including on 11th October 1968 when a tank in A Squadron was named after him.

Charles Garforth died at his home at Caravan 5, Lock Close, Ryland, Beeston, Nottinghamshire on 1st July 1973 and was cremated at Southern Cemetery Crematorium, Nottingham. His ashes were scattered in the Garden of Remembrance, where a memorial headstone was placed on 30th August 2008.

In addition to the VC, he was awarded the 1914 Star with 'Mons' clasp, British War Medal 1914-20, Victory Medal 1914-19 with Mentioned-in-Despatches oak-leaf, George VI Coronation Medal 1937 and Elizabeth II Coronation Medal 1953. His VC is held by the Imperial War Museum, Lambeth Road, London. Charles Garforth is commemorated at:

- National Memorial Arboretum, Alrewas, Staffordshire – 22 Berberis shrubs, each representing a Church Lads' Brigade VC, in the Church Lads & Church Girls Brigade Memorial Plot.
- Nottingham Castle – memorial to twenty Nottinghamshire VCs, including Charles Garforth, unveiled in May 2010.

SECOND LIEUTENANT BENJAMIN HANDLEY GEARY
4th attached 1st Battalion, The East Surrey Regiment

Benjamin Geary was born at Streatham, London on 29th June 1891, the youngest of eleven children. His second name was after his godfather, Handley Carr Glynn Moule (1841-1920). His father was the Reverend Henry Geary (1838-91) who was ordained priest in 1862 and was Curate of All Saints', Dalston 1862-63; St James's, Piccadilly 1863-64; Christ Church and Herne Bay, Kent 1864-74. He became Vicar of St Thomas', Portman Square, London from 1874 until his death. He was also Authorised Lecturer for the Palestine Exploration Fund and author of, '*The Doctrine of Holy Communion*' and '*The World's Opinion of the Church's Message*'. Benjamin's mother was Blandinah 'Blanch' Kesiah Ellen née Alport (1846-1923). Their marriage was registered during the 2nd quarter of 1870 at Blean, Kent. Amongst Benjamin's siblings:

Henry Ernest Geary (1871-1900) was ordained Deacon at Winchester in 1894, became Curate of Stoke-next-Guildford, Surrey 1894-95 and moved to Ceylon in 1897 to work as a tea planter and missionary.

Arthur Bernard Geary (1878-1961) was appointed to the Foreign Office as a Student Interpreter in the Consular Service for the Ottoman Dominions, Persia, Greece and Morocco. He was Assistant in the Levant 1904 and Vice-Consul at Constantinople, the Dardanelles, Monastir, Armenia and Alexandria. From 1914 he was registrar of the Alexandria Prize Court. Having been commissioned on 30th July 1916 on the General List, he arrived at Basra on 23rd September as Special Service Officer employed on intelligence duties at GHQ Mesopotamia Expeditionary Force. He was appointed Temporary Captain and GSO3 until 8th February 1917. Having relinquished his commission on 17th October 1917, he became Vice-Consul at Basra, Consul in the Levant 1st January 1918, Consul for Continental Greece and the Island of Negropont 17th June, Acting Consul-General at Alexandria 1918-19 and Consul at Cairo 1919-20. Arthur appears to have had a history of drinking and mental problems, which may explain his short military career and frequent moves. He was invalided out of the Consular Service by Lord Curzon in 1921. In April 1929 he appeared at Bow Street Court charged with being drunk and disorderly in Villiers Street, Strand on 8-9th March. He denied the charge, maintaining that the police and divisional surgeon had made serious allegations; the judge was not convinced and he was fined £2 with £2/2/- costs. On 6th March 1940, while a member of the Imperial Censorship Staff at Gibraltar, he was judged undesirable by the Governor and removed under 'The Aliens and Strangers Act 1935'. On returning to London he was suspended and served a writ against the Colonial Office for breach of contract on 19th March, believing he had been illegally deported from Gibraltar. Special Branch arrested him on 16th April and he wrote a rambling complaint from a mental institute (Banstead Hospital, Surrey), airing a host of grievances going back to 1916, when he claimed to be doing two jobs in Cairo, while contracting paratyphoid and serving as a Private-Corporal in the Alexandria Light Horse; as a result he came home on leave in February 1916. In the same letter he mentions being awarded the OBE for his consular services and managing to avoid that 'questionable distinction' (he was not awarded the OBE, but the letters appear after his name erroneously when appointed

Consul for Cairo in the LG dated 24th October 1919). The Censorship Department did not agree with his complaints and no further action was taken. What happened to him thereafter is not known.

Herbert Mashiter Geary (1882-1964) became a farmer in Canada. He returned to Britain in December 1915 and enlisted in the Inns of Court OTC as a Private (8631) on 3rd January 1916. He was commissioned in the Royal Sussex Regiment on 22nd November and joined the 3rd Battalion at Newhaven on 3rd December. On 23rd April 1917 he sprained his ankle playing football and embarked on SS *Cambria* in Calais for Dover on 1st May. He was declared fit again on 9th July, but was later wounded in the back while serving with 11th Royal Sussex. He embarked at Boulogne on 22nd October for Dover from 10 General Hospital at Wimereux and was treated at 2nd Western General Hospital, Manchester until declared fit on 9th November. Herbert was released on 30th May 1919, retaining the rank of Captain.

Winifred Mary Geary (1874-1930) married Henry Norman Stevens (1880-1959) in Montreal, Canada in 1904. Henry served in 1st (Lambeth Battalion) South London Regiment VTC before enlisting as a Private (5046) in the Inns of Court OTC on 22nd July 1915. He was commissioned in 9th East Yorkshire on 29th November and transferred to 22nd Northumberland Fusiliers later. He suffered from trench fever and a dilated heart in France in August 1916 and embarked on 4th September for Britain to be treated at Lady Violet Brassey's Hospital for Officers in Upper Grosvenor Street, off Park Lane, London. He was granted leave while recovering on the strength of 29th (Reserve) Battalion, Northumberland Fusiliers until declared fit for General Service on 16th April 1917. On 30th April 1918 he was examined by a medical board at Caxton Hall, London having returned from East Africa with enteritis, heart murmurs, nephritis, lumbar pains and albuminuria. He was loaned to the RAF and transferred on 28th October 1918 as a Lieutenant in the Administrative Staff and was later a Flying Officer in the Stores Branch until retiring on 18th March 1925.

Benjamin was educated at Dulwich College Preparatory School and St Edmund's School Canterbury January 1904 – July 1910. At St Edmund's he was Captain of East House and played first team football, hockey and cricket, becoming captain of football, vice-captain of cricket and captain of gymnasium and sports. He was a Lance Corporal in the Officer Training Corps and won the Music Instrumental Prize 1907-09 and the Stocks Memorial Prize for Mathematics 1909-10. He was awarded a Watson-Wagner Exhibition to Keble College, Oxford in 1910 (BA 8th August 1914). During his time at university he played rugby for Surrey in the

1913-14 season, was a member of the OTC and was employed as a teacher at Forest School, near Snaresbrook, Essex in 1913.

When war broke out, Benjamin was commissioned into 4th East Surrey (Special Reserve) on 15th August. He was based at South Raglan Barracks, Devonport prior to deploying to France on 26th September where he was attached to the 1st Battalion. In November, he removed a bayonet from an occupied German trench, for which he received the thanks of Divisional Headquarters. **Awarded the VC for his actions on Hill 60, near Ypres, Belgium on 20th – 21st April 1915, LG 15th October 1915.** He was evacuated to England on 28th April, having been shot in the head, losing the sight in his left eye and the right eye was also seriously impaired. Promoted Lieutenant 1st September.

His VC was presented by the King at Buckingham Palace on 9th December 1915. Benjamin was employed in a convalescent camp at Eastbourne from late 1915 and with the RFC on ground duties. He returned to France on 30th September 1916 as a Squadron Recording Officer with the RFC. Appointed Acting Captain 25th August 1917 while Assistant Instructor at a School of Instruction. Appointed Temporary Captain 1st December 1917 – 10th January 1918. He served with the 7th Battalion at some time and rejoined the 1st Battalion in Italy in January 1918, although medically he should not have been returned to active duty. Appointed Acting Captain 29th April while commanding a company. He returned to England on leave in June and rejoined his unit in France in August. At Achiet-le-Petit, near Bapaume, on 21st August he was wounded while commanding D Company; a bullet went through his abdomen and forearm. He was carried back by German prisoners and a blood transfusion saved his life before he was evacuated to England. Ill health caused by his wounds resulted in him retiring from the Army on 29th May 1919, retaining the rank of Captain.

Benjamin was awarded a MA in 1918 and studied theology at Wycliffe Hall, Oxford 1919-21. While at Oxford he was General Secretary of the Student Christian Union 1920. He was ordained deacon at Chelmsford Cathedral on 2nd October 1921, priest the following year and became Assistant Curate in West Ham 1921-23. He married Ruth Christiana née Woakes (1903-89) on 10th June 1922 at Holy Trinity Church, Marylebone. Ruth's father, Dr Claud Edward Woakes (1868-1936), was at various times Surgeon in charge of the Nose, Throat & Ear Department at Charing Cross Hospital, Senior Surgeon at the London Throat Hospital and Consultant Surgeon at the Hospital for Diseases of the Throat, Golden Square, London. He also served as a Surgeon-Captain in the City of London Volunteers. Ruth and Benjamin had two sons – Nevill John Geary, born on 28th June 1924, registered at Portsmouth (died 1971) and David Victor Geary, born on 24th May 1927, registered at Hartley Wintney.

In April 1923, Benjamin attended the unveiling of the Tomb of the Belgian Unknown Warrior in Brussels. He returned to the Army as Temporary Chaplain to the Forces 4th Class (Captain) on 5th October 1923 and became Chaplain to the Forces on 17th November 1926. He served at Chatham, Portsmouth, Crookham, Aldershot and Ewshot. Early in 1927 he was involved in a serious car accident. He was bound over for two years by Odiham Police Court on 23rd August 1927, having pleaded guilty to indecently assaulting two girls, his mind being affected by his war experiences and concussion in the car crash; the sentence was conditional on him seeking further medical advice, which he accepted. However, it meant the end of his military career and he resigned his commission on 1st October 1927.

The family emigrated to Canada in May 1928 and settled in Toronto. Benjamin was employed as Travelling Secretary of the World Alliance for Promoting International Friendship through the Churches. He had various other jobs – Continental Life Assurance Company 1930, Toronto Better Business Bureau 1935, Ontario Security Commission 1935 and Canadian National Institute for the Blind 1937. Ruth found it difficult to settle in Canada and left him in December 1930 to live with James Courtenay Sherren at Palmer's Green. Ruth and Benjamin were divorced on 1st August 1934 (decree absolute February 1935) and she subsequently married James Sherren.

Benjamin's second marriage was to Constance Joan née Henderson-Cleland (1906-72) on 2nd May 1935 at the Metropolitan United Church at St Thomas, Ontario, Canada. They lived at The Cottage, Woodbridge, Ontario and later at 329 Victoria Street, Niagara-on-the-Lake, Ontario. Constance's father, Fletcher Hayes Henderson-Cleland (born in India 1875), was commissioned in 3rd Battalion, Somersetshire Light Infantry on 5th June 1894, transferred to the Sherwood Foresters (Derbyshire Regiment) 1896, transferred to the Bedfordshire Regiment 1898 and was removed from the Army for absence without leave on 18th January 1899. He was Temporary Assistant Inspector of the Board of Agriculture from which he resigned in December 1901 and with his family emigrated to Ontario, Canada.

Benjamin was presented to George VI and Queen Elizabeth during their tour of Canada at Queen's Park, Toronto on 22nd May 1939. During the Second World War, he served in the Canadian Army as a Major from 2nd September 1940. He commanded an educational unit at Camp Borden, Ontario and was later Second-in-Command of a Basic Training Centre at Newmarket, Ontario until 27th December 1946. Back in civilian life he became Sergeant at Arms of the Ontario Legislature 1947-72 and its Official Historian until 1962. On 17th December 1971, the Speaker presented him with a Scroll from the Government of Ontario in recognition of his service to the Legislative Assembly. In October 1951 he was presented to HRH Princess Elizabeth and Prince Philip in Toronto.

Benjamin became involved with a large number of clubs, societies and organisations. He was Chairman of the British Legion in Canada, President and Life Member of the Imperial Officers Association of Canada, Life Governor of the Canadian Corps of Commissionaires, President of the Royal Canadian Legion's Woodbridge Branch and General Nelles Branch and Director of Kingsley Hall for Men (Toronto). He was also a member or honorary member of the Royal Canadian Military Institution, Royal Society of St George, St George's Society, Royal Commonwealth Society, Royal Canadian Legion, Canadian Institute for the Blind, VC & GC Association, Legion of Frontiersmen, University Club of Toronto, Empire Club, Aitken Club, Canadian Officers' Club, Civitan Club and Niagara Peninsular Armed Forces Institute.

Benjamin Geary later in life. The scar near his right eye is more apparent than in the earlier photograph.

Benjamin Geary died at Niagara Hospital, Niagara-on-the-Lake, Ontario, Canada on 26th May 1976 and is buried in St Mark's Anglican Church Cemetery, Niagara-on-the-Lake. In addition to the VC, he was also awarded the 1914 Star with 'Mons' clasp, British War Medal 1914-20, Victory Medal 1914-19, Canadian Volunteer Service Medal 1939-45, War Medal 1939-45, George VI Coronation Medal 1937, Elizabeth II Coronation Medal 1953 and the Canadian Centennial Medal. The medals disappeared from his funeral and it was not until September 1994 that they were returned having been discovered in a friend's attic. The family presented them to the Canadian War Museum in Ottawa, which still holds them. Benjamin's sons also had military careers:

Nevill was commissioned in the Royal Canadian Navy, qualifying as a Seaman Officer and was later a pilot in the Canadian Fleet Air Arm. Promoted Lieutenant 16th December 1945. He served at Naval Service HQ in Ottawa until June 1950, HMCS *Huron* 1950, HMCS *Shearwater* 1951, HMCS *Magnificent* 1953 and was promoted Lieutenant Commander on 16th December 1953. He commanded 881 Squadron (HMCS *Magnificent*) 1955-56, followed by tours at Naval Service HQ 1957, HMCS *Iroquois* 1960, HMCS *Bonaventure* 1963 and HMCS *Niobe* 1965. He retired in 1970 and was awarded the Canadian Forces' Decoration.

David was a Lieutenant Colonel in the Canadian Army and was also awarded the Canadian Forces' Decoration.

1685 RIFLEMAN GOBAR SING NEGI
2/39th Battalion, Garhwal Rifles

Gobar Sing Negi (now usually seen as Gabbar Singh Negi) was born on 19th October 1894 at Manjood Village, near Chamba, Tehri District, Uttaranchal, India. His date of birth has also been seen as 7th October 1893 and 21st April 1895. His father was Badri Sing Negi, but little else is known about his family. It is known he married, had children and his wife was alive in 1970.

Gobar enlisted in 2/39th Garhwal Rifles on 19th October 1912 and went to France with his unit when war broke out. **Awarded the VC for his actions at Neuve-Chapelle, France on 10th March 1915, LG 28th April 1915.** Gobar Sing Negi was killed during his VC action and has no known grave. He is commemorated on the Neuve-Chapelle Memorial, France (Panel 32 & 33). His VC was sent to the India Office on 28th July 1915.

In addition to the VC, Gobar Sing Negi was awarded the 1914-15 Star with 'Mons' clasp, British War Medal 1914-20 and Victory Medal 1914-19. The VC was acquired by the Officers' Mess, 39th Royal Garhwal Rifles and a duplicate was given to Gobar's widow, but the location of the original is not known.

Since 1925 the Gobar Sing Negi Fair has been held at the Negi Memorial at Chamba, Tehri District, Uttaranchal, India on 20th or 21st April, depending upon the Hindu calendar. In 1971 the Garhwal Regiment adopted the fair, bringing military traditions to the ceremonies and also using it for recruiting. The fair attracted many people from surrounding villages, but has been in decline recently.

13814 PRIVATE SIDNEY FRANK GODLEY
4th Battalion, The Royal Fusiliers (City of London Regiment)

Sidney Godly was born at North End, East Grinstead, Sussex on 14th August 1889. He became Godley due to a clerical error when he enlisted. His father was Frank Godly (1867-1930), a house decorator and sometime plumber. His mother was Avis née Newton (1861-96), a domestic servant cook. They were married at East Grinstead in the 4th quarter of 1886. One of Sidney's uncles, Henry George Godly, was a policemen involved in the hunt for Jack the Ripper. When his mother died on 3rd September 1896, Sidney, his brother and two sisters moved to Willesden, North London to live with an aunt and uncle. His father married Elizabeth (Lizzy) Keenan (1873-1948) at Marylebone in the 2nd quarter of

Recommendation written by Lieutenant F W A Steele immediately after the engagement at Nimy railway bridge.

In the defence of Railway Bridge near NIMY. 23rd Aug 1914. This afternoon Pte GODLEY of B. Coy shewed particular heroism in his management of the machine gun; Lt Dease having been severely wounded and each machine gunner shot; I called Pte. Godley to me in the firing line on the bridge and under an extremely heavy fire he had to remove 3 dead bodies and go to a machine gun on the right under a most deadly fire: This he did & not a shot did he fire except as I directed & with the utmost coolness until it was irretrievably damaged & he was shot in the head. He then left the firing line under orders to go to the rear.
23. Sept F.W.A.S[illegible]

1899. Sidney had two more brothers and five sisters from this marriage. He was educated at Henry Street School, St John's Wood, London and, following a family move, Sidcup National School until 1904.

Sidney was employed in an ironmonger's shop in Kilburn High Street before enlisting on 13th December 1909. In the Army he was an able runner, footballer and cricketer. The 4th Battalion was stationed at Parkhurst on the Isle of Wight at the outbreak of war and mobilised on 7th August 1914. It disembarked at Le Havre, France on 13th August. **He was awarded the first soldier VC of the war for his actions at Mons, Belgium on 23rd August 1914, LG 25th November 1914. Mentioned in Field Marshal Sir John French's Despatch dated 8th October 1914, LG 19th October 1914 (duplicated 20th October and reissued 9th December 1914).**

Taken prisoner on 23rd August 1914, he underwent extensive surgery in Berlin for bullet wounds and also had skin grafts. He was held at Doberitz and later at Delotz, where an official of the US Embassy informed him of the award of his VC. He was congratulated by the German Commandant, who allowed a parade to mark the occasion. When the guards abandoned the camp during the Berlin Revolution, Sidney walked out and with five others jumped a train to the Danish border. He returned to England in December 1918 and his VC was presented by the King at Buckingham Palace on 15th February 1919. He was officially welcomed home by the Mayor of Lewisham on 26th February 1919 and presented with fifty Guineas and a copy of the Lewisham Roll of Honour. He was discharged from the Army on 21st May 1919 and transferred to the Section B Reserve on 3rd June 1921. His brother, Sergeant Percival Henry Godley (1892–1916), was killed in action serving with 32nd Royal Fusiliers on 4th October 1916 and is buried in AIF Burial Ground, Grass Lane, Flers, France (X K 10).

'Mug' Godley, as he was known, while a prisoner of war in Germany (Colin Godley).

Sidney became a plumber and married Helen Eliza née Norman (1886-1963), a housemaid, on 2nd August 1919 at St Mark's Parish Church, Harlesden, Middlesex; she was a friend of one of his sisters. Claims he was married by the Reverend Edward Noel Mellish VC are without foundation; the marriage register was signed by Reverend E R Whalley; Mellish was in a nearby parish and may have attended. Sidney and Helen had two children – Stanley Sidney Godley, born on 13th May 1920 and Eileen Elizabeth, whose birth was registered in the 4th quarter of 1922 as Eileen V Godley.

In 1920, Sidney returned to his old school at Sidcup and was presented with an inscribed black marble clock and £150 of war bonds. From 1921 he was the caretaker of Cranbrooke School in East London until retiring in 1951. Although reputed to be the inspiration for 'Old Bill', the cartoonist Bruce Bairnsfather insisted the character was not modelled on a particular individual. Sidney became a prominent member of the Old Contemptibles Association and worked voluntarily for service charities, often dressing up as 'Old Bill'. During a visit to Mons in 1938, the Mayor gave a lunch at the Hotel de Ville at which Sidney was guest of honour. He was presented with a special gold medal and a plaque of the arms of the town. Amongst the guests was one of the children who brought him rolls and coffee on the morning of 23rd August 1914.

In the Second World War Sidney served in 8th (Home Defence) Battalion, Royal Sussex Regiment. After retiring he and his wife moved several times, ending up in

Sidney Godley (centre) with a group of former Royal Fusiliers in the square at Nimy during their visit in 1939.

Debden, Essex. Sidney died at St Margaret's Hospital, Epping, Essex on 29th June 1957 and is buried in St John's Churchyard, Loughton, Essex (Second F 3051). Reverend Edward Noel Mellish VC assisted at the funeral.

In addition to the VC, Sidney was awarded the 1914 Star with 'Mons' clasp, British War Medal 1914-20, Victory Medal 1914-19 with Mentioned-in-Despatches oak-leaf, George VI Coronation Medal 1937 and Elizabeth II Coronation Medal 1953. His medals were purchased by an anonymous collector for £230,000 at a Spink's auction on 19th July 2012. Sidney Godley is commemorated in a number of places:

- Lewisham National Reserve Club on Stanstead Road, Lewisham.
- Godley VC Housing Estate, Bexley, Kent, named after him in 1976.
- Housing block on Digby Street, Tower Hamlets, named after him on 8th May 1992.
- Plaque in Lewisham Civic Centre unveiled in May 1995 by Captain Philip Gardner VC, bearing the names of eight VC s from the town.
- Blue Plaque on council offices at East Court, East Grinstead, close to his birthplace unveiled on 23rd August 1998.
- Blue Plaque on his home at 164 Torrington Drive, placed in 2000 by Loughton Council.

Sidney Godley's grave in St. John's Churchyard, Loughton, Essex after renovation in 2012. (Colin Godley)

Sidney's grandson Colin at the 4th Royal Fusiliers memorial under Nimy railway bridge.

CAPTAIN FRANCIS OCTAVIUS GRENFELL
9th Queen's Royal Lancers

Francis Grenfell was born at Hatchlands, Guildford, Surrey on 4th September 1880, a twin with Riversdale. His father was Pascoe du Pré Grenfell JP DL (1828-96), a partner in Morton, Rose & Co, financiers specialising in American railroads. He was also Deputy Chairman of North British & Mercantile Insurance, Trustee of American Investment Trust, Director of Alliance Marine and General Assurance and sat on the London Committees of the Anglo-Austrian Bank, Bank of Romania and Imperial Ottoman Bank. Pascoe married his cousin, Sofia née Grenfell (c.1833-98), on 13th May 1858 at St Paul's, Princes Park, West Derby, Lancashire. The family homes were at 73 Eaton Place, London and Wilton Park, Beaconsfield. Wilton Park was used during the Second World War for Special Operations Executive training and later for senior German prisoners. The house was demolished in the 1960s to build the Army School of Education.

Francis' maternal grandfather was Vice Admiral John Pascoe Grenfell (1800-69), who served in the British East India Company, took part in the War of Chilean Independence, the Brazilian War of Independence and the Argentina-Brazil War in July 1826 during which he lost his right arm. He commanded a squadron in 1835-36, forcing the surrender of the rebel army in Brazil. He became Consul General in Britain in 1846 and commanded the Brazilian Navy in the war with Argentina in 1851. He returned to Britain in December 1851, was promoted Vice Admiral and resumed his duties as Consul General. His brother was Admiral Sidney Grenfell (1806-84), who served in the Royal Navy 1822-78. Amongst Francis' uncles were:

Field Marshal Sir Francis Algernon Wallace Grenfell (1841-1925), 1st Baron Grenfell of Kilvey PC GCB GCMG, who served in the 60th Rifles from 1859. He took part in numerous campaigns in Africa 1875-98 and was Governor and Commander-in-Chief Malta 1899-1903. He was Commander IV Corps 1903-04 and Commander-in-Chief Ireland 1904-08. He was also Francis' godfather.

John Granville Grenfell (1829-66), Commissioner of Crown Lands in New South Wales, who was killed defending the mail against bushrangers.

Vice Admiral Harry Tremenheere Grenfell KCB CMG RN (1845-1906), who commanded the paddle steamer *Cockatrice* during the Egyptian War in 1882. While stationed at Artaki in the Sea of Marmora on 13th February 1882 he was severely wounded in an affray with local shepherds; his companion, Commander Selby, was killed. When commanding HMS *Benbow* in 1895 he jumped overboard to rescue a boy in danger of drowning. He commanded HMS *Royal Sovereign* during operations in Crete 1896-97. Promoted Rear Admiral in 1901, hoisting his flag in HMS *Barfleur* and later HMS *Albion* as Second-in-Command on the China Station. Appointed Second-in-Command on the Mediterranean Station 1904 with his flag in HMS *Venerable*.

Francis and Rivy in Malta with their uncle, Lord Grenfell in April 1901.

Francis had eight brothers and four sisters; two other siblings died in infancy. After the death of their father in 1896 and mother in 1898, the children went to live with their uncle, Lord Grenfell. Francis was educated privately at Mr Edgar's School, Temple Grove, East Sheen and Eton College from 1894. He scored 80 not out against Harrow at Lords in 1897 and became Master of the Beagles in 1898, while his twin Rivy was Whip. Francis was a contemporary of Winston Churchill and John Buchan.

He was commissioned into 3rd (Militia) Battalion, Seaforth Highlanders on 1st September 1899 and embodied on 13th December 1899. He contracted typhoid and took a long sea journey to South Africa to recover, then served in Egypt for four months from November 1900. He transferred to Regular service with 4th KRRC on 4th May 1901 in Malta, where he was ADC to the Governor, his uncle, before moving to Ireland for a short period. He sailed from Cork to South Africa in the autumn of 1901 and saw service in the Boer War. While in South Africa he speculated profitably in diamonds. He returned to England briefly in 1903 before sailing for India, where he served until 1907. Promoted Lieutenant 28th January 1905 and transferred to 9th Lancers on 6th May 1905, having enlisted the support of Douglas Haig and Lord Kitchener. He returned to England and then went to South Africa in April 1908 to rejoin his Regiment. Promoted Captain 7th September 1912 and appointed Adjutant 1st November 1912 – 18th January 1914. Francis was a skilled linguist, being an interpreter in French, German and Hindustani. He studied German in Berlin for the Staff College examination and observed German military manoeuvres.

With his Regiment he disembarked in France on 16th August 1914. **He was awarded the VC for his actions at Audregnies, Belgium on 24th August 1914, LG 16th November 1914.** Francis wrote to his uncle, *"I have been through so much since June, that what would and should have made me yell with joy nearly causes tears. It gave me no great feeling of having achieved anything. I feel that I know so many who have done and are doing so much more than I have been able to do for England. I also feel very strongly that any honour belongs to my regiment and not to me. They have paid the toll and will go on paying until the road is clear."* **Mentioned in Field Marshal Sir John French's Despatch dated 8th October 1914, LG 19th October 1914 (duplicated 20th October and reissued 9th December 1914).** After his VC action he was evacuated to England for treatment at 17 Belgrave Square, London and recuperated with his uncle at Overston Park, Northamptonshire. While there he received news of his brother Rivy's death on 14th September 1914 and lost enthusiasm for everything but his Regiment thereafter. He returned to France to resume command of B Squadron on 15th October 1914 at Strazeele, but was wounded in the thigh at Messines on 31st October 1914. He was evacuated to Bailleul before being shipped to Dublin, where he made a slow recovery. His VC was presented by the King at Buckingham Palace on 22nd February 1915.

On 7th April, Francis gave a farewell dinner at Claridges in London; the guests included Lord Grenfell, Winston Churchill and John Buchan. He rejoined his unit on 20th/21st April at Meteren, Belgium. During the Second Battle of Ypres on 24th May 1915, Francis was shot in the back at Hooge, south of the Menin Road. A corporal bandaged his wounds, but he tore it off knowing the bullet had entered his heart. He died within half an hour and his last words are reputed to have been, *"I die happy. Tell the men I loved my Squadron."*

An American journalist, Frederic Coleman, reported, *"As the sun went down that evening their comrades of the 9th Lancers buried the bodies of Francis Grenfell and Algy Court* (Captain WHR Court). *Court's face wore a smile, as though he was quietly sleeping. Grenfell, shot through the heart at the height of the battle, bore, too, a look of deep peace, as if at last he had cheerfully gone to a better country, to join his beloved Rivy, from the shock of whose death, on the Aisne, Francis had never recovered."* He was buried in Vlamertinge Churchyard, but after the war his body was moved to Vlamertinge Military Cemetery (II B 14); Algy Court lies nearby.

A memorial service was held at Eaton Square, London on 2nd June 1915 and Lord Grenfell received telegrams from King George V and Field Marshal Sir John French. Francis is commemorated at St George's Chapel in Ypres, All Saints Church, Kilvey in Swansea, Glamorgan and at Lord's Cricket Ground, London. The twins are jointly commemorated at Canterbury Cathedral and a stained glass window in Beaconsfield parish church portrays them as Saul and Jonathan.

Probate was awarded to Albert Henry George Earl Grey and John Buchan, effects £40,569/12/6. In addition to the VC, Francis Grenfell was awarded the Queen's South Africa Medal 1899-1902 with four clasps, 1914 Star with 'Mons' clasp,

Francis Grenfell's grave in Vlamertinghe Military Cemetery.

British War Medal 1914-20 and Victory Medal 1914-19 with Mentioned-in-Despatches oak-leaf. His VC is held by the 9/12th Lancers Museum (Prince of Wales's) at the Derby Museum and Art Gallery.

His sister, Maraquita Masini Grenfell (1862-95), married John George Bulteel and one of their sons, Major John Crocker Bulteel DSO MC, Buckinghamshire & Berkshire Yeomanry, married Marie Dolores Reynolds (née Petersen) widow of Major Douglas Reynolds VC. Francis' cousin, Captain the Honourable Julian Henry Francis Grenfell DSO (1888-1915), son of 1st Baron Desborough was a war poet and author of '*Into Battle*'; he died of wounds on 26th May 1915 and is buried in Boulogne Eastern Cemetery (II A 18). Another son of Baron Desborough, 2nd Lieutenant the Honourable Gerald William 'Billy' Grenfell, 8th Rifle Brigade, was killed on 30th July 1915 in the same action as Gilbert Talbot, after whom Talbot House (Toc H) was named; Billy is commemorated on the Ypres Menin Gate Memorial (Panel 46-48 & 50). Francis' brothers also had military careers, many cut short by early deaths:

Pascoe St Léger Grenfell (1861-96) was killed in the Matabele War.

Cecil Alfred Grenfell (1864-1924) was a member of the Stock Exchange, rode in the 1896 Grand National and was MP for Bodmin in 1910. He served in South Africa in 1900 and as a Lieutenant Colonel in the Royal Buckinghamshire Yeomanry and Remount Service during the First World War (MID). He married Lady Lillian Maud Spencer Churchill, sister of Winston Spencer Churchill, in 1898.

Reginald du Pré Grenfell (1866-99) served with 17th Lancers in India from 1887.

John Pascoe Grenfell (1869-1948), a mercantile clerk and later financier, served in South Africa in 1900 as a Lieutenant in the Royal Navy and in the Great War as a Lieutenant Colonel in the Royal Buckinghamshire Yeomanry (MID).

Harold Maxwell Grenfell (1870-1929) was commissioned into 4th Brigade, Royal Artillery Militia, Scottish Division in 1888 and transferred to Regular service with 1st Life Guards in 1892. He was ADC to Major General Egypt 1897-98, including at Khartoum in 1898 (MID). In 1899 he was ADC for a few months before being appointed Assistant Military Secretary to his uncle, Governor and Commander-in-Chief Malta. In the Boer War 1900-02 he served with 2nd Brabant's Horse (MID). He commanded 3rd Dragoon Guards 1908-12 and in the First World War was a Brigade Commander (CMG MVO).

Francis and Rivy in August 1914.

Arthur Morton Grenfell (1873-1958), a financier, served in the Royal Buckinghamshire Hussars Yeomanry from 15th May 1901. In the First World War he was a Colonel in the Royal Buckinghamshire Yeomanry, 9th Lancers and Royal Flying Corps (DSO TD MID); he was wounded twice. One of his sons, Lieutenant Colonel Reginald Pascoe Grenfell KRRC married Joyce Irene Phipps on 12th December 1929; she is better known as the actress and comedienne Joyce Grenfell OBE.

Robert Septimus Grenfell (1875-98) was commissioned in 4th Bedfordshire Regiment (Militia) on 17th October 1894. He transferred to 12th Lancers and was killed in action while attached to 21st Lancers during the famous charge at Omdurman, Sudan on 4th September 1898. Captain P A Kenna and Lieutenant R H L J de Montmorency were awarded the VC for attempting to recover his body, to save it from further mutilation by the Dervishes.

Riversdale Nonus Grenfell (1880-1914) was commissioned into the Royal Buckinghamshire Hussars Yeomanry on 20th October 1904. As a Captain he was attached to 9th Queen's Royal Lancers and died of wounds shortly after being shot in the mouth north of the River Aisne, France on 14th September 1914. He is buried in Vendresse Churchyard, Aisne, France (1).

9016 SERGEANT JOHN HOGAN
2nd Battalion, The Manchester Regiment

John Hogan was born illegitimately at 134 Heyside, Royton, Oldham, Lancashire on 8th April 1884. His mother was Sarah Hogan (1860-1909), a cotton speed tenter. His father is unknown. Sarah married Matthew Creagan during the 2nd quarter of 1888 at Oldham and they sailed for Boston, USA from Liverpool aboard the *Cephalonia* on 22nd August 1895. Sarah had returned to Royton by the 1901 Census, when she was recorded as a widow living with her children at 35 Water Street. John had

three sisters from his mother's marriage to Matthew Creagan. He was educated at Waterhead Church Day School and was then employed as a piecer by J Taylor.

John enlisted in 6th Battalion, Manchester Regiment (Militia) on 5th December 1902 at Ashton under Lyne (No.8977). He was 5' 3½" tall, weighed 106 lbs, with fresh complexion, blue eyes and dark brown hair. He was living at 4 Hilton Street, Heyside, Oldham at the time. He then enlisted for regular service in the 2nd Battalion on 11th August 1903. From 22nd December 1904 he was in South Africa and was awarded a Good Conduct Badge on 11th August 1905. He served in India from 29th October 1906 with the 1st Battalion. Appointed Unpaid Lance Corporal on 14th October 1907 and received a second Good Conduct Badge on 11th August 1908. He qualified for Mounted Infantry duties on 15th August 1908. Promoted Lance Corporal 1st December 1908 and Corporal 11th February 1911. Having returned to England on 21st February 1912, he transferred to the Reserve on 19th April.

John became a postman in Heyside, Oldham, lodging at 36 New Radcliffe Street until being recalled on 5th August 1914. Promoted Sergeant 7th August 1914 and went to France with the 2nd Battalion on 15th August. **Awarded the VC for his actions near Festubert, France on 29th October 1914, LG 22nd December 1914.** He was wounded in the face by shrapnel on 14th December 1914 and almost lost an eye. On 17th December he was evacuated to England and recovered in a military hospital in High Street, Manchester (probably part of 2nd Western General Hospital located at more than 20 sites in Manchester and Stockport) and at Macclesfield Infirmary. During this time he was on the strength of the Depot. He heard of the award of his VC from the matron while helping to put up Christmas decorations in the ward.

John Hogan married Margaret Taylor née Hannon (1876-1926), widow of Robert Garlick Taylor (1873-1913), on 2nd January 1915 at St Mary's Catholic Church, Oldham. They were both living at 18 Miners Street, Oldham. Margaret had three children by Robert Taylor and two others died in infancy. John and Margaret had a son, John, born in the 4th quarter of 1919; he later served in the Royal Navy. **Mentioned in Sir John French's Despatch dated 14th January 1915, LG 17th February 1915.** His VC was presented by the King at Buckingham Palace on 20th February 1915. He transferred to 3rd (Reserve) Battalion on 20th July and 11th Battalion on 20th September 1915 for service at Gallipoli. On 23rd February 1916 in Egypt a Field General Court Martial reduced him to Private plus 28 days Field Punishment No 1 for being drunk on active service on the 19th. Appointed Unpaid Lance Corporal on 6th June 1916. Returned to France with 11th Battalion on 20th July 1916 and was appointed Unpaid Acting Sergeant 23rd May 1917. John transferred to 791st Area Employment Company, Labour Corps (No.398935), on 8th September 1917. The Company was in the St Valery area in the spring of 1918. Appointed Acting Sergeant 27th September and Sergeant 1st December 1917. He transferred to 43rd (Garrison) Battalion, Royal Fusiliers (No.GS/106493) on 13th September 1918 and served in Britain from 31st January until discharged on 1st March 1919. **Mentioned in Sir Douglas Haig's Despatch dated 16th March 1919, LG 8th July 1919.**

Post-war John struggled to find employment and sold matches on the streets in Manchester. A former soldier, Michael Lally, saw him standing in the street with a tray of matches and a notice, 'No Pension-Ex-serviceman'. He gave Hogan two shillings and said, *"I was in reserve to you and Mr Leach when you got your VC… Do you remember taking my bloody money before you got your VC? You had 100 Francs off me on my 20th birthday and spent it in the estaminet."* John was valet to Benny Ross, a variety star, for a short time. He and Margaret lived at 24 Franklin Street, 55 Frank Hill Street and 12 Alderson Street, Oldham at various times. He was a member of the VC Guard at the interment of the Unknown Warrior on 11th November 1920. John was an in-pensioner at the Royal Hospital Chelsea, 8th December 1932 – 15th February 1933. He worked in a munitions factory in 1939.

John Hogan in later life (Alec Armstrong).

John Hogan died at 449 Rochdale Road, Oldham, Lancashire on 6th October 1943 and was buried in Chadderton Cemetery, Oldham in the same grave (D9-63) as his wife and her previous husband. His death certificate stated he was living at 11 Beever Street, Oldham.

In addition to the VC, he was awarded the 1914 Star with 'Mons' clasp, British War Medal 1914-20 and Victory Medal 1914-19 with Mentioned-in-Despatches oak-leaf. He sold his VC in 1942 to a collector (Stanley Oldfield) for £60. It was resold in 1960 for £15. Mr R Souter of Stockport, Cheshire bought it in August 1967 for £785 from JB Hayward's. Hogan's family maintained it was stolen from his bedside after he died in hospital, but the row was resolved when Norman Stoller bought the medals for £9,750 in October 1983 and presented them to Oldham Civic Centre.

9376 LANCE CORPORAL FREDERICK WILLIAM HOLMES 2nd Battalion, The King's Own (Yorkshire Light Infantry)

Frederick Holmes was born at 23 Abbey Street, Bermondsey, Middlesex on 7th September 1891. His father was Thomas George Holmes (1859-99), a carman. His mother was Ann Mary née Hymns (born 1858). They were married at St Olave's, Southwark on 19th November 1875. The family lived at various times at 150 Wells Street, Camberwell and 9 Abbey Street, Bermondsey. Frederick had three brothers and a sister.

He was educated at Bermondsey London Board School (Neckinger Road London County Council School) and was a member of the Boys' Brigade. He enlisted on 28th September 1907 giving his date of birth as 27th September 1889. Frederick married Violet Imelda née Daley in Dublin in May 1914. She was known as Margaret. They had seven children – Victor Clarence Holmes born 10th January 1915, Sylvia Violet Holmes born 6th July 1916, Leola Eunice Holmes born 13th May 1918, Patricia Mary Holmes born 18th January 1920, Maureen Francis Holmes born 22nd March 1924, Frederick William Holmes born 8th March 1925 and Terence Michael Holmes born 3rd June 1926.

Frederick had been a reservist for a fortnight when recalled on 9th August 1914. He disembarked in France on 16th August. **Awarded the VC for his actions at Le Cateau, France on 26th August 1914, LG 25th November 1914. Mentioned in Field Marshal Sir John French's Despatch dated 8th October 1914, LG 19th October 1914 (duplicated 20th October and reissued 9th December 1914).** The officer who made the initial recommendation, Major H E Trevor, commanding D Company, 2nd KOYLI, later stated in a letter (Imperial War Museum VC files), that he regretted writing it as Holmes had been inaccurate in his account and others did equal work – what was meant by this is not known.

Frederick and wife Margaret flanking their daughter Maureen who is holding her first child (Haskins).

Awarded the French Medaille Militaire for taking a machine-gun to a platoon of struggling French soldiers on the Aisne, Army Order No 466 November

1914. Frederick was wounded in the ankle on 14th October 1914, but refused to have the foot amputated at a hospital in Lille and was evacuated to England on 30th November, where he was treated at Weybridge, Surrey and later at Aldershot and Millbank, London until June 1915. His VC was presented by the King at Buckingham Palace on 13th January 1915. Promoted Corporal by 23rd January 1915, when he attended a reception in Bermondsey and was presented with an illuminated address and a purse with gold. A further sum of money was held in trust for him to start his own business.

Frederick transferred to 1st Garrison Battalion, Yorkshire Regiment (21832) on 6th October 1915 and undertook recruiting duties until sailing for India with the Battalion on 24th December 1915. Promoted Sergeant 10th October 1915. Commissioned into the Yorkshire Regiment on 14th March 1917 (59609) and appointed Assistant Instructor at the Officer Training School at Kirkee, India. Later posted to Belgaum from where he took a draft of 200 men to join 9th Worcestershire at Basra in Mesopotamia in July 1917. He became Assistant Adjutant, but fractured his skull in October 1917 and was evacuated to Bombay in November and England in January 1918, where he required treatment until January 1919. Promoted Lieutenant 14th September 1918. Employed in the Infantry Record Office from October 1918. Appointed Assistant to Officer in Charge of London Infantry Record Office 4th April 1919 – 31st March 1921. He served in Ireland during the Rebellion before being discharged to the Reserve on 20th August 1921.

Frederick lived at 18 Wiverton Road, Sydenham and started his own business, which failed. He was forced to sell his medals and scrapbook in the 1920s. The scrapbook was found by Bill Gilbert a Peckham scrap dealer, in a pile of waste paper in 1962 and returned to Frederick after a worldwide search.

On 27th September 1939, Frederick attained the age limit of liability to recall and ceased to belong to the Reserve of Officers. Despite this he was appointed Lieutenant and Assistant Recruiting Officer on 15th April 1941 at the Royal Artillery Record and Pay Office in Sidcup, Kent. He also served in various administrative appointments in Infantry and Tank Record Offices until taken ill in June 1943 and discharged. He then served in the Observer Corps until the end of the war. At least two sons served in the Second World War. His daughter Sylvia served as a Civil Defence ambulance driver, married Sergeant Richard B Newnham USAAF and settled in California. His daughter Maureen served in the Women's Auxiliary Air Force.

Frederick Holmes with sons Fred and Mick in 1940. One of his sons reputedly joined the Navy and went down with his ship off Ceylon in 1943. There is no trace of him in CWGC records. This photograph shows Fred in Army uniform and Mick is dressed as a sailor. (Haskins)

Frederick represented the Disabled Soldiers and Sailors Association and the Earl Haig Fund 1945-51, calling on manufacturers for jobs and funds. He then became Chief Spares Order Clerk with Watford Electric and Engineering Company until 1957, when he was forced to give up work due to ill health. He was a champion for VC pensioners' rights and pleaded their cause on many occasions. Frederick emigrated to Australia with his wife, arriving on 18th January 1960. Daughters Leola and Maureen and son Frederick also settled there in the 1950s and 60s.

Frederick Holmes died at Port Augusta Hospital, South Australia on 22nd October 1969. He was buried in his wife's grave in Stirling North Garden Cemetery, Port Augusta (2 E 6). On his death certificate her name is given as Margaret Violet Holmes.

In addition to the VC, he was awarded the 1914 Star with 'Mons' clasp, British War Medal 1914-20, Victory Medal 1914-19 with Mentioned-in-Despatches oak-leaf, George VI Coronation Medal 1937, Elizabeth II Coronation Medal 1953 and the French Medaille Militaire. His VC (no other medals) was sold at auction by Morton & Eden on 3rd October 2003 for £92,000 and is held privately.

42617 BOMBARDIER ERNEST GEORGE HORLOCK
113 Battery, XXV Brigade, Royal Field Artillery

Ernest Horlock was born at Beech Farm, Alton, Hampshire on 24th October 1885. The family name is sometimes erroneously seen as Harlock. His father was John Horlock (1845-1932), a farm carter who worked on the Talbot-Ponsonby Estate. His mother was Emily née Hasted (1858-1933), a laundress; her maiden name also appears as Crocker, but the reason is not known. Their marriage was registered at Petersfield in the 2nd quarter of 1880. Ernest had four brothers and two sisters. The family lived at various times at Hartley Cottage in Hartley Maunditt and Laundry Cottage in Langrish, Hampshire and 5 Fitzalan Road, Littlehampton, Sussex. He was educated at Hartley School near Alton and Langrish Church School before being employed as a farm labourer.

Ernest enlisted in the Hampshire Regiment (No.7110) at Alton on 22nd February 1904 under the name Harlock, but transferred to the RFA soon afterwards and was posted to 113 Battery. He served at Fethard, Kildare, Dundalk and Athlone in Ireland and gained the 3rd Class Certificate of Education on 24th May 1907. When he returned to England he served at Sheffield, Colchester and Ewshot near Aldershot, from where his Battery was mobilised. He had been promoted Bombardier by 1914 and disembarked in France with the Battery on 16th August 1914. **Awarded the VC for his actions at Vendresse, France on 14th September 1914, LG 25th November 1914.** His VC was presented by the King at GHQ France, St Omer on 3rd December 1914 and he was appointed Acting Sergeant immediately afterwards. **Mentioned in Field Marshal Sir John French's Despatch dated 8th October 1914, LG 4th December 1914 (reissued 9th December 1914).** When he returned to England in August 1915 he received a purse of gold and a signet ring from Lord Peel at East Meon, Hampshire. Appointed Sergeant Major 22nd February 1916 and transferred to D/119 Battery. He transferred to A/119 Battery on 29th May 1916. On 18th December 1916 he joined CCCI Brigade Ammunition Column supporting 179th Brigade in 60th Division, which had moved to Salonika from France the previous month. He moved to the Base Depot in Egypt in July 1917 and returned to England in October.

Ernest and Ethel on their wedding day (Mike Hibberd).

Ernest Horlock married his cousin Ethel May née Hasted (born 1894), a domestic housemaid, on 13th October 1917. They had no children. Ernest was drafted back to Egypt on 28th November 1917 via Marseilles. His ship, HMT (formerly RMS) *Aragon* (9,588 tons), entered Alexandria harbour on 30th December 1917, but there were no berths and she was ordered out into the Roads. While awaiting permission to re-enter harbour she was torpedoed by UC-*34*, ten miles off Alexandria. The destroyer HMS *Attack* (took part in the Battles of Heligoland Bight, Dogger Bank and Jutland), pulled alongside to take people off, but *Aragon* went down before everyone got away. Many went into the water, including Ernest, where he helped rescue others until picked up by *Attack*. However, *Attack* was also torpedoed and he was killed instantly. Of the 2,500 men and women (160 VAD nurses) aboard *Aragon*, 610 were lost including the Captain, 19 of the crew and six VADs. Ernest's body was recovered the following day and he is buried in Alexandria (Hadra) War Memorial Cemetery, Egypt (F 171). His gravestone bore the name Harlock until corrected by the Commonwealth War Graves Commission in 1982.

A memorial service was held at the Royal Field Artillery Depot on 13th

HMT (formerly RMS) *Aragon* operated by the Royal Mail Steam Packet Company launched in 1905.

HMT *Aragon* sinking near Alexandria on 30th December 1917.

January 1918. His wife attended the dedication of the Royal Artillery Victoria Cross Memorial at the Garrison Church of St George, Woolwich in 1920; embarrassingly Ernest's name was not on it, but this was rectified soon after. The church was hit by a V1 in 1944 and is now a roofless shell, but the memorial survives. Ernest is also commemorated at St John the Evangelist Church, Langrish, Hampshire and on the Littlehampton War Memorial, Sussex.

In addition to the VC, he received the 1914 Star with 'Mons' clasp, British War Medal 1914-20 and Victory Medal 1914-19 with Mentioned-in-Despatches oak-leaf. His VC and a collection of artifacts were bequeathed to 10 (Assaye) Battery (successor to 113 Battery), 47th Regiment Royal Artillery on 14th November 1974 by Horlock's widow. She did not remarry and settled in Sussex, where she was living at Hillsboro Road, Bognor Regis in 1974.

Three of Ernest's brothers also served in the forces – 5869 Private William Henry Horlock (1883-1911) served in the Hampshire Regiment in 1900 and later in the Royal Marine Artillery; T/19225 WO1 Frederick Charles ASC (1884-1949) served in France from 17th August 1914 and was awarded the MSM (LG 14th June 1918); 8214 Private John Harry Horlock (1887-1916) served in the Persian Gulf from September 1914 and died of pneumonia while serving with 2nd Dorsetshire at Kut, Mesopotamia on 24th January 1916 and is buried in Kut War Cemetery (P 5). He had previously served in the Hampshire Regiment (1684) from 1906. Ernest's sister Louise was a Red Cross Sister and his nephew Reginald was a Royal Navy Telegraphist.

3976 LANCE CORPORAL CHARLES ALFRED JARVIS
57th Field Company, Royal Engineers

Charles Jarvis was born at Admiralty Buildings, Saltoun Place, Fraserburgh, Aberdeenshire, Scotland on 29th March 1881. His father, Charles Alfred Jarvis from Plymouth (1849-1900), ran the Westhaven Coastguard Station and was awarded the Royal Humane Society

Charles Jarvis being welcomed at a reception in Chelmsford in July 1915.

Bronze Medal for saving two boys at North Berwick on 27th July 1889. His mother was Mary Jane née Byth (1856-98), a domestic servant. Charles and Mary Jane married on 21st October 1879 at Fraserburgh. The family moved to Rattray Head Coastguard Station where Charles junior was educated at Crimond School. He had four younger sisters and a brother. The family moved to Carnoustie, where Charles was educated at Carnoustie School, later attended by George McKenzie Samson VC. Two uncles served as shipwrights in the Royal Navy.

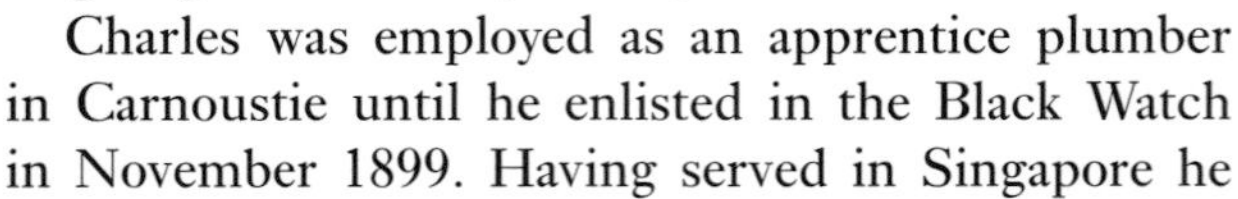

Charles was employed as an apprentice plumber in Carnoustie until he enlisted in the Black Watch in November 1899. Having served in Singapore he transferred to the Reserve in March 1907, finding employment as a telegraphist in London. He was living at Woodford, Essex when war broke out. Having been recalled to serve in the Royal Engineers, he disembarked in France with his unit on 16th August 1914. **Awarded the VC for his actions at Jemappes, Belgium on 23rd August 1914, LG 16th November 1914. Mentioned in Field Marshal Sir John French's Despatch dated 8th October 1914, LG 19th October 1914 (duplicated 20th October and reissued 9th December 1914).** After being wounded in September or October 1914, he learned of the award of the VC while recovering in hospital. Thereafter he was employed training recruits. The VC was presented by the King at Buckingham Palace on 13th January 1915. In early 1916 he was one of a number of technically skilled men asked to undertake munitions work in Fraserburgh (probably with the Consolidated Pneumatic Tool Co). He accepted, but on 29th December 1916 was handed his discharge papers by his works manager. In November 1917 he would have qualified for a pension after 18 years service and he was bitter about his service being cut short.

After the war he had a fishing tackle shop in Hannover Street, Portsmouth and was later employed in the Portsmouth Admiralty dockyard. His marriage to Janet Grace Bowden née Black (1882-1951) was registered at Basingstoke in the 1st quarter of 1940. Janet was the widow of Edgar Bowden (1873-1930), a former Corporal in the Royal Highland Fusiliers. Charles and Janet did not have any children. He was prosecuted for a blackout offence in November 1939; the charge was dismissed with costs of four shillings awarded against him. In the Second World War, he

Charles Jarvis is buried with his wife and her former husband.

served in the dockyard LDV and ARP and also worked in an aircraft factory. He returned to Scotland when his health began to fail in 1943 to live in St Monace, Fife and died at Dundee Royal Infirmary, Scotland on 19th November 1948. He is buried in Cupar Cemetery, Fife (G 176).

In addition to the VC, he was awarded the 1914 Star with 'Mons' clasp, British War Medal 1914-20, Victory Medal 1914-19 with Mentioned-in-Despatches oak-leaf and George VI Coronation Medal 1937. His VC is held by the Birmingham Museums Collection Centre in Dollman Street. Jarvis Place in Carnoustie and Charles Jarvis Court in Cupar are named after him.

CAPTAIN WILLIAM HENRY JOHNSTON
59th Field Company, Royal Engineers

William Johnston was born at 2 Madeira Place, Leith, Edinburgh, Scotland on 21st December 1879. His father was Major William Johnston (1834-1924), who served in the Royal Artillery as a soldier for almost 12 years before being commissioned as a Riding Instructor on 15th January 1864. He then served in England, India and Scotland before retiring in 1891 from Woolwich as an Honorary Major. His mother was Mary née Russell (c.1842-1918). William senior and Mary were married on 12th July 1863 at Saint Andrew By The Wardrobe, London. The family lived at various times at 37 Nightingale Vale and 27 Wood Street, Woolwich and 'Hurstleigh', Kew, Richmond, Surrey. William had two brothers and seven sisters and was educated at Bosworth and Stern's School, Barnes.

William trained at the Royal Military Academy Woolwich and was commissioned on 23rd March 1899. He served at Chatham until 12th April 1900, then went to Gibraltar to serve in the Intelligence Department until 1905. Promoted Lieutenant 19th November 1901. On returning to England he served in the Survey Department. Promoted Captain 23rd March 1908. He worked at the War Office June – July 1908, prior to being appointed GSO3 North China in Tientsin on 11th July 1908. He worked in intelligence in this appointment until 26th October 1911, visiting 11 of the 18 Chinese provinces. Appointed GSO3 South China in Hong Kong 27th October 1911 and was involved in the survey of the border between China and the New Territories. He relinquished this appointment on 27th July 1912 and returned to England to work in the Geographical Department of the War Office 2nd September 1912 – 9th August 1913. He was posted to Bulford, Wiltshire on 13th October 1913 and became a student at the Staff College 21st January – 3rd August 1914.

William Johnston's grave in Perth Cemetery (China Wall), Zillebeke (Sean Cripps).

Posted to 59th Field Company on 4th August 1914, he disembarked with the unit in France on 18th August 1914. **Awarded the VC for his actions at Missy-sur-Aisne on 14th September 1914, LG 25th November 1914. Mentioned in Field Marshal Sir John French's Despatch dated 8th October 1914, LG 19th October 1914 (duplicated 20th October and reissued 9th December 1914).** His VC was presented by the King at GHQ France, St Omer on 3rd December 1914. **Mentioned in Sir John French's Despatch dated 14th January 1915, LG 17th February 1915.** Commanded 172nd Tunnelling Company RE from March 1915. Appointed Brigade Major 15th Brigade on 2nd May 1915. Promoted Acting Major 3rd June 1915 (Brevet Major same date but not gazetted until 22nd June 1915, after his death). **Mentioned in Sir John French's Despatch dated 31st May 1915, LG 22nd June 1915.** William Johnston was killed by a sniper at Hill 60 near Ypres on 8th June 1915 and is buried in Perth Cemetery (China Wall), Zillebeke, Belgium (III C 12).

Major General Lord Edward Gleichen KCVO CB CMG DSO commanding 15th Brigade, wrote, *'He never spared himself an ounce. He was occasionally so nearly dead with want of sleep that I once or twice ordered him to take a night's sleep; but he always got out of it on some pretext or other ... he seemed to like getting shot at ... he was a wonderful fellow all round, always full of expedients and never disheartened by the cruel collapse of his plans by the wet weather.'*

William never married, but had a lady friend, Miss Lewis of Winchester. In addition to the VC, he received the 1914 Star with 'Mons' clasp, British War Medal 1914-20 and Victory Medal 1914-19 with Mentioned-in-Despatches oak-leaf. His VC is held by the Royal Engineers Museum, Gillingham, Kent. He is commemorated at:

- St Luke's Church, Kew Gardens, Richmond, Surrey.
- Royal Military Academy Woolwich VC Memorial Board in the Royal Military Academy Sandhurst library.

His older brother Robert was a surgeon and three of his sons also served – Eric was commissioned into the Royal Artillery in 1911, Stewart became a Royal Navy Surgeon Commander and Evelyn was commissioned into the Royal Artillery in 1915. William's younger brother John was also commissioned in the Royal Artillery in 1901.

6535 DRUMMER WILLIAM KENNY
2nd Battalion, The Gordon Highlanders

William Kenny was born at Drogheda, Co Louth, Ireland on 24th August 1880, not Malta, as is often quoted. His father Patrick (born c.1848) served as a Private (No.2674) in the 75th Regiment (Gordon Highlanders from 1882) 1866-89 at Gibraltar, China, Singapore, Hong Kong, South Africa, Ireland, Channel Islands, Aldershot, Chatham, Egypt and Aberdeen. He had a very chequered medical history, suffering at least three bouts of venereal disease and a number of other ailments. William's mother was Ann née Dollaghan (born c.1856). Patrick and Ann married on 24th August 1876, almost two years after his last reported case of syphilis. William had two brothers and six sisters, two of whom emigrated to the USA. He was educated at Drogheda.

William enlisted in 1897 aged 17, but his mother found out and bought him out. He ran away again in 1898 and re-enlisted. In the Army he was known as 'Paddy'. He served in South Africa 1899-1901 and later at Cawnpore in India, where he was present at the 1911 Dehli Durbar.

William disembarked with the Battalion at Zeebrugge, Belgium on 7th October 1914 attached to 5 Section, 2 Platoon and was appointed Bugler and Runner to Captain (later Major General) J L G Burnett, commanding A Company. The Battalion took part in the failed attempt to relieve Antwerp and the subsequent retreat from Ghent to Ypres. **Awarded the VC for his actions near Ypres, Belgium on 23rd October 1914, LG 18th February 1915. Mentioned in Field Marshal Sir John French's Despatch dated 14th January 1915, LG 18th February 1915.**

The Battalion tried to keep William out of danger, but he managed to slip into the front line occasionally. His VC was presented by the King at Glasgow Green on 18th May 1915. He broke his wrist in action later in 1915 and was hospitalised at Newton Abbott. **Awarded the Cross of the Order of St George 3rd Class (Russia), LG 25th August 1915.** William was granted the Freedom of Drogheda in 1915 and presented with a cheque for £120. He was also presented with a watch at the Mansion House, London. Promoted Serjeant and later appointed Drum Major. **Mentioned in Sir Douglas Haig's Despatch dated 13th November 1916, LG 4th January 1917.**

Drum Major William Kenny.

In 1917 William was at a communal bath when orders came to return to the trenches immediately. In their haste to dress William and one of his comrades grabbed the wrong clothing and identity discs. During the following action the comrade was killed and William was with a burial party when a Brigadier arrived and remarked about the loss of their gallant Drum Major. Kenny looked up to see his name on one of the crosses and had to explain about the mix up in the bathhouse.

On being discharged in 1919 he joined the Corps of Commissionaires, working on Bond Street, Berkeley Square and finally at the Park Royal. He lived in the Corps Barracks in the Strand, London. William was a member of the VC Guard at the interment of the Unknown Warrior on 11th November 1920. He never married.

William Kenny died at Charing Cross Hospital, London on 10th January 1936. At his funeral the pallbearers were former Gordon Highlanders who were also members of the Corps of Commissionaires. A wreath from General Sir Ian Hamilton on the coffin bore the message, "To a Gay and Gallant Gordon from a Gordon." He was buried in the Corps of Commissionaires Section, Brookwood Cemetery (199356). The grave marker was lost, but a headstone was erected nearby in 1999. William is commemorated on the Drogheda War Memorial, Co Louth, Ireland.

In addition to the VC, he was awarded the Queen's South Africa Medal 1899-1902 with four clasps, King's South Africa Medal 1901-02 with two clasps ('South Africa 1901' & 'South Africa 1902'), 1914 Star with 'Mons' clasp, British War Medal 1914-20, Victory Medal 1914-19 with Mentioned-in-Despatches oak-leaf, 1911 Delhi Durbar Medal and the Russian Cross of the Order St George 3rd Class. His VC is held by the Gordon Highlanders Museum, Aberdeen.

4050 SEPOY KHUDADAD KHAN
129th (The Duke of Connaught's Own) Baluchis

Khudadad Khan was born on 26th October 1888 at Dabb village, Chakwal, in the Jelum District of the Punjab, India. Little is known of his family and early life. Although he served in a Baluchi Regiment, he was a Pathan. Very few tribesmen of Baluchistan served in the Indian Army and the 127th, 129th and 130th Baluchi Regiments were recruited from Muslims of various tribes within India. In 1914 the 129th was composed of Punjabi Musalmans, Mahsuds and Pathans.

He was mobilised in August 1914 at Ferozepore, Punjab, India. **Awarded the first VC to a native born Indian for his actions at Hollebeke, Belgium on 31st October 1914, LG 7th December 1914.** Khudadad Khan was evacuated to England for treatment at the Indian Convalescent Hospital, Barton Court, New Milton, Hampshire. He received his VC from King George V on 26th January 1915. It is not known for certain where this took place, but it was probably at the Indian Convalescent Hospital, as the Commandant, Lieutenant Colonel J Chator-White IMS, was present at the investiture. Although Khudadad Khan was the first native-born Indian to be awarded the VC, the first to actually receive it was Naik Darwan Sing Negi, during the King's visit to France on 5th December 1914; Khudadad Khan was too ill that day.

Khudadad Khan served on the North West Frontier of India in 1919 and received a Viceroy's Commission to Subadar (Captain) in December 1929. He attended the VC Centenary Celebrations at Hyde Park, London on 26th June 1956 and the first VC Association Reunion at the Café Royal, London on 24th July 1958. He became a Committee Member of the VC and GC Association.

Khudadad Khan died at Chak No 25 Rukhan Tehsil Village, Phalia District, Mandi Bahauddin, Pakistan on 8th March 1971 and is buried in Rukhan Village Cemetery near Chakwal. There is a statue of him in the gardens of the Army Museum, Rawalpindi, Pakistan. A silver statuette was presented by his Regiment to the Quetta Staff College in 1951.

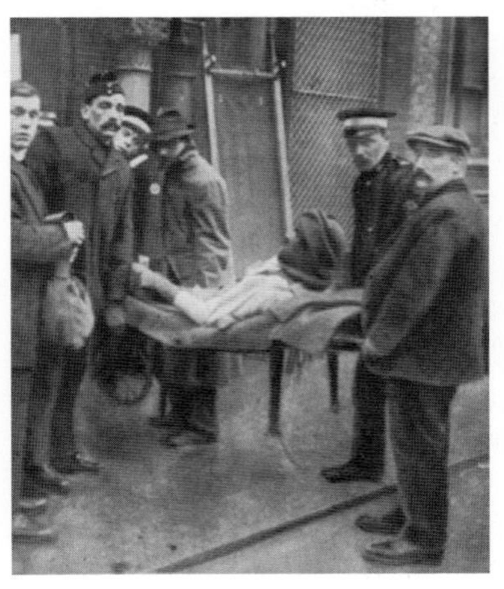

Khudadad Khan arriving at New Milton for treatment.

In addition to the VC, he was awarded the 1914 Star with 'Mons' clasp, British War Medal 1914-20, Victory Medal 1914-19, India General Service Medal 1908-35 with clasp 'Afghanistan NWF 1919', General Service Medal 1918-62 with clasp 'Iraq', George V Silver Jubilee Medal 1935, George VI Coronation Medal 1937 and

Barton Court Hotel in 1917. Almost all of it has since disappeared due to coastal erosion.

The Indian memorial at Barton-on-Sea. The remains of Barton Court are beyond the trees. (Ian & Tonya West)

Khudadad Khan after receiving a Viceroy's Commission as Subadar in December 1929.

Elizabeth II Coronation Medal 1953. His VC is reputed to be held by the Pakistan Army Museum, Eftikhar Road, Rawalpindi, Pakistan, but the Museum has no knowledge of it. The VC was reported stolen by Khudadad Khan in 1952 and an official replacement was neither applied for nor issued. A copy was made by the Birmingham company Fattorini and attempts have been made to sell it. 129th Baluchis continue to serve in the Pakistani Army as 11th Battalion, The Baloch Regiment.

SECOND LIEUTENANT JAMES LEACH
2nd Battalion, The Manchester Regiment

James Leach was born at Bowerham Barracks (now St Martin's College), Lancaster on 27th July 1894. He was registered at birth as James Edgar Leach. His father was James Leach (1860-1912), who served as a Colour Sergeant in 2nd, 1st and 3rd Battalions, The King's Own (Royal Lancaster Regiment) 1879-1901 (No 2959 later 2889), including in the West Indies 1880-81 and the South African War February 1900 – May 1901. On discharge in July 1901 he lived at 33 Cobden St, Moston Lane, Harpurhey, Manchester and became an agent for the Royal Liverpool Friendly Society Insurance Company. He was living at 62 Melrose Street, Leicester in 1911. His mother was Amelia Somerfield née Warren (1865-1913), a bookbinder in 1881. They married on 3rd October 1893 at Lancaster. James had four brothers and a sister and was educated at Bowerham Council School 1897-1901 and Moston Lane Municipal School, Manchester until 1907. He was then employed as an apprentice chemist.

When James enlisted in the Northamptonshire Regiment Special Reserve (No.8955) on 9th August 1910 he stated he was a fishmonger and added two years to his age. When he enlisted in 3rd Northamptonshire (No 9265) for Regular service on 23rd December 1910 he stated he was a labourer and both parents were dead. He did not nominate a next of kin. While at the Depot he gained 3rd and 2nd Class Education Certificates and trained as a signaller and scout. He was posted to 2nd Battalion on 4th January 1911 at Devonport and 1st Battalion on 15th March 1911. He gained the 1st Class Certificate of Army Education on 31st May 1911. Promoted unpaid Lance Corporal 7th November 1911 and Lance Corporal 30th May 1912. Awarded an Acting Schoolmaster's Certificate in February 1913. Trained in Transport Duties November 1913 and Sanitary and Water Duties February 1914. Promoted Corporal 23rd June 1914.

James was based at Aldershot when war broke out and disembarked in France on 13th August 1914. Promoted Sergeant after the Aisne battles. He was commissioned into the Manchester Regiment on 1st October 1914 and posted to 2nd Battalion on 9th October. **Awarded the VC for his actions at La Quinque Rue, near Festubert, France on 29th October 1914, LG 22nd December 1914.** He was concussed on 17th November 1914 and evacuated to England on 25th November for treatment at Lady Evelyn Mason's Hospital for Officers at 16 Bruton Street, London until 11th November. Medical Boards on 3rd and 17th December found him unfit for any service and he was sent on leave. Promoted Lieutenant 11th December 1914. He was declared fit for home service on 31st December and posted to 3rd (Reserve) Battalion at Cleethorpes, Lincolnshire on 1st January 1915. His VC was presented by the King at Buckingham Palace on 13th January 1915. He took part in a recruiting drive at Manchester on 13th February. **Mentioned in Sir John French's Despatch dated 14th January 1915, LG 17th February 1915.**

James was declared fit for general service on 1st March and returned to the Battalion on 15th April. He was concussed again two days later and evacuated to Britain on the *St Andrew* on 20th April. Having been treated at Taplow Priory, Buckinghamshire he was found unfit for service for two months and sent on leave until 20th June. A Medical Board next day found him fit for light duties and he was

James Leach seated second from the right outside the Gate of Honour of Gonville and Caius College, Cambridge with staff of the Army School of Signalling.

posted to 15th Royal Fusiliers, 7th Reserve Brigade at Purfleet, Essex. A Medical Board on 21st July found him fit for service. He was posted on 20th August to No 1 Army School of Signalling, HQ First Army Central Force, Caius College, Cambridge and declared fit for general service on 31st August 1915.

James Leach married Gladys Marguerite Digby (1896-1916) at Cambridge on 23rd December 1915, but she died a few months later. Appointed Temporary Captain 1st January 1917. James Leach married Josephine née Butt (born c.1895) on 3rd March 1917 at Old Clee Parish Church, near Cleethorpes, Lincolnshire; her father was a Grimsby trawler owner. They had three children – James Walter Barry Leach born 1st June 1918, Donald Anthony Leach born 19th May 1925 and Josephine Anna Wendy Leach born 22nd November 1927.

James returned to France on 23rd March 1917, joined 30th Infantry Base Depot next day and rejoined 2nd Manchester on 17th April. He returned to 30th Infantry Base Depot 19th June – 2nd July to attend a Lewis Gun Course and was sent on leave on 24th August. While in Britain he was medically examined and found unfit again. Medical Boards on 13th September, 16th October and 20th November each declared him unfit for service for four months. He was in various hospitals between each Board and spent some time at Craiglockhart Hospital in Edinburgh, indicating he was suffering some form of mental breakdown. On 2nd January 1918 a Medical Board declared him permanently unfit for further service and he was placed on half pay on 9th February. The following month he was appointed Adjutant, South-West London Cadet Battalion. A Medical Board on 24th July found him unfit for further service and he retired on 7th August 1918.

James next served in the Royal Irish Constabulary, Auxiliary Division (Black and Tans) from 6th January 1921 until early 1922 (No.81618), stationed at Glengarrif, Co Cork. He was then employed by his father-in-law in a clerical position at Grimsby fish docks while studying to become a Fellow of the Chartered Institute of Secretaries (FICS). In 1927 he worked at the Bank of England but lost the position in the Depression of 1930-31. His next position was as a chartered secretary with a copra exporting business in the Fanning Islands in the South Pacific until 1934, during which time he left his family at home. He then worked for stockbrokers Foster and Braithwaite in the City.

When his father-in-law died in 1936 there was sufficient money to enable him to give up work and read for the Bar. He had not completed the training before being cited as correspondent in a divorce case at Devon Assizes with the wife of a company director. Costs of £500 were awarded against him. In 1939 he worked for the Ministry of Aircraft Production and later moved to the legal department of Osrams, the lighting company, in Hammersmith.

James was appointed Lieutenant 2nd December 1941 in 27th City of London (Roehampton) Battalion, Home Guard; the same unit as George Dorrell VC. His last appearance in the Home Guard List was in March 1943. His third marriage to Mabel F Folland (born 1910) was registered in the 1st quarter of 1945 at Brentford.

Post war he worked for the Danish Bacon Company and was a Conservative Councillor in Hammersmith Borough 1949-55. James Leach died at No 4 The Lodge, Richmond Way, Shepherd's Bush, London on 15th August 1958 and was cremated at Mortlake Crematorium, where his ashes were scattered in Plot 8.

In addition to the VC, he was awarded the 1914 Star with 'Mons' clasp, British War Medal 1914-20, Victory Medal 1914-19 with Mentioned-in-Despatches oak-leaf, George VI Coronation Medal 1937 and Elizabeth II Coronation Medal 1953. Since 2010 his VC has been owned by the Lord Ashcroft VC Collection and is displayed in the Lord Ashcroft Gallery of the Imperial War Museum. His son James was commissioned in the Royal Fusiliers on 6th September 1937 (Supplementary Reserve, Category B). He was mobilised on 24th August 1939, promoted Lieutenant 6th February 1940, Captain Regular Army Reserve of Officers 6th February 1947 and last appears in the Army List in August 1948.

71787 DRIVER FREDERICK LUKE
37 (Howitzer) Battery, VIII (Howitzer) Brigade, Royal Field Artillery

Frederick Luke was born at Lockerley, near West Tytherley, Hampshire on 29th September 1895; he was registered as Frederick John Luke at birth. His father was William Luke (1867-1950) a grain miller's vanman at Elwood Mill. His mother was Kate née Luffman (1868-1914). Their marriage was registered at Stockbridge in the 4th quarter of 1890. Frederick had six brothers and six sisters. The family lived at Monks Cottage, Romsey Extra, Hampshire. Frederick was educated at Lockerley School and then worked as a farm labourer at East Dean Farm.

He enlisted at Winchester in January 1913 and disembarked in France on 19th August 1914. **Awarded the VC for his actions at Le Cateau on 26th August 1914, LG 25th November 1914. Mentioned in Field Marshal Sir John French's Despatch dated 8th October 1914, LG 19th October 1914 (duplicated 20th October and reissued 9th December 1914).** His VC was presented by the King at Army HQ, Locon, near Béthune, France on 1st December 1914. The first he knew about it was in the trenches near Béthune when a field officer informed him that the King wanted to see him. There was no time to clean up before he was in the King's inspection line at Locon and only then was he informed he was to receive the VC. The King told Luke not to lose his medal in the mud, but to give it to his commanding officer to send home. At the VC Garden Party in 1920 the King recalled the incident.

Frederick was wounded on 2nd May 1915 during Second Ypres and sent to Todmorden, West Yorkshire and Glasgow to recover. He later served with D/180 Battery in 16th Division, returning to France in January 1918. Promoted Sergeant. He was a member of the VC Guard at the interment of the Unknown Warrior on 11th November 1920.

Frederick was discharged to the Reserve in 1919 and worked as a clerk at the Labour Bureau in Glasgow before becoming a janitor at Glasgow High School for Boys. He married Jane 'Jeannie' Wilson née Husband (1898–1974) at Queen's Cross United Free Church, Glasgow on 4th April 1919. They met while he was in hospital. They lived at Top Green, Lockerley, Hampshire and later at 208 Alison Road, Glasgow. Frederick and Jeannie had three children all born at Kelvin, Glasgow – William Husband Luke born 5th February 1920, Frederick Frank Luke born July 1922 and Mattie (Martha) Luke born 1935.

Frederick was discharged from the Reserve in 1929. He enlisted in the RAF as a Ground Gunner on 29th July 1941 and joined No 744 Defence Squadron at Dyce, Scotland on 1st November 1941. The Squadron renumbered as No 2744 on the formation of the RAF Regiment on 1st February 1942. Frederick was a temporary Sergeant within a year of enlisting. He attended the Artillery School in May 1942 and rejoined his Squadron, which had moved to the RAF Regiment Depot at Belton Park, Lincolnshire, where he became an instructor. In May 1942 he was with the Squadron's No 6 Flight at Filey, Yorkshire. In November 1943 he transferred to the RAF Marine Branch as a Boat Crewman, relinquishing his rank and reverting to Aircraftman 1st Class. He served at Oban for most of 1944 and was discharged on 22nd August 1945. His son William served in the Merchant Navy and his son Frederick served in the RAF as an air gunner.

After the war Frederick became a gauge and tool storeman at Weirs of Cathcart, Glasgow until about 1960 and also worked for a short time as a petrol pump attendant in 1967. In 1962 he returned to Le Cateau for the 48th anniversary of the battle and received the Freedom of the town. He went back for the 50th anniversary along with 93 (Le Cateau) Battery. Frederick Luke became the oldest man living to hold the Victoria Cross. At a dinner at Buckingham Palace for surviving VC winners he presented the First World War veterans to the Queen. He regularly attended VC reunions and ceremonies. In February 1981 he spent a week with 93 (Le Cateau) Battery at Paderborn, West Germany. A champagne lunch was held at Le Cateau and at Paderborn he took the salute at a special parade. Major General Richard Vickers, commanding 4th Division, expressed the hope they would never have to go to war again. Luke replied, *"Well if you do and you need any help, just give me a call!"*

Frederick Luke died at his daughter's home at 597 Castlemilk Road, Croftfoot, Glasgow on 12th March 1983 and was cremated at Linn Crematorium, Glasgow, where his ashes were scattered. He is commemorated on the Royal Artillery VC Memorial in the ruins of St George's Chapel, the former Garrison Church at Woolwich, which was reduced to a roofless shell by a V1 in 1944. 93 (Le Cateau)

Battery, successor to 37 (Howitzer) Battery, comprises Drain, Luke and Reynolds Troops.

In addition to the VC, which he held for a record 69 years, he was awarded the 1914 Star with 'Mons' clasp, British War Medal 1914-20, Victory Medal 1914-19 with Mentioned-in-Despatches oak-leaf, Defence Medal 1939–45, British War Medal 1939-45, George VI Coronation Medal 1937 and Elizabeth II Coronation Medal 1953. In 1969 a duplicate VC was put into circulation by a fraudulent dealer. The real VC and other medals were purchased privately in 1999 and are held by the Lord Ashcroft VC Collection in the Lord Ashcroft Gallery of the Imperial War Museum.

Frederick Luke (3rd from right) at the 50th anniversary dinner at Le Cateau in 1964.

8185 PRIVATE JAMES MACKENZIE
2nd Battalion, Scots Guards

James Mackenzie was born at West Glen, New Abbey, Kirkcudbrightshire on 2nd April 1884. His father was Alexander McCortie Mackenzie (1859-1900), a mason. His mother was Marion Carnduff née Millar/er (1859-1939). Alexander and Marion married on 8th June 1883 at West Glen. The family was living at 65 Eglinton Street, Glasgow in 1883, 23 Galloway Street, Maxwelltown by 1891 and at 22 Terregles Street, Maxwelltown in 1900. James had a brother and six sisters.

James was educated at Maxwelltown School (now Laurieknowe Primary School), also attended by Captain James Edward Tait VC MC, 78th Canadian Infantry Battalion. After school, James was employed at Locharbank farm at Bankend, on his maternal grandparents farm at Barncleugh, Irongray and later as a joiner with Messrs Williamson in Maxwelltown.

When he enlisted on 16th February 1912, he gave his age as 23 although he was 27, to ensure he got in, and gave his occupation as groom. He went to France with his unit on 7th October 1914. **Awarded the VC for his actions at Rouges Bancs,**

France on 19th December 1914, LG 18th February 1915. He was killed in action the same day and is commemorated on the Ploegsteert Memorial, Belgium.

James never married and the VC was sent to his mother on 9th March 1915. In addition to the VC he was awarded the 1914 Star with 'Mons' clasp, British War Medal 1914-20 and Victory Medal 1914-19. His mother later presented his medals to the Regiment and they are held by Regimental Headquarters Scots Guards, Wellington Barracks, London. James Mackenzie is commemorated in a number of places:

- 'Mackenzie VC Block' at the Infantry Training Centre, Catterick, Yorkshire opened by the Regimental Colonel Scots Guards, Major General J T Holmes, on 25th April 2003.
- Named on the family gravestone and on a plaque at Troqueer Parish Church, Maxwelltown, Dumfriesshire.
- Maxwelltown War Memorial.
- Roll of Honour at Laurieknowe Primary School.

LIEUTENANT CYRIL GORDON MARTIN
56th Field Company, Royal Engineers

Cyril Martin was born at Foochow, China on 19th December 1891. His father was the Reverend John Martin (c.1857-1921), principal of the Church Missionary Society College in Foochow, China, later Examining Chaplain to the Bishop of Fuh-Kien and became vicar of Grandborough, near Rugby, in November 1916. His mother was Sarah Eliza née Goldie (1850-94), born at Arcot, Tamil Nadu in India. She was the daughter of John Henry Goldie (1817-94) an Indian Civil Service Judge. John and Sarah married in 1883. After his mother died, Cyril was brought up by two aunts at 12 Somerset Place, Bath. By 1901 he was living with his aunt, Emma Sophia Georgina Goldie (1854-1923), at Rivers Street, Bath, together with his brothers and sister – John, Francis and Dorothy. Another sister, Olive died in 1894. John Martin married again in 1910 to Louisa Howard Edmonds (1871-1949) at St John's Cathedral, Hong Kong and they had two sons – Ronald and Dennis.

Cyril was educated at Hamilton House at Bath, Bath College, Clifton College and then trained at the Royal Military Academy Woolwich. He was commissioned on 23rd December 1911 and succeeded Lieutenant Philip Neame (VC 1914) in 56th Field Company at Bulford on Salisbury Plain. Promoted Lieutenant 15th July and proceeded to France on 16th August 1914. **Awarded the DSO for holding a post with his section at Le Cateau on 26th August 1914, after the infantry had been driven from it and remained under heavy fire until relieved, LG 9th November 1914.** He was shot through the shoulder and bayoneted in the hand on this occasion and returned to England on 23rd October 1914. **Mentioned in Field Marshal Sir John French's Despatch dated 8th October 1914, LG 19th October 1914 (duplicated 20th October and reissued 9th December 1914).**

Having recovered, Cyril returned to France on 21st February 1915. **Awarded the VC for his actions at Spanbroekmolen, Belgium on 12th March 1915, LG 19th April 1915.** He was wounded in this action and returned to England. **Mentioned in Field Marshal Sir John French's Despatch dated 31st May 1915, LG 22nd June 1915.** The VC was presented by the King at Buckingham Palace on 12th July 1915. While recuperating he was presented with a sword of honour by the citizens of Bath in October 1915.

Cyril was appointed Assistant Instructor, School of Military Engineering 27th October 1915 – 19th May 1916. He then served with the Egyptian Army in various appointments 10th July 1916 – 16th January 1925. He took part in operations in Sudan against the Lau Nuer, in the Nyima Hills and in Nuba Mountains Province 1917-18. During Allenby's Palestine campaign he served with the Egyptian Expeditionary Force 30th June – 31st October 1918 in the Egyptian Army Public Works Department. Promoted Captain 26th June 1917.

Cyril Martin married Mabel née Hingston (born c.1896) at Chatham on 20th August 1917. His father performed the service. Mabel was the daughter of Major Edward Hingston (1870-1915), who was killed in action in France on 28th March 1915 commanding 54th Field Company RE and is buried in Estaires Communal Cemetery and Extension, France (II H 8). Cyril and Mabel had three children – Cyril Edward Hingston Martin, born 14th November 1919 in Egypt; Richard Francis Hingston Martin, born 17th February 1923; and Mabyn Elizabeth Martin born 24th August 1924, both registered at Medway, Kent.

Back in Egypt he was attached to the Sudan Defence Force 17th January – 14th July 1925 as Assistant Director of the Works Department. **Awarded the Order of the Nile 4th Class, LG 21st September 1923.** After nine years in Egypt and Sudan, Cyril returned to take up the appointment of Assistant Instructor Field Works and Bridging, School of Military Engineering, Chatham on 15th July 1925 until 17th August 1928. Promoted Major 10th August 1928.

Cyril moved to India, where he took part in operations on the Northwest Frontier 1930-31. **Mentioned by Field Marshal Sir William Birdwood for distinguished services during operations on the Northwest Frontier**

Cyril Martin towards the end of his military career.

of India during the period 23rd April – 12th September 1930, LG 26th June 1931. Mentioned by General Sir Philip Chetwode for distinguished service on operations on the Northwest Frontier of India during the period October 1930 – March 1931, LG 6th May 1932. Brevet Lieutenant Colonel 6th May 1932. Appointed GSO2 India 4th May 1933 – 15th September 1936. Brevet Colonel 6th May 1935. Promoted Lieutenant Colonel 15th March 1936. Took part in operations on the Northwest Frontier of India 1936-37. **Awarded CBE, LG 16th August 1938 for services on operations in Waziristan 16th September – 15th December 1937. Mentioned by General Sir Robert Cassels for distinguished service on operations in Waziristan, Northwest Frontier of India 17th January – 15th September 1937 and 16th September – 15th December 1937, LG 18th February and 16th August 1938.** He was appointed Commander Royal Engineers India 7th February 1937 – 29th July 1939. Promoted Colonel 30th July 1939, with seniority from 6th May 1935 and appointed Deputy Chief Engineer, Northern Command.

On 23rd April 1941 he was promoted Acting Brigadier and Chief Engineer British Troops Iraq until 27th February 1942. He was Temporary Brigadier from 23rd October 1941. **Mentioned by the War Office for gallant and distinguished services in Iraq, Syria and Persia during the period April 1941 – February 1942, LG 14th January 1943.** Appointed Brigadier Royal Engineers Middle East 15-27th February 1942. After a lengthy period abroad, Cyril returned to Britain to be Commandant of the Royal Engineers Officer Cadet Training Unit at Newark, 1942-43. He was retained on the Active List while supernumerary to establishment 13th July 1943. This was not for long, as he was appointed Commandant School of Military Engineering Roorkee, India and Temporary Brigadier on 9th October 1943. Appointed Chief Engineer North Western Army, India 13th March 1945 – 1946. Appointed ADC to the King 22nd January 1945 – 15th December 1946.

Cyril retired from the Army on 15th December 1946 and on 26th March 1947 was appointed Honorary Brigadier. He ceased to belong to the Regular Army Reserve of Officers on attaining the age limit of liability to recall on 19th December 1949. He was employed by the Forestry Commission, served as a Lieutenant in the Devon Army Cadet Force 9th December 1951 – 8th February 1955 and was on the Committee of the Victoria Cross and George Cross Association. Cyril was a Freemason – Khartoum Lodge No 2877, Jamrud Lodge No 4372, Stewart Lodge No 1960.

Cyril Martin died at Morden College Hospital, Blackheath, London on 14th August 1980 and was cremated at Eltham Crematorium, London. His ashes were scattered on Pew Tor on Dartmoor. He is commemorated on the Royal Military Academy Woolwich VC Memorial Board in the Royal Military Academy Sandhurst library.

In addition to the VC, CBE and DSO, Cyril was awarded the 1914 Star with 'Mons' clasp, British War Medal 1914-20, Victory Medal 1914-19 with Mentioned-in-Despatches oak-leaf, India General Service Medal 1908-35 with clasp 'North West Frontier 1930-31', India General Service Medal 1936-39 with clasp 'North West Frontier 1936-37', 1939-45 Star, 1939-45 Defence Medal, War Medal 1939-45 with Mentioned-in-Despatches oak-leaf, George V Silver Jubilee Medal 1935, George VI Coronation Medal 1937, Elizabeth II Coronation Medal 1953, Elizabeth II Silver Jubilee Medal 1977, Order of the Nile 4th Class (Egypt) and Khedive's Sudan Medal 1910-22 (Egypt) with two clasps ('Nyima 1917-18' & 'Lau Nuer'). Although entitled to Mentioned-in-Despatches oak-leaves on both India General Service Medals, he retired before an Army Order in September 1947 permitted them to be worn on inter-war medals and he may not have been aware of this. His children, Richard and Mabyn presented his medals to Major General G S Sinclair, Engineer-in-Chief on 2nd December 1980. They are held by the Royal Engineers Museum, Gillingham, Kent. Amongst his siblings:

Francis Henry Martin (1888-1917) was commissioned on 4th June 1917 and served in 84th Field Company, Royal Engineers. He was killed in action on 24th November and is commemorated on the Cambrai Memorial, Louverval, France (Panels 1 and 2).

Anne Dorothy M Martin (1890-1957) married the Right Reverend Howard West Kilvington Mowll (1890-1958). He was a tutor at Wycliffe College, Toronto, Canada in 1913 and Deacon to the Bishop of London for the Colonies 21st September 1913. He was ordained on 7th June 1914 and returned to Canada as Professor of History at Wycliffe College in 1916. He served as a Chaplain on the Western Front and became Assistant Bishop for West China on 24th June 1922 and Diocesan Bishop in 1928. They emigrated to Australia, where Howard became Anglican Archbishop of Sydney on 1st March 1934. He became Primate of Australia in 1948 and was awarded the CMG in 1954. Howard purchased a 60 hectare property at Castle Hill, Sydney on which Dorothy established the first retirement village in Australia for missionaries returning from China. She was awarded the OBE in 1956.

Amongst his cousins:

George Henry Goldie (1888-1914) was commissioned in 1st Loyal North Lancashire Regiment on 29th August 1906, promoted Lieutenant 1st January 1910 and was killed in action on 14th September 1914. He is commemorated on La Ferté-sous-Jouarre Memorial, Seine et Marne, France.

Noel Barré Goldie (1882-1964) was commissioned in 1st Lancashire Battery, Lancashire Brigade RGA on 15th January 1915. Acting Lieutenant 15th July 1915, Staff Capt 30th March 1916, Temporary Captain 15th May and Lieutenant 1st June. He was promoted Captain 27th October 1920 and appears in the Army list until April 1921 with 4th West Lancashire Medium Battery RGA. He was elected Conservative MP for Warrington in 1931 and retained the seat until defeated in the Labour landslide in 1945. He was knighted in the Birthday Honours June 1945.

Cyril's sons served in the Second World War:

Cyril was commissioned in the Royal Engineers on 1st July 1939 (95080), promoted Lieutenant 1st January 1941 and Temporary Captain 25th August 1942. He was killed in action on 28th February 1944 in Italy, serving with 2nd Parachute Squadron Royal Engineers and is buried in Sangro River War Cemetery (X C 24).

Richard was commissioned in the RAF General Duties Branch (122157) on 7th March 1942. Promoted War Substantive Flying Officer 1st October 1942, War Substantive Flight Lieutenant 7th March 1944, Flight Lieutenant 7th September 1945 and Squadron Leader 1st January 1953. He retired on 17th February 1966.

LIEUTENANT ARTHUR MARTIN-LEAKE
5th Field Ambulance, Royal Army Medical Corps

Arthur Martin-Leake was born at 'Marshalls', High Cross, near Ware, Hertfordshire on 4th April 1874. His father was Stephen Martin Leake (1826-93), a barrister and author of legal texts. His '*Precedents of Pleadings in Common Law*', compiled with Edward Bullen in 1860 has been much updated and the 17th edition was published in 2011. Stephen was a prominent member of the Juridical Society founded in the 1850s to promote the scientific study of law. In 1863 he left practice to became a county magistrate and continue writing – '*Principles of the Law of Contracts*' 1867, '*A Scheme of a Digest of Law: With a Specimen Digest of the Law of Bills of Exchange*' 1868 (in print in 2010), '*Elementary*

Digest of the Law of Property in Land' 1874, '*Elementary Digest of the Law of Contracts'* 1878 and '*A Digest of the Law of Uses and Profits of Land'* 1888. Arthur's mother was Isabel née Plunkett (1835-1924). Stephen and Isabel were married on 24th September 1859 at Cheltenham. Arthur had five brothers and two sisters and the family lived at 2 Maitland Park Terraces, St Pancras, London before 'Marshalls'.

Arthur's paternal grandfather, Stephen Ralph Martin Leake (1782–1865), was Assistant Secretary to the Treasury and one of the founders of the Victorian Civil Service. A distant relative, Sir John Leake, Commander-in-Chief of Queen Anne's fleet, left his estates to his brother-in-law, Captain Stephen Martin, who honoured his benefactor by changing his name by Royal Warrant on 19th December 1721 to Martin-Leake.

Arthur was educated at Grange Preparatory School at Stevenage, Westminster School September 1888 – June 1891 and privately. At University College Hospital, London (MRCS & LRCP 1898), he was assistant demonstrator to various surgeons and studied under Sir Victor Alexander Haden Horsley CB, the foremost neurosurgeon of his time. He was employed as House Physician at University College Hospital, London, a locum at Surrey County Lunatic Asylum, Brookwood and became House Surgeon and Assistant Secretary at West Herts Infirmary, Hemel Hempstead in October 1899.

When the Boer War broke out, he enlisted as a trooper (No 5778) in 42nd (Hertfordshire) Company, Imperial Yeomanry in December 1899 and departed from Tilbury on 3rd March 1900 aboard the *Cornwall*. Landing at Cape Town on 28th March, he saw some action before taking leave of the Yeomanry on 18th October at Krugersdorp. He was attached to the RAMC as a civilian surgeon at the military hospital at Pienaar's Poort, 19 kms east of Pretoria, and later at Barberton, in Eastern Transvaal. Disillusioned by the pay and work he transferred to Baden-Powell's Police (South Africa Constabulary) as Surgeon Captain on 24th May 1901. He was assigned to the SAC Hospital at Meyerton, near Johannesburg and in October transferred to C Division at Cyferfontein, between Val Station and Heidelberg. Arthur was critical of British Army medical officers being more interested in military procedure than patients, particularly about their failure to prepare for the predictable typhoid epidemic in 1900.

During the attack on Vlakfontein on 8th February 1902, Arthur was with a patrol of 150 men of C Division when it came across a Boer force, commanded by Commandant Piet Viljoen, hidden in a deep hollow at Van Tonders Hoek, near Vlakfontein (55 kms southeast of Johannesburg). The patrol was outnumbered and forced to withdraw, fighting rearguard actions at Van Tonders Hoek and Vlakfontein on the way. Many men were wounded. At Van Tonders Hoek, Arthur attended Sergeant W H Waller while under heavy fire from 40 Boers only 100m away. He then went to assist the mortally wounded Lieutenant TOP Abraham. While trying to make Abraham comfortable, Arthur was shot three times in the right arm and left thigh, but did not give up until he collapsed through loss of blood. The position was overrun by the Boers, who expressed regret for having shot him, but refused to take the prisoners and left him with the other eight wounded lying in the area. Relief arrived some hours later and Arthur refused water until he was sure the other wounded had received sufficient. Major General Robert Baden-Powell, commander of the South African Constabulary, recommended him for the VC following a Board of Officers convened by Major Fair to collect statements from members of the unit, including Sergeant Waller. The recommendation was forwarded to Commander-in-Chief South Africa, Lord Kitchener, on 3rd March 1902. Kitchener and his predecessor, Lord Roberts, believed Martin-Leake was only carrying out his duty and recommended the DSO, but Sir Redvers Buller thought he deserved the VC. Under pressure from William St John Brodrick, Secretary of State for War, Roberts, by then Commander-in-Chief in London, made the recommendation to the Military Secretary, '*Submit to the King for the VC*'. King Edward VII approved the award on 8th May 1902, the last VC of the Boer War. **Awarded the VC for his actions at Vlakfontein, South Africa, LG 13th May 1902. Mentioned in Lord Kitchener's Despatch dated 8th March 1902, LG 25th April 1902.** His VC was presented by King Edward VII at St James's Palace on 2nd June 1902.

Arthur was treated at the SAC Hospital at Heidelberg, before being granted six months leave and invalided home to recover. In June 1902 his former tutor, Sir Victor Horsley, operated on his injured hand. Horsley was later a Colonel in the RAMC and died of heatstroke in Mesopotamia on 16th July 1916 (Amfara War Cemetery, Iraq – IX F 6). Arthur's ulnar nerve had been severed and, despite surgery, the hand remained inflexible and partially paralysed. As a result he failed to qualify as a surgeon in 1902, but succeeded on 11th June 1903 (FRCS University College Hospital, London). However, a surgical career was not possible. As a result of his injuries he was awarded disability and wound pensions of £100 per annum each from SAC funds in February 1903.

He was appointed Chief Medical Officer of the Bengal – Nagpur Railway in January 1904 and on 28th April 1905 also became Surgeon Lieutenant with the Bengal – Nagpur Railway Volunteer Rifle Corps. Promoted Surgeon Captain on 6th October 1905. Arthur was in England on leave in October 1912 when the Balkan War between Montenegro and Turkey broke out. He volunteered to serve with the British Red Cross in Montenegro, arriving there on 25th October 1912. He was very critical of the Red Cross, which had plenty of medical equipment but few drugs and its staff and equipment were poorly distributed. He returned to England in May and India in June 1913. Awarded the Order of the Red Cross by King Nicholas of Montenegro in recognition of valuable services to the Montenegrin Red Cross during the Balkan Wars 1912-13. This award is often quoted incorrectly as the Order of Prince Danilo I. Arthur was also awarded the British Red Cross Society Balkan War Medal (1912-13) with clasp 'Montenegro', which was presented to him in absentia by Queen Alexandra at Marlborough House on 8th July 1913.

When war broke out in Europe in 1914, Arthur gave the Railway notice and travelled directly to France, arriving in Paris on 30th August 1914. He was almost arrested as a spy, wearing his Indian volunteer uniform, but the British Embassy arranged for him to serve with the RAMC. He reported to 5th Field Ambulance at Chaumes, southwest of Paris, on 6th September and his commission as a Temporary Lieutenant was backdated to 3rd September. **Awarded a Bar (the first ever) to his VC for his actions near Zonnebeke, Belgium 29th October – 8th November 1914, LG 18th February 1915. Mentioned in Sir John French's Despatch dated 14 January 1915, LG 17th February 1915, corrected LG 7th April 1915.** Appointed Temporary Captain on 5th March 1915. He was awarded the British Medical Association's Gold Medal on 30th June 1915, but did not receive it until 25th July 1922, when visiting Glasgow on leave from India. His VC Bar was presented by the King at Windsor Castle on 24th July 1915. Arthur had left India in such haste that he forgot his VC and it had to be sent for by the Military Secretary to have the Bar added before the investiture.

Arthur was recalled to England on 22nd November 1915, promoted Major on 27th November and departed on 1st December with the British Adriatic Mission to assist the Serbian Army. He deployed to Corfu on 28th January 1916 with elements of 143rd Field Ambulance, but the mission was short lived and when the French took over he returned to England on 6th March. He went to France as second-in-command of 30th Casualty Clearing Station on 22nd March 1916 and served briefly with the RFC in September, until being recalled due to a shortage of doctors. Appointed to command 46th Field Ambulance on 19th March 1917. Acting Lieutenant Colonel 3rd April 1917 – 12th September 1918. Captain Noel Chavasse VC & Bar was seen by Arthur as he passed through 46th Field Ambulance after being mortally wounded in August 1917. **Mentioned in Sir Douglas Haig's Despatch dated 7th April 1918, LG 25th May 1918.** Appointed to command 42nd Casualty Clearing Station 13th June – 12th September 1918.

Arthur did not return to the Bengal – Nagpur Railway until 16th January 1920 and did not rejoin the Volunteers. **However, he was awarded the Indian Volunteer Forces Officers' Decoration for 18 years volunteer service, Gazette of India 6th September 1924**. He joined the Bengal Flying Club in 1927, qualified as a pilot in 1928 and purchased a Gypsy Moth. Arthur may have been a misogynist, as he openly disliked nurses, hated 'railway wives', disapproved of suffragettes and had no time for vicars' wives and village do-gooders. However, he made an exception for his future wife, as they both loved India, enjoyed hunting and the outdoor life. Arthur Martin-Leake married Winifred Frances Carroll née Nedham (c.1885-1932), at Christ Church, Westminster on 1st October 1930. She was the widow of Charles W A Carroll, a Railway employee who died in July 1929. Arthur and Winifred had no children and he was the only one of eight siblings to marry. Winifred committed suicide in their railway saloon carriage at Chandla Road

Arthur Martin-Leake's impressive set of medals, held by the Army Medical Services Museum.

Station, Central Provinces, India on 14th October 1932. She was buried without inquest or post-mortem examination in a tiny churchyard adjacent to St Augustine's Church, at Bilaspur.

Arthur was co-author, with RDT Alexander DSO OBE TD of *'Some Signposts to Shikar'* 1932, a record of their adventures tracking and shooting in India and Burma, which included his line drawings and photographs. In 1936 he flew himself for a safari in Nyasaland and Portuguese East Africa. Arthur retired and left India on 1st October 1937. During the Second World War he set up and commanded a mobile Air Raid Precaution unit at the White House Inn at High Cross, near Ware, Hertfordshire in May 1940. He taught First Aid classes there and at nearby Puckeridge and his mobile unit won many prizes in inter-unit competitions.

Arthur Martin-Leake died at 'Marshalls' on 22nd June 1953. His remains were cremated at Enfield and his ashes buried in the family grave in the churchyard of St John the Evangelist, High Cross, near Ware. The grave was refurbished by the RAMC in 1989. He left £110,320/12/-; probate 19th May 1954.

In addition to the VC and Bar, he received the Queen's South Africa Medal 1899-1902 with three clasps ('Cape Colony', 'Transvaal' & 'Wittebergen'), King's South Africa Medal 1901-02 with two clasps ('South Africa 1901' & 'South Africa 1902'), 1914 Star with 'Mons' clasp, British War Medal 1914-20, Victory Medal 1914-19 with Mentioned-in-Despatches oak-leaf, George V Silver Jubilee Medal 1935, George VI Coronation Medal 1937, Elizabeth II Coronation Medal 1953 and the Indian Volunteer Forces Officers' Decoration. His VC is held by the Army Medical Services Museum, Keogh Barracks, Mytchett, Surrey, having been presented on 26th June 1955 by his cousin, Dr Hugh Martin-Leake. Arthur is commemorated in a number of places:

- Parish church of St John the Evangelist, High Cross, Hertfordshire.
- RAMC Memorial Grove, National Memorial Arboretum, Alrewas, Staffordshire – an Acer 'Royal Red' tree was dedicated to him on 18th October 2000.
- Army Medical Services VC & GC Roll of Honour at AMS Regimental HQ, the former Army Staff College, Camberley, Surrey.

- Martin Leake House, Territorial Army Centre, Stoke-on-Trent, Staffordshire, named after him on 22nd August 1992.
- Martin Leake Ward at the MOD Hospital Unit, Frimley Park Hospital, Surrey, a 27-bed acute surgical ward established in February 1996 alongside Chavasse Ward.

Arthur's siblings also had interesting lives:

Stephen 'Steenie' (1861-1940) was an assistant engineer on the Bengal and North Western Railway and helped construct the Bengal – Nagpur Railway. He became a musketry officer in the Great War until 1916, when he retired.

Georgiana 'Sittie' (1863-1949) worked in a convalescent hospital at Ware during the Great War.

William 'Willie' (1865-1947) was a trooper in Methuen's Horse, raised during the expedition to Bechuanaland 1884-85. He was commissioned in 1st Cheshire on 4th May 1887 and saw action in Burma 1886-89, on the Chin Lushai Expedition 1889-90 and in South Africa in the Transvaal and Cape Colony 1901-02. Willie retired on 29th May 1907 as a Captain, but was recalled in 1914, promoted Major and Brevet Lieutenant Colonel on 25th November. He served in France from 1st December 1914 until invalided home with rheumatism on 5th February 1915 and took up a staff appointment in the Adjutant General's Department at Hounslow, Middlesex.

Richard 'Dick' (1867-1949) was also an assistant engineer on the Bengal and North Western Railway and helped construct the Bengal – Nagpur Railway. He too became a musketry officer in the Great War.

Francis (1869-1928) served in the Royal Navy from September 1884 – Lieutenant 1st April 1892, Commander 31st December 1903 and Captain 22nd June 1911. He commanded 4th Destroyer Flotilla and was wounded when the cruiser HMS *Pathfinder* was torpedoed by U-21 on 5th September 1914; *Pathfinder* was the first warship sunk by a submarine. William Cotter, cousin of William Richard Cotter VC, drowned in the same action. Francis later commanded HMS *Achilles* and was awarded the DSO (LG 22nd June 1917) for sinking the German raider *Leopard* on 16th March 1917. He was also Mentioned in Despatches and awarded the American Distinguished Service Medal, LG 12th December 1919. He retired as a Rear Admiral in 1921 and was made CB, LG 3rd June 1922 and ADC to the King.

Isabel 'Bella' (1871-1930) ran the family home 'Marshalls, where all the siblings lived.

Theodore Edward (1878-1907) was a Royal Engineer, commissioned on 23rd March 1899. He served in the China Expedition 1900-01 and in Peking on general duties with the 1st Brigade. He transferred to the Balloon Section at Aldershot. On 28th May 1907 he gave a demonstration for King Edward VII and Prince Fushimi of Japan, but the balloon was later found off the Dorset coast near Abbotsbury and both he and Lieutenant Caulfield were drowned.

7504 PRIVATE HENRY MAY
1st Battalion, The Cameronians (Scottish Rifles)

Henry May was born at 246 Nuneaton Street, Bridgeton, Glasgow on 29th July 1885. His father William Henry May (c.1856-1933) was born in Ireland. He was working as a general labourer in 1881, as a city cleansing carter when his son was born and as a gas stoker in 1901. Henry's mother Margaret (Maggie) née Fyfe (c.1857-1921), a paper mill finisher, was born at Madras in India, the daughter of a Royal Artillery sergeant. They married on 26th December 1879 at Bridgeton, Glasgow. The family lived at 198 Boden Street, Barony, near Glasgow in 1881 at 41 Dunn Street, Glasgow at the time of the VC's birth and later at 29 Hozier Street and 262 London Road. Henry had three brothers and two sisters and was educated at Dalmarnock Public School, Bridgeton and the Royal Technical College Glasgow (now the University of Strathclyde).

He was employed as an apprentice mechanic at J Brown & Sons weaving factory on Adelphi Street from 1899. Henry enlisted on 29th August 1902, giving his age as 18, his employment as labourer and declaring previous service in 4th Volunteer Battalion Scottish Rifles. He joined 1st Provisional Battalion in Chatham next day. Promoted Lance Corporal on 18th January 1903 and posted to 1st Battalion on 27th January. He was reduced to Private for misconduct on 16th February and posted to 2nd Battalion on 4th March, serving with it in South Africa until 27th May 1904. Despite his misconduct he received a Good Conduct Badge on 29th August 1904.

Having transferred to the Reserve on 31st January 1905, he returned to J Brown & Sons and from 1907 he was a power loom mechanic. Henry May married Christina née Dewar (1888-1968) on 5th June 1908 at Chalmers Street Hall, Glasgow. They lived at various times at 38 Colvend Road, Bridgeton and 903 Cumbernauld Road, Riddrie, Glasgow. They had three children – Agnes (Nessie) May, born 24th April 1909; Henry May, born 1st March 1911 (died 1931); and Margaret May, born 12th January 1914 (died 1985). Henry May's gravestone records two other children, James (possibly born in 1925) and George, who may have pre-deceased him. From 1912, Henry was employed by Forrest Frew Co Ltd, muslin manufacturers, as a tenter at their Rutherglen Bridge factory, at Bridgeton, Glasgow.

Henry was recalled from the Reserve on 5th August 1914 and disembarked in France on 15th August. **Awarded the VC for his actions near La Boutillerie, France on 22nd October 1914, LG 19th April 1915.** He was wounded by shrapnel in the face at Ypres on 2nd November 1914, evacuated to Britain and returned to France in mid-January 1915. When he was sent on leave on 31st July 1915, the Lord Provost's representative and former colleagues from Forrest Frew met him at Glasgow Central Station. He attended a civic reception on 4th August and addressed a group of Clyde munitions workers a week later. His VC was presented by the King outside Buckingham Palace on 12th August 1915. Having been posted to the Depot on 16th August 1915, he was discharged on 28th August at the end of thirteen years Regular and Reserve service.

Henry was reputedly employed as an inspector in a munitions factory, but he stated in a military document that he was a fitter with Albion Motor Company in Glasgow. He re-enlisted on 27th October 1917 in the Army Service Corps (Motor Transport) (M/348285). His employment was given as power loom tooler and fitter. He attended officer training at No 1 Company, ASC Cadet School, declaring his employment as textile mechanic and motor fitter. He was commissioned into the ASC (MT) on 4th March 1918 and posted to Grove Park MT Depot the same day. He reputedly had another child, Paul May Hamilton, as a result of a relationship on

Henry May at a reception in Bridgeton. It is unusual that he is dressed in a civilian suit rather than uniform. It is known that he attended a reception at Bridgeton on 4th August 1915, but in the picture he is wearing his VC, which was not presented until 12th August. It is unclear what event is portrayed here, but it may have taken place in the period 28th August 1915 - 27th October 1917 when he was not serving in the Army.

Armistice night. Henry was posted to Sydenham on 10th February 1919, returned to Grove Park on 12th March and moved to Edinburgh on 21st March. He served in North Russia from 29th March until returning to Leith on HMT *Kalyan* on 17th November, suffering from rubella and was treated at Edinburgh City Hospital until 30th November. Promoted Lieutenant 4th September 1919 and resigned his commission on 15th November, retaining his rank.

Post-war he joined the Glasgow Manufacturing Co (a hosiery firm) and later became a partner. He attended the Garden Party hosted by George V at Buckingham Palace for 324 VC holders on 26th June 1920. He was a Freemason (Lodge of Glasgow No 441). Henry May died at the Royal Infirmary, Glasgow on 26th July 1941 and was buried in Riddrie Park Cemetery (B 146). Four VCs attended the funeral – John McAulay, Robert Downie, David Lauder and Walter Ritchie. The original gravestone carried two of his children's names, but not his own until a new headstone was dedicated on 12th September 2006.

In addition to the VC, Henry was awarded the 1914 Star with 'Mons' clasp, British War Medal 1914-20, Victory Medal 1914-19 and George VI Coronation Medal 1937. Henry's VC is held by the Cameronians Museum Collection, Low Parks Museum, Hamilton, Lanarkshire, having been purchased by the Ogilby Trust on behalf of the Regiment for £18,250 by Wallis and Wallis on 7th June 1994.

Henry May is commemorated with the two other Bridgeton VCs – John Simpson Knox and James Cleland Richardson – on a memorial paving unveiled on 23rd August 2010, part of the Bridgeton Burns Club Memorial. Henry May's younger brother, 9762 Lance Corporal James May, was killed in action serving with 2nd KOSB at Lille, France on 18th October 1914 and is commemorated on the Le Touret Memorial. Henry's great grandson, Lance Corporal Alan Murray, served in Iraq in 2003.

10531 PRIVATE ROBERT MORROW
1st Battalion, Princess Victoria's (Royal Irish Fusiliers)

Robert Morrow was born at Sessia, New Mills, Dungannon, Co Tyrone, Ireland on 7th September 1891; one of nine children. His father was Hugh Morrow. His mother, Margaret Jane née Ingram (born c.1857), was a farmer. Robert was taken into care by the Presbyterian Orphan Society after his father died and was educated at Carland and Gortnaglush National Schools in Co Tyrone.

After finishing school, Robert ran the family farm until he enlisted in late 1910. Following training with the 3rd Battalion at the Depot, Gough Barracks, Armagh, he transferred to the 1st Battalion at Headley, Hampshire. The Battalion was at Shorncliffe, Kent when war broke out and he went with it to France on 22nd August 1914. **Awarded the VC for his actions near Messines, Belgium on 12th April 1915, LG 22nd May 1915.** Robert was the Regiment's first VC winner.

He was also awarded the Russian Medal of St George 3rd Class, LG 25th August 1915.

Robert was fatally wounded on 25th April 1915 while carrying wounded soldiers to safety under heavy fire during the Battalion's attack at St Julien. He died of wounds at St Jean, near Ypres, Belgium on 26th April 1915 and is buried in White House Cemetery, St Jean-les-Ypres (IV A 44). His brother, Richard, served with 12th Royal Inniskilling Fusiliers during the War.

As he never married, the VC was sent to his mother by post on 19th July 1915. This was the practice at the time for posthumous awards, but on 29th November 1916 the King presented it to her formally at Buckingham Palace. In addition to the VC, Robert was awarded the 1914 Star with 'Mons' clasp, British War Medal 1914-20, Victory Medal 1914-19 and the Russian Medal of St George 3rd Class. Although quite poor, his mother donated the medals to the Regiment in August 1919 rather than sell them. In return the Regiment purchased a piece of land she wanted to add to her farm and presented her with a sum of money. The medals are held by the Royal Irish Fusiliers Museum, Sovereign's House, The Mall, Armagh. Robert Morrow is commemorated in a number of places:

- St Anne's Cathedral, Belfast.
- Carland Presbyterian Church.
- New Mills Church.
- A memorial in New Mills raised by public subscription was knocked over several times by passing vehicles; the Burmah Oil Company restored it after one of its vehicles knocked it over on the third occasion.

LIEUTENANT PHILIP NEAME
15th Field Company, Royal Engineers

Philip Neame was born at Macknade Farm, Faversham, Kent on 12th December 1888. The farm was worked by the Neame family for over 150 years. Just about every generation of the family from Philip's great great grandfather Thomas onwards were members of the Faversham Farmers Club, which claims to be

Philip Neame's father, Frederick.

the oldest dining club in England, having been founded in 1727. In 1864 the Neame family went into partnership with the Faversham brewery, now known as Shepherd Neame. His father, Frederick Neame (1847-1932), was also a land agent for Earl Sondes and served in the East Kent Yeomanry 1865-78. In 1870 he started his own flock of Kent/Romney Marsh sheep and in 18 years received 218 awards, including seven champions, six reserve champions and 60 first prizes. At various times he was Treasurer of the Faversham Agricultural Association, Secretary and Treasurer of the East Kent Cart Horse Society, Director of the Kent Fire Office and a Commissioner for East Kent Sewers. In 1905 he represented the hop industry on Joseph Chamberlain's Tariff Reform Committee. Philip's mother was Kathleen née Stunt (1851-1935). She was Frederick's cousin and they married on 20th January 1880 at St Mary's Church, Higham, Rochester, Kent; Reverend Thomas Hayes Belcher, Frederick's brother in law, conducted the ceremony. Philip had four brothers and a sister:

Frederick Ivo (1880-1955) was a surveyor and succeeded his father as agent for Earl Sondes and other estates. He served in the RGA (Volunteers) and competed at Bisley.

Margaret (1882-1960) spent much of her life blind.

Geoffrey (1884-1918) took over the running of the farm from his father in 1912. He was commissioned on 1st November 1914 and served as an Acting Major in B Battery, 190th Brigade RFA. He was awarded the MC (LG 19th November 1917) and was killed in action at Bucquoy on 2nd April 1918. He is buried in Bienvillers Military Cemetery, France (XII D 6). As he left no will, Letters of Administration were granted in September and his estate was valued at £5,063/7/7.

Thomas (1885-1973) gained experience in factories all over Europe before becoming Department Manager with Stewarts and Lloyds Ltd of Birmingham. He applied for a commission in the Worcestershire Regiment on 16th August 1914 and was highly recommended because he was a fluent German speaker. He served with 9th Worcestershire from November onwards. In the assault on Sari Bair, Gallipoli on 10th August 1915 he received a gun shot wound to the left buttock. He was evacuated on 16th August to Imbros, then Malta and arrived on 30th August at Southampton on SS *Grantully Castle*. Having been treated at Lady Islington's Hospital, 8 Chesterfield Gardens, Curzon Street, off Park Lane, London, a Medical Board at Caxton Hall on 8th September declared him unfit for six weeks and he was sent on leave. A Medical Board on 19th October at Fort Pitt, Chatham found him fit for general service, but he did not return to active duty. Instead he reported to Messrs Stewarts & Lloyds Ltd for munitions work on 25th October. After the war he partnered his father in hop, fruit, dairy, poultry and pig farming, winning several milk and dairy trials and was three times second in the Silcock All-England Dairy Herds Competition. He promoted cooperative marketing and was a driving force in forming East Kent Packers Ltd. He was also Chairman of East Malling Research Station, served on the Council of the Royal Horticultural Society, Trustee of the Royal Agricultural Society of England, High Sheriff of Kent 1948-49 and Master of the Worshipful Company of Farmers 1958-59. He was knighted for services to fruit growing, LG 11th June 1960. Thomas married Astra Desmond (1893-1973), born Gwendolyn Mary Thomson, the contralto singer and musical author (CBE, LG 1st January 1949).

Humphrey (1887-1968) was a surgeon (MRCS and LRCP 1910, FRCS 1913). He served as a Captain in the RAMC in France from 25th October 1915 with 2nd Lancashire Field Ambulance and was awarded the French Croix de Guerre.

Philip was educated at St Michael's School Westgate (now Hawtrey's Preparatory School) and Cheltenham College, where he was a member of the Rifle Corps. He trained at the Royal Military Academy Woolwich 1906-08 and was commissioned on 29th July 1908, following which he attended the School of Military Engineering at Chatham, Kent 1908-10. Promoted Lieutenant on 18th August 1910 and served in 56th Field Company at Bulford until 1913 under Major Clifford Coffin (VC 1917). Philip was replaced by Lieutenant Cyril Martin (VC 1915). He served in Gibraltar from October 1913, but returned to England on the outbreak of war to join 15th Field Company.

Astra Desmond, Philip's sister-in-law.

Philip went to France with his unit on 5th November 1914. **He was awarded the VC for his actions near Neuve Chapelle, France on 19th December 1914, LG 18th February 1915. Mentioned in Sir John French's Despatch dated 14th January 1915, LG 17th February**

1915. Promoted Captain February 1915, backdated to 30th October 1914. He was wounded on 10th March 1915, but it must have been relatively minor, as he became Adjutant 8th Division RE on 30th March. He received a civic reception in Faversham, Kent on 17th July, during which he was driven with his parents in an open carriage, preceded by a band and mounted escort of the Royal East Kent Mounted Rifles, to the Guildhall, where he was welcomed by the Mayor. The VC was presented by the King at Windsor Castle on 19th July.

Appointed GSO3, HQ 8th Division on 11th October. **Mentioned in Sir John French's Despatch dated 30th November 1915, LG 1st January 1916. Awarded the DSO for outstanding services, LG 14th January 1916.** Appointed Brigade Major 168th Brigade on 13th February. The DSO was presented by the King at Buckingham Palace on 8th April. Promoted Temporary Major and appointed GSO2, HQ XV Corps 29th November. Brevet Major 1st January 1917. Appointed GSO2, HQ First Army on 17th December. Promoted Temporary Lieutenant Colonel and appointed GSO1, 30th Division on 20th June 1918. Appointed GSO1, No 2 Tank Group 15th November. **Also awarded Croix de Chevalier of the Legion d'Honneur (France) LG 7th January 1919, Croix de Guerre (France) LG 21st July 1919 and Croix de Guerre (Belgium) LG 4th September 1919. He was Mentioned in Sir Douglas Haig's Despatches dated 13th November 1916, LG 4th January 1917; 7th November 1917, LG 11th December 1917; 16th March 1919, LG 5th July 1919.**

Philip was appointed GSO1 Instructor at the Staff College, Camberley 1st March 1919 – 30th April 1923. He was a member of the VC Guard at the interment of the Unknown Warrior on 11th November 1920. His '*German Strategy in the Great War*', based on lectures delivered at the Staff College, was published in 1923. Brevet Lieutenant Colonel 24th June 1922. He was a member of a hockey team with fellow VC George Roupell, which in 1923 was in the top six teams in England. Appointed Brigade Major Aldershot 31st January 1924 – 15th March 1925. Philip was a member of the British team at the 1924 Olympic Games, winning gold and bronze medals for running deer rifle shooting and is the only VC with an Olympic gold medal. Promoted Major 1st January 1925. He served with the Bengal Sappers and Miners from December 1925. Promoted Lieutenant Colonel 24th June 1926. He attended the Imperial Defence College in 1930 and the Senior Officers' School at Sheerness in 1931. During the 1930s he purchased 'Woodlands' house in Selling as a family home and named it 'Brooke's Croft'. Promoted Colonel and appointed GSO1, Waziristan District, India 17th June 1932. In India he was frustrated working alongside political authorities lacking long-term policies.

Having been severely injured by a tigress while hunting, he spent months in hospital with blood poisoning and fever, during which time he was placed on half pay 12th December 1933 – 6th May 1934. His arm was about to be amputated when he made an unexpected recovery. He was looked after at Lansdowne Hospital, Simla, by a Lady Minto nurse, Harriet Alberta née Drew (1906-94). They were married on 12th April 1934. Philip and Harriet had four children – Gerald David born 16th December 1935, Veronica Kathleen born 20th October 1937 and twins Nigel and Philip born 27th February 1946.

Philip Neame, later in his career as a Colonel in the early 1930s.

Philip was promoted Temporary Brigadier and appointed Brigadier General Staff, Eastern Command, India 3rd July 1934 – 5th February 1938. He was a member of the 1936 Mission to Lhasa, Tibet led by (later Sir) Basil John Gould of the Indian Civil Service, to advise the Tibetan authorities on military reforms and modernisation. Philip and family conducted a two month tour of Burma, Malaya, Singapore, China and Japan in the spring of 1937.

Philip was appointed the last Commandant of the Royal Military Academy Woolwich on 28th February 1938 and his promotion to Major General was backdated to 19th December 1937. When war broke out the Academy closed and afterwards it merged with Sandhurst. **Awarded the CB, LG 2nd January 1939, while Commandant of the Royal Military Academy Woolwich.**

Philip was appointed Deputy Chief of the General Staff, British Expeditionary Force 4th September 1939. Appointed to command 4th Indian Division in the Western Desert 14th February 1940. Appointed Acting Lieutenant General and General Officer Commanding Palestine, Trans-Jordan and Cyprus on 5th August 1940. Appointed General Officer Commander-in-Chief and Military Governor of Cyrenaica (Western Desert Force) 28th February 1941, replacing General Sir Richard O'Connor, who became Commander-in-Chief Egypt.

The Western Desert Force was drastically reduced to send formations to Greece. Rommel attacked on 31st March 1941 and Wavell sent O'Connor back to replace Neame, whom he believed had lost control. O'Connor realised Neame faced overwhelming enemy forces and massive logistical issues and refused to replace him, but agreed to act as adviser. Neame and O'Connor were taken prisoner on 6th April 1941 when their small convoy ran into a German reconnaissance battalion at night. They were held at Villa Orsini at Sulmona in Sicily and Castello di Vincigliata near Florence with other senior prisoners, including Major General Adrian Carton de Wiart VC. There were many escape attempts. Having been released following the Italian capitulation on 10th September 1943, Neame, O'Connor and Air Marshal Owen T Boyd had many narrow escapes from the Germans. They reached the Allied lines at Termoli on 20th December in a fishing boat out of Cattolica. Their escape was organised and led by Captain Jimmie Ferguson RE and Lieutenant Pat Spooner 2/8th Gurkha Rifles. They were driven to Bari to meet Generals Alexander and

Philip Neame (right) with fellow escapers General Sir Richard O'Connor (left) and Air Marshal Owen T Boyd (centre) following their return to Allied lines in December 1943.

Eisenhower and then flew to Tunis to be welcomed by Air Chief Marshal Tedder and also met Churchill there. After flying via Algiers and Marrakesh they landed at Prestwick in Scotland on Christmas Day and took the train to London, arriving on 26th December 1943. **He was twice Mentioned in Despatches, LG 26th July 1940 and 1st April 1941.**

Philip was Colonel Commandant Royal Engineers 1st February 1945 – 1955. He was appointed Local Lieutenant General and Lieutenant Governor of Guernsey 25th August 1945 – 1953. **Awarded the KBE, LG 13th June 1946, as Colonel Commandant Royal Engineers. Awarded the Knight of Grace of the Venerable Order of the Hospital of St John of Jerusalem, LG 28th June 1946 while Lieutenant Governor of Guernsey, and Knight of the Order of the White Lion (Czechoslovakia).** He retired as Honorary Lieutenant General on 17th July 1947 and published *'Playing with Strife, the Autobiography of a Soldier'* the same year. He worked on these memoirs while a prisoner in Italy and the draft was returned to him in November 1944 soon after the monastery where he hid them was liberated. **His wife was awarded the Order of St John (Sister), LG 5th January 1951.** In retirement Philip was busy with a number of appointments:

- Vice President National Rifle Association.
- Honorary Colonel 131st Airborne Regiment RE (TA) 1948-58.
- Honorary Colonel Kent ACF Regiment RE 1952-58.
- President of the Institution of Royal Engineers 1954-57.
- Deputy Lieutenant Kent 4th January 1955.
- Fellow of the Royal Geographical Society.

Philip was also a freemason, Old Cheltonian Lodge No 3223. In April 1967 he was involved in a car crash in which his cousin, Alan Bruce Neame, was killed. Philip Neame died at his home 'The Kintle', Selling Court, Selling, near Faversham, Kent on 28th April 1978 and is buried in St Mary The Virgin Churchyard, Selling. His estate was valued at £7,540; probate 17th August 1978.

In addition to the VC he was awarded the CB, KBE, DSO, Order of St John, 1914 Star with 'Mons' clasp, British War Medal 1914-20, Victory Medal 1914-19 with Mentioned-in-Despatches oak-leaf, 1939-1945 Star, Africa Star, Italy Star, 1939-45 Defence Medal, 1939-45 War Medal, George V Jubilee Medal, George VI Coronation Medal, Elizabeth II Coronation Medal, Elizabeth II Silver Jubilee Medal 1977, French Legion d'Honneur, Belgian Croix de Guerre, French Croix de Guerre and the Czechoslovakian Order of White Lion. His VC is held by the Imperial War Museum. He is commemorated on the Royal Military Academy Woolwich VC Memorial Board in the Royal Military Academy Sandhurst library. Philip's sons all had military careers:

Gerald was commissioned in the Royal Engineers 1954-60.

Nigel was commissioned in the Royal Artillery on 5th August 1967 and retired as a Lieutenant Colonel on 1st October 1992. He then ran 'Sterling Travel', a specialist business travel consultancy.

Philip was commissioned into the RAF Regiment on 6th September 1968 and transferred to the Army (Parachute Regiment) on 9th October 1974. He attempted Mount Everest twice and made the first ascent of Lamjung Himal in 1974. During the Falklands War he commanded D Company, 2nd Battalion, Parachute Regiment under Lieutenant Colonel H Jones VC OBE (MID, LG 11th August 1982). Promoted Lieutenant Colonel 30th June 1988, commanded 10th Battalion, Parachute Regiment from 5th March 1990 and retired on 1st November 1994. Philip became Vice President and Trustee of the Reserve Forces Ulysses Trust (patron Prince of Wales), supporting challenging projects by Cadets and Reservists. He ran 'Integral Mobile Data', providing software for access to databases by handheld computers.

Amongst his nephews:

Basil Desmond Neame (born 1921) was commissioned in the Royal Engineers on 13th June 1942 and later served as a Major (MID).

Geoffrey Desmond Neame (1924-57) served as a Leading Aircraftsman in the RAF from 1942 and was commissioned as Probationary Pilot Officer 28th July 1943. Later Flight Lieutenant and served until 1945.

Christopher Desmond Neame (born 1927) was appointed High Sheriff for Kent in December 1976.

John Humphrey Neame (born 1926) was a member of the unsuccessful Cambridge team in the 1946 Boat Race. Served as a National Service Captain in the RAMC 12th July 1952 (seniority 9th July 1951). Captain Army Emergency Reserve of Officers 9th January 1956.

Amongst his cousins:

Gerald Tassell Neame (1885-1916) was killed in action on 1st July 1916 serving as a Captain in 7th East Kent (Buffs) and is buried in Delville Wood Cemetery (XXIII Q 9).

Arthur Laurence Cecil Neame OBE (born 1883) served as a Colonel in the Royal Engineers. Sheriff for Kent 1934-36.

Godfrey John Neame (1886-1947) in 1925 married Phyllis Rose Boothby, daughter of Guy Newell Boothby, the prolific Australian-born novelist. Brevet Major Royal Engineers 3rd June 1919.

Douglas Mortimer Lewis Neame (born 1901). As a Royal Navy Lieutenant he was granted a temporary commission in the RAF as a Flying Officer on attachment for four years from 4th January 1927. As a Lieutenant Commander he returned to the Royal Navy on 26th July 1931. As a Commander he was awarded the DSO (LG 23rd February 1940) for his part in the action against the *Graf Spee* while serving aboard HMS *Ajax*. He received a Bar to the DSO (LG 8th September 1942) as a Captain for a successful convoy to Malta.

33419 SERGEANT DAVID NELSON
L Battery, Royal Horse Artillery

David Nelson was born at Darraghlan, Stranooden, Co Monaghan, Ireland on 3rd April 1886. His father was George Nelson and his mother was Mary Anne, known as Annie. David had three brothers and a sister. He was educated at the village school in Darraghlan and Monaghan Grammar School before being employed as a shop assistant.

David enlisted on 27th December 1904 and achieved 2nd Class Education on 22nd February 1905. Having been posted to 98 Battery RFA on 22nd December 1905, he was appointed Acting Bombardier 7th April 1906 and achieved 1st Class Education on 30th October. He was admitted to hospital in Colchester 5-10th December 1907 with a sprain, extended his service on 19th December and reverted to Gunner on being posting to L Battery RHA on 28th December. He was paid as Bombardier from 8th September 1908 and admitted to hospital at Newbridge, Hampshire 1st-8th July 1909 with inflamed tissue. Appointed Assistant Signalling Instructor 9th December 1909. Promoted Bombardier 18th May 1910 and Corporal 7th January 1911. He attended the Short Gunnery Course at Shoeburyness on 1st March 1913 and was awarded a First Class Gunnery Certificate. Promoted Sergeant 5th August 1914.

David Nelson disembarked in France with L Battery on 15th August 1914 and was slightly wounded on 24th August. **Awarded the VC for his actions at Néry, France on 1st September 1914, LG 16th November 1914. Mentioned in Field Marshal Sir John French's Despatch dated 8th October 1914, LG 4th December 1914 (reissued 9th December 1914).** He was wounded during the action at Néry in the leg, right lung and ribs and evacuated to a field hospital at Baron, which was overrun by the Germans on 2nd September. Despite his wounds, he managed to escape on the 5th, reached the French lines and was taken to hospital in Dinan, where a piece of shrapnel was removed from his right lung. He returned to England on 20th October 1914 and was treated at 1st London General Hospital 25th October – 16th November.

David Nelson's marriage to Ada Jane Jessie née Bishop (born 1884) took place in the 4th quarter of 1914 registered at Dartford. A son, Victor Cyril, was born in the 4th quarter of 1915, registered at Rochford. David was commissioned 15th November 1914 and according to the Army List his date of birth was 27th December 1886. His VC was presented by the King at Buckingham Palace on 13th January 1915. Appointed Instructor in Gunnery at the School of Gunnery Shoeburyness 1st March 1915 until he returned to France on 11th December 1917. While at Shoeburyness he became a Freemason, a member of Priory Lodge (No.1000) meeting at Southend-on-Sea, Essex. Promoted Temporary Lieutenant 3rd June 1915, Lieutenant 9th June 1915 and Temporary Captain 12th October 1916. Joined C Battery, LIX Brigade RFA on 18th December 1917 and transferred to A Battery, LVIII Brigade on 31st December. Appointed Acting Major 1st March 1918 to command D Battery, LIX Brigade. He received multiple shell wounds to the left forearm, right foot and back and a compound fracture of the skull on 7th April 1918. He died next day at No 58 Casualty Clearing Station at Lillers, France and was buried in Lillers Communal Cemetery (V A 16).

In addition to the VC, he was awarded the 1914 Star with 'Mons' clasp, British War Medal 1914-20 and Victory Medal 1914-19 with Mentioned-in-Despatches oak-leaf. His VC is owned by L (Néry) Battery RHA and is loaned to the Imperial War Museum. David Nelson is commemorated at:

- Presbyterian Church and Church Hall, Ballybay, Co Monaghan.
- Royal Artillery VC Memorial in the ruins of St George's Chapel, the former Garrison Church at Woolwich, which was reduced to a roofless shell by a V1 in 1944.

His wife was living at 'Deraghland', 34 Cowper Street, Ipswich from 1930.

3697 CORPORAL CECIL REGINALD NOBLE
2nd Rifle Brigade

Cecil Noble was born at 18 Tower Road, Boscombe, Bournemouth, Hampshire on 4th June 1891. He did not like his name and was generally known at Tom or Tommy. His father was Frederick Leopold Noble (c.1866-1916), a painter and decorator. His mother was Hannah née Smith (1862-1945). Their marriage was registered during the 4th quarter of 1888 at Christchurch, Hampshire. The family also lived at 36 Lincoln Avenue, 335 Holdenhurst Road and 175 Capstone Road, Malmesbury Park, Bournemouth at various times. Frederick Riggs, who won the VC in October 1918, also lived on Capstone Road. Tommy had two brothers, both of whom died in infancy, and a sister. He was educated at St Clement's School and the Art and Technical School in Bournemouth, following which he was employed as a decorator.

Tommy enlisted on 31st March 1910 and joined at Winchester next day, claiming previous service with 6th Hampshire Battery RFA. He gave his father's name as Alexander (deceased) of 335 Holdenhurst Road, Bournemouth. His uncle, Louis Alexander Noble, had lived at 337 Holdenhurst Road until his death in 1901. His next of kin was recorded as his mother, living at 172 Capstone Road.

Tommy joined the 1st Battalion in Dublin on 11th August 1910. On 24th February 1911 he was charged with using obscene language to a NCO and detained for seven days. He was posted to the 2nd Battalion in India on 10th November. He gained the 3rd Class Certificate of Education on 22nd March 1913 and became a Pioneer on 9th September.

The Battalion sailed from Bombay on 20th September 1914, landed at Liverpool on 22nd October and moved to Hursley Park, Winchester where it joined 25th Brigade, 8th Division. Tommy landed at Le Havre, France with C Company on 7th November. He was appointed Unpaid Acting Corporal 23rd November. **Awarded the VC for his actions at Neuve Chapelle, France on 12th March 1915, LG**

28th April 1915. Tommy Noble died of wounds at Longuenesse, France on 13th March 1915 and is buried in Longuenesse (St Omer) Souvenir Cemetery (I A 57). His VC was sent to his mother by post on 12th June 1915 and was presented to her formally by the King at Buckingham Palace on 29th November 1916.

In addition to the VC, Tommy was awarded the 1914 Star with 'Mons clasp', British War Medal 1914-20 and Victory Medal 1914-19. His VC is held privately. He is commemorated in a number of places:

- St Clement's School, Bournemouth.
- Blue Plaque on his former home at 175 Capstone Road, Bournemouth – his service record gives his mother's address as 172 Capstone Rd.
- Reginald Noble Court, 66 Surrey Road, Bournemouth was named after him on 18th October 1980 – the flats run by the Royal British Legion Housing Association offer sheltered accommodation for retired ex-service personnel.

3556 LANCE CORPORAL MICHAEL JOHN O'LEARY
1st Irish Guards

Michael O'Leary was born at Kilbarry Lodge, Inchigeelagh, near Macroom, Co Cork, Ireland on 29th (2nd on his enlistment forms) September 1888. His father was Daniel O'Leary (born 1852), an agricultural labourer and staunch Nationalist. His mother was Margaret née Lucy (born c.1867). Daniel and Margaret married on 24th August 1886 at Inchigeelagh Parish Church. Michael had two brothers (one died in infancy) and two sisters. He was educated at Kilbarry National School and was then employed as a labourer on his father's farm.

Michael served in the Royal Navy (K3106) as a Stoker on HMS *Vivid* from 1909 and was invalided out on 29th April 1910 with rheumatism in the knees. Rather surprisingly for a man suffering from rheumatism, he enlisted in the Irish Guards on 2nd July 1910 and joined for duty at Caterham on the 7th. He gained the Third Class Certificate of Education on 28th February 1912, was posted to the Depot on 27th February 1913 and transferred to the Reserve on 2nd July.

He joined the Royal North-West Mounted Police in Regina, Saskatchewan, Canada as a Constable (No 5685) on 2nd August 1913 and was posted to Battleford, Saskatchewan. Following a two-hour running gun battle he captured two robbers and was awarded a gold ring, which he wore for the rest of his life. His Superintendent

The Illustrated War News.

AFTER THE KING HAD PINNED THE V.C. ON HIS BREAST: SERGEANT MICHAEL O'LEARY AT HOME ON LEAVE.

A relaxed but posed image of the VC hero for the Illustrated War News of 30th June 1915.

became concerned when he lost a lot of weight and transferred him to the Depot Division, Regina in May 1914 to be more closely supervised by the Surgeon.

Michael was granted a free discharge on 22nd September 1914 and rejoined the Irish Guards on 22nd October. Having been posted to the 1st Battalion, he went to France on 22nd November and was appointed unpaid Lance Corporal on 5th January 1915. **Awarded the VC for his actions at Cuinchy, France on 1st February 1915, LG 18th February 1915.** Promoted Sergeant 4th February. His VC was presented by the King at a private ceremony at Buckingham Palace on 22nd June.

Michael O'Leary was the first Irish VC of the war and the first ever in the Irish Guards. An O'Leary Fund was set up for widows and orphans of Irish troops and he was warmly received at a massive recruiting drive (O'Leary Day) in Hyde Park in July. The Daily Mail published a poem about him and George Bernard Shaw wrote a short play based upon his exploits entitled 'O'Flaherty VC'. Although he was warmly greeted on his return to Macroom, his father was not so complimentary, commenting that he himself had laid out 20 men with a stick at Macroom fair and his son could only kill eight armed with rifle and bayonet. **Awarded the Cross of the Order of St George 3rd Class (Russia), LG 25th August 1915 (invested 30th January 1916).**

Michael attended a short course at GHQ Cadet School in France before being granted a Regular commission in 2nd Connaught Rangers on 23rd October 1915. He was involved in recruiting based in Dublin and was jeered by Ulster Volunteers during a recruiting drive in Ballaghaderrin, which led to questions in the House of Commons on 6th December. On 2nd February 1916 he was attached to 30th Reserve Battalion, Northumberland Fusiliers at Catterick for recruiting duties until he was posted to 3rd Connaught Rangers at Kinsale on 25th August. He arrived at Salonika on 11th January 1917 and joined No 1 Entrenching Battalion on the 17th before serving with 5th and later 2nd Battalions of the Connaught Rangers. Promoted Lieutenant on 1st July. He moved to Egypt on 2nd October and joined HQ RFC Middle East in Cairo on 1st January 1918 for flying training at Heliopolis and Aboukir (No.3 School of Military Aeronautics). **Mentioned in Lieutenant General George Milne's Despatch dated 25th October 1917, LG 28th November 1917.**

Recruiting poster to stir up support for the war in Ireland. Because of the tense political situation over Home Rule, conscription was never introduced on the island.

Michael was constantly in and out of hospital with malaria from September 1917 and was found unsuitable for the RFC on 21st February 1918. He was recommended for return to Britain by a medical board on 26th July and left Alexandria on the New Zealand Hospital Ship *Maheno* on 19th August. He joined 3rd Connaught Rangers at Dover and served until discharged to the Regular Army Reserve of Officers on 10th June 1920 with a gratuity.

Michael married Margaret (Greta) née Hegarty (1889-1953) in 1919 at Ballyvourney, near Macroom, Co Cork and they had six sons and a daughter – Daniel and Jeremiah O'Leary (twins), born 8th October 1920; Matthew N O'Leary, birth registered 1st quarter 1930 at Hendon; Mary T O'Leary, birth registered 3rd quarter 1931 at Hendon. Liam, Timothy and

O'Leary during a recruiting event possibly in Hyde Park, London.

William were born in Canada. They lived initially at Home Farm, Ballyvourney. Michael returned to Canada on 4th March 1921, leaving the family in Ireland while he toured as a lecturer and worked for a publishing company, which went out of business in July 1921. He then became a licence inspector for the enforcement of the Ontario Temperance Act with the Ontario Provincial Police. His family sailed on SS *Carmania* on 30th July 1921 to join him. He resigned from the Ontario Provincial Police on 15th June 1923 and next day became a detective sergeant at Bridgeburg, Ontario with the Michigan Central Railway Police (the line crosses southern Ontario). He encountered a great deal of smuggling and bootlegging and was arrested twice in 1925; once when accused of smuggling an alien over the border to Buffalo and on a second occasion over an irregularity in a search for liquor. He was probably set up by bootleggers and was acquitted in both cases, but was not reinstated in his job.

He worked as a timekeeper for a while and sent his family home on SS *Letitia* in October 1926 when he was unemployed. An uncle in Ireland promised to look after the family, but could not afford the £79 passage fees, which was provided by the City of Hamilton, Ontario. Michael remained in Canada, having secured employment with the Attorney General of Ontario. Bouts of malaria recurred and he was eventually advanced the cost of his passage back to Ireland by the authorities around 1929. The family then lived at 3 Oakleigh Avenue and Limesdale Gardens, Edgware, London. He was initially a packer at the British Legion poppy factory before becoming head linkman at the Mayfair Hotel, London.

Michael was mobilised from the Regular Army Reserve of Officers on 24th August 1939 and appointed Lieutenant in the Middlesex Regiment, with seniority from 1st July 1937. Appointed Camp Commandant, HQ III Corps on 25th October 1939 and went to France with the BEF, but was invalided home before Dunkirk as a diabetic. Appointed Temporary Captain (specially employed) on 2nd February 1941 and transferred to the Pioneer Corps on 24th December. He then served on the staff of POW Camps in the south of England and was forced to relinquish his commission on 19th March 1945 due to disability. He was granted the honorary rank of Captain.

Returning to civilian life once again, Michael was employed in the building contracting trade until retiring in 1954. During the VC Centenary Review in Hyde Park on 26th June 1956, a 64 year-old wheelchair bound attendant at an Uxbridge theatre, Thomas Meagher, impersonated O'Leary. He spoke to the Queen, who was concerned that he did not feel well enough to attend the VC/GC Dinner. Several other VC recipients were suspicious, but did not feel they could embarrass the Queen at the time.

Michael O'Leary died at Whittington Hospital, Islington, London on 2nd August 1961 and is buried in Mill Hill Cemetery, London (G-3 1930). He is commemorated on a plaque at the Royal Canadian Mounted Police Museum, Regina, Saskatchewan, Canada and O'Leary Lake in northeast Saskatchewan was named after him as part of the Saskatchewan Geo-Memorial Project.

In addition to the VC, Michael was awarded the 1914-15 Star, British War Medal 1914-20, Victory Medal 1914-19 with Mentioned-in-Despatches Oakleaf, 1939-45 Defence Medal, 1939-45 War Medal, George VI Coronation Medal, Elizabeth II Coronation Medal and Russian Cross of St George 3rd Class. His medals were loaned to the Irish Guards by the family in 1962 and were purchased by the Regiment in 1982. They are held by the Irish Guards at Wellington Barracks, Birdcage Walk, London. Michael's sons also had military careers:

> Daniel enlisted in the RAFVR (1386126) rising to Sergeant. He was commissioned in the RAFVR as a Pilot Officer (133045) in General Duties Branch on 27th September 1942. Promoted Flying Officer (War Substantive) 27th March 1943 and Flight Lieutenant (War Substantive) 27th September 1944. He was awarded the DFC while serving with 680 Squadron (LG 29th September 1944). After the war he was commissioned in the RAF on extended service (four years on active list) as a Flying Officer and transferred to the Aircraft Control Branch on 27th September 1947 with seniority from 27th September 1944. Promoted Flight Lieutenant January 1948, backdated to 27th September 1947. Appointed to a Permanent Commission on 12th October 1948, retaining rank and seniority. He transferred to Fighter Control Branch on 7th July 1949. Promoted Squadron Leader 1st January 1956 in General Duties Branch (Ground Section) Fighter Control and retired on 8th April 1971.
>
> Jeremiah Michael enlisted in the RAFVR (1386554) and trained as an air gunner. As a Warrant Officer in 114 Squadron he was awarded the DFC (LG 25th April 1944) – in an attack on a railway station where there was a large concentration of enemy troops, he raked the anti-aircraft defences with his machine guns hitting many vehicles and enabling the pilot to complete a successful bombing run. He had previously completed a large number of sorties. He was commissioned in the RAFVR (Emergency Commission) as a Pilot Officer in General Duties Branch on 29th March 1945 (196883). Promoted Flying Officer (War Substantive) 29th September 1945. He was appointed to a Permanent Commission in the RAF as Pilot Officer and transferred to Catering Branch on 20th February 1947 (seniority 29th March 1945). Promoted Flying Officer 29th March 1947 and Flight Lieutenant 19th November 1953. He forfeited two years seniority from 23rd February 1956 and was dismissed from the RAF by a General Court Martial on 3rd September 1958.
>
> Amongst three of the other four boys (Liam, Tim and William), two served in the Royal Navy as Chief Petty Officers and another was a Master Sergeant in the United States Army Air Force. Matthew was too young to serve in the Second World War.

CAPTAIN HARRY SHERWOOD RANKEN
Royal Army Medical Corps attached 1st Battalion, The King's Royal Rifle Corps

Harry Ranken was born at 17 Carndrum Street, Glasgow on 3rd September 1883. His father was the Reverend Henry Ranken (1852-1937). He was a teacher in 1881 and in 1883 became Rector of George Stiell's Institution, Tranent, Haddingtonshire, which provided free education to 150 children. In 1887 he was Assistant at Trinity Parish, Edinburgh and was ordained as Minister of John Knox Parish Church, Mounthooly, Aberdeen on 16th March 1888. He transferred to Irvine Parish, Ayrshire as Assistant on 1st October 1891 and succeeded as Minister on 29th January 1893 until he retired in 1928. Henry joined the Volunteer Force as Acting Chaplain in 1st Volunteer Battalion, Royal Scots Fusiliers at Kilmarnock, Ayrshire on 9th January 1892. On the formation of the Territorial Force he was appointed Second Class Chaplain to the Territorial Force (Lieutenant Colonel) on 1st April 1908 (with precedence from 9th January 1892), attached to 4th (formerly 1st Volunteer) Battalion, Royal Scots Fusiliers. Promoted First Class Chaplain to the Territorial Force (Colonel) on 9th January 1912, remaining attached to the 4th Battalion. Awarded the Territorial Decoration, LG 9th August 1912. A compilation of his sermons dedicated to his late wife, '*In the Morning Sow Thy Seed: Morning Seed Sown in Irvine Kirk and Parish*' was published in 1931. Henry was Chairman of the Irvine School Board, President of the Irvine Burns Club for 1895 and a Member of the Craft of Hammermen of Irvine. Harry's mother was Helen McCormick née Morton (c.1848-1929). Henry and Helen married on 10th August 1882. The family lived at The Manse, Irvine 1893 – 1928. Harry had a younger brother, Alan.

Harry Ranken while working in Glasgow (University of Glasgow).

Harry was educated at Montgomery School in Irvine (later attended by Ross Tollerton VC), Irvine Royal Academy and Glasgow University Medical School from 1900 (MB ChB 1905). During his training he was awarded eight prizes, included three for surgery under Professor Sir William Macewen, a pioneer of many modern surgical techniques, who helped found the Princess Louise

Scottish Hospital for Limbless Sailors and Soldiers at Erskine in 1916. With the help of nearby Yarrow Shipbuilders Ltd, Macewen designed the Erskine artificial limb. Harry was appointed house physician and surgeon at the Western Infirmary in Glasgow and was later an assistant medical officer at Brook Fever Hospital in London.

Harry was commissioned as a Lieutenant in the RAMC on 30th January 1909, gaining top place in the entrance examination. He became a member of the Craft of Hammermen of Irvine on 1st October 1906, having been proposed by his father. He became a Freemason on 31st January 1910 and was a member of Mother Kilwinning Lodge No 0, reputed to be the oldest in the world. MRCP 1910. Appointed by the Tropical Diseases Committee of the Royal Society to assist in research on the treatment of trypanosomiasis (sleeping sickness). Harry was the author and co-author of numerous articles for the '*British Medical Journal*', '*Proceedings of the Royal Society*' and the '*RAMC Journal*' and was awarded the Tulloch Medal for Military Medicine, the de Chaumont Prize for Hygiene and the Tropical Medicine Prize. He was seconded to the Egyptian Army from 17th August 1911 for service with the Sudan Government Sleeping Sickness Commission as Commandant of the Sleeping Sickness Camp at Yei in the Lado enclave. Promoted Captain 30th July 1912. Away from his work, Harry was a big-game hunter, a scratch golfer and a member of the Automobile Club. While serving with the Egyptian Army he had the rank of Bimashi, Ottoman Turk for Major, a term adopted throughout the Egyptian and Sudanese forces.

When war broke out Harry was on leave and immediately volunteered for active service, being attached to 1st KRRC. He was officially transferred back to the Home establishment from the Egyptian Army on 8th August 1914. He disembarked in France on 13th August. **Awarded the Croix de Chevalier de Legion d'Honneur (France) for gallant conduct in the retreat from Mons 21st-30th August 1914, LG 3rd November 1914. Awarded the VC for his actions near Soupir, France on 19-20th September 1914, LG 16th November 1914.** The citation states the action took place at Haute-Avesnes, but this is a commune west of Arras, 120 kms northwest of Soupir. **Mentioned in Field Marshal Sir John French's Despatch dated 8th October 1914, LG 19th October 1914 (duplicated 20th October and reissued 9th December**

Harry Ranken's grave in Braine Communal Cemetery, eight kilometres southwest of Soupir.

1914). Harry Ranken died of wounds at No 5 Clearing Hospital, Braine, France on 25th September 1914 and is buried in Braine Communal Cemetery (A 43).

Harry never married and his VC was presented to his father by the King at Buckingham Palace on 29th November 1916. In addition to the VC and Legion d'Honneur, he was awarded the 1914 Star with 'Mons' clasp, British War Medal 1914-20 and Victory Medal 1914-19 with Mentioned-in-Despatches oak-leaf. His VC is held by the Army Medical Services Museum, Keogh Barracks, Mytchett, Surrey. Harry is commemorated in a number of places:

- Irvine – War Memorial, Ranken Drive, Ranken Crescent, tablet in Old Parish Church and family headstone in the churchyard.
- RAMC Memorial Grove, National Memorial Arboretum, Alrewas, Staffordshire.
- Painting of his VC action at the TA Centre, Braganza Street, Walworth, London.
- His parents founded the 'Captain H S Ranken VC Memorial Prize', awarded annually since 1924 by the University of Glasgow to the undergraduate demonstrating the highest level of excellence in Pathology/Mechanisms of Disease.
- Ranken House, Queen Elizabeth Hospital, Woolwich.
- Alexander Elder War Memorial Chapel at Glasgow Western Infirmary, in memory of 22 House Physicians and House Surgeons of the Infirmary who gave their lives in the Great War.

His brother, Alan Rain Ranken (1889-1974), was a solicitor, Company Secretary of Dandua Coal Co Ltd of Glasgow until 1912, partner in Wilson, Chambers and Hendry of Glasgow from 1921 and Director of Corwall & Co Ltd of Glasgow until 18th December 1961, when it was voluntarily wound up. He enlisted in 4th Lowland (Field Artillery) Brigade as a Driver on 6th December 195 (No 1885 then 665499). He was transferred to the Army Reserve until mobilized on 11th December. Appointed paid Acting Bombardier 4th January 1916 and transferred to 1st Provisional Battery on 20th February. On 4th March he was attached to TF Records Office at Woolwich and appointed Acting Orderly Room Corporal. He applied for a commission in the ASC on 28th October, but it appears he was not accepted due to his B1 medical grading. He was posted to 6 Depot on 31st March 1917 and struck off the strength of 4 Depot on 22 May on proceeding to the Garrison Officers Cadet Battalion, Jesus College, Cambridge. Alan was commissioned in the Labour Corps on 15th July 1917, was released from Kinross on 3rd April 1919 and relinquished his commission on 13th October 1920, retaining the rank of Lieutenant. During the Second World War he served in the Royal Artillery again.

Alan was executor to Harry's will jointly with Dr George Haswell Wilson. After all bills had been paid in Egypt and Sudan and his gratuity and back pay were added, £404/11/9 was forwarded by the Command Cashier Egypt to the War Office. Harry's estate was valued at £1,400/1/4. In addition, a war gratuity of £45 was paid by the War Office in 1919.

7079 BANDSMAN THOMAS EDWARD RENDLE
1st Battalion, The Duke of Cornwall's Light Infantry

Thomas Rendle was born at 113 Mead Street, Bedminster, Bristol on 14th December 1884, the eldest of seven children, one of whom died in infancy. His father was James Rendle (1864–1928), who was employed variously as a painter and decorator, paper merchant's packer and stevedore. His mother was Charlotte née Gillard (1865–98), a domestic servant. James and Charlotte's marriage was registered at Bedminster in the 2nd quarter of 1883. After Charlotte died on 4th October 1898, James was forced to split up his children. Thomas and daughter Charlotte (Lottie) initially remained with him, while William, Henry (Harry), Elizabeth and Maud either went to live with relatives or were taken into the workhouse. By 1901, Charlotte was boarding at the Devon and Exeter Reformatory and Refuge for Girls, Polsloe Road, Exeter and Elizabeth was residing at Carlton House Certified Industrial School, Southwell Street, Bristol. Thomas was educated at St Luke's School, New Cut, Bedminster and Kingswood Reformatory in Bristol.

On 7th June 1904, The Bristol Emigration Society arranged for William, Harry and Maud to go to Canada aboard the *Lake Erie*, departing Liverpool and arriving at Quebec on 17th June. On arrival, children were placed by the Immigration Agent at St John, New Brunswick; a few went to Marchmont Home in Belleville, Ontario, some girls were placed through the Women's Protective Society of Montreal and others went to local homes, Industrial Schools and Reformatories. It is not known where William, Harry and Maud lived.

Having failed to gain a place in the Gloucestershire Regiment, Thomas enlisted in the DCLI on 5th September 1902, giving his date of birth as 30th November 1884. He was posted to the 1st Battalion at Stellenbosch, Cape Colony on 3rd January 1903 and served at Middelberg and Wynberg from July 1904. Awarded Good Conduct Badges on 5th September 1904 and 1907.

Thomas Rendle married Lilian Sarah née Crowe (1883–1959) at Wynberg, Cape Colony, South Africa on 7th February 1906. Lilian was the daughter of a 60th Rifles bandsman. She had returned to England after her father's death to become nursemaid to the children of Captain Turner DCLI. She went back to South Africa with the Turner family and subsequently met Thomas Rendle. Thomas and Lilian had two children – Ruby Lilian Jessie Rendle, born 23rd May 1907 registered at Plympton; and Edward William Wootton Rendle, born 10th October 1909, registered at Gravesend.

The 1st Battalion was posted to Crownhill, Plymouth, England in 1906. Thomas and his family departed South Africa on 12th March 1906 on HMT *Soudan*, arriving on 5th April 1906. The Battalion moved to Woolwich in 1907, where Thomas was appointed Bandsman on 15th September. Further moves took place to Gravesend in 1908, where the family lived at 34 Peppercroft Street, Tidworth in 1911 and the Curragh in Ireland in 1913. The Battalion was temporarily in Newry, Ireland in March 1914 for the Home Rule troubles.

Thomas went to France with the 1st Battalion on 13th August 1914. **Awarded the VC for his actions at Wulverghem, Belgium on 20th November 1914, LG 11th January 1915.** His sight was affected by high explosives a few days after the VC action. He was evacuated to England and sent to Voluntary Aid Hospital No 1 (West of England Eye Infirmary), Exeter. His family moved to be close to him and lived with Thomas' sister Lottie at 225 Monks Road, Heavitree, Exeter. Thomas returned to the Depot on 4th January 1915. He was given a civic reception at the Guildhall, Launceston, Cornwall on 28th January and was posted to the 3rd Battalion at Falmouth on 1st February. There he was employed as a recruiter and musketry instructor and later at Aldershot. Promoted Corporal 24th March, Acting Sergeant 25th March and later substantive Sergeant from the same date. The 3rd Battalion moved to the Isle of Wight in May. His VC was presented by the King at Buckingham Palace on 12th July 1915. Thomas was the only VC recipient in the DCLI during the war. **Mentioned in Field Marshal Sir John French's Despatch dated 14th January 1915, LG 17th February 1915. Awarded the Cross of the Order of St George 4th Class (Russia), LG 25th August 1915.**

While based on the Isle of Wight, Thomas became a Freemason, Initiated into the Needles Lodge No 2838 on 2nd August 1916, Passed on 6th September and Raised on 4th October; he was appointed Assistant Secretary. Posted to No 2 Reception Battalion on 8th September 1918, but returned to 3rd Battalion on 10th December.

Thomas Rendle leaving Buckingham Palace, having been presented with his VC by King George V on 12th July 1915. On his right is Lance Corporal Leonard James Keyworth VC, London Regiment and to his left is Company Sergeant Major Frederick Barter VC, Royal Welch Fusiliers and Sergeant John Ripley VC, Black Watch.

Thomas returned to Ireland (Ballyshannon) in early 1919 with 3rd Battalion, where it formed the cadre for the reformation of 1st Battalion on 29th August. Appointed Band Sergeant 4th October. Thomas moved with the Battalion to Ballykinlar. He was discharged on 12th November 1920 no longer physically fit for war service. His final Army Number was 5429038.

The family emigrated to South Africa in February 1921, where he was employed as caretaker and stationery controller of Standard Bank, Strand Street, Cape Town. He was also part time Bandmaster of the Duke of Edinburgh's Own Volunteer Rifles in Cape Town. Thomas organised the annual Battle of Mons dinner on 23rd August each year in Cape Town. He joined the 'Memorable Order of Tin Hats' (Moths) in 1927 and was nicknamed 'Provincial Old Bill'. In 1936-37 a former soldier, Joseph William Randell, impersonated Thomas, wearing a replica VC bought in London for 15/-. Randell moved from Lancaster to Glasgow, where he wore the VC at British Legion functions and was appointed President of the Govan branch. Thomas Rendle read a newspaper article about 'Rendle VC' at a British Legion parade in Glasgow, which he did not attend and so he alerted the police through the newspaper. Randall was fined £5 and lost his job, but he also wrote Thomas an apologetic letter. Thomas became Bandmaster of the Citizen Force for a short time, but returned to the Dukes in early 1938.

Thomas Rendle died at Groote Schuur Hospital, Cape Town, South Africa on 1st June 1946 and is buried in Maitland No 1 Cemetery (24598). In addition to the VC, he was awarded the 1914 Star with 'Mons' clasp, British War Medal 1914-20, Victory Medal 1914-19 with Mentioned-in-Despatches oak-leaf, George V Silver Jubilee Medal 1935, George VI Coronation Medal 1937, Army Long Service and Good Conduct Medal, Efficiency Medal (Union of South Africa) and Cross of St George 4th Class (Russia). His VC is held by the DCLI Museum, The Keep, Bodmin, Cornwall.

There is a framed tribute to Thomas Rendle at the Royal Military School of Music, Kneller Hall, Twickenham, Middlesex. The Moths branch at 345 Koeberg Road, Rugby, Cape Town (originally at Maitland and later at Brooklyn) was named the 'Tommy Rendle VC Shellhole' in his honour. A number of his relatives also served:

Thomas Rendle in the uniform of Bandmaster of the Duke of Edinburgh's Own Volunteer Rifles.

Brother William enlisted in the Canadian Army (No.410534) as William J Randle on

18th March 1915, giving his date of birth as 26th June 1895. He was described as a farmer, 5' 4" tall, of ruddy complexion with brown eyes, brown hair and his religious denomination was Wesleyan. He was assigned to D Company, 38th Battalion (Ottawa), Canadian Expeditionary Force and served in Europe during the Great War.

Thomas Rendle's grand daughter, Mrs Barbara Braime, on the left, at her grandfather's grave on the 50th anniversary of his death in June 1996 (Barbara Braime).

Brother Harry enlisted in 67th Regiment (Militia) and served for one year before enlisting in 26th Battalion, (New Brunswick), Canadian Expeditionary Force (No 69816) on 20th November 1914, giving his date of birth as 2nd August 1896. He was described as a labourer, 5' 5" tall, with sandy complexion, brown eyes, sandy hair and his religious denomination was Baptist. His next-of-kin was Saul Gallagher, of East Central, Carleton County, New Brunswick. Corporal Henry John Rendle was killed in action on 26th February 1917 and is buried in Ecoivres Military Cemetery, Mont-St Eloi, France (IV D 29).

Sister Maud served as a nurse and she and William returned to Canada after the war, where sister Lottie and her husband Frederick James Parsons joined them in 1920.

Cousin, 4/79609 Private Edward James Gillard, Welsh Regiment died, on 7th October 1918 and is buried in Barry (Merthyr Dyfan) Burial Ground (A 428).

Nephew, Lieutenant Thomas Oliver Turner, Gloucestershire Regiment attached Border Regiment, was killed on 3rd February 1945 and is buried in Taukkyan War Cemetery, Burma (18 J 24).

His sister Elizabeth Victoria Rendle (1888-1968) adopted the beliefs of Wiccan witchcraft. She was promised aged 15 to a silversmith in Exeter, but after the arranged marriage she fled to London. As Lysbeth Victoria Rendle she married Thomas William Turner, registered in the 4th quarter of 1915 at Kensington. She answered Wiccan Gerald Gardner's call to arms in 1940, when witches from the south of England met in the New Forest to cast a protective charm over England and a spell on Hitler's designs. She became Gardner's high priestess. Her daughter

Joan married Norman Arthur Botting (1912-1943) in the 3rd quarter of 1939, registered at St Ives, Huntingdonshire and they had three children. Norman served as a Warrant Officer Navigator (No.520680) in 49 Squadron (DFC, LG 14th May 1943) and was commissioned as Pilot Officer on 23rd April 1943 (No.51975). He was posted to 617 Squadron under Wing Commander Guy Gibson VC and later Wing Commander Leonard Cheshire VC. Norman was killed when his aircraft was shot down over Germany on 16th September 1943. He is buried in Reichswald Forest War Cemetery, Germany (24 H 12). After his death, Joan had an affair with Leonard Cheshire and they had a daughter, Merle Elizabeth Botting, birth registered in the 1st quarter of 1946 at Tavistock, Devon. Joan was baptised as a Jehovah's Witness in September 1948, but Cheshire converted to Roman Catholicism in December; Joan moved out and emigrated to Canada with her children in 1954. Joan's son, Gary Botting and other members of their family were also Jehovah's Witnesses. During Lysbeth's visit to Canada in 1966, she lamented to Gary's future wife Heather Harden, also a Jehovah's Witness, that 'the old religion' of Wicca would be lost. Heather abandoned her faith, was initiated into witchcraft by Lysbeth and eloped with Gary in October 1966. Heather formed 'Coven Celeste', the first Wiccan coven in Canada. She and Gary published *'The Orwellian World of Jehovah's Witnesses'* in 1984, an exposé focusing on the mental regulating of Witnesses through isolationism and dogma, comparing it to the thought control depicted by Orwell in 'Nineteen Eighty-Four'.

CAPTAIN DOUGLAS REYNOLDS
37 (Howitzer) Battery, VIII (Howitzer) Brigade, Royal Field Artillery

Douglas Reynolds was born at 5 Miles Road, Clifton, Bristol on 21st September 1881. His father was Captain (later Honorary Lieutenant Colonel) Henry Charles Reynolds (1842-99) who served in the Royal Engineers 1862-81. His mother was Sarah Eleanor Baker née Goodwyn (1846-1930). They married at Clifton, Gloucestershire on 17th April 1877. After Henry left the Army the family settled at 44 Royal York Crescent, Clifton. Douglas had three brothers, including Basil, who died in 1896 aged 12, and a sister. Douglas was educated at Glyngarth Preparatory School, Cheltenham and Cheltenham College, where he was a member of the Rifle Corps.

His grandfather, Major General James Williams Reynolds (1816-75), served in 11th Hussars 1840-71. On 18th May 1840 he upset his commanding officer, Lord Cardigan, in the 'black bottle affair'. Reynolds had a bottle of Moselle on the mess table. Cardigan believed it to be porter or beer, which he had banned and had Reynolds arrested.

Douglas entered the Royal Military Academy Woolwich in 1898 and was commissioned on 6th January 1900. Promoted Lieutenant 3rd April 1901 and served with mounted infantry in South Africa for the last four months of the war. With the RFA he served with 148 Battery, XLIX Brigade at Aldershot, 4 Battery, VII Brigade at Newcastle in Natal, 42 Battery, II Brigade at Bradford, 78 Battery, VII Brigade at Neemuch, Bombay and commanded No 1 Ammunition Column at Campbellpore and later Nowshera, India in 1911. He was a keen sportsman and an excellent shot, spending most of his leave in Kashmir and the Baltistan mountains. Promoted Captain 1st June 1908. In June 1912 while in India he became a freemason, a member of Kitchener Lodge, Simla, No 2998 – Major Herbert Carter VC and General Sir O'Moore Creagh VC were also members.

Douglas was in Ireland with his unit when war broke out and disembarked in France on 20th August 1914. **He was awarded the VC for his actions at Le Cateau on 26th August and at Pisseloup on 9th September 1914, LG 16th November 1914. Mentioned in Field Marshal Sir John French's Despatch dated 8th October 1914, LG 19th October 1914 (duplicated 20th October and reissued 9th December 1914).** He was seriously wounded on the Aisne on 15th September 1914 when a shrapnel bullet passed through his side and up into his breast, from where it could not be extracted. Promoted Major 30th October 1914. **Awarded the French Croix de Chevalier de Legion d'Honneur, LG 3rd November 1914.** His VC was presented by the King at Buckingham Palace on 13th January 1915. On recovering from his wound, he trained a new howitzer battery in LXXXIII Brigade RFA, which he commanded and took into action.

Douglas Reynolds married Doris (later known as Maria Dolores) née Petersen (1895-1953) of Heron's Ghyll, East Sussex on 29th March 1915 at Epsom, Surrey. She was the daughter of Danish ship owner, William (later Sir William KBE) Petersen (1856-1925). He was Chairman of Petersen & Co Ltd, European and Brazilian Shipping Co Ltd and the British Committee of the International Shipping Registry. He founded London American Maritime Shipping Co and Royal & Uraneum Passenger Lines, as well as being Director of the Thompson Steam Shipping Co and Honorary Commander RNR. Douglas and Maria had a son, Douglas William Sinclair Petersen 'Peter' Reynolds, born at the end of January 1916.

Mentioned in Field Marshal French's Despatch of 30th November 1915, LG 1st January 1916. Douglas was knocked out by a gas shell in December 1915 and appeared to recover, so stayed with his battery, but subsequently died of septicaemia at No 1 Red Cross Hospital (Duchess of Westminster's Hospital),

Le Touquet on 23rd February 1916. He is buried in Etaples Military Cemetery, France (I A 20). Will probate to Public Trustee – £6,771/12/-. Douglas Reynolds is commemorated in various places:

- The family grave at St Peter's Church, Leckhampton, Cheltenham.
- Cheltenham College.
- Two Cheltenham War Memorials.
- Royal Artillery VC Memorial in the ruins of St George's Chapel, the former Garrison Church at Woolwich, which was reduced to a roofless shell by a V1 in 1944.
- Royal Military Academy Woolwich VC Memorial Board in the Royal Military Academy Sandhurst library.
- 93 (Le Cateau) Battery, successor to 37 (Howitzer) Battery, comprises Drain, Luke and Reynolds Troops.

In addition to the VC, he was awarded the Queen's South Africa Medal 1899-02 with three clasps, 1914 Star with 'Mons' clasp, British War Medal 1914-20, Victory Medal 1914-19 with Mentioned-in-Despatches oak-leaf and the French Croix de Chevalier de Légion d'Honneur. The medals were part of a collection owned by Sir John Roper Wright, which were presented to the Royal Artillery in the 1940s and are now held by the Royal Artillery Museum 'Firepower' at the Royal Arsenal, Woolwich.

Douglas' sister, Esme, married Colonel Arthur William Neufville Taylor, 10th Gurkha Rifles, and settled in British Columbia, Canada. His brother-in-law, 2nd Lieutenant William Sinclair Petersen (1892-1914) Essex RHA Battery TF, was commissioned on 21st May 1914 and attached to 2nd Life Guards on 17th October 1914; he was killed in action on 6th November 1914 and is buried in Zillebeke Churchyard near Ypres, Belgium (C 3).

Maria Reynolds married Major John Crocker Bulteel DSO MC, Buckinghamshire and Berkshire Yeomanry (1890-1956) in the 4th quarter of 1919 at Watford. He was the nephew of Francis Grenfell VC. John and Maria lived in Australia until 1938. He was an official of the Jockey Club and was created KCVO (LG 9th June 1955). In 1951 he conceived the 'King George VI and Queen Elizabeth Stakes' while Clerk of the Course at Ascot.

Douglas and Maria's only son, 67903 Lieutenant D W S P Reynolds, Supplementary Reserve Irish Guards 16th May 1939, was mobilised on 24th August 1939 and killed in action at Boulogne on 23rd May 1940 while serving with 2nd Irish Guards. He is buried in Outreaux Communal Cemetery, France (B 4).

6016 PRIVATE JACOB RIVERS
1st Battalion, The Sherwood Foresters (Nottinghamshire and Derbyshire Regiment)

Jacob Rivers was born at House 4, Court 12, Bridge Gate, St Alkmund, Derby on 17th November 1881 (also seen as 28th March 1882). His father was George Rivers (1859-93), a bricklayer's labourer and later a railway labourer. His mother was Adeline née Holmes (1857-1937), a servant. Their marriage was registered during the 1st quarter of 1876 at Derby. The family was living at House 21, Court 11, St Alkmund in 1891, Court 11, Number 10 Building, Bridge Gate in 1901 and Court 12, House 4, Wide Yard, Bridge Gate by 1911. Jacob had four brothers and six sisters, but two brothers and two sisters died in infancy.

His uncle, Enoch Holmes (1859-98), enlisted in the Derbyshire Regiment in May 1876 (474). He was posted to Cork and went absent without leave in January 1877, resulting in 27 days in prison. In October he was admitted to hospital in Dublin with syphilis and went absent again in November, resulting in another 15 days imprisonment. Enoch transferred to the Dorsetshire Regiment in India on 21st September 1878. He was admitted to hospital at Rangoon, Burma on 12th March 1879 having been wounded and suffering from fever. He was imprisoned for another 42 days in February 1880 and returned to India in May. His behaviour improved, as he was awarded Good Conduct Pay on 3rd April 1882, but his health did not and he was sent to the Convalescent Depot at Landour 7th April – 20th November. He served on the Reserve from 25th March 1883 until 16th October 1892. The following January he enlisted in 3rd Battalion, The Sherwood Foresters (Militia) and was still serving when he died in 1898.

Jacob was educated at Orchard Street School, off Chapel Street (renamed Lancaster School and later demolished) and was then employed as a riveter with Phoenix Foundry Company, Derby. He enlisted in 3rd Battalion, The Derbyshire Regiment (Militia) on 22nd April 1898 (6263) giving his age as 17. On 3rd June 1899 he enlisted for regular service in the Royal Scots Fusiliers (6129) giving his age as 18 years and one month. He joined at Ayr on 7th June, but was soon in trouble with the military authorities and was imprisoned by his CO 5-13th December. On 15th March 1901 he moved to India to join the 1st Battalion and also served in Burma. He extended his service to complete eight years on 1st April 1904, but fell foul of authority again, having his pay reduced to 3d per day on 7th April 1905. Having broken out of barracks on 14th October, he was sentenced by Court Martial to imprisonment until 1st November. His pay was restored to 4d per day on 20th April 1906.

Jacob left India on 28th February 1907, transferred to the 2nd Battalion at Tidworth on 1st March and was discharged to the Reserve on 3rd June. He returned to Derby and was employed as a labourer for a coal agent in 1911 and was later a gang labourer on a Midland Railway Company ballast train. He was discharged from the Reserve on 2nd June 1911.

Jacob Rivers as a young soldier while serving in 3rd Battalion, The Derbyshire Regiment (Militia), prior to enlisting for regular service with the Royal Scots Fusiliers.

Jacob was in trouble with the police on a number of occasions. Early on 27th July 1909, Jacob and George Rivers were stopped by Constable Mortimer coming from the Great Northern yard in possession of pegs and nets used to catch game. Mortimer knew both men previously as poachers, but they denied the charge. In court Superintendent Clamp said there were 20 records against George for various offences, but none against Jacob. George was fined £1 and costs or a month in jail and Jacob 10/- and costs or 14 days in jail. On 1st January 1912, Jacob was drunk and disorderly in Derby and was fined 10/- plus costs or 14 days confinement. A few months later he was charged with stealing or receiving a silver English lever watch from Robert Holgate, a pensioner, who was knocked to the ground and kicked by a man unknown after visiting the White Hart at Bridge Gate, Derby on 6th April. A witness saw George Rivers and a boy helping Holgate to his feet after the incident. Jacob attempted to pawn the watch, using Mrs Elizabeth Smith. He denied stealing it, but was fined £2 plus costs or one month's hard labour. On 23rd June he was charged with George and another man with being drunk, disorderly and causing a nuisance at Bridge Gate; they were fined 5/- each.

Jacob re-enlisted on 18th August 1914, joining 1st Battalion, The Sherwood Foresters on 10th November. He went to France on 11th December and was admitted to No 4 Stationary Hospital with frostbite of the feet on 23rd January 1915. It seems more likely he was suffering from trench foot, as he was discharged on the 29th. **Awarded the VC for his actions at Neuve Chapelle, France on 12th March 1915, LG 28th April 1915.** He was killed during the VC action and is commemorated on the Le Touret Memorial (Panel 26 & 27).

The Princess Mary Christmas Box presented to him in 1914 was pierced by a bullet, indicating he was shot through the heart; it was the only possession returned to his mother. The Derby Daily Telegraph set up a Shilling Fund to assist her as she was living in poverty. The fund reached £50 within three weeks, but was only just over £60 when it closed in June 1915.

In addition to the VC, he was awarded the 1914-15 Star, British War Medal 1914-20 and Victory Medal 1914-19. The VC was initially sent to his mother by registered post on 15th October 1915, but was presented to her formally by the King at Buckingham Palace on 29th November 1916. She received the freedom of the City of Derby in recognition of her son's achievements during a ceremony at the Drill Hall on 24th March 1923, on the same occasion as Earl Haig and the Duke of Devonshire. Her funeral on 4th March 1937 was attended by two men who had been at Neuve Chapelle with Jacob – Captain Warmer, who had been a lance corporal stretcher-bearer and Private R Hardy, who was awarded the Croix de Guerre for bringing up ammunition although wounded.

In accordance with Adeline's wishes, her daughter, Mrs Elizabeth Potter, presented Jacob's medals to Major General Sir Frederick Maurice at the Regimental Depot on 7th April 1937. Following the ceremony the dignitaries lunched in the Officers' Mess while Mrs Potter and her relatives were entertained in the Sergeants' Mess. Jacob's VC is held by the Sherwood Foresters Museum at Nottingham Castle. He is named on a brass plaque at St Alkmund Church, Kedleston Road, Derby and is also commemorated on his mother's headstone in Nottingham Road Cemetery, Derby.

Jacob's brother, George (1877-1964), enlisted in London in the Royal Engineers Labour Battalion as a Pioneer (125034) on 19th October 1915 and served in France from 29th November. He transferred to the Labour Corps, 710 Labour Company (295859) on 31st July 1917 and was discharged on 28th January 1918 (probably for defective vision) and was awarded the Silver War Badge. Jacob's brother, Isaac (1887-1962), served three years in the Grenadier Guards from 9th October 1905 and was recalled from the Reserve when war broke out (12400) to serve in the 3rd Battalion. He went to France on 26th July 1915, was wounded in October and discharged on 22nd May 1916 (Silver War Badge). His sister, Lucy (1879-1957), married Isaiah Fieldhouse (1876-1932),

Jacob's sister, Mrs Elizabeth Potter, presenting his medals to Major General Sir Frederick Maurice, Colonel of the Sherwood Foresters, at the Regimental Depot, Normanton Barracks, Derby on 7th April 1937. Also present were the High Sheriff of Nottinghamshire, the Chief Constable of Derbyshire, the Mayor of Derby and a number of other civil and military dignitaries. The presentation was preceded by an inspection of recruits. It rained heavily throughout the ceremony.

who served in 1st Battalion, The Sherwood Foresters from October 1895. He took part in the Tirah Campaign (Indian General Service Medal 1854–95 with clasp 'Punjab Frontier') and the South African War, in which he was wounded in the right shoulder at Klip River on 12th February 1902 (Queen's South Africa Medal with four clasps). He transferred to the Reserve on October 1902.

11340 PRIVATE HENRY HOWEY ROBSON
2nd Battalion, The Royal Scots (Lothian Regiment)

Henry Robson was born at 40 Hampden Street, South Shields, Co Durham on 27th May 1894. He was known as Harry. His father was Edward Robson (1859-1921) a coal miner and his mother was Mary née Morris (1864-1939), a papermaker. Edward and Mary's marriage was registered at Sunderland, Co Durham in the 2nd quarter of 1884. The family was living at 87 Victoria Street, Shotton Colliery, Castle Eden, Co Durham by 1911. Henry had six brothers and a sister and was educated at Mortimer Road Council School, South Shields. Thereafter he was employed as a miner, probably at St Hilda's Colliery, where his father worked.

Jacob Rivers as a young soldier while serving in 3rd Battalion, The Derbyshire Regiment (Militia) prior to enlisting for regular service with the Royal Scots Fusiliers.

Henry enlisted in September 1912 and served at Plymouth. He went to France with his Battalion on 11th August 1914. **Awarded the VC for his actions at Petit Bois, near Wytschaete, Belgium on 14th December 1914, LG 18th February 1915.** He was evacuated to England as a result of his wounds. His VC was presented by the King at Buckingham Palace on 12th July 1915 and three days later he was given a civic reception in South Shields. On 6th October he received the Freedom of South Shields and during the ceremony was presented with £73 raised through a Shilling Fund by the Mayor of South Shields.

He returned to his old school on 24th May 1916 and was presented with a gold watch by the pupils. Having returned to France on 3rd November, he was wounded at Serre on 13th November and never returned to the front. Henry served in the Labour Corps (349894), probably at the Scottish Command Labour Corps Depot, Blairgowrie.

Post-war he worked in the shipyards, for the South Shields Corporation Highways Department and as a steward on oil tankers running between Britain and South America for two and a half years. He sold his VC to a doctor for £80 and used the money to pay for his passage to Canada on SS *Marburn*, arriving at St John, New Brunswick on 18th March 1923. He found employment as a streetcar conductor with the Eglinton Division, Toronto Transportation Commission.

Henry Robson married Alice Maude née Martin (1897-1964) in Toronto on 9th February 1924. She was a nurse from Portobello, Midlothian, who had emigrated there. They had a son Henry 'Harry' (1928-83) and four daughters (Doreen, Patricia, Victoria and Betty), all of whom settled in Canada.

Henry became a civil servant in the Parliament Buildings in Ontario in 1934. He was presented to King George VI and Queen Elizabeth at Queen's Park, Toronto on 22nd May 1939. Henry was Sergeant at Arms of the Ontario Legislature for six years and then became an information clerk, showing visitors around Parliament until retiring in 1954. He devoted much of his time to the welfare of former servicemen and women.

Henry returned to England in 1953 for the Coronation and in 1956 for the VC Centenary celebrations. In 1951 his VC was bought by a Dunfermline solicitor, who lent it to him to wear at the 1956 VC Centenary Review in Hyde Park. It was never returned to the solicitor.

Henry Robson died at Sunnybrook Hospital, Toronto, Canada on 4th March 1964. He was buried in the Veteran's Section, York Memorial Cemetery, Toronto (B 302). A commemorative terracotta bust was unveiled at South Tyneside Library, South Shields in March 2008. Henry Robson Way, Tedco Business Park, South Shields was named after him.

In addition to the VC, Henry Robson was awarded the 1914 Star with 'Mons' clasp, British War Medal 1914-20, Victory Medal 1914-19, George VI Coronation Medal 1937 and Elizabeth II Coronation Medal 1953. His VC was presented to the Royal Scots Museum, Edinburgh Castle by his daughter, Mrs Patricia Gaskin of Toronto.

CAPTAIN GEORGE ROWLAND PATRICK ROUPELL
1st Battalion, The East Surrey Regiment

George Roupell was born at Tipperary, Ireland on 7th April 1892. His father, Colonel Francis Frederick Fyler Roupell (1848-1916), was commissioned in the 70th Foot on 5th October 1867. He was Adjutant 1876-78 and Deputy Assistant Adjutant General (Musketry) Bengal 1881-83. He served in the Afghan War and on the Masoud Waziri Expedition 1880-81 (MID). Promoted Major 1st August 1882 and appointed Adjutant Auxiliary Forces 1884-89. On 21st June 1895 he was promoted Lieutenant Colonel to command 1st East Surrey. Promoted Colonel 18th

November 1901 to command Regimental District No 31 (Surrey) at Kingston-upon-Thames until he retired on 29th July 1903. Francis was a keen rifle shot and held many appointments on the Council of the Army Rifle Association, the Kingston and Surbiton Rifle Club and was a life member of the Bengal-Punjab Rifle Association. He won numerous shooting awards and captained the Army Rifle team in India in 1898. When he retired, he presented the Roupell Cup to the Army Rifle Association, which is still competed for each year at Bisley. He offered his services as a musketry instructor at the outbreak of the Great War, but the strain of his appointment led to his death in October 1916.

George's mother, Edith Maria née Bryden (1855-1938) is believed to be related to Dr Brydon, one of the very few survivors of the retreat from Kabul in January 1842. George had three siblings:

Francis Leyland Lyster Fyler Roupell, (1890-1965) served in the Royal Garrison Artillery 1911-41, retiring as a Lieutenant Colonel. He was awarded the MC (LG 1st January 1918) and a Bar (LG 16th September 1918); during an intense bombardment, although wounded by shrapnel in the leg and unable to walk, he refused to leave until nearly surrounded and the guns put out of action. Appointed Honorary Colonel on 26th July 1947.

Charles Frederick de Coetlogon Roupell (1897-1980) was a Cadet on the School Ship *Conway* at Rock Ferry, Cheshire before going to Germany to study for the Sandhurst entrance examination. He was interned there throughout the Great War.

Editha Violet Prioleau Roupell (1888-1962).

George was educated at Rossall 1907-10 and trained at the Royal Military College Sandhurst. He was commissioned on 2nd March 1912 and promoted Lieutenant on 29th April 1914. He was serving in Dublin, Ireland when war broke out and deployed to France with the Battalion on 16th August. Following the Battle of the Aisne, he was given command of a company. Appointed Temporary Captain 29th December 1914 – 20th April 1915. **Mentioned in Sir John French's Despatch dated 14th January 1915, LG 17th February 1915. Awarded the VC for his actions at Hill 60, near Ypres, Belgium on 20th April 1915, LG 23rd June 1915.** He was evacuated to England on 23rd April 1915.

His VC presented by the King at Buckingham Palace on 12th July 1915. **Awarded the Order of St George 4th Class (Russia), LG 25th August 1915.** Appointed Temporary Captain 2nd September 1915 – 20th April 1916 and returned to France on 8th September 1915 as Adjutant. Promoted Captain 21st April 1916. Appointed GSO3 HQ XVII Corps 25th May and GSO3 HQ Third Army 1st September – 28th December.

On 26th October 1916 he was returning to England to attend his father's funeral when HMT *Queen* was halted by German destroyers *V80* and *S60*. He escaped into the boats disguised as a crewman before the ship was sunk and had to row the rest of the way. Appointed Brigade Major 105th Brigade 29th December 1916 – 8th May 1918. **Mentioned in Sir Douglas Haig's Despatch of 7th November 1917, LG 11th December 1917.** Appointed Temporary Major and GSO2 HQ 8th Division 9th May – 29th June 1918. Appointed Acting Major 22nd October – 12th December while a Battalion 2IC. He was wounded twice more. Appointed Acting Lieutenant Colonel and CO 13th December 1918 – 1st March 1919. Appointed Acting Major 2nd March – 21st April. Appointed GSO3 Vologda North Russian Force 1st-21st July. On 20th July he was taken prisoner on the Archangel front while visiting a White Russian unit that had mutinied. He was held in Butyrka prison, Moscow in very poor conditions and not released until May 1920. In his absence, he was replaced by Captain A M Toye VC. **Awarded the French Croix de Guerre, LG 7th January 1919.**

George was a member of the VC Guard at the Interment of the Unknown Warrior on 11th November 1920. Appointed Staff Captain Eastern Command 27th April 1921 – 22nd January 1922. George married Doris Phoebe née Sant (1890-1958) on 30th March 1921 at Christ Church, Lancaster Gate, London. She was the daughter of Captain Mowbray Sant (1864-1943), Chief Constable of Surrey. George and Doris had two children – Phoebe Irene Sant Roupell born 30th January 1922 registered at Hambledon and Peter George Francis Mowbray Roupell born 24th June 1925 registered at Great Ouseburn.

In 1922 George attended the Staff College at Camberley. He was a high quality hockey player and a member of a team in 1923 that included Philip Neame VC and was amongst the top half-dozen in England. Appointed Staff Captain Northern Command 1st May 1924 – 30th September 1926. Appointed Brigade Major Eastern Command 1st October 1926 – 30th April 1928. Promoted Major 18th November 1928. Appointed GSO2 Canadian Royal Military College, Kingston, Ontario 16th March 1929 – 16th April 1931. He commanded the East Surrey Depot at Kingston-upon-Thames July 1931 – 1934. Appointed GSO2 China Command 15th October 1934 – 21st November 1935. Promoted Lieutenant Colonel to command 1st East Surrey 21st December 1935 – 1938. Promoted Colonel 27th August 1939 with seniority backdated to 21st December 1938. Appointed Temporary Brigadier 27th August 1939 – 14th July 1942 as Commander 36th Brigade in the BEF.

On 19/20th May 1940, 36th Brigade was attacked by armoured forces and Stukas. Completely surrounded at 4.00 a.m. on 21st May, George gave orders for his men to split up and escape independently. He and two other officers (GSO3 and a French LO) avoided capture and worked on a farm at Perriers-sur-Andelle near Rouen until the Resistance got them out through Spain in 1942. The French LO went to Paris and joined the Resistance. Appointed Commander 105th Infantry Brigade, the same formation of which he had been Brigade Major 1916-18. Appointed Temporary Brigadier 28th March – 31st October 1943 and 14th November – 22nd December 1943. Appointed Commander Chatham Garrison. He was a supernumary from 31st December 1944 and retired as Honorary Brigadier 20th February 1946. That was not quite the end of his military career, as he commanded the South East Surrey Home Guard 1952-56. Appointed DL Surrey 30th June 1953. **Created CB (Military Division), LG 31st May 1956 while Colonel, South East Surrey Home Guard.**

While touring Canada, Hong Kong and Australia in 1955-56, he and his wife stayed with Benjamin Handley Geary, who was also awarded the VC serving with 1st East Surrey on Hill 60. George was the last Colonel of the East Surrey Regiment before amalgamation with the Queen's Royal Regiment 1954-59. Doris died in 1958 and George married Rachel Kennedy née Bruce (1911-2010) on 3rd November 1959. She was previously married to Eric W Kennedy. He was President of the Old Contemptibles Association in 1973.

George Roupell died at his home, Little Chartham, Shalford, near Guildford, Surrey on 4th March 1974 and was cremated at Guildford Crematorium, where his ashes were scattered.

In addition to the VC and CB, he was awarded the 1914 Star with 'Mons' clasp, British War Medal 1914-20, Victory Medal 1914-19 with Mentioned-in-Despatches oak-leaf, 1939-45 Star, 1939-45 Defence Medal, War Medal 1939-45, George VI Coronation Medal 1937, Elizabeth II Coronation Medal 1953, Russian Order of St George 4th Class and French Croix de Guerre with Bronze Star. His medals are held privately.

His son Peter was commissioned in March 1944 and saw action in the last few weeks of the war in Europe. He was granted a Regular Commission in the East Surrey Regiment and served in Greece, was attached to the Malay Regiment 1950-53 and attended Staff College in 1958. He served in Germany, Berlin and the Gulf before retiring in 1973 as a Lieutenant Colonel. Peter's son, Anthony Charles Roupell, born in 1948, was commissioned in the Grenadier Guards in June 1967 and left the Army in 1974.

George Roupell just before he retired from the Army.

6423 PRIVATE JAMES ALEXANDER SMITH
3rd attached 2nd Battalion, The Border Regiment

James Smith was born at 17 Back Henry Street, Peels Yard, Workington, Cumberland on 5th January 1881. His birth was registered as James Alexander Glenn. His father was Alexander Glenn (c.1836-1918), a blast furnace labourer. His mother was Ellen née Smith (c.1841-1906). Both parents were from Co Down, Ireland. Ellen had been married previously as Middleton. The family also lived at 6 Marsh Side, Workington. James had a sister, four half brothers and a half sister.

It is not known where he was educated or where he worked afterwards, but in 1901 he enlisted under his mother's maiden name. He served in Burma 1902-05 and South Africa 1905-07, following which he transferred to the Reserve. By 1911 he was a blast furnaceman, boarding at 30 Leven Street, North Ormesby, Middlesbrough.

James was recalled from the Reserve when war broke out and went to France with the 2nd Battalion on 26th November 1914. **Awarded the VC for his actions at Rouges Bancs, France on 21st December 1914, LG 18th February 1915. Mentioned in Sir John French's Despatch dated 14th January 1915, LG 17th February 1915.** When asked for details of his VC action he replied, "*It was now't, just the usual thing*".

James received a gunshot wound to the arm on 12th March 1915 and was evacuated to England. His VC was presented by the King at Buckingham Palace on 22nd April. While he was recovering he married Eliza Jane née Reynolds (1875-1937) at North Ormesby Parish Church in Middlesbrough in the 2nd quarter of 1915, as James A Glenn. He returned to the Battalion on 8th October and transferred to munitions work on 2nd January 1917.

Post-war James was employed as a labourer by Middlesbrough Council. His wife died in 1937. James served in the Home Guard in the Second World War and married Ada Parkes née Stewart (1887-1966) in the 4th quarter of 1949 at Middlesbrough. There were no children to either marriage. Ada had married Joseph H Parkes (1884-1926) in 1917 and had a son, William, in 1919. James was one of the many VC holders to attend Queen Elizabeth II's 1953 coronation.

James Smith died at his home, 73 Thorntree Avenue, Brambles Farm, Middlesbrough on 21st May 1968. At the time he is believed to have been the oldest living VC (87). His funeral on 25th May 1968 at St Thomas's Church, Brambles

Farm, was attended by four VCs (Edward Cooper, Tom Dresser, Stanley Hollis and William McNally) and was followed by cremation at Acklam Crematorium, Middlesbrough. His ashes were scattered in the May section of the Garden of Remembrance.

In addition to the VC he was awarded the 1914-15 Star, British War Medal 1914-20, Victory Medal 1914-19 with Mentioned-in-Despatches oak-leaf, 1939-45 War Medal, George VI Coronation Medal 1937 and Elizabeth II Coronation Medal 1953. His VC is held by the Border Regiment Museum, Queen Mary's Tower, Carlisle Castle, Cumbria.

7281 PRIVATE ROSS ANDERSON TOLLERTON
1st Battalion, The Queen's Own Cameron Highlanders

Ross Tollerton was born at the Constabulary Office, Hurlford, Ayrshire, Scotland on 6th May 1890. His father was James Tollerton (c.1854-1933), a Police Sergeant, who married three times. His first wife, Isabella née Thomson, died on 13th April 1883. Ross Tollerton's mother was Jane ('Jeanie') née Anderson (c.1865-95); she married James Tollerton on 25th April 1884 at 10 Greenhill, Waterside, Dalmellington, Ayrshire. On 1st September 1895, she gave birth to an unnamed child, who died within an hour at the Constabulary Station, Kilwinning, Ayrshire. Jeanie developed puerperal fever and died on 3rd September 1895. James' third wife was Janet née Gillespie (born c.1866) a domestic servant; they married on 19th January 1898 at Kilwinning, Ayrshire. Janet had an illegitimate son, James. By 1901 the family was living at 61 East Road, Irvine and by 1908 James was an insurance agent. Ross had two brothers and a sister, plus two half/step brothers and two half sisters from his father's first and third marriages. He was educated at Montgomery School in Irvine, which was earlier attended by Harry Ranken VC. Ross is reputed to have been educated at Laurieknowe (Maxwelltown) Primary School, Dumfries (also attended by James Mackenzie VC and Lieutenant James Tait VC), but this is nowhere near Irvine and there is no evidence of a family move there.

Ross enlisted in 1st Battalion, The Royal Scots Fusiliers at Kilwinning in October 1905. He served in South Africa from 1906 and Hong Kong, North China and India 1909-12, until being transferred to the Reserve. Initially employed in Irvine Shipyard as an engine keeper and later labourer. Ross Tollerton married Agnes née

Muir (born c.1869), a tailoress, on 26th December 1913 at 4 Kirkgate, Irvine. They had no children.

When war broke out he was recalled and reported to Inverness, then Edinburgh. He joined the Queen's Own Cameron Highlanders, which is unusual as Reservists generally returned to their former regiments, and disembarked in France on 14th August 1914. **Awarded the VC for his actions at Chivy, France on 14th September 1914, LG 19th April 1915.** He was wounded and hospitalised at Invergordon. His VC was presented by the King at Glasgow Green on 18th May 1915. Ross visited Montgomery School, Irvine, where he had been a pupil. He returned to the Western Front and was promoted Sergeant. After discharge from the Regular Army in 1919 he joined the Irvine Company, Royal Scots Fusiliers and later became a CSM.

In civilian employment Ross was a janitor at Bank Street School, Irvine. He was a Freemason (Irvine St Andrew's Lodge No 149). As the local VC, he laid the first wreath on Irvine's War Memorial in April 1921. Ross Tollerton died at his home at 15 High Street, Irvine, Ayrshire on 7th May 1931 and was buried in Knadgerhill Cemetery, Irvine (C 104) with full military honours. Major James Sutherland MacKay Matheson, who Tollerton saved in his VC action, attended the funeral. Ross is commemorated at Tollerton Drive, Irvine. On 11th September 1932, Brigadier J W Walker CMG DSO unveiled a memorial erected by the British Legion at Knadgerhill Cemetery.

In addition to the VC, he was awarded the 1914 Star with 'Mons' clasp, British War Medal 1914-20 and Victory Medal 1914-19. The medals were left to his stepmother in his will and she successfully sued his widow for possession. His VC is held by The Highlanders Museum, Fort George, Inverness-shire. Three of his brothers served in the Army, including S/12358 CSM James G Tollerton, 1st Cameron Highlanders, who served in France from 9th July 1915.

CAPTAIN JOHN FRANKS VALLENTIN
1st Battalion, The South Staffordshire Regiment

John (Jack to the family) Vallentin was born at 109 Lambeth Road, London on 14th May 1882 and was baptised at Hythe, Kent on 8th October. His father was Grimble Vallentin (1850-1911), a distiller and Master of the Worshipful Company of Distillers 1883, 1893 and 1906-07. He owned the Red Cross pub, Barbican, London in 1909. His mother, Lucy Ann née Finnis (c.1856-1935), was born in India, but her family home was at Hythe, Kent. Grimble and Lucy married in the 4th quarter of 1876, registered at West Ham. The family home was at 116 Albert Place Mansions, Battersea Park, London. Lucy lived at 33 Prince of Wales Mansions, Prince of Wales Road, Battersea Park, London after Grimble died in 1911. John Vallentin had two sisters and was educated at Wellington College.

His paternal grandfather, Sir James Vallentin (1815-70), also a distiller, was Knight Sheriff of the City of London 1869 and Master of the Worshipful Company of Distillers 1869. His maternal grandfather, Lieutenant Colonel John Finnis (1804-57), was commanding 11th Bengal Native Infantry Regiment when he was murdered at Meerut on 10th May 1857 on the first day of the Indian Mutiny.

John was commissioned into 6th (Militia) Battalion, Rifle Brigade on 9th August 1899. The Battalion was embodied 5th December 1899 at the Curragh, County Kildare, Ireland. Promoted Lieutenant 25th July 1900. When the Battalion disembodied in December 1900, he transferred to 3rd (Militia) Battalion, Royal Sussex Regiment and served with it in South Africa, taking part in operations in Orange River Colony April – December 1901 and Transvaal until May 1902. He transferred to 2nd Battalion, Royal Garrison Regiment at Standerton, Transvaal as 2nd Lieutenant on 29th July 1903.

John gained a regular commission in the Royal Garrison Artillery in July 1903 and transferred to 1st South Staffordshire on 7th June 1905. Promoted Lieutenant 7th September 1907. He served on the North West Frontier in India, fighting Pathans. He captained the Regimental Polo Club and was also highly skilled in musketry. Promoted Captain 12th June 1909 and served in Gibraltar in 1911.

He disembarked in France with his Battalion on 5th October 1914. Having been wounded on 30th October, he was treated in hospital in Ypres. **Awarded the VC for his actions at Zillebeke, Belgium on 7th November 1914, LG 18th February 1915. Mentioned in Sir John French's Despatch dated 14th January 1915, LG 17th February 1915.** John Vallentin was killed during his VC action at Zillebeke, Belgium on 7th November 1914 and has no known grave. He is commemorated on the Ypres (Menin Gate) Memorial, Ypres, Belgium.

His VC was sent to his mother by post on 9th March 1915, but was presented formally to her by the King at Buckingham Palace on 16th November 1916. In addition to the VC, he was awarded the Queen's South Africa Medal 1899-1902 with five clasps (two of which are 'Orange Free State' & 'Transvaal'), India General Service Medal 1908-35 with clasp 'North West Frontier 1908', 1914 Star with 'Mons' clasp, British War Medal 1914-20 and Victory Medal 1914-19 with Mentioned-in-Despatches oak-leaf. His VC is held by Wellington College, Crowthorne, Berkshire.

John Vallentin never married and his mother administrated his will; he left £1,613/7/2. He is commemorated at St Leonard's Parish Church, Hythe, Kent and the Garrison Church, Whittington Barracks, Lichfield. His mother presented a set of silver to the Regiment in his memory. A number of his uncles led notable lives:

The memorial plaque erected by his mother at St Leonards Church, Hythe (Ian Dunster).

Rupert Eugene White Vallentin (1858-1934) was commissioned in 1st Battalion, The Cornwall Volunteer Regiment on 3rd October 1917. He was a noted naturalist who conducted independent expeditions to the Falkland Islands 1897-1911. His work was used by several authors notably:

> '*On some Crustaceans from the Falkland Islands collected by Rupert Vallentin*' by Reverend Thomas Stebbing in '*Proceedings of the Zoological Society of London*' 22nd May 1900.
>
> '*The Falkland Islands, with notes on the natural history by Rupert Vallentin*' by VE Boyson 1924.
>
> '*A List of the Fishes Collected by Mr Rupert Vallentin in the Falkland Islands. With Notes by the Collector*' by GA Boulenger in '*Annals and Magazine of Natural History*' 1900.

John Maximilian Vallentin (1865-1902), was commissioned into 2nd Somerset Light Infantry on 7th February 1885, served in Burma 1886-87 and attended Staff College 1897. At the outbreak of war in South Africa he was Brigade Major at Ladysmith (9th April 1898 – 8th October 1899). When brigades were redistributed within the Natal Field Force, he became Brigade Major to Lieutenant General Sir Ian Hamilton from 9th October 1899. At Elandslaagte, he behaved with conspicuous gallantry rallying the flank attack during the most critical phase of the assault. He served throughout the siege of Ladysmith (Mentioned in Sir George White VC's Despatch of 2nd December 1899 and on three other occasions) until January 1900, when he contracted enteric fever. On recovering he served under Hamilton at Bloemfontein as Deputy Assistant Adjutant General from 26th April 1900. After the occupation of Heidelberg on

27th June 1900, he became its Commissioner. He was sent with one of Field Marshal Earl Roberts' proclamations to a Boer Commando in the autumn of 1900 and lived with it for a week while discussions took place. From 22nd October 1900 he saw much service with the South African Constabulary. Brevet Major 29th November 1900. On 4th January 1902 at Onverwacht, Ermelo District he was with a patrol of 50 men pursuing a party of several hundreds Boers under Oppermann and Christian Botha when he was killed; Oppermann was also killed in this engagement.

Henry Edward Vallentin (1870-1949) trained at the Royal Military Academy Woolwich and was commissioned in the Royal Field Artillery on 15th February 1889. As a Major with 27th Battery RFA he was awarded the DSO for withdrawing his guns by hand under heavy fire near Ligny-en-Cambresis, France during the Battle of Le Cateau on 26th August 1914, LG 9th November 1914. Promoted Lieutenant Colonel 30th October 1914 and was specially employed at the War Office 8th October 1916 – 31st October 1919, when he was placed on half pay. Also awarded the OBE and Mentioned in Despatches.

Robert Francis Finnis (1840-68) served as a Lieutenant in the Indian Navy before becoming a sheep farmer at Tandil, Buenos Aires, Argentina.

Two of John's cousins are also of interest:

Archibald Thomas Pechey (1876-1961), through his aunt Alice's marriage to John Thomas Primrose Pechey, was a lyricist and author who adapted the name 'Valentine' as his pseudonym. He wrote lyrics in conjunction with composer James W Tate. His songs include '*Love Will Find a Way*' and '*A Paradise for Two*', both in 1917 from '*The Maid of the Mountains*'. He wrote novels such as '*The Adjusters*' 1922 and '*An Exploit of The Adjusters: The Man Who Scared The Bank*' 1929. He also wrote over 45 crime novels as Mark Cross between 1934 and 1961, including '*The Shadow of the Four*' and '*Who Killed Henry Wickenstrom*'. Archibald married Bijou Sortain Hancock in 1908 and their daughter, Phyllis Nan Sortain Pechey (1909–94), married Johnnie Cradock and became the restaurant critic, writer and television chef, Fanny Cradock.

Claude Max Vallentin (1896-1961), through his uncle Henry, was commissioned in the Royal Field Artillery 16th September 1914, served throughout the war in France from 11th November 1914 and was awarded the MC (LG 1st January 1919) as an Acting Major. He served in Russia 16th August – 12th October 1919. Between the wars he attended Staff College and was a staff officer with the RAF 1935-36. Appointed Acting Brigadier and CRA 5th Indian Division on 28th April 1942 (later substantive from same date). On 5th

June he was taken prisoner in a counter-attack on the 'Cauldron' at Bir Hamat, North Africa. He escaped with his batman, Lance Corporal W Snailum, from Villa Orsini following the Italian surrender on 8th September 1943, posing as peasants as they trekked through the mountains to rejoin Allied forces. He was Mentioned in Despatches 15th December 1942, retired from the Army in 1948 and served for many years as Under-Sheriff of the City of London.

9553 PRIVATE GEORGE WILSON
2nd Battalion, The Highland Light Infantry

George Wilson was born at Milne's Court, Lawnmarket, Edinburgh on 29th April 1886. His father James (born c.1849), was a merchant navy seaman and later a dock labourer. His mother was Mary née Hunter (c.1852-90). They married on 30th April 1872 at 5 Cockburn Street, Edinburgh. George had two brothers and five sisters. He was educated at Castlehill Board School and became a newspaper seller for the Evening Dispatch at Leith Walk and on the corner of Edinburgh High Street and George IV Bridge.

George enlisted in the Royal Field Artillery at Piershill Barracks, Edinburgh before enlisting in the HLI on 28th September 1904. He reported

Royal Field Artillery at Piershill Barracks, Edinburgh before the First World War.

to the Depot on 1st October and joined the 2nd Battalion on 7th January 1905. For refusing to obey an order he was put in detention 6-16th June 1905. On transferring to the Reserve on 27th September 1907 he worked in the pits at Niddrie before returning to selling newspapers.

The day after being recalled from the Reserve when war broke out, he stopped a runaway horse outside his house. Told by his sister, Mrs Mary Devlin, that he deserved the VC he replied, *"Jist bide 'til I get back frae the front an' I'll hae it right here"*, slapping his chest. He disembarked in France on 10th August 1914. **Awarded the VC for his actions near Verneuil, France on 14th September 1914, LG 5th December 1914. Mentioned in Field Marshal Sir John French's Despatch dated 8th October 1914, LG 19th October 1914 (duplicated 20th October and reissued 9th December 1914).** His VC was presented by the King at the Quartermaster General's office at HQ BEF in St Omer, France on 4th December 1914. He was the first Edinburgh man to be awarded the VC in the First World War and became known as 'The Newsboy VC'. He was in hospital in France on 16th January 1915 and evacuated to Britain on the 29th. While in Britain George's disciplinary record was not good:

SCOTTISH V.C. HERO IN HOSPITAL IN GLASGOW.

Thrilling Story of How He Won Coveted Medal.

George Wilson in hospital at Glasgow (Dundee Courier 2 February 1915).

- Confined to barracks for nine days on 28th May 1915 for being absent overnight and breaking bounds.
- Confined to barracks for three days on 31st May 1915 for smoking while under escort.
- Confined to barracks for four days on 11th June 1915 for being absent from Tattoo.
- Fined 28 day's pay on 1st July 1915 for overstaying his pass, using obscene language and resisting his escort.

He returned to France on 5th July 1915, but came back to England on 18th March 1916 and was discharged unfit for further service on 3rd July.

He worked on the Polton Farm Colony (part of the Royal Victoria Tuberculosis Trust) from September 1916, then with Edinburgh Corporation for a while; both

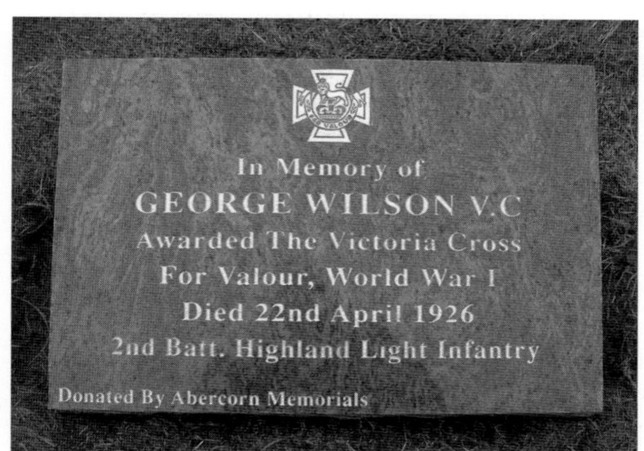

The turfstone in Piershill Cemetery, Portabello, Edinburgh, marking George Wilson's grave.

jobs were secured by the Lord Provost of Edinburgh. Eventually he returned to selling newspapers. The Silver War Badge was awarded on 22nd November 1916. He re-enlisted for garrison duties on 29th July 1919 (No.76852) and went to France on 17th August. On 26th August he was admitted to No 14 Surgical Hospital at Wimereux with pleurisy, was evacuated to Britain on 4th September and was in hospital in Edinburgh from 8th September. He returned to France to serve in D Company, 23rd Battalion on 5th November 1919, but was reprimanded on 8th December for being in town, returned to England on the 29th and was discharged as a Corporal on 7th January 1920, no longer fit for Army service.

George did not marry or have children. He became increasingly dependent upon alcohol, sold his VC for £5 and lived with his sister Mary Devlin and her husband at 20 Bank Street, Edinburgh. George Wilson died at Craigleith Hospital, Edinburgh on 22nd April 1926. Craigleith Poorhouse and Hospital was taken over by the military in 1914 as 2nd Scottish General Hospital and after the war reverted to its previous use, but was used by the Ministry of Pensions and was often referred to as the Ministry of Pensions Hospital or Craigleith Military Hospital; it was renamed the Western General Hospital in 1930. He was buried in an unmarked grave in Piershill Cemetery, Portabello, Edinburgh. The grave was marked by a turfstone by the Royal Highland Fusiliers on 21st August 2003.

In addition to the VC, he received the 1914 Star with 'Mons' clasp, British War Medal 1914-20 and Victory Medal 1914-19 with Mentioned-in-Despatches oak-leaf. His VC is held by the Royal Highland Fusiliers Museum, Sauchiehall Street, Glasgow. His brother John served with 2nd Royal Scots Fusiliers and was wounded at Ypres in 1914 while carrying a message over fire swept ground.

SECOND LIEUTENANT GEOFFREY HAROLD WOOLLEY
9th (County of London) Battalion, The London Regiment (Queen Victoria's Rifles)

Geoffrey Woolley was born at St Peter's Vicarage, Bethnal Green, London on 14th May 1892. His father was Reverend George Herbert Woolley (1846-1926). Before being ordained, George was a wine merchant in partnership with his father, trading as Charles Woolley & Son at 12 Mark Lane, London and also as the Macon Wine Agency at 13 Old Bond Street. He was Curate of St Matthew's, Upper Clapton, London and by 1901 was Vicar of St Peters, Bethnal Green. Geoffrey's mother was Sarah née Cathcart (1853-1909). George and Sarah married on 8th December 1874 at Holy Trinity, Tulse Hill, London. Geoffrey was one of 11 children (four brothers and six sisters), including:

George Cathcart Woolley (1877-1947), who worked for the North Borneo Chartered Company 1901-32 in the unexplored interior. He returned to North Borneo in 1934 as the Colonial Administrator and Ethnographer. His collections formed the basis of the Sabah Museum, which opened in 1965. George was interned by the Japanese at Batu Lintang, Kuching, Sarawak until September 1945. When rescued by the Red Cross he was close to death, but refused to give the names of his captors on the grounds that it served no Christian purpose. His health was ruined by his treatment and he died on 6th December 1947 at Jesselton, North Borneo.

Charles Leonard Woolley (1880-1960) was Assistant Keeper of the Ashmolean Museum, Oxford 1905-07. He worked with T E Lawrence on archaeological digs at the Hittite city of Carchemish 1912-14. At the outbreak of war he was commissioned in the Royal Artillery and engaged in intelligence work in Egypt and the Middle East. In 1916 his ship hit a mine while landing agents on the Syrian coast and he was held by the Turks for two years (MID and French Croix de Guerre, LG 21st April 1917). In 1919 he worked on digs in the Sinai and in 1922 was appointed Director of Excavations for the Egypt Exploration Society. 1929 saw his greatest discovery, the burial site of the Mesopotamian royal family at Ur of Chaldees in Iraq. The excavations catapulted his career and by 1934 he had his own series on BBC radio. He was knighted for his archaeological achievements, LG 3rd June 1935. During the Second World War he served on the General Staff and was promoted Lieutenant Colonel in 1943. Agatha Christie spent time with him and his wife and later married Charles' assistant, Max E L Mallowan. One of her Hercule Poirot novels, '*Murder in Mesopotamia*' 1936, is set around one of Charles' digs and he appears as one of the characters with a fictitious name. He was the author of many books including '*The Sumerians*' 1928, '*Digging Up the Past*' 1930, '*Ur of the Chaldees*' 1938, '*A Forgotten Kingdom*' 1953, '*Spadework: Adventures in Archaeology*' 1953 and '*Excavations at Ur: A Record of 12 Years Work*' 1954.

Geoffrey's brother Leonard Woolley, on the right, with T E Lawrence during a dig at Ur.

Alice Mary Woolley (1882-1915) was an artist who studied in Paris. She married the famous Belgian artist, Felix Eyskens (1882-1967) in 1907.

Herbert Martin Woolley (1883-1916) served as a Rifleman (No.3844) in 1/5th London (London Rifle Brigade) and was killed in action on the Somme on 9th October 1916. He is commemorated on the Thiepval Memorial.

Edith Pearce Woolley (1885-1970) married Matthew Henry Laxton, who was related to Eustace Laxton Jotham VC.

Amy Kathleen Woolley (1887-1976) became a teacher in Tokyo, Japan.

Frances Rachel Woolley (1889-1979) was headmistress of a diocesan school in India, having previously taught in Jamaica.

Geoffrey was educated at Parmiter's School, Bethnel Green 1900-02 (moved to Garston Hertfordshire in 1977), St John's School Leatherhead 1902-11 and Queen's College Oxford 1911-14 (BA awarded under war service conditions), where he was a member of the OTC. He was commissioned in 5th Essex on 26th August 1914 and transferred in September to 9th London. He went with the Battalion to France on 4th November and was one of the street liners when Lord Roberts' body began its journey back to England.

In the trenches a mortar bomb landed in the section he was occupying without exploding. He promptly picked it up and threw it back. **Awarded the VC for his**

actions at Hill 60, near Ypres, Belgium on 20th-21st April 1915, LG 22nd May 1915; the first VC won by a member of the Territorial Force. He was badly affected by gas on 23rd April, but returned to the Battalion two days later. A few days after he was sent to a rest camp and then No 2 Red Cross hospital at Rouen before being evacuated to Osborne, Isle of Wight. Appointed Acting Captain 27th April. While convalescing he helped train Cambridge University OTC and ran various courses. **Mentioned in Sir John French's Despatch of 31st May 1915, LG 22nd June 1915.** Appointed Temporary Captain 17th June. The VC was presented by the King at Buckingham Palace on 6th July 1915.

Geoffrey was promoted Lieutenant 5th September and returned to France to command B Company. Appointed Temporary Captain 24th January 1916. He attended the first course of instruction at the Fourth Army School at Flixecourt in February. Appointed Instructor at Third Army Infantry School at Auxi-le-Chateau in March. Promoted Captain 1st June. Appointed GSO3 HQ Third Army 5th August. Returned to Third Army School 7th December. Appointed Assistant Instructor 17th March 1917. Appointed GSO3 HQ 17th Division, returning to HQ Third Army on 21st April 1918.

While on leave on 8th July 1918 he married Janet Beatrix née Orr-Ewing (1890-1943); his father conducted the service. Her father was a MP and she was the widow of Captain George Culme-Seymour KRRC. He was attached as Adjutant to 9th London and was killed on 7th May 1915; commemorated on the Ypres (Menin Gate) Memorial. Janet was the niece of Alexander Gore Arkwright Hore-Ruthven VC CB GCMG DSO, later Earl of Gowrie, who won his VC on 22nd September 1888 in the Sudan. Her mother's third marriage was to Thomas Sopwith, founder of Sopwith Aviation, producers of the famous Camel fighter. Her son, Mark Charles Culme-Seymour (born 1910), served as a Major in the Rifle Brigade in the Second World War and was married four times – Babette Patric-Jones 1935, Princess Hélène Marie de la Trémoïlle 1941, Patricia June Reid-Graham 1956 and Mary Darrall Riely 1973. Her daughter, Angela Mary Culme-Seymour (born 1912), also married four times – John George Spencer-Churchill 1934, nephew of Winston Churchill; John Patrick Douglas Balfour 1938; Count René Guillet de Chatellus 1948; and Mehmet Ali Bulent Rauf 1977. Geoffrey and Janet had two children – Harold Lindsay Cathcart 'Rollo' Woolley, born 7th October 1919 and registered in Fulham and Janet 'Janetta' E Woolley, born 31st December 1921 and registered in Kensington.

Geoffrey was demobilised on 1st February 1919 and restored to the establishment of 9th London. **Mentioned in Sir Douglas Haig's Despatch of 8th November 1918, LG 20th December 1918. Awarded the MC for distinguished services in connection with military operations in France and Flanders, LG 3rd June 1919.**

Having returned to Queen's College, Oxford 1919-20 (Dip Th 1920 and MA 1924), he then went to Cuddesdon College near Oxford for an ordination course. He was a member of the VC Guard at the Interment of the Unknown Warrior on

11th November 1920. He was ordained in Coventry Cathedral on 19th December 1920 with a licence as a curate at Rugby parish church and was employed as an Assistant Master at Rugby School 1920-23. At Rugby School he was seconded for service with the Officers Training Corps 16th December 1920 – 27th September 1923.

He joined the hastily formed Defence Force against strikes, being granted a temporary commission as Captain in 7th (Defence Force) Battalion, Royal Warwickshire Regiment on 12th April 1921. He commanded a company in Coventry, tasked with ensuring local demonstrations by striking miners did not get out-of-control. On demobilisation of the Defence Force he relinquished his commission on 5th July 1921 and resigned his Territorial commission on 5th December 1923, retaining the rank of Captain.

In May 1923 he was presented with a College living, the benefice of Monk Sherborne cum Pamber near Basingstoke, by the Provost and Fellows of Queen's College, which he held until 1927. He led School Empire Tours to Australia in 1926 and Canada in 1928 and 1939. He was an Assistant Master at Harrow School 1927-39 and Chaplain there from 1932.

Geoffrey was appointed Chaplain 4th Class (16517) on 1st February 1940 (Regular Army Emergency Commission) and served at Woolwich and Pirbright until appointed Chaplain 3rd Class as Senior Chaplain Algiers in November 1942. He sailed aboard the Cunard liner, RMS *Scythia*, which was bombed while anchored at Algiers, but he was unharmed.

In Algiers he immediately faced the problem of providing alternative entertainment for troops other than the notorious wine shops in the city, the source of a great deal of indiscipline. With the help of other chaplains and a number of ladies from various Allied nations, he set up 24 improvised clubs, some able to stage concerts and put on films. He faced many problems supplying them with even basic commodities such as milk, but it was done and the situation in Algiers eased considerably. He ran these clubs until the official welfare services took them over in August 1943.

His son Rollo graduated from Queen's College, Oxford, (BA Modern Languages) in 1940 and enlisted in the RAFVR (916237). He was commissioned (89816) on 28th December 1940 with seniority from 15th December and on completion of pilot training was retained as a flying instructor. Promoted Flying Officer 28th December 1941 (seniority 15th December) and was posted to 152 Squadron, which moved to Tunisia in November 1942. On 2nd December 1942 he shot down a German fighter before being shot down himself. He was posted 'missing believed killed' until his wrecked Spitfire was found months later. His body was recovered after the campaign in Tunisia and buried in Massicault War Cemetery, Tunisia (III L 7).

Geoffrey suffered another bereavement when his wife died of pneumonia in February 1943. He fell ill with pleurisy and pneumonia in May, also contracting dysentery in hospital. He returned to duty after six weeks, but never felt fully fit the rest of the time he was in North Africa. **Awarded the OBE (Military Division) for gallant and distinguished services as Chaplain to the Forces in North Africa,**

LG 16th September 1943. In December 1943 he was invited by Captain Spencer-Churchill to accept the living of Harrow, a curacy that included Pinner. The War Office would not release him for six months until he undertook the appointment of Senior Chaplain in Rome. He agreed and was posted to Naples, pending the fall of Rome. While returning from a visit to Salerno, his vehicle was overtaken by an American convoy at the same time as an Italian car passed in the opposite direction. Geoffrey's driver swerved off the road and they overturned in a field. He suffered a back injury and was hospitalised before being moved to a rest station at Sorrento and was eventually evacuated to England. He was not active from 1944, but appeared in the Army List until August 1948. He relinquished his commission on 14th May 1952 and was granted the honorary rank of Chaplain to the Forces 3rd Class.

Geoffrey after the Second World War.

He became Vicar of St Mary's, Harrow 1944-52. On 12th June 1945, Geoffrey married Elcie Elisabeth née Nichols (1908-79). Amongst her siblings were:

- Henry Wilfrid Lee Nichols (1894-1968), a doctor who served as a Lieutenant Colonel.
- Charles Alfred 'Godfrey' Nichols (1898-1986) was a Royal Navy Captain on HMAS *Shropshire* 1944-46. He also commanded the Australian Squadron October – December 1944 (MID, DSO, MVO and US Bronze Medal).
- Reginald Frederick Nichols (1900-84) was a Royal Navy Captain and Deputy Chief of Naval Staff in Australia 1940-43.

Geoffrey and Elcie had a son, Geoffrey Nicholas Woolley, born in the 2nd quarter of 1946, registered at Hendon. After Harrow, Geoffrey became Rector of West Grinstead, Sussex 1952-58. He was a member of the Royal Commonwealth Society, the first Vice-Chairman of the VC and GC Association 1956-68, a member of the Church of England Commission on Ordination Candidations and President of the Harrow Branch of the British Legion and the Old Contemptibles' Association.

His autobiography, '*Sometimes a Soldier*', was published in 1963. He also wrote, '*The Epic of the Mountains*' 1929, '*Fear and Religion*' 1930, '*A Journey to Palestine*' 1935 and '*A Pocket-Book of Prayers*' 1940. On 27th June 1964 he led the Old Contemptibles Golden Jubilee Service at the Royal Albert Hall, organised by Ralph Reader of 'Gang Show' fame.

Geoffrey Woolley died at Hunter's Barn, West Chiltington, near Pulborough, Sussex on 10th December 1968 and is buried in St Mary's Churchyard, West Chiltington. In addition to the VC, OBE and MC, he was awarded the 1914 Star with 'Mons' clasp, British War Medal 1914-20, Victory Medal 1914-19 with Mentioned-in-Despatches oak-leaf, 1939–45 Star, Africa Star, Italy Star, 1939–45 Defence Medal, War Medal 1939–45, George VI Coronation Medal 1937 and Elizabeth II Coronation Medal 1953. His medals are held privately. Geoffrey Woolley is commemorated in a number of places:

St Mary's, Harrow where Geoffrey was Vicar 1944-52.

- Woolley House, Parmiter's School, Garston, Hertfordshire.
- Parmiter's School memorial in St George's Church, Ypres, Belgium unveiled on 6th June 2007.
- His chaplain's stole displayed at the TA Centre, Davies Street, London.
- Woolley VC Memorial Cup, donated by Jack Hinton VC in January 1969, awarded by the Auckland Area Horse Society to the winner of the 'A' Grade Pony Class.
- Geoffrey Woolley House (a block of 17 flats), Pollard Street, Bethnal Green, London, opened on 20th February 2013.
- Royal British Legion Headquarters, Northolt Road, South Harrow. The dedication reads:

> "THIS HALL WE BUILT AND LEAVE FOR YOUR USING,
> IN HOPE THAT YOU, OUR SONS, WILL FIND HEREIN
> THAT LIVING SPIRIT WHICH, THEIR FUTURE LOSING,
> OUR COMRADES BREATHED, ETERNITY TO WIN.
> THEIR LIVES THEY GAVE, PEACE-LOVING, YET IN STRIFE;
> TO SERVE WITH LOVE IN DUTY, – THIS IS LIFE;
> CHOOSE YE THEIR PATH; GOD BLESS YOU IN YOUR CHOOSING.
> REV GH WOOLLEY VC OBE MC MA."

His daughter Janet 'Janetta' E Woolley married three times:

Humphrey Richard Hugh Slater (1906-58) in 1940. He spent his childhood in South Africa and studied at the Slade School of Art in London. He Joined the Communist Party of Great Britain and was a reporter for '*Imprecor*', the

English-language newspaper of the Comintern. In 1936 he joined the Popular Front forces in the Spanish Civil War, became a political commissar in the British Battalion and was later Chief of Operations for the International Brigades. In July 1940 he became an instructor in guerrilla warfare at the Osterley Park Home Guard Training School, but in 1941 was dismissed as unsuitable because of his communist sympathies. He enlisted as a Private and served in an anti-aircraft unit. After the war he was editor of '*Polemic*' 1945-47 and author of a spy novel, '*The Conspirator*' 1948, made into a film starring Elizabeth Taylor, Robert Taylor and Honor Blackman. After they divorced, Humphrey married Moyra Sutherland in 1947.

While married to Slater, Janet had a long affair with Kenneth William C Sinclair–Loutit (1913-2003), which resulted in a daughter, Nicolette Sinclair-Loutit in 1943. At Cambridge, Kenneth developed an interest in politics and visited Germany in 1934 and 1935. Concerned at the growth of fascism, he became an active opponent of Mosley's British Union of Fascists. He trained at St Bartholomew's Hospital and in August 1936 went to Spain with twenty other volunteers and a mobile hospital, formed by the Socialist Medical Association's Spanish Medical Aid Committee. He was Administrator of the Field Unit and he and Thora Silverthorne, matron of Granen Hospital, became lovers and married in 1937. He completed his medical degree and joined the Holborn branch of the Labour Party, joining forces with Stafford Cripps and Aneurin Bevan in the campaign against appeasement. They were threatened with expulsion by the National Executive Committee for appearing on the same platforms as Communists. Early in the Second World War he was Medical Officer in Paris to the Polish Relief Fund and returned to St Bartholomew's at the beginning of 1940 to help establish Finsbury Health Centre on principles that became the bedrock of the National Health Service. He was also Medical Officer for Civil Defence in Finsbury. For helping to rescue survivors in a collapsed block of flats in Stepney during the Blitz he was awarded the MBE, LG 25th April 1941. In 1941 he left Thora to live with Janetta and when she fell pregnant with Nicolette she changed her name by deed poll to Sinclair-Loutit. When he was offered a post in the Balkans in July 1944, Janetta objected, but he went anyway and was appointed Director of the United Nations Relief and Rehabilitation Administration in Belgrade. In 1945 he returned to collect Janetta and Nicolette, but by then Janetta had fallen in love with Robert Kee and refused to leave. Sinclair-Loutit married Angela H De Renzy-Martin in 1946. In 1950 he became World Health Organisation Medical Adviser in Bangkok. He was next WHO Medical Advisor to the UNICEF office in Paris, responsible for programmes in Africa, Europe and the Middle East. In 1961 he took over the WHO office in Rabat and also liaised with the government in Algeria. When he retired in 1973, he and Angela settled in Morocco, where he started a communications and electronic engineering company, carrying out many projects, including the country's first mobile radio telephone.

Janetta married Robert Kee (born 1919) in 1948. He was born in Calcutta, India and served in the RAF during the Second World War. He was shot down over the Netherlands and made several escape attempts before succeeding after a difficult journey across Poland. Janetta and Robert had a daughter, Georgiana, in 1949. They divorced in 1950/51 after he had an affair with Janetta's half-sister, Angela Culme-Seymour.

Janetta's third husband was Derek Ainslie Jackson (1906-82) in 1951. He worked under Professor Lindemann at the Clarendon Laboratory, Oxford and was appointed lecturer in spectroscopy in 1934. He rode but fell in the Grand National in 1935. He joined a group of researchers working for the Admiralty at the Clarendon until released by Lindemann to join the RAF as a navigator in 1941. As Chief Airborne Radar Officer of Fighter Command he was involved in trials of chaff and jamming German night defences. He flew 1,100 hours on active service (DFC 1941, AFC 1944, OBE 1945, US Officer of the Legion of Merit). Appointed Professor of Spectroscopy at Oxford in 1947. He rode in the Grand National in 1947, but fell, and again in 1948 when his horse refused the penultimate fence while lying second. He was a research professor in spectroscopy at the Laboratoire Aimé Cotton at Bellevue, Paris and later at Orsay (Chevalier of the Légion d'Honneur 1966). Janetta and Derek had a daughter, Rose Janetta in 1953. They divorced in 1956. Jackson married twice before Janetta and three times afterwards. His second wife was Pamela Freeman Mitford, whose sister Diana married Oswald Mosley, the British fascist leader.

CAPTAIN THEODORE WRIGHT
57th Field Company, Royal Engineers

Theodore (Dodo to the family) Wright was born at 119 Lansdowne Place, Hove, Sussex on 15th May 1883. His father, William Walter Wright (c.1825–1911), born in Philadelphia, USA, was a Minister of the Catholic Apostolic Church. His mother was Arabella née Tarbet (1845–1927). William and Arabella married at the Catholic Apostolic Church, Canning Street, Liverpool on 15th October 1874. The family lived at Weston House and Talgai at Albury Heath, Guildford, Surrey. Theodore had a brother and four sisters. His maternal grandparents lived in Abercromby Square, Liverpool, where the parents of Ernest Alexander VC and Noel Chavasse VC & Bar lived at various times.

Theodore was educated at Clifton College and the Royal Military Academy Woolwich. At the Academy he represented the Army in a cricket match against Hampshire. Having been commissioned on 1st October 1902, he continued training at Chatham. Promoted Lieutenant on 21st June 1905. He served with the Balloon Section at Aldershot, then Gibraltar until December 1906, followed by 2nd Fortress Company in Cairo and returned to Aldershot in October 1912. Having attended the advanced course at Chatham, he was posted to 56th Field Company at Bulford Camp, Wiltshire as Adjutant 3rd Division RE. Promoted Captain on 1st October 1913. He disembarked at Rouen, France on 17th August 1914. **Awarded the VC for his actions at La Mariette, near Mons, Belgium on 23rd August and at Vailly, France on 14th September 1914, LG 16th November 1914. Mentioned in Field Marshal Sir John French's Despatch dated 8th October 1914, LG 19th October 1914 (duplicated 20th October and reissued 9th December 1914).** Although wounded in the head on 23rd August he remained at duty, but was killed at Vailly, Aisne on 14th September 1914, assisting wounded men into shelter. He is buried in Vailly British Cemetery (II B 21). He is commemorated on the Royal Military Academy Woolwich VC Memorial Board in the Royal Military Academy Sandhurst library.

His VC was presented to his mother by the King at Buckingham Palace on 16th November 1916. In addition to the VC, he was awarded the 1914 Star with 'Mons' clasp, British War Medal 1914-20 and Victory Medal 1914-19 with Mentioned-in-Despatches oak-leaf. Theodore's medals, memorial plaque, letters relating to the award of the VC and his wooden grave marker passed to his nephew, Peter Heath, who donated them to the Royal Engineers on his death. They are held by the Royal Engineers Museum, Gillingham, Kent.

The grave of Captain Theodore Wright in Vailly British Cemetery (II B 21).

Theodore's younger brother, Major Godfray Tarbet Wright, served in the Army Service Corps from 1907. An older sister, Arabella (1876-1950), married Brigadier John Bayford Wells (1881-1952); he served in the Loyal North Lancashire Regiment in the Second Boer War (DSO and MID), in the First World War in France, Gallipoli and Egypt (CMG and MID) and was later Colonel of the Regiment (CBE). Arabella and John's son, Captain Theodore John MacDonald Wells, Loyal North Lancashire Regiment, was killed in Tunisia on 30th April 1943 and is buried in Massicault War Cemetery (V F 2).

5854 LANCE CORPORAL GEORGE HARRY WYATT
3rd Battalion, The Coldstream Guards

George Wyatt was born at Britannia Road, Whitstones, Worcester on 5th September 1886. His father, Arthur Digby Wyatt (1862-1938), worked as a groom for a veterinary surgeon until 1889 and was then employed by the Dowager Lady Hindlip as a coachman at Hindlip Hall for the next 20 years. While in her employ the family moved to Hadzor. George's mother was Sarah Ann née Mason (1864–1918). Arthur and Sarah married at Worcester on 2nd December 1883. George had six brothers and two sisters and was educated at Hindlip School and Holloway School in Droitwich. He sang in the local choir and after school was employed as a blacksmith's boy.

George enlisted at Birmingham on 23rd November 1904 and served in the 2nd Battalion in England until being posted to the 3rd Battalion in Egypt on 16th September 1906. He gained the Third Class Certificate of Education on 25th February 1907 and undertook Mounted Infantry training November 1907 – March 1908. Having returned to the 2nd Battalion in England on 7th October 1908, he transferred to the Section B Reserve on 23rd November.

George became a policeman in Barnsley on 9th January 1909 and boarded at 16 Highfield Terrace, Churchfield, Barnsley. He married Ellen née Graham (1891–1972) at Whitehaven, Cumberland on 1st January 1912. They had seven children – Arthur Digby Wyatt, born on 28th November 1912; Ellen Wyatt, born on 29th April 1914; George Harry Wyatt, born on 10th December 1916; John G Wyatt, registered in the 4th quarter of 1919; Annie E Wyatt, registered in the 1st quarter of 1922; Maud A Wyatt, registered in the 2nd quarter of 1923; and Jeffery F Wyatt, registered in the 3rd quarter of 1925. George transferred to the Doncaster Police on 19th May 1914 and trained as a mounted officer.

George Wyatt while serving in Egypt.

On 5th August 1914, George was recalled to the Colours and disembarked with 3rd Battalion in France on 12th August. He was evacuated to England on 8th September with a gunshot wound to the scalp received on 1st September. **Mentioned in Field Marshal Sir John French's Despatch**

dated 8th October 1914, LG 19th October 1914 (duplicated 20th October and reissued 9th December 1914). While in England he was on the held strength of the 4th Battalion and returned to France on 11th November 1914 to join 2nd Battalion. Appointed Unpaid Lance Corporal 12th November and promoted Lance Corporal 18th December 1914. He received another gunshot wound to the scalp at Cuinchy on 26th February 1915 and was evacuated to England on 9th March, where he was on the held strength of 4th Battalion. He served the rest of the war in England, transferring to 5th Battalion on 12th August 1915.

3rd Battalion's recommendations for awards in August and early September 1914 were compiled in great haste by the Second-in-Command, Major Torquhil Matheson, in a field on 9th September. George Wyatt's name was on the list, but no particular award was recommended and he was only Mentioned. In the summer of 1915, the Russians were looking to honour an especially brave act. Lieutenant Colonel Fielding, who commanded 3rd Battalion at Landrecies and was temporarily commanding 4th (Guards) Brigade, saw the letter from GHQ and alerted Matheson. **Awarded the Cross of the Order of St George 3rd Class (Russia), LG 25th August 1915.** Information was then requested on what happened at Landrecies. Matheson, by then commanding 46th Brigade, wrote to the then commanding officer of 3rd Battalion, Lieutenant Colonel JV Campbell (VC September 1916), recommending Wyatt be put forward for the VC. **Awarded the VC for his actions at Landrecies on 25/26th August and Villers Cotterets, France on 1st September 1914, LG 18th November 1915.**

His parents were living at the Pear Tree Inn, Hindlip, where his father was landlord and baker, when they learned of George's VC through the local newspaper, 'The Berrow Worcester Journal'. Following a distinguished performance on a bombing course at Godstone, Surrey, George was appointed First Class Bomb Throwing Instructor on 25th January 1916. His VC was presented by the King at Buckingham Palace on 4th March 1916. Appointed Acting Corporal 28th February 1917 and Acting Unpaid Lance Sergeant 12th September 1917.

George Wyatt being congratulated on being awarded the VC.

George returned to the Doncaster Police on 19th December 1918, but was not formally discharged to the Class Z Reserve until 14th January 1919. The Chief Constable and former police colleagues presented him with a gold watch and his wife received a silver cream jug and sugar bowl. He was discharged from the Army Reserve on 31st March 1920. On 30th June 1924 he stopped a runaway horse at great personal risk for which he was awarded a guinea. George was a keen swimmer and won numerous prizes while serving with the Police.

George Wyatt in police uniform post-war.

George retired on 10th February 1934 and became a small holder. He died at Sprotborough, near Doncaster, Yorkshire on 22nd January 1964 and was buried in Cadeby Churchyard, Sprotborough. A memorial plaque was placed there in 1999. George Wyatt was a freemason (Bulwer Lodge of Cairo No 1068). In addition to the VC, he was awarded the 1914 Star with 'Mons' clasp, British War Medal 1914-20, Victory Medal 1914-19 with Mentioned-in-Despatches oak-leaf, George VI Coronation Medal 1937, Elizabeth II Coronation Medal 1953 and the Russian Cross of St George 3rd Class. While attending a Remembrance Service in London he lost the original Cross of St George, which was issued with the standard bow ribbon. The Regiment presented the family with a replica in August 1988, but it is incorrectly suspended from a 4th Class ribbon. The VC is held privately and its location is not known.

MAJOR CHARLES ALLIX LAVINGTON YATE
2nd Battalion, The King's Own (Yorkshire Light Infantry)

Charles Yate was born at Ludwiglust, Mecklenburg, Germany on 14th March 1872. He was known as 'Cal' from his initials. His father was Prebendary George Edward Yate (1825-1908), Missionary Canon of St Paul's Cathedral in Calcutta, India 1852-56, Honourable East India Company chaplain at Kiddepore 1856-59, Vicar of St Michael's Madeley, Shropshire 1859-1908 and Prebendary of Hereford 1905. His mother, Louisa Georgina Harriet Caroline Adolphine née Petersen (c.1833-84), was George's second wife. They married in the 2nd quarter of 1871

at Wellington, Shropshire. Charles had five sisters, four from his father's previous marriage to Margaret Maria née Bishop (c.1828-69). Charles was to be educated at his father's old school, Shrewsbury, but he was a delicate boy and was sent to Weymouth College instead so that the sea air and mild climate would improve his health. He left in December 1890.

Charles trained at the Royal Military College Sandhurst and passed out 9th when he was commissioned on 13th August 1892. He joined the Battalion in Bombay. Promoted Lieutenant 7th February 1894. Served with the Tirah Expeditionary Force on the North-West Frontier 1897-98 before moving to Mauritius, where he studied for the Staff College examination. Promoted Captain 26th July 1899. The Battalion went to South Africa when the Boer War broke out aboard HMS *Powerful*. Charles received a gunshot wound to the abdomen at Enslin on 25th November 1899 during the Battle of Graspan. He returned to Madeley to convalesce and on arrival local miners met the train, took the place of the horses and pulled his carriage home in celebration of his many acts of bravery. He returned to duty on 18th October 1900 as part of the peace negotiation party sent to negotiate with General Botha. **Mentioned in Lord Roberts' Despatch of 4th September 1901, LG 10th September 1901.** Attended Staff College in 1901. Appointed Staff Officer Transvaal and Orange River Colony 1st August – 21st September 1902.

Charles Yate married Florence Helena Burroughs née Brigg (1870-1924) on 17th September 1903 at St George's, Hanover Square, London; they had no children. Florence was divorced from George Edward Elton Burroughs in 1898. Charles was a keen horseman, riding with the Allbrighton hounds and played polo. He also played football and skied at Arosa, Switzerland. He wrote an article, '*Moral Qualities in War*', for 'Blackwood's Magazine'.

Cal Yate between the end of the South African War and the outbreak of World War One. He is wearing the distinctive double crossbelt Sam Browne favoured by a number of regiments.

Charles was sent to Japan representing the Infantry in a British Army Mission. He was appointed Military Attaché with the Japanese during the Manchurian War 26th July 1904 – 28th February 1905 and was present at the siege of Port Arthur, being one of the first to enter the stronghold. **Awarded the Japanese War Medal for Manchuria with clasp 'Port Arthur' and the Order of the Sacred Treasure 4th Class, the latter being presented by the Emperor; neither appeared in the London Gazette.** Charles returned to England through Liverpool on 22nd

Major Yate pictured by the Germans in transit to a prison camp in Germany. Yate regarded capture as dishonourably as the Japanese, with whom he served as an observer some years before. Although he survived the battle, he was dead within a month.

March 1906 and was appointed Staff Captain and GSO3 in Cape Colony District, South Africa 16th June 1906 – 8th February 1908. He was a skilled linguist, being an interpreter in French, German and Japanese and also spoke Hindustani and Persian. Appointed GSO3 at HQ of the Army in London 9th February 1908 – 31st March 1909. Appointed GSO2 at the War Office 8th March 1910 – 7th March 1914. Promoted Major 7th February 1912. He returned to the 2nd Battalion in March 1914 and was one of the first 10 officers selected for training as air observers at Netheravon, commencing on 13th July 1914.

Charles refused a post on General Joffré's staff when war broke out and returned to his Battalion as a company commander, disembarking in France on 16th August 1914. **Awarded the VC for his actions at Le Cateau on 26th August 1914, LG 25th November 1914. Mentioned in Field Marshal Sir John French's Despatch dated 8th October 1914, LG 19th October 1914 (duplicated 20th October and reissued 9th December 1914).** He adopted a very Japanese view of being taken prisoner unwounded and tried to shoot himself on the battlefield.

He was held initially at Cambrai, France and arrived at Torgau Prison, Germany on 8th September, having attempted to jump train en route and being roughly handled by civilians on the way. At Torgau he was interviewed about his pre-war work in Germany and believed the Germans thought he was a spy. He became agitated about this and wanted to escape before the next interview. Knowing his wife was ill in Switzerland, he intended heading there. On the night of 19th September 1914, dressed in civilian clothing, he was assisted over the wall by Lieutenant Breen and Captain Roche. He had previously swapped his safety razor for Breen's cutthroat. There are a number of versions of what happened next. However, a post-war investigation revealed that the following morning Charles was challenged by civilians on their way to work on the Torgau – Mühlburg road south of Lehndorf. His clothing was suspicious as he had no hat and his cloak was too small. While being questioned he slashed his own throat a number of times, staggered 40m and fell dead.

Charles was originally buried in Martinkirchen churchyard. No British officer was allowed to see the body or attend the funeral, but the German pastor officiating at the burial cabled Florence Yate in Switzerland, confirming his death and burial.

After the war his remains were moved to Berlin South Western Cemetery, Stahnsdorf (II G 8) and in November 2004 Queen Elizabeth II laid a wreath on his grave.

Cal Yate's grave in Berlin South Western Cemetery at Stahnsdorf. His body was moved here from Martinkirchen churchyard after the war (Alain Chissel).

Charles is commemorated at St Aldhelm's Church, Weymouth, Dorset and St Michael's Church, Madeley, Shropshire. Probate to his wife, £2,114. In addition to the VC, he was awarded the India Medal 1895-1902 with 'Punjab Frontier 1897-98' clasp, Queen's South Africa Medal 1899-1902 with four clasps (Belmont, Orange Free State, Transvaal and South Africa 1902), 1914 Star with 'Mons' clasp, British War Medal 1914-20, Victory Medal 1914-19 with Mentioned-in-Despatches oak-leaf, George V Coronation Medal 1911 and the two Japanese awards already mentioned. His VC was originally sent to his widow by post on 11th January 1915, but was presented to her formally by the King at Buckingham Palace on 2nd August 1919. His VC is held by the King's Own Yorkshire Light Infantry Museum, Doncaster Museum & Art Gallery.

Charles's cousin, Charles Yate of Madeley Hall, was created a Baronet in 1921. Florence Yate died in 1924 in Monaco.

Sources

The following institutions, individuals and publications were consulted.

Regimental Museums.
Museum of the 9/12th Royal Lancers, Derby; Royal Army Medical Corps Historical Museum, Aldershot; The Duke of Cornwall's Light Infantry Regimental Museum, Bodmin; Light Infantry Office (Yorkshire), Pontefract; RHQ The Royal Scots, Edinburgh; 15th/19th The King's Royal Hussars Museum, Newcastle upon Tyne; The Cameronians Regimental Museum, Hamilton; Royal Engineers Museum, Chatham; Lancashire County and Regimental Museum, Preston; Museum of the Manchesters, Ashton-under-Lyne; RHQ Worcestershire and Sherwood Foresters, Beeston; Gordon Highlanders Museum, Aberdeen; Royal Leicestershire Regiment Museum, Leicester; Royal Green Jackets Museum, Winchester; The Royal Irish Fusiliers Regimental Museum, Armagh; Regimental Headquarters Coldstream Guards, London; HQ Scots Guards, London; Green Howards Museum, Richmond, Yorkshire; RHQ Queen's Lancashire Regiment, Preston; Border Regiment and Kings Own Royal Border Regiment Museum, Carlisle; Scottish United Services Museum, Edinburgh; Royal Artillery Historical Trust.

Individuals
Mr and Mrs H Acton, Granville Angell, Doug and Richard Arman, Alec Armstrong, Jock Asbury-Bailey, Brian Best, Mrs K Best, Mary Borst, Barbara Braime, Laryn Brown, Judy Burge, Merrill Burns, Mike Chapman, Roger Coleman, Bill Cooper, Maj John Cotterill, Jean Crichton, Sandra Daniels, Mrs N Dobson, Walter Garforth, Colin Godley, Tony Grant, Lord Julian Grenfell, David Harrison, David Harvey, Kathy Haskins, Mike Hibberd, Terry Hissey, Donald Jennings, Tom Johnson, Alan Jordan, J Barry Luke, Frederick Luke, Alasdair Macintyre, Robert Mansell, Richard Martin, Alison McIntosh, Alistair and Mary Melville, Honourable Mrs C Mieckowska, Col Gerald Napier, Lt Col Philip Neame, John Oxley, Stuart & Carol Peel, Maj JIR Phillips, June Pickering, Edith Quaggin, Edna Rendle, Maj Malcolm Ross, Peter Roupell, Derek Seaton, Adrian Sissons, Brandon Smith, John Starling, Anthony Staunton, Iain Stewart, Neil Storey, Vic Tambling, Iain Tidey, Margery Turner, Goodwin Wilson, Lt Col Les Wilson MBE, Freda Wood, Michelle Young.

Record Offices, Libraries and Local Museums
Birmingham Central Library, Derby City Museum, Leicester County Record Office.

Newspapers
North Eastern Evening Gazette; Leicester Mercury.

Schools and Universities
Cheltenham College; Clifton College, Bristol; Edinburgh Academy; Eton College; University of Glasgow; Harrow School; Irvine Royal Academy; Marlborough College; St Edmund's Canterbury; Stonyhurst College; Wellington College; Winchester College.

Divisional Histories
The Guards Division in the Great War. C Headlam. 1929. Two volumes.
The History of the Second Division 1914-18. E Wyrell. 1921. Two volumes.
Iron Division, The History of the 3rd Division. R McNish. 1976.
The Fifth Division in the Great War. Brig Gen A H Hussey and Maj D S Inman. 1920.
A Short History of the 6th Division August 1914 – March 1919. Editor Maj Gen T O Marden. 1920.
The Seventh Division 1914-18. C T Atkinson. 1927.
The Eighth Division in War 1914-18. Lt Col J H Boraston and Capt C E O Bax. 1926.

Brigade Histories.
A Short History of the 5th Infantry Brigade. Maj G D P Young. 1965.
The Doings of the Fifteenth Infantry Brigade August 1914 to March 1915. Major General Lord Edward Gleichen. 1917.

Regimental/Unit Histories
In regimental seniority:

The Ninth Queen's Royal Lancers 1715 – 1936. Maj E W Sheppard. 1939.
The History of the 15th (The King's) Hussars 1914 – 22. Lord Carnock. 1932.
Royal Artillery Journal, Volume LIV, No 3, 1927-28 – Néry, 1914. Maj A F Becke.
The Royal Artillery War Commemoration Book. Anon. 1970.
The Royal Regiment of Artillery at Le Cateau 26th August 1914. Maj A F Becke. 1919.
History of the Royal Regiment of Artillery, Western Front, 1914-18. Gen Sir M Farndale. 1986.
Horse Gunners, The Royal Horse Artillery, 200 Years of Panache and Professionalism. W G Clarke. 1993.
ARTYVICS – The Victoria Cross and The Royal Regiment of Artillery. Marc J Sherriff.
History of the Corps of Royal Engineers, Volume V, The Home Front, France, Flanders and Italy in the First World War. Anon. 1952.

Demolitions Carried Out at Mons and During the Retreat 1914. Maj Gen Sir R U H Buckland. RE Journal Mar-Jun 1932.
The Grenadier Guards in the Great War of 1914-18. Lt Col Sir F Ponsonby. 1920. Three volumes.
The Coldstream Guards 1914-18. Lt Col Sir J Ross of Blankenburg. 1928. Two volumes with a separate volume of maps.
A History of the Coldstream Guards Victoria and George Cross Holders. Sergeant L Pearce. 1995.
The Scots Guards in the Great War 1914-18. F Loraine Petre, W Ewart and Maj Gen Sir C Lowther. 1925.
The Irish Guards in the Great War. R Kipling. 1923.
The Micks, The Story of the Irish Guards. P Verney. 1970.
The Royal Scots 1914-19. Maj J Ewing. 1925. Two volumes.
The Royal Fusiliers in the Great War. H C O'Neill. 1922.
Royal Fusiliers Chronicle.
The 16th Foot, A History of the Bedforshire and Hertfordshire Regiment. Maj Gen Sir F Maurice. 1931.
The Story of the Bedfordshire and Hertfordshire Regiment Volume II – 1914-58. Compiled by Lt Col T J Barrow DSO, Maj V A French and J Seabrook Esq. 1986.
History of the 1st and 2nd Battalions The Leicestershire Regiment in the Great War. Col H C Wylly. 1928.
The Green Howards in the Great War 1914-19. Col H C Wylly. 1926.
The Green Howards – For Valour 1914-18. Anon. 1964.
The History of the Green Howards – 300 Years of Service. G Powell. 1992.
Beyond Their Duty; Heroes of the Green Howards. Roger Chapman.
A Short History of the Cameronians (Scottish Rifles). Col H C Wylly. 1924.
History of the Cameronians (Scottish Rifles), Volume II 1910-22. Col H H Story. 1961.
History of the East Lancashire Regiment in the Great War 1914-18. Edited by Maj Gen Sir N Nicholson and Maj H T McMullen. 1936.
History of the East Surrey Regiment, Volume II 1914-17. Col H W Pearse & Brig Gen H S Sloman. 1924.
The History of the Duke of Cornwall's Light Infantry 1914-19. E Wyrall. 1932.
The Story of the 1st Battalion Duke of Cornwall's Light Infantry. Lt H N Newey. 1924.
The Border Regiment in the Great War. Col H C Wylly. 1924.
Tried and Valiant, The History of the Border Regiment 1702-1959. D Sutherland. 1972.
A History of the South Staffordshire Regiment 1705-1923. J P Jones. 1923.
History of the South Staffordshire Regiment. Col W L Vale. 1969.
The 1st and 2nd Battalions The Sherwood Foresters (Nottinghamshire and Derbyshire Regiment) in the Great War. Col H C Wylly. 1924.
History of the King's Own Light Infantry in the Great War, Volume III 1914-18. Lt Col R C Bond. 1930.

The King's Own Yorkshire Light Infantry, Register of Officers 1755-1945. C P Deedes.
The Annals of the King's Royal Rifle Corps, Volume V The Great War. Maj Gen Sir S Hare. 1932.
The King's Royal Rifle Corps Chronicles 1914, 1915, 1916 and 1917.
History of the Manchester Regiment, Volume II 1883-1922. Col H C Wylly. 1925.
Proud Heritage, The Story of the Highland Light Infantry, Volume III 1882-1918. Lt Col L B Oates. 1961.
The 2nd Battalion Highland Light Infantry in the Great War. Compilers Maj A D Telfer-Smollett, Maj C J Wallace and Capt H Ross Skinner. 1929.
The Life of a Regiment Volume 4, The Gordon Highlanders in the First World War 1914-19. C Falls. 1958.
Historical Records of the Queen's Own Cameron Highlanders, Volumes III and IV. Anon. 1931.
The Royal Irish Fusiliers 1793-1950. M Cunliffe. 1952.
The 1st Battalion The Faugh – A – Ballaghs in the Great War. Brig Gen A R Burrowes. 1926.
The History of the Rifle Brigade in the War 1914-18. Volume I August 1914 – December 1916. R Berkley. 1927.
As above. Appendix – List of Officers and Other Ranks of the Rifle Brigade awarded Decorations or MID for services during the Great War. Compiled by Lt Col T R Eastwood and Maj H G Parkyn. 1936.
Rifle Brigade Chronicles 1915 – 1920. Editor Col W Verner.
A Rifle Brigade Register 1905-63, Part 1 – A Roll of Officers who have served in the Regiment. Compiled by Col W P S Curtis. 1964.
The History and Records of Queen Victoria's Rifles 1792-1922. Compiler Maj C A Cuthbert Keeson. 1923.
Not Least in the Crusade, A Short History of the Royal Army Medical Corps. P Lovegrove 1951.
History of the Great War, Medical Services, Volume IV General History. Maj Gen Sir W G MacPherson. 1924.
Medical Officers in the British Army, Volume II 1898-1960. Lt Gen Sir R Drew. 1968.
The Royal Army Medical Corps. R Mclaughlin. 1972.
The Medical Victoria Crosses. Col WEI Forsyth-Jauch. 1984.
The Army Medical Services Magazine.
The Fourth Battalion, Duke of Connaught's Own Tenth Baluch Regiment in the Great War, 129th DCO Baluchis. WS Thatcher. 1932.
Historical Record of the 39th Garhwal Rifles Volume 1 1887-1922. Brig-Gen J Evatt. 1922.
With the Royal Garhwal Rifles in the Great War from August 1914 to November 1917. Brig-Gen DH Drake-Brockman. 1934.
The Frontier Force Rifles. Brig WEH Condon. 1953.

General Works

A Bibliography of Regimental Histories of the British Army. Compiler A S White. S 1965.

A Military Atlas of the First World War. A Banks & A Palmer. 1975.

Mons, The Retreat to Victory. J Terraine. 1960.

The Soldier's War 1914-18. P Liddle.

Into Battle 1914-18. E Parker. 1964.

The Times History of the Great War.

Topography of Armageddon, A British Trench Map Atlas of the Western Front 1914-18. P Chasseaud. 1991.

The Battle Book of Ypres. B Brice. 1927.

Before Endeavours Fade. R E B Coombs. 1976.

British Regiments 1914-18. Brig E A James. 1978.

Orange, Green and Khaki, The Story of the Irish Regiments in the Great War 1914–18. T Johnstone. 1992.

1914. L McDonald. 1987.

The Ypres Salient, A Guide to the Cemeteries and Memorials of the Salient. M Scott. 1992.

Wipers, The First Battle of Ypres. T Carew. 1974.

1915, The Death of Innocence. Lyn McDonald. 1993.

Norfolk and Suffolk in the Great War. G Gliddon. 1988.

Farewell, Leicester Square – The Old Contemptibles 12th August – 20th November 1914. Kate Caffrey. 1980.

A Walk Round Plugstreet – Cameos of the Western Front – South Ypres Sector 1914-18. Tony Spagnoly and Ted Smith. 1997.

Salient Points – Cameos of the Western Front – Ypres Sector 1914-18. Tony Spagnoly and Ted Smith. 1995.

The Battles of Neuve Chapelle, Aubers Ridge, Festubert 1915 – An Illustrated Pocket Guide. Michael Gavaghan. 1997.

The Story of a Nonentity; The Autobiography of Alf Bastin. 1998 (with Sidney Godley as POW).

Battle of the Aisne, 13th-15th September 1914, Tour of the Battlefield. War Office. 1934.

With the Indians in France. Gen Sir James Willcocks 1920.

The Indian Corps in France. Lt Col JWB Merewether & Sir Frederick Smith 1919.

In The Line of Battle. Walter Wood 1916.

The Affair at Néry, 1 September 1914. Patrick Takle. 2006.

Aisne 1914. Jerry Murland. 2013.

Battleground Europe – Sanctuary Wood and Hooge. N Cave. 1993.

Biographical

The Dictionary of National Biography 1901-85. Various Volumes.

The Cross of Sacrifice, Officers Who Died in the Service of the British, Indian and East African Regiments and Corps 1914-19. S D and D B Jarvis. 1993.

Whitaker's Peerage, Baronetage, Knightage & Companionage 1915.
Our Heroes – Containing Photographs with Biographical Notes of Officers of Irish Regiments and of Irish Officers of British Regiments who have fallen or who have been mentioned for distinguished conduct from August 1914 to July 1916. Printed as supplements to Irish Life from 1914 to 1916.
The Bond of Sacrifice, A Biographical Record of all British Officers Who Fell in the Great War. Volume I Aug – Dec 1914, Volume II Jan – Jun 1915. Editor Col L A Clutterbuck. 1916 and 1919.
The Roll of Honour Parts 1-5, A Biographical Record of Members of His Majesty's Naval and Military Forces who fell in the Great War 1914-18. Marquis de Ruvigny. 1917-19.
Birmingham Heroes. J P Lethbridge. 1993.
The Last Post – Being a Roll of all Officers (Naval, Military and Colonial) Who Gave Their Lives in the South African War 1899-1902. M G Doorner.
The Dictionary of Edwardian Biography – various volumes. 1904-08 reprinted 1985-87.
Morayshire Roll of Honour.

Specific Works on the Victoria Cross

A Tiger and a Fusilier, Leicester's VC Heroes. Derek Seaton. 2001.
Sometimes a Soldier. Reverend G H Woolley VC OBE MC. 1963.
Francis and Riversdale Grenfell: A Memoir. John Buchan. 1920.
Martin-Leake: Double VC. Ann Clayton. 1994.
Playing with Strife, the Autobiography of a Soldier. Lt Gen Sir Philip Neame VC KBE CB DSO. 1947.
Drummer Spencer John Bent VC. H L Kirby & R R Walsh. 1986.
Benjamin Handley Geary VC 1891-1976. Jock Asbury-Bailey.
The Register of the Victoria Cross. This England. 1981 and 1988.
The Story of the Victoria Cross 1856 – 1963. Brig Sir J Smyth. 1963.
The Evolution of the Victoria Cross, A study in Administrative History. M J Crook. 1975.
The Victoria Cross and the George Cross. IWM. 1970.
The Victoria Cross, The Empire's Roll of Valour. Lt Col R Stewart. 1928.
The Victoria Cross 1856 – 1920. Sir O'Moore Creagh and E M Humphris. 1920.
Victoria Cross – Awards to Irish Servicemen. B Clark. Published in The Irish Sword summer 1986.
The Medical Victoria Crosses. Col WEI Forsythe-Jauch. 1984.
VC's of Wales and the Welsh Regiments. W A Williams. 1984.
Brave Railwaymen. A Stanistreet. 1989.
The Seven VC's of Stonyhurst College. H L Kirby and R R Walsh. 1987.
For Conspicuous Gallantry, A Brief History of the recipients of the VC from Nottinghamshire and Derbyshire. N McCrery. 1990.
For Valour, The Victoria Cross, Courage in Action. J Percival. 1985.

VC Locator. D Pillinger and A Staunton. 1991.
VCs of the First World War: 1914. G Gliddon. 1994.
VCs of the First World War: The Western Front 1915. P F Batchelor & C Matson. 1997.
Black Country VCs. B Harry. 1985.
VC Heroes of the War. GA Leask. 1916.
The VC Roll of Honour. J W Bancroft. 1989.
A Bibliography of the Victoria Cross. W James McDonald. 1994.
For Valour – The History of Southern Africa's Victoria Cross Heroes. Ian Uys. 1973.
Canon Lummis VC Files held in the National Army Museum, Chelsea.
Recipients of the Victoria Cross in the Care of the Commonwealth War Graves Commission. 1997.
Victoria Cross Heroes. Michael Ashcroft. 2006.
Monuments to Courage. David Harvey. 1999.
The Sapper VCs. Gerald Napier. 1998.
Liverpool Heroes – Book 1. Ann Clayton.
Beyond the Five Points – Masonic Winners of The Victoria Cross and The George Cross. Phillip May GC, edited by Richard Cowley. 2001.
Irish Winners of the Victoria Cross. Richard Doherty & David Truesdale. 2000.
Nottinghamshire Victoria Cross Heroes. Nottinghamshire VC Committee. 2010.
Merseyside Heroes. Sid Lindsay. 1988

Other Honours and Awards

Distinguished Conduct Medal 1914-18, Citations of Recipients. 1983.
The Distinguished Service Order 1886-1923 (2 volumes). Sir O'Moore Creagh and E M Humphris. 1924.
The Old Contemptibles Honours and Awards. 1915.
Burke's Handbook to the Most Excellent Order of the British Empire. 1921.
South African War – Honours and Awards 1899-1902.

University and Schools Publications

The Royal Technical College Glasgow, Sacrifice and Service in the Great War.
The OTC Roll – A Roll of Members and Ex-members of the OTC Gazetted to Commissions in the Army August 1914 – March 1915. 1989.
Harrow Memorials of the Great War Volume 5. 1920.

Official Publications and Sources

History of the Great War, Order of Battle of Divisions. Compiler Maj A F Becke.
History of the Great War, Military Operations, France and Belgium. Compiler Brig Gen Sir J E Edmonds. Published in 14 volumes with 7 map volumes and 2 separate Appendices. 1923-48.
Location of Hospitals and Casualty Clearing Stations, BEF 1914-19. Ministry of Pensions 1923.

List of British Officers taken Prisoner in the Various Theatres of War between August 1914 and November 1918. Compiled from Official Records by Messrs Cox & Co, London. 1919.
London Gazette.
Census returns, particularly 1881, 1891, 1901 and 1911.
Births, Marriages and Deaths records formerly in the Family Records Centre, Islington, London, now in the National Archives.

National Archives:

War Diaries under WO 95
Medal Cards and Medal Rolls under WO 329 and ADM 171.
Soldier's Service Records under WO 97, 363 and 364.
Officer's Records under WO 25, 76, 339 and 374.
RAF Officer's Records under Air 76.
Royal Navy Records under ADM 139, 188, 196 & 340.

Official Lists

Navy Lists.
Army Lists – including Graduation Lists and Record of War Service.
Air Force Lists.
Home Guard Lists 1942-44.
Indian Army Lists 1897-1940.
India List 1923-40.

Reference Publications

Who's Who and Who Was Who.
The Times 1914 onwards.
The Daily Telegraph 1914 onwards.
Kelly's Handbook to the Titled, Landed and Official Classes.

Websites

I hesitate to include websites because they change frequently, but the following were very useful:

Victoria Cross – www2.prestel.co.uk/stewart – Iain Stewart.
Commonwealth War Graves Commission – www.cwgc.org
www.spartacus.schoolnet.co.uk
Births, Marriages and Deaths – www.freebmd.com

Periodicals

This England.
Coin and Medal News.
Orders and Medals Society Journal.
Journal of the Victoria Cross Society.

Useful Information

Accommodation – there is a wide variety of accommodation available in southern Belgium and northern France. Search on-line for your requirements. There are also numerous campsites, but many close for the winter from late September.

Clothing and Kit – consider taking:
Waterproofs.
Headwear and gloves.
Walking shoes/boots.
Shades and sunscreen.
Binoculars and camera.
Snacks and drinks.

Customs/Behaviour – local people are generally tolerant of battlefield visitors but please respect their property and address them respectfully. The French are less inclined to switch to English than other Europeans. If you try some basic French it will be appreciated.

Driving – rules of the road are similar to UK, apart from having to drive on the right. If in doubt about priorities, give way to the right. Obey laws and road signs – police impose harsh on-the-spot fines. Penalties for drinking and driving are heavy and the legal limit is lower than UK (50mg rather than 80mg). Most autoroutes in France are toll roads.

<u>Fuel</u> – petrol stations are only open 24 hours on major routes. Some accept credit cards in automatic tellers. The cheapest fuel is at hypermarkets.

<u>Mandatory Requirements</u> – if taking your own car you need:
Full driving licence.
Vehicle registration document.
Comprehensive motor insurance valid in Europe (Green Card).
European breakdown and recovery cover.
Letter of authorisation from the owner if the vehicle is not yours.
Spare set of bulbs, headlight beam adjusters, warning triangle, GB sticker, high visibility vest and breathalyzer.

Emergency – keep details required in an emergency separate from wallet or handbag:

Photocopy passport, insurance documents and EHIC (see Health below).
Mobile phone details.
Credit/debit card numbers and cancellation telephone contacts.
Travel insurance company contact number.

Ferries – the closest ports are Boulogne, Calais and Dunkirk. The Shuttle is quicker, but usually more expensive.

Health

European Health Insurance Card – entitles the holder to medical treatment at local rates. Apply online at www.nhs.uk/NHSEngland/Healthcareabroad/EHIC or call 0300 3301350. Issued free and valid for five years. You are only covered if you have the EHIC with you when you go for treatment.

Travel Insurance – you are strongly advised to also have travel insurance. If you receive treatment get a statement by the doctor (*feuille de soins*) and a receipt to make a claim on return.

Personal Medical Kit – treating minor ailments saves time and money. Pack sufficient prescription medicine for the trip.

Chemist (*Pharmacie*) – look for the green cross. They provide some treatment and if unable to help will direct you to a doctor. Most open 0900-1900 except Sunday. Out of hours services (*pharmacie de garde*) are advertised in Pharmacie windows.

Doctor and Dentist – hotel receptions have details of local practices. Beware private doctors/hospitals, as extra charges cannot be reclaimed – the French national health service is known as *conventionné*.

Rabies – contact with infected animals is very rare, but if bitten by any animal, get the wound examined professionally immediately.

Money

ATMs – at most banks and post offices with instructions in English. Check your card can be used in France and what charges apply. Some banks limit how much can be withdrawn. Let your bank know you will be away, as some block cards if transactions take place unexpectedly.

Credit/Debit Cards – major cards are usually accepted, but some have different names – Visa is Carte Bleue and Mastercard is Eurocard.

Exchange – beware 0% commission, as the rate may be poor. The Post Office takes back unused currency at the same rate, which may or may not be advantageous. Since the Euro, currency exchange facilities are scarce.

Local Taxes – if you buy high value items you can reclaim tax. Get the forms completed by the shop, have them stamped by Customs, post them to the shop and they will refund about 12%.

Passport – a valid passport is required.

Post – postcard stamps are available from vendors, newsagents and tabacs.

Public Holidays – just about everything closes and banks can close early the day before. Transport may be affected, but tourist attractions in high season are unlikely to be. The following dates/days are public holidays:

1 January
Easter Monday
1 May
8 May (France only)
Ascension Day
Whit Monday
14 July (France only)
21 July (Belgium only)
15 August
1 & 11 November
25 December

In France many businesses and restaurants close for the majority of August.

Radio – if you want to pick up the news from home try BBC Radio 4 on 198 kHz long wave. BBC Five Live on 909 kHz medium wave can sometimes be received. There are numerous internet options for keeping up with the news.

Shops – in large towns and tourist areas they tend to open all day. In more remote places they may still close for lunch. Some bakers open Sunday a.m. and during the week take later lunch breaks. In general shops do not open on Sundays.

Telephone

To UK – 0044, delete initial 0 then dial the rest of the number.
Local Calls – dial the full number even if within the same zone.
Mobiles – check yours will work in France and the charges.
Emergencies – dial 112 for medical, fire and police anywhere in Europe from any landline, pay phone or mobile. Calls are free.
British Embassy (Paris) – 01 44 51 31 00
British Embassy (Brussels) – 02 287 62 11

Time Zone – one hour ahead of UK.

Tipping – a small tip is expected by cloakroom and lavatory attendants and porters. Not required in restaurants when a service charge is included.

Toilets – the best are in museums and the main tourist attractions. Towns usually have public toilets where markets are held; some are coin operated.

Index

Notes

1. Armed force units, establishments, etc are grouped under the respective country, except Britain's, which appear under the three services.
2. Cemeteries/crematoria, churches, hospitals, schools and universities appear under those headings.
3. Commonwealth War Grave Commission cemeteries and memorials appear under that heading.
4. All orders, medals and decorations appear under Orders.